When the School Says No…
How to Get the Yes!

When the School Says No… How to Get the Yes!

Securing Special Education Services for Your Child

VAUGHN K. LAUER

Jessica Kingsley *Publishers*
London and Philadelphia

First published in 2014
by Jessica Kingsley Publishers
73 Collier Street
London N1 9BE, UK
and
400 Market Street, Suite 400
Philadelphia, PA 19106, USA

www.jkp.com

Library of Congress Cataloging in Publication Data
Lauer, Vaughn.
  When the school says no, how to get the yes! : securing special education services for your child /
Vaughn Lauer.
    pages cm
  Includes index.
  ISBN 978-1-84905-917-6 (alk. paper)
  1. Children with disabilities--Education. 2. Individualized education programs. 3. Children with disabilities--Services for. I. Title.
  LC4015.L38 2013
  371.9 2 23
                          2013008813

British Library Cataloguing in Publication Data
A CIP catalogue record for this book is available from the British Library

ISBN 978 1 84905 917 6
eISBN 978 0 85700 664 6

Printed and bound in Great Britain by Bell & Bain Ltd, Glasgow

This book is dedicated to Bryn, who we thank for inspiring this project and teaching us so much without saying a word.

Disclaimer

All names and identifying information have been changed including parents', children's, and educators' names, school names, and the names of cities and towns. Some names of programs and medications were not changed, but in no way is the author or this book promoting the use or disuse of any cited products or programs.

Acknowledgments

First, I want to thank all the parents who submitted their stories, who were willing to refine and clarify their scenarios in the hope that their experiences and my analyses would benefit parents of children with disabilities. Each took a significant period of time out of their lives to make this book a reality. I have a great deal of respect and appreciation for each one of them.

I want to thank my wife, Mary, for all her support and encouragement throughout the writing of this book and her willingness to listen to my *many* thoughts on the scenario submissions.

I want to thank Stephanie Allen Crist for her thorough review of the book chapters, for reminding me of my audience and for her "suggestions" for rephrasing the text. Also, I wish to thank Mary Ellen Web for her critical eye in locating text errors and for her helpful comments.

And finally I also want to thank my friends Marie-Ann Aghazadian and Kathy Snow, and Eleanor Voldish, all of whom reside in different parts of the country and who are long-time, dedicated advocates for children with disabilities and who assisted me in locating parents whose stories could be told.

Contents

Preface

The idea for this book started with a chance conversation I had with a parent of a child with autism. We already knew each other professionally, but we had never spoken about things of personal importance. I do not recall how our conversation started but what I do remember clearly is how the parent, an M.D., responded once she learned that I had decades of professional experience in the field of special education. She revealed that she and her husband, a Ph.D., had a child with autism. She added that she had wanted to write a book about the difficulties she had experienced with her child's school district. She wanted to help parents somehow, so they could deal with school systems more effectively than she and her husband had been able to do.

I explained that by coincidence I had recently developed a collaborative approach to working with schools that would not require compromise: parents could readily use the approach in Individualized Education Program (IEP) meetings to guide the IEP team to answer key questions that were based on the child's needs. Further, by applying the "Structured Collaborative IEP Process," the end result would be an IEP with real meaning—one that had been developed based on the answers agreed on and reached by the IEP team. The meeting would end with the team feeling confident that the IEP would indeed meet the child's needs and that the child's needs had not been superseded by those of an individual or institution.

To test the book concept, she and her husband wrote a scenario (experience) of working with their school district. I then conducted an analysis of the scenario by using the six key questions that should be asked during an IEP meeting, which embodies the Structured Collaborative IEP Process. After reading the analysis of her scenario, she commented that this was exactly what she and her husband had hoped for and they knew that the resulting book would be helpful to parents who wanted to learn how to approach school systems.

They felt that the analysis was understandable, diagnostic, prescriptive, and not written in a "gotcha" format, and would result in the IEP team collaborating. We agreed that a book of scenarios and analyses would help parents to see a variety of school/parent interactions. And, through the analyses, they would understand how the Structured Collaborative IEP Process would help improve IEP meetings and meet the needs of many parents (and educators).

I am hopeful that those reading it will indeed find the process practical and easy to use. Of course, practice does make perfect. Those using the Structured Collaborative IEP Process will only get better at it and they will also see the benefits as the process favorably impacts their child's learning. They will experience IEP meetings carried out in a collaborative fashion with each child's needs being the focus of the IEP meeting. And that is where the focus should be.

When I began this project, I felt confident that I had a process that would enable parents and advocates to take the lead during an IEP meeting, or any kind of school meeting, while using a collaborative approach. The approach may seem slightly "academic," but I wanted to help parents to participate actively during IEP meetings and have their child's needs as the focus of those meetings. I wanted the time spent on developing IEPs to be shorter and, quite frankly, easier and less stressful. I also wanted there to be an end (or at least a major reduction) to the number of IEP meetings that would go on for hours and hours without reaching a conclusion, requiring additional meetings to be held just to complete the IEP. I wanted every step of the process to end in agreement, so that when the team moved to the next question and began developing appropriate answer(s), they would be basing their decisions on the agreements reached during the previous discussion—and they would always be focused on the child's needs. This would be collaboration at its finest, with each step of the process directed toward meeting the child's needs—those needs identified and agreed to at the onset of the meeting.

As I spoke with each parent involved with the project and listened to their stories—and then re-read, edited, and analyzed their submissions/scenarios—a number of realizations struck me. The first was that this was indeed more than simply, if you will please excuse the word, an "academic" venture. I found that I was connecting with the parents, and even more so with their perspectives. With an even greater depth of understanding, I saw how often issues of disagreement came about because a parent or educator incorrectly understood a policy. I read how parents could become so involved in the events and processes that they lost perspective of their child's needs. I observed parents' wishes become paramount in developing IEPs that were only loosely related to their child's needs. And I read how IEPs were primarily constructed without the team fully understanding the child's needs. Just as striking were the number of non-existent policies presented that were nevertheless "stood by," preventing a service from being provided—until the parent or advocate requested a copy of "the policy" to review, only to discover that there was no such policy.

I also saw where parents were doing their very best to have the schools provide their children with appropriate services, but they did not fully know how to go about it. They might have the data, but they did not know how to share them in an understandable format, so they were not understood by the medical professionals or school personnel. I saw that parents had the information to show what their child's needs were, but they did not know how to ensure those needs were addressed in the IEP.

These were not new observations for me. They were issues I had heard or experienced before. I have attended thousands of IEP meetings, but through the development of this book I looked more closely at the IEP process and the interpersonal relationships—good or bad—between parents and school personnel. Do I remain confident in the Structured Collaborative IEP Process? I most certainly do! Why? Because of the number of times that parents had unknowingly applied portions of the process with success. Because I have observed this process to be effective during IEP meetings, even under strained situations. And because several parents told me that, following our conversations regarding IEP meetings they were about to attend for their child, they found using the key questions of the process to be productive.

They added that it helped them to think through just what their child's needs were and what information (data) existed to support their observations. They explained how they were better able to describe their child's behaviors to the educational staff, so that new and old staff alike could "picture" what the parents were describing and could "see" what the parents saw. The parents also noted how the meeting atmosphere changed and how staff came to recognize what expectations the parents had for future IEP meetings.

I am confident in this process because several parents said, "Thank you, it did work." Even better, they understood why it worked—that "Aha" moment! They experienced the value of asking questions that required the full IEP team to respond and for those responses to be based on previously agreed-to answers and decisions. They also noted that they felt more a part of the IEP process and more in control of the direction of the meeting.

Not all IEP meetings in this book were as successful, for different reasons; but having read the book you will know which ones were not and, most importantly, why. The purpose of this book is to help you achieve that recognition. I hope, too, that these "lessons learned" will be sufficient, once you've read them, to prepare you to be better able to avoid stalemates or your own IEP meetings ending without a completed IEP. Of course, should you experience these unfavorable and temporary outcomes, you may certainly seek skilled facilitators (e.g., advocate, attorney, or IEP facilitator) who are capable of bringing the two "sides" back to a point where they can implement the Structured Collaborative IEP Process.

Introduction

Understanding the Approach

A successful Individualized Education Program (IEP) meeting requires the collaborative use of data. Parents, teachers, therapists, and support personnel all need data to recognize what works and what doesn't. Unfortunately, parents often don't have the training and experience to compile and use data effectively. In the eyes of most parents, it's the teachers, therapists, and support personnel—the school staff—who are responsible for compiling and using data, not them. Regrettably, many of those same educators, therapists, and support personnel—administrators, teachers,— were also not trained on how to use data effectively, either. As a result, the IEP team doesn't always use data to benefit the child. Sometimes there are not enough data. Sometimes they're the wrong data. Sometimes they're the right data used in the wrong way.

The failure to use data effectively is not simply ignorance. We use data all the time to make decisions. But when we put ourselves in the setting of an IEP meeting, everything is complicated by educational jargon and legislation. Ideally, the entire IEP team would receive the training they need. That's not always possible, but there is still a lot you can do to ensure the best outcome for your child. The process for making informed decisions is easier than you might think—even when faced with educational jargon and legislation. We use this process all the time. What we need to remember is to apply those same decision-making strategies, regardless of setting. Simply put, we don't have to be afraid of data (which we will refer to in the plural) when we make IEP decisions; we need to use them effectively.

The Car Analogy

You already know how to make decisions. You make them every day, often without much thought. Even when we don't have to think consciously about our decisions, we are processing data and making informed decisions. Take our near-daily experience of driving. We don't need to think consciously about it when we go to the car, open the door, get in, start the car, and then decide to move in one direction or another. We remember to check to make sure we are safe and that we will cause no harm to others, property, or ourselves. How do we do that? We ensure that before we move, we buckle the seatbelt and look in all directions to see where everything is in relation to where we are. We may choose to back up, using rearview mirrors and turning around to look behind us before moving. If we see that all is clear, we proceed. If there is an oncoming car or a child on a bicycle headed our way, we may choose to wait, or we may decide that there is sufficient time to back out without consequence.

Our decision to move is based on the car's position, the information we pick up from around us, and where we want to go. Processing all these inputs helps us know "where we are." In our mind, we have a plan on where we want to go and how we want to get there—a mental roadmap of sorts. We process data throughout our trip as we follow our roadmap and make driving decisions: we slow down, speed up, change lanes—responding in any number of ways given the information that we are provided. We also compare how the car responds (how the brakes work, sensitivity of the gas pedal, etc.) to our previous experiences with our car to determine its level of performance. We evaluate large amounts of data as we make a variety of decisions in order to reach our destination.

The Approach: Start with Behaviors

The good news is that the process of making educational decisions parallels the driving experience. You do not need to be an expert in education any more than you need to be an expert in building roads to get from point A to point B. What you do need is to understand the inputs required to make the best educational decisions possible. So, the remainder of our discussion will concentrate on your child's behaviors and how these behaviors make up the inputs, or data, by which all educational decisions will be made.

You have talked about your child's behaviors before. During an IEP meeting, they may have been grouped under the heading "Academic Achievement and Functional Performance" or "Present Levels of Educational Performance." Perhaps you have been involved in developing a behavior intervention plan (BIP). You may also have talked about your child's behaviors during a parent-teacher conference. But what do we mean by behaviors?

For our purposes, behaviors include academic skills (reading, math), social skills (interpersonal interaction), sensory skills (auditory, tactile, and visual), motoric skills (gross-motor and fine-body movements), or mobility (a person's skills of maneuvering within his or her environment). If you cannot describe a behavior (an action), then you cannot observe it. Simply put, behaviors are those actions that are both observable and measurable by anyone. Furthermore, every behavior is a form of "communication." It tells us something about the child. Thus, behaviors are the essential inputs the IEP team needs in order to make decisions.

It is not enough simply to say, "I observed (saw) a behavior." The IEP team needs to know more. For example, it is important to know how often that behavior occurred. Was it just once, or was it eight times? Knowing how often a behavior occurs helps us "picture" the importance of this behavior. We want to increase some behaviors and decrease others. So, the frequency of a behavior (how often a behavior occurs) is a key part of our description of the behavior.

We also want to describe how long a behavior lasts. Suppose that we want to change the amount of time a child cries. It is not enough to know what crying means to us and how often the child cries. We need to know how long the behavior lasts, or its duration. If we decide that this is a behavior we want to change, then this information is important, because we can use the frequency and duration to measure how the behavior changes over time. If our ultimate goal is to end the behavior, then we need these measurements to show when our interventions begin to reduce the time the child cries. That way we know our strategies are working!

Behavior intensity is another form of measurement, and it describes the magnitude of the behavior. To put it another way, a behavior's intensity is its level on some sort of scale. Suppose we say that the child throws tantrums. Now, "throws tantrums" is not a well-defined behavior, which is problematic in itself, but for now we are just going to define and measure it in terms of intensity. We might know that the child's tantrums range from stomping his or her feet to throwing chairs. That is quite a range of behaviors, but it describes the degree or level of the tantrums we might expect. Wouldn't you like to know how intense a particular child's tantrums might be before you actually experience it—especially if throwing furniture is on that scale?

It is equally important to identify when and where the behavior is observed and when and where it is not. We call these "when" and "where" conditions. For example, we might know that if the child is presented with a crayon when he or she is standing up, then he or she immediately scribbles on any object within reach. If, however, he or she is given a piece of paper with a drawing on it, such as a coloring book page, followed by a crayon, then he or she begins to color in the spaces on the drawing. The behavior differs when the circumstances change. These are our conditions. Both sets of conditions are helpful when describing his or her behavior, therefore they are useful data to know and collect when measuring an existing behavior or a change in behavior.

So, a behavior is an action that is observable by anyone. Behaviors are measured based on their frequency (how often), their duration (how long), and their intensity (how much). Behaviors are further described by the conditions (where and when) under which they occur. Finally, it is important to note that all behaviors are measured in terms of whether they increase, decrease, or remain the same. All this information is called data and these data are the inputs we need to make educational decisions.

Many people, both in the general population and in the educational field, shy away from the word "data." However, the term simply means information. So, now that you know what goes into describing a behavior, you can see how important it is to describe a behavior correctly, including the various relevant parts. But it is not enough simply to describe a behavior in a useful way. What you do with those data is just as important.

The premise of this book is that parents and educators need to define, observe, measure, and use a student's behaviors (behavioral data) in order to make sound educational decisions with respect to creating an IEP that clearly defines the child's needs, the services that will meet those needs, and the setting in which those services will be delivered. Now, you might be asking yourself, "What do I do with all this information?" What if:

- you did not need to know all the special education laws, regulations, and policies

- you did not need to be a statistician or even be great with math

- you did not need to have a background in collecting data?

And you knew:

- key questions to ask during IEP meetings that would help determine where your child "is" and where you want him or her to "go"

- how to use the behavioral observations from home and school to make educational decisions for your child

- what to ask and do if, during a meeting, you disagreed with a school proposal.

And what if:

- your IEP team cooperated in a collaborative way, focusing on your child's needs, because you knew that achieving collaboration stems from answering key questions?

As you read the upcoming scenarios, you will learn how to determine which data are important and which are not. You will also discover how to ask questions that will help your team get the information you need to make informed decisions. You will learn what questions to ask and of whom, so that the necessary information is provided or sought before a decision is made. You will also learn how to evaluate whether an intervention, program, or service is working. You will see how to do this by asking questions, not by becoming an expert in education or special education law. This does not mean that you may never need assistance; rather, this means you will know if and when you need assistance, from whom, and, most importantly, why. Let's begin by discussing how we will get to where we need to go—how, based on the child's needs, the IEP team will develop and provide the appropriate programming and services.

Mapping Out a Plan: The Questions to Ask

If you're going on a road trip, you'll probably gather as much information as you can about the possible routes you can take, and make a map or a plan of which route you will follow. You'll look up the different highways and interstates you can use. You may consider appropriate sightseeing opportunities or places to stay overnight. You might consider accessibility to restaurants, gas stations, and other services on each route. You make your decisions based on where you need to go, how long you have to get there, and what you'll need along the way. You create a plan to ensure you get there on time without enduring unnecessary hardships, such as running out of gas ten miles from the nearest gas station or finding yourself on a long stretch of empty road when you need a place to rest.

Your child's education is a lot like a road trip, and your IEP is the route you and your team plan for how to get your child where you want him or her to go. Of course, the tools and information you need to make good decisions are different, but the process is the same. You need to ask the right questions to get the information you need to make the best decisions possible. The questions you ask and the answers your team provides need to be specific enough to provide you with useful information. For example, if you're going on a road trip, it's not enough to know that you'll be using a vehicle. Will it be a gas-sipping economy car or a gas-guzzling SUV? The answer makes a difference to how you plan your route, because you'll need more frequent refueling stops in an SUV. That's pretty straightforward, but what if it's a diesel-powered truck or a battery-powered car? That really changes things! The questions you ask in an IEP meeting work the same way, and the answers you get need to be as specific as possible.

It's not enough to say, for example, that you want your child to talk more or to do better in school. You have to ask the questions and get the answers needed to define what that means for your child, given his or her current level of performance and the expectations placed on him or her in the school environment. You and your team can only move forward once you have the necessary information (the answers to your questions). You can't make a good plan if you haven't agreed upon what it is you're planning to do. If you haven't defined it, you can't plan to achieve it. If you don't know what you're trying to achieve, you can't determine whether you achieved it when you're done. So, you need to ask questions and get answers in order to define what you're planning, and you have to write the plan in such a way that it captures the definitions you used to make the plan.

These are the six basic questions we will use to help develop a plan:

1. What do we know? (What don't we know? Where are we? What do we need to know?)

2. Where do we want to go? (Where are we going? What do we need to accomplish?)

3. How will we get there? (What do we need to get there?)

4. How do we know that we are getting there?

5. Who is responsible for this plan?

6. How do we know when we have arrived? (What do we do when we get there?)

Once we've implemented the plan, there are two additional questions to consider:

1. How do we keep what we have?

2. When is it time to move on?

Imagine yourself standing at the edge of a cliff, blindfolded. Someone spins you around and around until you're dizzy, and then that person asks you to take a step in any direction you choose. How will you know which way to go—safely? Before you move, you'll want to know where you are in relation to the cliff, so you can choose a different direction—away from the danger. Sometimes the decisions you face in an IEP meeting can feel like you're standing at a cliff's edge. In order to know the best way to go, you have to know where you are. You need as much usable information as possible to understand and define what you and your team already know about your child. That is why an IEP meeting should start with, "What do we know?"

The next question is, "Where do we want to go?" Imagine yourself back on the cliff's edge. The obvious choice is to step away from the edge, but what if you really want to get to the other side? That changes the choices you're likely to make. So, it's not enough to know where you are; you also have to know where you are going.

Once you and your team agree on what you know and where you want to go, the next question you need to ask is, "How will we get there?" A question that goes along with that is, "What do we need to get there?" Imagine you're standing at the cliff's edge. In asking, "What do we know?" you learned that there's a rope bridge ahead. In asking, "Where do we want to go?" you learned that you're trying to get to the other side. If you and your team agree, you might decide to take the rope bridge across, but you might not. Perhaps you remember that in previous attempts to use a rope bridge, you always fell. So, you need to plan a way to use that bridge safely. Or maybe you decide to ignore the obvious choice of the rope bridge and make plans to build a hang glider to get yourself across. You see, you have to make sure you plan a way to get to where you want to go. Sometimes that means coming up with modifications or accommodations to make a tried-and-failed solution work, but sometimes it means coming up with a whole new solution. It's not enough just to use the tools you have on hand; you need to use the right tools to accomplish your goal.

The next question to ask is, "How do we know that we are getting there?" If you're busy making that hang glider, you want to know that the hang glider is designed to carry your weight, that it will fit your body comfortably, and that you'll have enough of a runway to get the speed you need to reach the other side. You also want to know anything else that might help you determine whether your plan is on track. You don't want to wait until you're in mid-air to think about these things. Neither do you want to wait until the middle of the school year to start thinking about how you will know if your IEP plan is working. So, when you're planning your IEP, you want to make sure you build a means of keeping your team on track. That way everyone agrees on what to keep track of and what to look out for, so that you can determine whether the plan is working or not. It is crucial that we know that we are headed in the right direction and getting closer to our goal and not going the wrong way, or worse, going nowhere.

It is also important to ask, "Who is responsible for this plan?" As you work with your team, reaching an agreement on the answers to these questions, it's also important to determine who is responsible for each part of the plan. Imagine yourself back at that cliff. If everyone on your team is working independently to build your hang glider, it is important that each of you is working on the right parts of the hang glider; otherwise you might end up with an abundance of wings, but no structure, and therefore, no hang glider. When fulfilling the educational needs of a child, you often have a lot of people working on a lot of different things. You need to know who's responsible for what, so that you all know what you are expected to do to keep the child on track.

Last, but not least, you need to ask, "How do we know when we have arrived?" If you get in the hang glider and you take off, you need to know when you've reached the other side, so you can prepare for your landing. But getting to the other side of that cliff is rarely the end of the journey. There's always a next step. When you're planning an IEP, you need to know when you've reached your goals. It's also important to try not to lose the gains you've made as you move on to the next obstacles in your journey. So, you'll want to ask, "How do we keep what we have?" and "When is it time to move on?"

If you are thinking that this sounds familiar, you are right. It is quite similar to the development of an IEP or a new product in the business world. These are questions we ask when planning for a desired outcome. It's when we don't ask these questions or when we don't get the answers we need that a breakdown occurs. Now, let's look at these questions in more detail.

One might wonder about the origin of the six key questions. They are, in fact, a culmination of use and experiences from several disciplines. First, if we look at the IEP process (the steps involved in creating the IEP), we see that the questions follow the steps to be carried out during the development of an IEP. Those steps stem from, at least in the U.S., the federal regulations that, for example, first require the IEP team to define the child's needs. That is, by pooling from formal and informal assessments, observations, and other data collected from a variety of sources, the team defines what they know about the child's "present levels of academic achievement and functional performance." By changing this to a question, you have "What do we know?" and in answering this we may well ask "What don't we know?"

If you think about how the GPS system in your car or smart phone operates, it, too, begins with a determination of "Where are you?" (literally) and then asks you "Where do you want to go?" (physically). Clearly if you, or the GPS, do not know where you are, you will never know how to get to where you want to go, or think you want to go. In the IEP, we write measurable goals to answer the question "Where do we want to go?" The GPS can answer your question of "How are we going to get there?" by showing you step-by-step directions. The IEP answers the same question by delineating the services needed to get "there." Continuing with this analogy, the GPS can show you the progress you are making toward reaching your destination. Similarly, with an IEP, we receive progress reports that help us know if we are getting there. If progress is not being made, then we call for another meeting to discuss options for getting there, in the same way the GPS can give us alternative routes to our destination. And so it continues.

These questions are also quite similar to how businesses set out to develop new products. Companies no more create new products to sell than we should just write an IEP without answering a number of questions. Businesses do the same. They will begin with asking the question of "What do we know?" The answers to this single question will bear much information about what is known of their product, but may provide no information on their competitor's similar product. That alone will cause the developers to list out those things that they do not yet know and devise a plan for obtaining them. In writing IEPs, when we reach a point where we recognize that there are things we don't know, we may decide to carry out literature reviews or conduct evaluations. Likewise, businesses will conduct research that could involve various types of studies, consumer surveys, focus groups, etc. to learn what they do not know. This is all in the name of answering the questions of "What do we know?" and "What don't we know?" and then to answer the next questions of "Where do we want to go?," "How do we know that we are getting there?," and so forth.

My own experiences in submitting research proposals, competitive grants, and business proposals confirm the value and use of similar questions listed in this book. All have one major component in common and that is knowing that we can't get to "there" if we don't know where "here" is. And there is no way to develop a plan to get "there" or know "if we are getting there," much less know where "there" is or to know "when we have arrived," without answering that first question of "What do we know?"

Simple questions? Perhaps, but they are very powerful if used in the right sequence and one knows what to listen for in the answers. They are, in some form or another, used across disciplines, successfully in organizations and businesses, and now in developing IEPs.

In this book, you will see some of the questions worded in slightly different ways. This is only because there are several ways to ask the same question. Slight modifications are completely acceptable and it is likely you will find some more preferable than others. The point here is that the questions do need to be asked and in the correct order to carry out the Structured Collaborative IEP Process if the goal is to develop an effective IEP in collaboration with the school staff.

What Do We Know?

As with the driving example, it is essential first to know where we are by answering the question, "What do we know about this child?" We will use the answers to this question as the basis for every other decision—hence, the need for the information to be accurate and complete. Data consist of anything that is made available to the IEP team for discussion and that applies to the child's need(s) under discussion. The data can be formal and informal. They can come from the school, and may range from student work to individually administered norm-referenced tests. The information can also include data from parents or others who have observed the child first-hand. For our purposes, it is the form and format of this information that is important. Data must be comprised of measurable and observable behaviors, regardless of the source.

Looking at the data, the team needs to ask, "Which of the pieces of information show measures of change or no change at all?" "Can we explain the change in terms of the conditions under which we observed the behaviors and the frequency or accuracy of the behaviors?" "Can it be determined how long the behavior has presented itself and where it can be observed?" "Can we assess the intensity of that behavior? Do we know when and where the behavior does *not* occur?" We ask these questions to understand what we know about the child and the child's educational needs. We may well discover that there are things that we do not know. What we know and what we don't know are equally important.

A note of caution regarding the "age" of information is in order. In particular, formal evaluations lose their value over time, and the team must decide if that information continues to define the child's behaviors accurately. In some cases, it is important to gather data over a period of time for the information to be of value. Team members will have to determine the information's usefulness in making educational decisions.

Where Do We Want to Go?

Another way of asking this is, "What goals do we want the child to achieve?" "What is it we want to accomplish?" Specifically, we are setting out a course of achievements we want our child to reach or accomplish. For example, suppose we have identified our child's needs in the area of reading; more precisely, we know that he or she recognizes and can state ten letters of the alphabet. One goal we may want him or her to achieve, let's say in two months of instruction, is to state all the letters of the alphabet. Another goal might be that, in four months, we want our child to be able to make the sounds of both the short and long vowels, and in eight months, to say one-syllable words with short and long vowel sounds. These are our goals for the IEP. They are based on what he or she knows (he or she can state the names of the first ten letters of the alphabet). Furthermore, we would know, by answering the first question ("What does he or she know?"), how long it took for him or her to learn the first ten letters. If it took a year to learn those ten letters, then the goals just established would be unreasonable. However, if it only took two weeks to state the first ten letter sounds, it might be more reasonable to believe that he or she might achieve the goals as laid out in the IEP, because they are in line with his or her rate of learning. We now have a direction in which we want to go. We know what we want to accomplish and have tied the answer of the first question to that of the second ("Where do we want to go?").

If we find it difficult to determine where we want to go or what we want to accomplish, then we still might need to ask, "What don't we know?" and "What do we need to know?" It is impossible to establish these things in a meaningful way if we are missing data, or if the information we have is incomplete, out of date, or not understandable. To put this simply, we cannot state where we want to go if we do not know where we are. For example, if we have not agreed on what the child's behavior is, if we do not know how the child's behavior has changed over time, or if we cannot state when and where we would reasonably expect to see the behavior, then how could we possibly state what behavior could or should ultimately be observed? When we do decide where we are going, we will state that goal in behavioral and measurable terms that will include conditions under which these behaviors will be observed.

How Will We Get There?

Remember, behaviors are observable and measurable actions that are described so that any observer can identify them, and this description includes the conditions under which an observer could expect to see the behavior or expect not to see it. The frequency (how often), duration (how long), and intensity (how much) of the behavior, if relevant, should also be known. All this information is important when trying to agree on what the behavior is and what change the team wants to accomplish. Once agreement is reached, the team can begin to describe, discuss, and determine the best manner to reach the goal. The team will review various possible interventions, instruction, programs, or services, planning how to change the behavior from what it is to what it is to be, in order to answer the question, "How will we get there?"

It is also important to know what methods have already been tried, what's worked, what hasn't, and why it has/hasn't. Agreeing on all of this may be a challenge, especially if the behavior is novel or has not made the degree of progress previously expected. Getting the answers you need may involve carrying out more trials, researching alternatives, gathering evidence, or carrying out some additional assessments. It is worth noting that sometimes, when seeking the appropriate methodology, an informed series of trials and errors is the only option available.

In other cases, your team can find alternative solutions by conducting further research, such as a review of pertinent literature produced by other professionals, visiting other programs, or collaborating with personnel outside of the current team. The team may also need more behavioral evidence or to review the evidence already gathered more thoroughly. Finally, the team may need a formal assessment to identify a problem or challenge that has previously been overlooked.

Whether the team can readily make a decision based on the information they have or whether they must decide to seek further information because they cannot make a decision with confidence, the team must first have a well-defined behavior (both what the current behavior is and what you want it to be, its frequency, duration, etc.).

And when making a decision on what service to provide or the setting in which to provide it, remember that it is far too easy, and far too dangerous, simply to say, "This is the approach I want to use." The team needs a rationale for its choice. This rationale should be built on the answers to the first two questions, and the team should agree to these answers. What a comfortable feeling it is to have made a decision based on useful data and to have a group of people working to meet the child's needs agree on that decision—we call it "collaboration," and we call the process used to reach this kind of agreement "structured collaboration."

Taking a Breath

Up to this point, we have discussed what a behavior is, and we have noted the importance of describing the behavior in terms of what it is and the conditions under which an observer could expect to see or not to see it. To explain further the child's behavior, we noted the importance of several ways of measuring the behavior— including its frequency, duration, and intensity—when relevant. Without all of this descriptive information, the team cannot be certain it is discussing the same behavior, and they cannot reach agreement regarding what the behavior is. When agreement is reached, the team can determine which intervention, instruction, program, or service will answer the question, "How will we get there?"

The intervention will need to be written with the same level of detail used to identify and describe the original behavior. It will need to consist of a clear statement of what the target behavior is, what behavior we expect to see as a result of the intervention, when and where it will occur, and its frequency and/or accuracy.

The difference when writing this into an IEP is that we are stating the behavior in terms of the effects of the intervention. We want to determine how much change is expected to be due to the program and related services the team deemed necessary when answering the previously asked questions. The plan should not be so complicated that the intervention negatively impacts the child's learning or the teacher's ability to implement it.

How Do We Know That We Are Getting There?

When working with children, we need feedback on what effect the intervention is having on the child and whether the effects (changes in behaviors) are going to enable him or her to reach the goal. How are we going to measure if change takes place? We don't want to wait until the end of, let's say, six weeks or until the annual review. That's too late, especially if we discover that we should have been making changes because of lack of progress or because the wrong behaviors were learned.

So, in the plan, the IEP team needs to devise a way to collect data that will show the effects of the implementation of the plan. The system should not require a computer strapped to the teacher, or to the child for that matter. Instead, the method should be as easy as possible in order to increase the likelihood that the measurement will take place a sufficient number of times to show the effects of the intervention on the child's behavior.

The IEP team needs to establish a timeline for the intervention to begin and include specific notations of when the behavior will be assessed (measured). We also need to determine the steps to take if the intervention is not working. In essence, the plan is somewhat fluid and dependent on the change (or lack of change) in the child's behaviors. There should be latitude to adjust instruction without the need for a meeting, as long as the behavior measured shows progress toward the desired outcome.

Who Is Responsible for This Plan?

With some goals, the person responsible will be obvious, but there will also be times when several team members may be jointly responsible for a single goal. At other times it may not be immediately clear who the person or persons responsible should be. No matter which of these situations an individual goal falls under, the plan should clearly state who is responsible for each part of the plan—not by name, but, by title (e.g., teacher, occupational therapist, etc.).

How Do We Know When We Have Arrived?

There must be agreement as to when a meeting should be called to discuss how the plan is going, and a way of sharing progress. The team might also, for example, establish a date by which, if intervention A is not working, then intervention B will be implemented. In any case, timelines for implementation, assessment, and the sharing of progress are major components of the plan.

How Do We Keep What We Have?
When Is It Time to Move On?

This is not the time to say, "Well, we are here, and we have done our job." We need to continue to receive scheduled reports to know that any gains are not lost and that, if appropriate, we will maintain a particular behavior at some predetermined proficiency level. The scheduled times for reporting on IEP progress are found in the IEP. It is important that you review those reports when you receive them from the school to verify that you are seeing similar behaviors at home.

Of course, another choice after reaching a goal is to change it in some way, such as increasing the frequency, the accuracy, or some other measure. But the basis for change should continue to be grounded in what we know.

Summary

In conclusion, a behavior is an action that is observable by anyone, one that may be measured based on its frequency, duration, and intensity. A behavior is also described by the conditions under which it does and does not occur. A behavior may increase, decrease, or stay the same. These inputs are used to determine what we know, where we want to go, how we will get there, how we will know when we are getting there, who is responsible for getting us there, and how we will know when we've arrived. We also want to figure out how to keep what we have and when it's time to move on. We answer these questions by working together and reaching agreement in a collaborative fashion.

The answers to these questions have then become the plan. It is abundantly clear that each answer is dependent upon the answer to the previous question(s), making each question asked and its response integral to the completion of the plan. It is from this set of questions that each of the scenarios presented in this book will be reviewed. A discussion will be presented in the context of these questions and plan components, whether they were or were not in place and how they might have been included. More importantly, through this process, you should learn how this information can be used in future discussions about your child's educational needs and how to get from here to there.

How to Get Assistive Technology for the Nonverbal Child with Autism

The Bradshaws are well-educated professionals who, like so many parents, did not know how to get the school to say "Yes;" at least, not in the beginning. Unfortunately, because they were able to afford it, Brint's parents purchased a very expensive piece of assistive technology (AT) to address his communication skills. The Bradshaws intuitively knew that by improving his ability to communicate, his behaviors would be favorably affected. They were showing—literally, via use of a video camera—the school that he could use and benefit from the AT device that was key. Sadly, the school had elected not to consider conducting a full AT evaluation—something they had the capability to do. The Bradshaws' scenario leads the book, because it illustrates, with absolute detail, how to get the "Yes" when the school says "No."

The Bradshaws' Story

"The team asked us why we hadn't agreed to it, then. We had no answer."

Having a child with a disability changes your life forever. What we have learned as our child grows is that rather than being disabled, he really is "differently-abled." We cannot say we did not go through a period of grief; my wife, Susan, and I certainly did. We also went through our periods of hope that he could potentially speak. All children are born nonverbal, so when our son failed to speak by the age of three, we were not alarmed. Perhaps he is slow, we thought. Even Albert Einstein did not speak until he was about five, and, despite his early speech difficulties, he was a genius.

Brint is 12, and, even after years of intense and expensive speech therapy, he cannot speak. He is frustrated. He has thoughts, but his brain is like spaghetti loops of crossed wires. The connections are crossed, so the signals do not go through correctly, and thus he has trouble expressing his needs and wants. Autism is a processing disorder. Information comes in, but is not processed as one would expect. This lack of ability to communicate and process information makes cognitive ability difficult to assess. Brint has trouble with body awareness; ergo, he has trouble toileting. Because he has difficulty communicating, he has trouble communicating the need for toileting. So, rather than toileting when he needs to, he has been placed on a toileting schedule. He has learned much of his self-help skills, such as getting dressed or brushing his teeth, via rote memorization and habit training. The frustration for him and for us is that he cannot communicate effectively. We kept thinking that if he could speak, then somehow he could communicate better.

When Brint had just turned nine, we were at a breaking point. His frustration had been building, and he would bite his finger, bang his head, and cry out of frustration. The school system had only offered picture exchange communication system (PECS™) boards, as he was five. It was not flexible enough to express complex thoughts and it was difficult for him to use, because he lacked the dexterity necessary to pick up the cards. He has recently been diagnosed with cerebral palsy (CP), which explains his fine-motor difficulty.

He had a wonderful teacher who spent a lot of time getting him to isolate his pointer finger to point at pictures. She suggested we look into a speech-generating device (SGD) for him. We wondered how well he would do with another device that would require pointing because we felt that the CP would continue to impede his accuracy in pointing. So we waited—a big mistake. In time, the teacher left the school system. At the time we did not realize how exceptional she was.

We went through a horrible period with the new, first-year teacher who had little experience with children with autism spectrum disorders (ASDs). He descended into what is termed "learned helplessness." He could do a task such as toileting or self-feeding. However, he would initially need assistance, moving slowly and wavering as he executed the task. Untrained caregivers tend to do the work for individuals because it is easier and faster than training. When this occurred repeatedly, Brint gladly accepted the assistance and essentially learned not to do the task himself; hence, the term "learned helplessness." His teacher was simply not trained to help Brint communicate or develop his self-help skills.

A lack of training leads to instinctive babysitting. Without training, we tend to resort to what we know rather than implementing research-based practices. For example, our son required assistance with self-feeding. Because of the cerebral palsy, Brint had trouble scooping yogurt onto a spoon. He could do it, but he was messy. He needed simple verbal prompts when self-feeding, such as, "Scoop it, eat it, and wipe your mouth with a napkin." Instead, at first his teacher would place his lunch in front of him and leave him to it. Daily, he would come home with a new hairdo, stiff with yogurt, and with food all over his clothes. After we told her that he needed assistance, she just fed him like a baby. There were numerous incidents that culminated in our increasing frustration.

Brint was not being educated in either academic or life skills. Basically, he was left to self-stimulate with toys and other items in the classroom, thereby undoing the hard work we did at home. The regression was obvious and painful to watch. The worst part was that the school kept telling us to give the teacher more time. We were told that she was "learning." When Susan went to the principal for help, she was told, "Mom to mom, you need to be careful not to complain too much, because you do not want to create a bad relationship with your son's teacher." The school system kept promising us the teacher would get better. They were "helping" her. Finally, one day Susan went to the classroom and saw an aide spray Brint with air freshener, rather than help him clean up after toileting. That was the final straw.

Susan wrote this email to an attorney friend of hers:

> He cried his heart out this morning trying so desperately to tell me something and he just couldn't do it. I held him to keep him from banging his head and biting his finger in anger. His frustration level has continued to increase dramatically this year. He is getting older and wants his needs met. When he beats his hands against the sides of his head it breaks my heart.

We had gone to a friend's house and her daughter had an SGD called a DynaVox®. She was able to touch the screen, and it said, "I want a drink" for her. This was exactly the kind of device that Brint needed. We wanted to know how we could get one for our son to use in school. We kept kicking ourselves, recalling that Brint's former teacher had specifically told us such a device would be perfect for him. Why hadn't we agreed to have him try the DynaVox® when we had the support? We kept telling ourselves it was his lack of manual dexterity that had inhibited us, but, now we realize that at the time we did not understand what the device could do.

No matter what, we wanted the device but had no idea how to get one. It cost about $5,000, and the school system was not going to pay for it readily. Naively, Susan thought that if she just told the school Brint needed one, then the school would give it to him. That began the fight that changed our lives and forced us to learn law, precedent, and obstruction tactics.

Our initial attempt was to call an emergency IEP meeting at the beginning of December. We told our autism coordinator the reason and asked an attorney friend of ours with experience in special education law to come to the meeting. We were expecting the usual kind of meeting, with our standard IEP team plus the AT specialist.

When we arrived, we were surprised to see a number of people we had not seen before, including the director of special programs. The Office of Special Education was ready for a contest; we were not. They listened to our argument that our son needed a DynaVox® to help him communicate. They got us with the first question, "Why a DynaVox®? What can it do that other SGDs cannot?" We hadn't done our homework and so were unprepared. Neither Susan nor I could compare it with any other device, because it was the only device we had seen. We did not even know that other devices existed.

We explained that the DynaVox® was appropriate because his former teacher had endorsed it, describing it as "more motivating." The team asked us why we hadn't agreed to it then. We had no answer. Meekly, Susan said it was because our son did not have the ability to point properly at the time. They asked what made us think he could do it now. We had no appropriate answer for this. They calmly suggested that we start with a much simpler device, called a "Communication Builder," and see whether our son had sufficient abilities to use an SGD. We had no idea about "other" SGDs, so we agreed to a trial using this simpler and less-expensive device for one month and then meet again.

That night we received the following email from our attorney friend who had helped us at the meeting:

> From my perspective, you lost the support you had been building with other IEP members when the AT specialist asked you what specific features of a voice output device you thought your son needed. You were not prepared to explain why the DynaVox® solution you proposed had the specific features that matched his communication need…features which are unavailable on the less expensive voice output devices in the school's inventory. To be candid, the AT specialist made reasonable arguments based on the actual features of the DynaVox® solution you had proposed as to why, in her professional opinion as a speech therapist, that device might be inappropriate for your son. Without being in a position to discuss one product's features in comparison to the features of other products, you were unable to rebut her arguments effectively.

He was right.

The following week our son was provided with a "Communication Builder." It was a "low-tech" device, requiring manual recording for a 12-frame overlay. If a particular word or activity was not on those 12 frames, you had to take out the sheet and replace it with one that had the required choice. While we appreciated what the device could do, it was cumbersome to use and quickly became very frustrating for Brint and for us! We spoke to the parent who had first shown us the DynaVox®, and she was not surprised at the school's tactic. She said she had eventually resorted to a court proceeding before the school agreed to purchase the DynaVox® for her child.

Rather than go down this long and potentially expensive track, we opted for the short, but probably equally expensive track, and bought our own DynaVox®. Bear in mind that these events took place well before the Apple iPad™ was available. We found out that rather than $5,000, it cost closer to $8,000. We reasoned we would have had to spend that kind of money on attorney fees anyway, so why waste the time? He needed help now. The school system was not prepared for this option. Now we could prove that we were right.

At the initial AT meeting we had asked whether our son's teacher and aides would receive training on a DynaVox® if he had one, to which they had agreed. We worked hard with our son at home, having him use his DynaVox® at every opportunity where there was the most chance for success. We wanted him to see that it could give him an instant reward for making a correct choice. Food items and play options were our focus. We took many videos of him using the device. We sent a DVD to the AT team to view before our next meeting. They were stunned. We showed Brint using the device effectively to communicate his basic needs and wants, having had the device for only three weeks!

At the end of the agreed one-month trial with the "low-tech" device, we entered the next IEP team meeting with renewed confidence. Our argument was that a simple device such as the "Communication Builder" could not be made to do more complicated things as our son's abilities improved. On the other hand, the DynaVox® could be made as simple as needed, and complexity could be introduced gradually. Brint would also be learning on the same device over time, rather than having to change devices as his needs changed and learn how to use new ones each time. We were sure that now our son could start making real progress with his communication, at home and at school. "Not so fast" was the message we received! The next tactic the school system used was that our son could not bring his own SGD to school, as it would not be properly insured. Our lawyer friend, who was at the meeting, said, "That is like saying to a child who cannot walk that he must check his wheelchair at the door and crawl to class because his device is not insured." Our son could not speak, so the DynaVox® was his voice. After a heated discussion, the AT team agreed to rent a DynaVox® for a one-month trial at school. What could go wrong?

Here is where we made our next mistake. We didn't ask to see the content of the proposed trial and assumed they would be testing our son's ability to make correct choices. So, when we reconvened at the end of April, we were told that our son had "failed the trial." Why? Because they had conceived of a trial to test not only our son's ability to make choices, but also his ability to move between the digital pages to reach particular screens. In their mind, for them to purchase a DynaVox®, the child must demonstrate expertise in its use. Susan and I felt foiled again! We complained that this was not a fair trial. They somewhat agreed, but said, "Oh dear, there won't be enough time left this school year to complete another trial." To which we replied, "Oh yes, there will!"

The next evening, we went to a special education advisory committee meeting and spoke to the director of special education there. She had delayed meeting with us, despite repeated requests. This time my wife, Susan, who is a physician, had sent her an email to document that we had spoken and to ensure that a meeting would indeed take place.

The director of special education then met with us. When she heard the whole saga, she was very understanding and surprisingly accommodating. She said, "Of course there was time for a re-trial and, if successful, the school system would insure the device while it was on school property. No problem." We were stunned and pleased.

We hastily arranged another meeting with the AT team, this time including the director of special education. We were pleasantly surprised at the sudden change of attitude and transparency. We reached agreement on a trial that was fair and would test our son's ability to use the device to the best of his current ability. We agreed on the symbols and range of choices to be on each page for the trial. The school would tabulate its use at school and we would do the same at home. We would collect data on success and failure rates at making correct choices. The trial started at the beginning of May, and we met again before the end of the school year. The trial was a success, meaning our son could bring our DynaVox® to school and our son's teacher would receive further training on the device over the summer.

All this had taken five months, involving countless hours of writing emails and attending meetings, together with lost sleep and indigestion. Most importantly, our son had lost five months of time to make progress with communication.

We will never know whether we would have been as successful in getting the school system to agree to the DynaVox® five months earlier had we approached the director in the first place. Regardless, we learned that being thankful and asking for help, rather than making demands, got the results that we needed for our son. We sent the director another email thanking her for her attendance at the meeting and for supporting the trial to be conducted before the end of the year. We noted that it would have been beneficial had the AT team made us aware of devices that could have been of benefit to Brint for purposes of discussion as a team. We also thanked the director for her time and understanding of our concern, ending with a suggestion to review the procedures in place to avoid a repeated instance in the case of other parents of children with disabilities.

The Bradshaws' Final Thoughts

Looking back, there are many things we could have done to expedite the final outcome, and there were many things the school system should have done. The school system should have discussed AT with us at each IEP meeting.

As parents, we should have been better informed of our legal rights and should have been aware that our son had unmet communication needs for AT. Being nonverbal, he had no means of engaging in discussions with teachers about the classroom curriculum or having social conversations with peers. This negatively affected his involvement and progress in the general curriculum. Likewise, because he had not been trained to use a vocal output device that produces synthesized speech, he had no ability to engage in social conversations with non-disabled peers at school or to participate successfully in non-academic activities. Only a vocal output device that produces synthesized speech would meet his communication needs at school.

The DynaVox®-type technology was too expensive for the school system to adopt for all nonverbal children with ASD, and so they resorted to an obstructionist policy. Now, with iPads™, the technology is less expensive and readily available to all. With the right application, even our iPhones™ can be used as effective communication devices. However, the adjunct and ongoing problem is training, even with the much less expensive iPads™. If the teacher and aides do not know how to use a device appropriately, then no matter how inexpensive or expensive it is, it will never be effective or useful. Training takes time and money. Sympathetic bodies rather than trained professionals and paraprofessionals will never be effective, no matter how much technology is at their disposal.

Analysis of the Bradshaws' Scenario

What Do We Know?

It is impossible to include every piece of information in the framework of this scenario or book. What we do know is what the parents have provided, and all that follows will be limited to that information, but many useful observations and conclusions can be made from this scenario.

Initially, we know that the Bradshaws' son was nine years old and that the IEP team had previously determined a diagnosis of autism and, more recently (he is now 12), cerebral palsy. There appear to be four major concerns presented:

1. Their son has no verbal communication skills.

2. The parents question the appropriateness and utility of the PECS™ (where the yet-to-be-diagnosed cerebral palsy interferes with the pointing accuracy requirements of the presently used communication system).

3. The weak skills of the teacher and aide are resulting in their son's behavioral regression (i.e., "learned helplessness" in toileting and eating).

4. Parents have limited familiarity with the regulations specific to children with disabilities.

We learn that the appropriateness of the DynaVox® was observable, taped, and reviewed later, but this was after the family purchased their own DynaVox® for use at home.

We do not have any information from the school; accordingly, discussion will be limited to the information provided by the parents. We do not have the parents' concerns stated using any of the behavioral components outlined earlier in the Introduction; that is, the behavioral functioning (levels of communication or accuracy of pointing) related to use of PECS™ are not stated in observable or measurable terms. We have no measures of progress or even regression from the child's use of the PECS™.

The result is that the school and parents have not yet agreed on how to describe what the behaviors are or the level of educational functioning that those behaviors produce. This failure to come to an agreement on these two important issues results in the school and the parents trying to work without a common framework. From there, they will move in separate directions and with different outcomes. However, had the full membership of the IEP team reached agreement on what we know and where we are, they would have taken the first step in collaboration. In other words, they would have had a shared understanding of the concerns presented initially by the parents and an agreed description of the specific educational behavior(s) to be discussed during the remainder of the IEP meeting. Instead, the divide continued to widen.

What should have taken place is for the parents to have stated their concerns, noting as much in behavioral terms as possible. They should have asked the school to do the same, showing student work or documentation of how the PECS™ was being used, under what circumstances, and what behaviors they were expecting to change and achieve, as well as the results of the initial PECS™ intervention over time. Then, as a group working together (collaborating), they would have reached a common agreement on the needs and degree of progress made using the current form of communication. From here, the team could then determine the answer to where we want to go with respect to the noted concerns—the goal they wish to establish.

Where Do We Want to Go?

In other words, "What goal do we want to establish?" Currently, the school and the parents want to go in two separate directions. Because school staff have neither identified nor introduced the issues raised, we will focus on what it is that the parents are requesting for their son—that is, a DynaVox®. This particular piece of AT would be able to address his motoric difficulties of pointing and foster communication between their son and those around him. The device could also be adjusted to meet the child's changing skill levels.

Certainly, there is nothing wrong with parents stating a desire for something to be included in an IEP. However, just as with any programming or services placed in an IEP, there must be a reason for its inclusion. In other words, the team must know the purpose and have an intention for its selection that is based on the child's needs and knowing what it will accomplish toward meeting those needs.

The parents saw a device for generating speech that they thought would provide their son with a way of communicating and would allow him to express his needs and respond to his environment in a manner that anyone could understand. They also saw that the DynaVox® helped achieve word-choice selection despite inaccurate pointing. However, when asked why they wanted the DynaVox®, they replied only by noting he was ready to point, albeit inaccurately. Had the team answered and agreed to the previous question ("What do we know?"), they would have recognized that the goal they all wanted was to improve communication, because, at this point, there had been minimal growth, and they would have agreed to the difficulty of pointing with accuracy, agreeing that progress was limited. The goal(s) would have been easy to identify, but the school skipped to questioning why the parents wanted the DynaVox®. The parents and the school needed to recognize that the motoric skills negatively impacted the present system of communication ("What do we know?"). Then, they needed to agree that the goal was to improve communication ("Where do we want to go?"). But both the parents and the school missed the essential step of reaching an agreement.

By now, we should have collectively and collaboratively reached two points of agreement, with the second based on the first. The first is that, using the present communication system, the child has limited communication skills and has difficulty pointing accurately, which is directly interfering with him making progress. The second is that the goal (where we want to go) is increasing communication skills and addressing his ability to point with accuracy.

How Will We Get There?

We are not going to get there—not without considerable effort and backtracking—as the parents and school have failed to answer, much less agree on the answers to, the first two questions. From this point on, the presentation will focus on what could have been done to circumvent the unnecessary delay in the appropriate AT selection. And we return to "What do we know?"

The parents want to employ the DynaVox®. Even without a rationale, parents have the right to make the proposal. Unfortunately, without understanding the benefits of any program, service, or intervention, it becomes difficult to understand its value. When a school is presented with an unknown program or intervention it is not unusual for the school to ask parents what this is and what, in terms of meeting needs, it might do. However, in this case, the school already had an AT specialist who could have, and should have, answered those questions. She did not, and this is where the parents needed to put additional questions to the specialists to explain the differences between the PECS™, the "Communication Builder," and the DynaVox®.

It is also not unusual for members of the IEP team to have different perspectives (e.g., parents and school, teachers and teachers, teachers and related service personnel, etc.), and this should not be surprising. In this example, the school was electing to intervene with something other than what the parents had requested. The first impression might be that school staff simply did not want to spend large amounts of money for an unknown in terms of student benefits. They should not be blamed for that. But, as those in attendance at this meeting had not reached any level of agreement to the first two questions, it is no wonder the direction of intervention—action taken to achieve a goal—was different from what the parents wanted.

As a result, a trial plan was to be developed and implemented. The parents felt this plan did not address the concerns they presented, because the "Communication Builder" was too similar to the PECS™ in terms of the level of manual dexterity required to operate it. So, they made a personally expensive decision and purchased their own DynaVox®, implemented it, and this time video-recorded its use. By doing so, they ingeniously found a way to:

1. explain the behaviors they wanted to change in an observable way

2. present the conditions under which the behaviors would be observed

3. show the effectiveness of their chosen intervention.

This is actually the purpose of a plan and the very components that should be in the plan.

The parents presented the results of the DynaVox® use at home to the IEP team, and also stated that a major difference between the "Communication Builder" and the DynaVox® is that the DynaVox® could be adjusted with the child's needs. After a heated discussion, the school agreed to another trial, but the trial plan was not developed with the parents. This, as the parents found out, was a mistake, because by not participating there was no assurance that the concerns they presented and discussed would be assessed in a fair way. Not surprisingly, the result of them not participating in the trial's development was that their son had "failed the trial." He failed because the trial was not designed to measure his ability to use the DynaVox® or its benefits to his communication skills, considering his manual dexterity. The school's plan was based upon an evaluation of his skills to "master" the use of the DynaVox®. Worse, when the parents complained that the issues presented were not measured through the trial, they were told there was no time for another trial.

Two issues appear from this last IEP meeting. The first is that parents should participate in all aspects of the IEP process, including the development of a trial plan. A plan is actually going to answer the questions of how we will get there, if we are getting there, and if we are there. In developing the trial, it is essential that the educational behaviors in the plan are the same as those under discussion, and this is exactly what the parents did when they video-recorded their son's use of the DynaVox®.

It is important that the conditions under which the intervention is employed are the same as those for the expected behavior that is currently observed. The conditions, once changed, can affect the behavior, much as it would to work with a child using a computer keyboard for writing, but then to evaluate his skills using paper and pencil. The results would be different.

Key to a plan is that, in order to know if we are getting there, we also need to know how the behavior will be assessed (when, where, and how often), how (measures of accuracy, time period, or frequency), and when the data will be collected, along with a timeline for the implementation, including starting and ending dates. These measures, assessed during the trial, will let us know if we are likely to meet the stated goal or achieve the target behavior.

A concern arises when there is dissatisfaction with the decision of the school. The Bradshaws elected to go to the director of special education and voice their concerns, which entailed having to relay the entire history. Another avenue would have been to ask the school representatives what recourse/options they, as parents, had under the federal rules and regulations. By law, the person asked must inform you of those options/rights. While this does not negate the possibility of contacting a higher level of staff, it can circumvent the need to do so. At the very least, it will provide more information regarding what steps could be taken regarding the issues of the disagreement.

When the Bradshaws were asked why they wanted the DynaVox® and what the device could do, they could have:

1. asked the AT specialist what it could do

2. asked what options there were in determining the appropriate AT device, or

3. directly asked for an assistive technology evaluation to determine the needs for AT.

Keep in mind that it is always appropriate to ask about federal options and parental rights—or state and local regulations, policies, and procedures—when there appears to be an impasse, or even if you just want to know the answer for your own general information. Follow this up by asking to be shown the regulations, having them explained, and requesting a copy to be made for future reference.

How Do We Know When We Have Arrived?

The answer to this question might seem obvious, but it is important to ask so that everyone agrees on the answer. Ultimately, the answer will be, "When the stated goal has been achieved." What this looks like and what criteria will be used will be determined by how the goal is written in the plan. Another question that goes along with this is, "First, how do we keep what we have?" This is not the time to say, "Well, we are here, and we have done our job." We need to ensure that any gains are not lost. The school and the parents need to stay informed, to receive scheduled reports to ensure the child is not losing skills. If either the school or the parents find the child is losing skills, you will need to revisit these topics. There are no maximum numbers of reviews. The minimum is to review progress (or regression) and the IEP once annually.

At any time, a parent may ask what the particular regulations are with respect to any item found within an IEP. You may also ask to see the pertinent section and may request to see the state regulations and any local policies and procedures that might apply to the topic under discussion. You may request all three, and expect to receive them and to have them explained to you so that you understand them. It is important to remember that if you do not understand something, you have both the right and the responsibility to ask for clarification. No one expects you to know all of the laws, rules, and regulations.

In this scenario, there remained a major disagreement between the school's and the parents' proposal. The parents could have asked for a full AT evaluation to be conducted by the school, or asked for an independent educational evaluation, specific to AT needs, to be carried out by someone outside of the school system.

When it comes to AT, it is not enough simply to say that none is provided, therefore none is needed. The parents and the school must work together to determine if any of the needs identified in the IEP may require the use of AT to meet the goals established in the IEP. This process starts by identifying the needs of the child and identifying the goals for the child. Then, you must consider how those needs can be met, so that those goals can be achieved. This does not mean that parents should present a smorgasbord list of desired technologies. Neither does it mean that the school should assert that technologies can only be used at some predetermined proficiency level. It means that parents and the school should work together to match needs with assistance, in the context of the goals, which may or may not include the use of AT.

The scheduled times for reporting on IEP progress should be written into the IEP. It is important for you to review the reports you receive from the school to verify that what you are seeing at home is similar to what you are seeing at school.

Of course, another choice after reaching a goal is to change it in some way, such as increasing the frequency, the accuracy, or some other measure. But the basis for change should continue to be grounded on what we know through data.

Who Is Responsible for This Plan?

In all cases, it is important that parents know who is going to provide the various services and ensure integrity of application. Parents share responsibility for this. Specifically, parents are responsible for monitoring their child's progress and for carefully reviewing the progress reports sent home. The point is, the entire team as individuals is responsible for the implementation of the plan and for monitoring the child's progress. Simply stated, parents need to remain vigilant in attending to the child's educational growth and for remaining in contact with the child's teachers.

Key Regulations to Know

All IEPs require that the areas of communication and AT be discussed during:

1. the initial IEP writing

2. an annual review meeting, or

3. any other time that the team determines a need for an IEP meeting to be held.

Again, the justification of need and benefit in attaining the goal is required and was the issue in this particular case.

Although there are a number of AT assessment procedures that could be used, we will discuss the Student, Environment, Task, and Tools (SETT) Framework, which is an exemplary structure for moving through the process of considering AT needs (Zabala 2010[1]). The steps of the process are very similar to the IEP process presented in this book. It is a decision-making process that is also based on a collaborative format. The framework is summarized in the following paragraphs.

Briefly, the entire IEP team must first consider the student and his or her needs, strengths, and weaknesses. The next step is to assess the environment in which the child receives services. The environment here refers to everything that is currently available to the child, from materials and equipment (including desks) to the space

---

1 www.joyzabala.com, accessed on June 21, 2013.

in the hallway, and from student attitudes to general access to staff, for example. Tasks reference the educational demands or activities that are required or available that relate to the IEP, enabling participation in the school curriculum and activities.

Key to the SETT is that it is a set of steps used to assess the child's needs and then to determine what the child might need to enable participation in the school educational community and to support student achievement. It should not be considered a process to determine which AT device to select. It is equally important to note that the process might result in the team determining that there is no need for technology. Finally, implementation of the SETT Framework incorporates many of the very questions we have used in this scenario.

Key Points

- Although there are a number of minor points that could be discussed, there is a major one that warrants special attention. The fact that the parents rather than the school purchased a DynaVox® may be perceived as the largest issue. However, there was one basic question that could have been posed during the IEP meeting that could have negated that purchase.

- That question is what do the laws and regulations say with regard to AT and the trial of various AT devices? The result would have been a full evaluation of Brint's needs, abilities, and recommendations for appropriate AT devices.

- It is essential to note that the parents knew what their child's communication difficulties were and that their focus was on his needs—not theirs—and they could identify those needs. What happened is that they did not know how to present their "case" to the team with measurable data to show the value and utility of the DynaVox® and, when challenged at the IEP meeting, they realized this. But it was not their responsibility to do so.

- The parents were under no obligation to compare and contrast various AT devices. That is the purpose of an "AT meeting" and the function of the specialist. Here was an opportunity to ask what the regulations were regarding AT and to ask several questions, beginning with, "Can you please show me your measures of progress on the communication goals and objectives?" That is the "Where are we?" question and the beginning of any IEP meeting. It would have shown that Brint was not making progress using the current intervention. And the next questions would have been, "Where do we want to go?" and "How will we get there?"

- Unfortunately, the Bradshaws began the meeting with what they wanted to be provided, and the school immediately challenged that request, disputing the need and the value of the intervention (DynaVox®): "Where are we?" "Where do we want to go?" "How will we get there?" The school was right in wanting the answers, but the school was responsible for providing those answers.

- When the Bradshaws returned, they were able, via video, to show the team what Brint could and could not do using the purchased DynaVox®. They did the school's job, but, not having asked about the law and the school's policies on AT, they felt this was their only recourse—and a successful one.

As pointed out earlier, you can't get to "there" from "here" if you don't know where "here" is. When the parents showed the IEP team the video, it became clear what the needs were (where we are) with respect to communication. The video also showed the possibility for improved communication (where we want to go) and the ways the DynaVox® could help (how to get there). And, of course, by helping to write the plan of use, they would know if they were getting there, when they were there, and whether to change the goal at the end of the IEP. One answer provides the basis for the next question, with each answer being agreed upon, reached through a collaborative process.

Summary

Very quickly, the reader will recognize the similarities between the development of an IEP, the questions to ask found in this book, and the SETT process described earlier. This process of collaboration is also supported by research. This book will focus on the application of these steps. The major tenet of this book is to ask key questions in a specific order, recognizing that the team is collaborating—building on small steps of agreement—to answer each question, and that each question relates directly to the child and the child's needs.

Finally, the reader should see that each question is based firmly on the answers to the previous question. It is the child's needs that are to be programmed for and met, and not the institutional or personal needs of anyone. The end product is much stronger because a team of people have created it, agreed to it, and committed themselves to its implementation—and success. And, so, you can get from "here" to "there" if you know where "here" is and where "there" is, and if you know why you want to go "there."

CHAPTER 2

The IEPs Went Right, But Their Expectations Were Too Low

This story portrays the struggles that Holly Editor experienced when trying to determine what it was that made her three children with autism "different." She knew something was different and attempted to explain to the medical professionals what she saw in her children, but the words failed her. Frustration continued until a family member pulled her aside to share her observations, as a nurse, and her conclusions with Mrs. Editor. With that, Mrs. Editor began her trek to find assistance for her three sons who exhibit three levels of autism—mild, moderate, and severe. In her scenario, she provides insightful observations—recognized in hindsight—that you will find very helpful, including concerns over special education labeling and educators' possible preconceptions based on those labels.

The Danger of False Assumptions

"…I couldn't put what I saw into words, the kind of words the professionals needed to hear. So, my concerns were dismissed."

As the mother of four children, three of whom have diagnoses on the autism spectrum, I have found that many people look at my life with a miserable sort of awe. I am a writer and an advocate, so people expect me to have the answers. Few can imagine themselves in my shoes. Few realize that I'm just doing the best I can. Fewer still realize that sometimes I don't have the answers; sometimes I get it wrong; sometimes I need help. They come to me for advice, information, encouragement, and direction. I gladly give it when I can. But sometimes I'm the one in need. Though I've been very lucky in getting some great teams at some great schools, though I've been dedicated and involved in the Individualized Education Program (IEP) process, I've still hit a brick wall that I don't know how to tear down. I need help.

It's not an unfamiliar feeling. I had my first child, Tommy, when I was 19, exactly nine months and eight days after marrying my husband. I'd taken a child development class in the tenth grade, so I knew sometimes children were born unhealthy or with developmental disorders. I knew there was a chance for a high quality life even with such a disorder. But the examples the teacher used in that class were the kind of disorders that were pretty obvious, like Down syndrome, or ones discovered by a medical test of some kind, like sickle cell anemia. She never mentioned autism. The only things I knew about autism I had learned from the movie *Rain Man*[1].

There were signs that something was different from the very beginning. Tommy didn't like gentle touches, especially while eating. He wouldn't engage in social games. Tommy babbled and talked on schedule, but his younger brother, Bradley (who was born about a year after he was), didn't. Then, Tommy regressed, losing the ability to speak and to regulate his sensory system. Had I known about autism or sensory defensiveness, I might have understood. But I didn't; I thought it was my fault.

It probably doesn't help that I experienced a serious bout of post-partum depression, exacerbated by birth control hormones, after Bradley was born. It certainly didn't help that everyone seemed to think I was too young to be a mother, and that my husband and I were too poor to provide our children with the opportunities necessary for optimal development. All around us was this pervasive disapproval, and whether at the doctor's office or at the local clinic, it seemed that every time I raised my concerns about my children's development, they weren't taken seriously. *I* wasn't taken seriously.

I tried to get help, but I was perceived as "one of those mothers," the kind of mother who read the baby books and "freaked out" when things didn't go her way; except, I really wasn't one of those mothers. I didn't take my child to the doctor for a case of the sniffles. I didn't obsess over every little thing. I wasn't making something out of nothing. Something was seriously, truly, objectively wrong. For a long time, despite being a writer, I couldn't put what I saw into words, the kind of words the professionals needed to hear. So, my concerns were dismissed.

That began to change when I received an invitation to attend Child Development Days, during which the local elementary schools invite kids from their neighborhoods, kids who are too young to have started school, to have their developmental progress assessed. The idea behind this program is to catch kids who

---

1 1988, directed by Barry Levinson, distributed by MGM.

need special education services when they're young, in the hope that they'll be ready for school when it's time for kindergarten. So, we took the boys in to be assessed.

There was a line, of course. By the time it was our turn, I already knew we needed their help. The other kids laughed and played. They engaged with their parents, with the other kids, and with the teachers. The other kids behaved like all the kids I'd grown up with. But not mine. My kids screamed and cried, throwing tantrums on the floor or in my arms. In a room full of kids, my kids stood out, and not in a good way.

The teacher who screened them referred us to a program—Birth to Three—that would provide special educational services to help our kids get on track. The boys had speech and fine-motor developmental delays, so we received speech therapy and occupational therapy. We tried putting Tommy into the pre-K classroom, but all he did was scream and throw tantrums. So, we stuck with the therapies that were provided in our home. Slowly, we made progress.

We made the mistake of assuming that Bradley's delays were somehow a reaction to Tommy's delays. I figured once we had Tommy on track, Bradley would naturally follow. A lot of people have made that assumption since then, but it's never happened. Tommy is Tommy; Bradley is Bradley. Helping one child doesn't really do much to help the other. So, like I said, I've made some mistakes over the years.

Of course, providing the boys with special education services was only the first step. We knew they had developmental delays, but not why. I accepted the lack of explanation for too long. Actually, it took a family gathering held at a restaurant—the big family dinner to celebrate my sister-in-law's wedding—before we got that final nudge.

Every time we brought the boys into the restaurant, the sensory stimuli would overwhelm them, and they would cry and scream. When we took them out, they'd calm down. When we brought them back in, they'd start crying again. As obvious as the pattern was, we didn't see it. We were too immersed in the experience and too ignorant of the symptoms of autism to recognize what was happening. But my husband's grandmother knew that, whatever it was, it was more than just developmental delays. She told us we needed to get help.

It still took several months for us to find a diagnostician who could tell us Tommy had autism. (And, again, I decided it was best to wait with Bradley.) The first diagnostician couldn't offer us any services. So, we sought another provider for a second opinion, and this one promised services in its online documentation. But the services they offered weren't what we had in mind. The doctor recommended we institutionalize Tommy. We refused.

It was a couple of years later, after Bradley got his own diagnosis, that we were contacted once again—this time by someone who worked with Tommy and Bradley in the Birth to Three program. She was the newly created autism waiver coordinator for our county. Finally, the boys would get the services they needed to treat their autism. And, even there, we made another mistake. We stuck with a provider even after the relationship turned sour.

I know a lot about autism and special education—now. A lot of people consider me an expert. But, if I'm an "expert," I assure you that experts don't know everything. We become experts by making mistakes, by learning from them, and by doing research to prevent more mistakes. Even experts need help. Even experts need to consult with people who know more than we do. That's how we learn.

I know a lot about special education, I know even more about autism, and I know still more about my boys. But I've hit a brick wall. Like I said, I need help.

You see, my three sons with special needs are something of a study in the spectrum that is autism. Tommy, my oldest child, fit the criteria for a classic autism diagnosis when he was first assessed, developing "typically" and then regressing. He became almost completely nonverbal, threw tantrums, cried out in pain in response to stimuli that "shouldn't" hurt (e.g., he said that his hair hurt when it was being cut), and basically manifested the stereotypical autistic behaviors. Then, with interventions, he "recovered" to the point that he can be mainstreamed in school (inclusion). He has friends, talks, plays, and even longs for his first girlfriend. It's shocking, at least for those who assume that autism is a tragedy. Some would claim he's not autistic any more, but he is and does as well as he does because of modifications, interventions, adaptations, and assistance. In short, by traditional standards, we got things right with Tommy. (When, in fact, Tommy is just a different child with different needs.)

Bradley is another story. He never regressed. He simply never followed a traditional developmental trajectory. Bradley is primarily nonverbal, meaning that he cannot use speech to communicate effectively. His sensory system is on near-constant overload, meaning he cannot experience a typical environment without discomfort. And both his social skills and his social desires are atypical, meaning that, while he craves affection and interaction, he cannot interact "normally" and he is not motivated by "normal" social impulses.

For example, when Bradley wants the attention of an adult, he'll grab a hand and pull toward whatever he wants. This is an effective form of communication for him. On the other hand, he rarely engages with other children, even his own brothers. If another child initiates an interaction in a way Bradley understands, he will participate—but he rarely initiates. Mostly, he stands back and watches other children, or ignores them altogether.

Despite his nonverbal status, Bradley is disruptively loud on a near-constant basis. He cannot handle a large variety of sensory inputs and tends to lash out aggressively, either due to communication challenges or sensory overload. Ironically, noise is the biggest thing that bothers him. Did I mention that Bradley is loud?

I mean, he's fire-siren loud! I assume it's a coping mechanism, but his means of communication are not yet sophisticated enough for him to communicate why he makes these loud, disruptive noises, at least not in a way any of the adults I've spoken with can understand. Bradley's physical control of his own body—from walking to fine motor, from toileting to dressing—is impaired. Simply put, Bradley is at the severe end of the autism spectrum and our attempts to help him have been largely inadequate. (Again, he is a very different child with different needs.)

Just to round things off, Jimmy, my youngest, is somewhere in between. He is not as far along as Tommy, but his developmental trajectory arcs right between his brothers. He already talks more effectively than Bradley, but not quite as effectively as Tommy. He doesn't have Tommy's physical control, but he can do more than Bradley can. Jimmy's therapies and interventions have been more successful than Bradley's, but aren't enough to launch him into the mainstream the way Tommy's have. He also has aggressive tendencies.

Jimmy is very self-centered. If he wants something, he'll take it. If the person who has it resists, he'll pinch them. If that doesn't work, he'll kick or bite them, depending on whether his foot or mouth is closer. If you try to stop him from doing something, he'll kick, bite, or pinch you. And sometimes he pinches, bites, or kicks for no apparent reason.

For years, Bradley took Jimmy's mistreatment, without returning any of the same. Then, Bradley had enough and started fighting back. This is not meant to imply that we don't intervene. We certainly do. It's just that we haven't found a way consistently to prevent these behaviors before they start.

All of this stands as a testament to the spectrum nature of autism—severe, moderate, and mild (relative to each other). Our goals for Bradley and Jimmy aren't to make them like Tommy, just like our goal for Tommy isn't to make him like Cody (their oldest brother and my stepson). But, and this is a big but, there's a difference between my boys having different developmental trajectories and one of my boys not receiving the educational services he needs. And that's my brick wall. There's a fundamental misassumption going on here, and that's the barrier I need to break down for the sake of my sons.

What Do Our IEPs Look Like?

Before we get into that, I think it's important to acknowledge that, relative to the experiences of many parents, our IEPs are something of a dream. It's also important to acknowledge that, aside from doing my part, these results are not something that I achieved alone. Our IEP meetings are a team effort that rely on the combined knowledge, experience, and dedication of people who are committed to doing right by their charges.

So, what does a good IEP meeting look like?

I receive an informal notice when an IEP meeting is coming up. I tend to keep my calendar pretty flexible, but with medical appointments that are set three to six months in advance, it's important to ensure there's no overlap. My IEP team mates from the school have always been very accommodating in that regard, which is important.

When the IEP meeting date is getting close, I receive a formal notice, which I am expected to sign to indicate that I will be attending. If I forget, they'll be sure to have a copy for me at the meeting. I also get another notice the day before the meeting in the form of a note in the communication log, a spiral-bound notebook that goes back and forth to school with the boys.

This routine was started by staff in the boys' Three to Five preschool program, which I have continued as the boys have progressed to other schools. The communication log is a way for parents and teachers to communicate on a daily or as-needed basis, without having to resort to phone calls or emails. It's like passing notes, except the notebook serves as a record of the communications.

It's also important to note that my husband, Kenneth, does not attend IEP meetings. He attended one, and that was enough educational bureaucracy for him. But he does want to provide his input. The teachers call throughout the year, and especially close to upcoming IEP meetings, to converse with him about his concerns and expectations. This helps Kenneth to feel included in the process, without any unnecessary childcare expenses and without forcing him to endure any bureaucratic procedures.

Daytime IEP meetings are usually a bad fit for me, so we tend to schedule the meetings for after school. My husband is a stay-at-home dad, so he's responsible for getting the kids off the bus and orienting them to the home routine, but I'm also a work-at-home mom (one of the benefits of being a freelance writer), and part of their routine is to get time with me. The result is that I'm often late to meetings. Staff could take this as a sign of disrespect, or as if I didn't care, but they don't. They understand and they accommodate these delays.

The meeting starts with a review of what we know. We talk, about where the particular boy is in regards to development, skill acquisition and retention, health, behaviors, and anything else that seems pertinent. We can spend anywhere from 20 to 45 minutes on this.

Once we've agreed on my son's current behaviors and progress, we cover any recent testing results. Testing may be government-required standardized testing, in which case they discuss not only the scores, but the accommodations, how successful they were, and how engaged the child was during the test. If it's a re-evaluation or an assessment to determine whether he qualifies for a new service, that can take much longer than the 10 to 15 minutes we might spend on a lower level assessment—perhaps a full meeting is devoted to such discussion.

We will next address past goals in terms of progress made toward meeting those goals, and new goals simultaneously for each section. The teacher or therapist most responsible for the set of goals presents the past goal followed by a discussion on the amount of progress made. We often rely more heavily on anecdotal evidence, rather than numerical data, but we also use measurements, such as "three out of four trials," to keep our perceptions in check. The teacher or therapist most responsible for the goal usually then proposes a new one. Sometimes it is a variation on the old one where, if the child has achieved a goal of "three out of four trials," we might bump it up to "four out of five trials" until we're confident that the skill has been mastered.

Once all goals in a particular set are covered, we discuss whether additional goals are needed, or if we want to try a new approach toward achieving the goals. One risk here is that we—usually me—can go off on tangents. These are relevant tangents, but tangents nonetheless. It is important to discuss what happens at home, too. This helps to better understand the child, and can assist in devising approaches to issues than we might otherwise do with only a partial set of information. This can take an hour to an hour and a half.

Much of what we cover in IEP meetings is based on decisions we've made in the past, so the hard work has already been done and now we just have to push it a little further as the boys' progress. On the other hand, sometimes we need to cover a larger issue that has recently surfaced.

When these issues occur, which we know about ahead of time and often schedule meetings exclusively to deal with, we devote a significant amount of time to brainstorming. The teachers or therapists may have a particular approach in mind, but that is not to say they've already made up their minds. The issue, and approach, or possible approaches are presented and discussed by all team members. The approach may be tweaked, or it may be changed radically, or we, as a team, may decide to go in a totally different direction. To me, this process is the primary reason our IEP meetings are so successful and so effective.

We all have something—knowledge, expertise, experience—to bring to the table, and it's this combination that makes for a stronger, more effective whole. It's much more time consuming when we're considering major changes, because there are a lot more data to present—both anecdotal and numerical. Before we make changes, we need to know what is going on, what the problem is, what the solutions are, and what the data tell us. Without that, and the discussion among team members, we're just shooting in the dark.

We then cover the hours of services, transportation, and other things that rarely change. We also discuss accommodations, modifications, and technologies, which tend to fluctuate a bit more as the boys get older and make progress in their development.

All told, an IEP meeting can take anywhere from two to three hours. It's a long, tiring process, but in order to share the information we need to make the best decisions we can, it needs to be a long process.

Now here's the caveat: as someone who's been trained in business, I have to note that, while we rely on information to make informed decisions, the information we use is primarily qualitative. In other words, it is very subjective. We don't analyze the statistics of specific behaviors. Our approach to understanding the numerical aspects of the data is limited to whether they achieved "three out of four trials," or whether they succeed more or less often than targeted.

I'm familiar with the Applied Behavior Analysis (ABA) approach. ABA usually involves an extensive use of data tracking and the processing of many numerical values to achieve a graph-like picture of the child's progress. The data can be tedious and yet demonstrate tangible nuggets of information. However, that information often does little good, in my experience. This isn't because the information isn't valuable, but because the time and effort to gather the information, and then to present and process it, takes up time without increasing gains. So you need to ensure any data you intend to collect are worth the time-sacrifice of collecting them.

For example, when Bradley was receiving intensive in-home therapy, using a strict ABA approach, the therapist would spend 15 minutes orienting herself by reviewing past data (since that therapist's last visit), spend 10 to 20 minutes working on a goal, spend 5 to 20 minutes recording data, and then move on to the next goal—losing Bradley's attention and cooperation in the intervening wait time of recording the goals. A less strict ABA approach requires less time to process past data and record current data, leaving more time to work with the child and shorter intervals in which the child may be diverted away from the "work" of therapy.

I've found that a more subjective approach provides more time to instruct, instead of number crunching. Generally speaking, personal testimony can be just as useful, while simultaneously requiring less data-management time, which takes away from actual learning time. In fact, knowing the surrounding circumstances (which are often not included in numerical presentations) can be more important than knowing the specific behaviors. If Bradley is in a noisy, busy environment, he's not going to be on-task—the data prove that. We don't need to know how much of that time is spent biting his wrist versus bouncing in his chair. What we need to know is that this noisy environment is not an effective setting for Bradley. Nonetheless, records of time-consuming, detailed observations can be essential when the team is having trouble figuring more complex behavioral issues that are not so obvious.

The Segregated Classroom

Even a great team doesn't always agree. When we do agree, that doesn't necessarily mean that I get what I want. When Bradley was transitioning from the Three to Five program to elementary school, I experienced my first IEP-related "thwarted desire" as a parent.

I went into the meeting firm in my belief that I did not want my son to be placed in a "segregated classroom." I knew that, while this school district placed students in inclusion classrooms when they reached a certain developmental level, they typically segregated students like my son. I knew that it would be a battle to get full inclusion for Bradley.

I had recently attended an excellent parent training program and was full of the possibilities of what parents could do. I knew that, had it not been through the efforts of parents who had come before me, children with disabilities would not have been entitled to an education at all. So I went into this IEP prepared to do battle for my son's right to be placed in an inclusive environment. If, for example, Bradley were to be placed in a segregated classroom, it meant that he would be transferred to a school that his brothers did not attend. I did not like that thought.

When I say I was prepared to do battle, I must note that I did not have or want a combative relationship with the school staff. Our interactions, even when we disagreed, were positive and constructive. Keeping these relationships was important.

I brought a bag full of documentation proving that what I wanted was possible. The Three to Five program was already a fully inclusive environment—students without disabilities also attended so that the students with disabilities had positive peer models. I just wanted that environment to continue for Bradley, as it had for Tommy.

How can I describe this meeting? I can't remember the precise events or words. I know that, despite being on distinctly different sides, it wasn't combative. They weren't there to ensure I lost, and I wasn't there to ensure I won. We were there to ensure that Bradley *received the support he needed*, though we saw that need differently.

Everyone already knew what I wanted and how much and why I wanted it. I spoke in spurts, gushing one minute, listening silently the next. As the meeting progressed, they described in brutal detail the support they knew Bradley needed and why he needed it. They knew just how extensive that support was, and they described it all, using data to show everything they did to support Bradley in the educational environment, from safety to education, from helping him to manage his aggression to verbal skills, just everything. They didn't talk about where he'd receive this support. They didn't make their case for a particular kind of setting, as I wanted to do. They just laid out exactly what Bradley needed.

And I couldn't disagree. I knew the supports Bradley needed to access his education and how extensive those supports were. I knew how much of that support would continue to be needed for years to come. After all, I had helped to design the level and nature of supports he received during all the previous IEP meetings.

After we had talked for nearly two hours about the support Bradley needed, the subject of where and how to provide that support came up. I jumped in, claiming they could do for Bradley what they did for Tommy—they could mainstream him with an aide. But it wasn't the same and I knew it. Tommy can, for the most part, keep up with the mainstream curriculum. When he needs modifications, the team of regular education teachers receives assistance from the therapists and a group of teachers and a special group of therapists specially trained on providing services and support to students with autism—and it's enough.

For Tommy, in grade school, it was mostly a matter of using more pictures, making assignments shorter, or blowing up the assignments on a copy machine to give him more space to write. The aide kept him on-task and helped him exit the room gracefully when he needed a break. Bradley needed so much more support than that.

The teachers didn't need to modify Bradley's assignments. Bradley needed totally different assignments. Without the language component in place—without the ability to use either receptive or expressive language at grade level—Bradley couldn't keep up with his peers academically. For Bradley to succeed, the entire approach needed to be modified, and to be implemented by trained professionals.

He needed more technology to facilitate his education and fewer demands to demonstrate his understanding. He needed more support for the basic daily living skills, too, and he also needed curricula designed to teach him to develop those skills. In short, he needed the full special education package, instead of special education supplementing his regular education package.

They could not provide him with that level of support and services in the home school. They had the therapists there already, of course, but they would have to hire a teacher just for him. And that wasn't even the most difficult hurdle. The school was an older building, built solidly of brick and cement blocks, and they did not have a room that could be modified to adapt to Bradley's sensory needs—open spaces where he could move freely while learning, or multiple quiet areas (at least one for learning and one for down-time) which he could use to better regulate himself. In contrast, the school they recommended was a recently built school with rooms designed to accommodate the needs of children just like my Bradley, rooms segregated from their mainstreamed peers.

It was a sad moment. The inevitability of the decision, the sympathy of the staff, and the overwhelming sense of failure hit me hard. I don't cry easily or often. If I have to cry, I save it for when I am alone, or at least at home. But I cried then. And I wasn't alone.

After the meeting was over, before I left the building, one of the team members took me aside. She gave me a brief account of what I would need to do to "take on" the school district. She wasn't trying to talk me out of my decision, but she wanted me to understand what it would take. She laid it out, and assured me that if I decided to do this, I would have support.

But, there was also an easier way to get most of what I wanted. All the support Bradley would need would be at the other school, and as Bradley made gains he could be incorporated more fully into the regular classrooms at that school. And, with my dedication, I could also propose completely new solutions within that environment. It was something of a consolation prize, and I knew it.

I don't regret that decision. I can only fight so many battles before I wear myself out, and when it comes to giving my children the best chance they can have at a high quality of life, it seems like the entire world is my battle ground. Besides, I did get them to try some new things to expose Bradley to regular education peer models, and to expose those peers to him. The kids loved it.

I had proposed bringing peer models to visit Bradley in his classroom, instead of taking Bradley to the regular classroom. It became a privilege to be the student who got to go, relying on good behavior and setting a positive example to earn the privilege. With coaching from the special education teacher and the aides, Bradley and his regular education peer would engage in parallel play and turn-taking. The peers got to see the work Bradley was expected to do, and how a lot of that work was made into play-like activities. It was fun for all of them.

The "Cognitive" in Disability

The biggest problem, in my experience, with a segregated classroom for children labeled with "cognitive disabilities" is the assumption that a child placed in such a classroom must therefore have a cognitive disability. Now, this isn't a problem if you use "cognitive disability" to mean a disability in which a person has greater difficulty with some mental tasks. Unfortunately, our linguistic gymnastics to create a politically correct way to refer to people whose IQs are lower than average—the language for which has been hi-jacked almost exclusively to mean something prejudicially bad—has, in the minds of many, made "cognitive disability" into something synonymous with mental retardation or intellectual disability. Cognitive disability is an umbrella category that covers a great many disabilities. But if you assume that a child in such a classroom *must* have a lower IQ, then we have a problem.

Autism is a cognitive disability, but tells you nothing about IQ. Autism tells you that a child has difficulties with language, socialization, and sensory processing—all of which is true in the case of my son, Bradley. His severe disability in each of these categories readily explains his present performance levels. But none of it informs us of his IQ. Yet, some have assumed that, because Bradley was in this classroom and his performance doesn't prove otherwise, he must be mentally retarded.

I want to make it perfectly clear that I wouldn't be offended by the label or the assumption that my son is mentally retarded if that was the whole story. I wouldn't love or value my son any less because of it. I wouldn't be offended by the label if it was accurate. Having said that, I *am* offended by the label that my son is mentally retarded because *it's not an accurate description*.

I am offended by the way this assumption has made people treat my son. Part of this is because *nobody* should be treated that way. I'm offended that anyone would assume that my son can't learn something, because they assume that there's not enough intellectual potential for him to learn.

For whatever unknown reason, Bradley's ability to communicate is severely impaired. But that does not mean that his ability to *think* is severely impaired. Bradley's ability to *socialize* is severely impaired. But that does not mean that his ability to *acquire knowledge* is severely impaired. It does mean, however, that his ability to demonstrate his skills is severely impaired. It also means that his *motivation* to communicate (i.e., his desire to interact in socially acceptable and expected ways) is severely impaired.

Case in point: Bradley will not consistently complete the exercises that demonstrate his knowledge of the English alphabet. He won't consistently show us that he knows his letters. And why should he? He can't rattle off his letters. He can't sing the alphabet song. He can do worksheets, but why should he? I mean, really? The *reason* for doing those worksheets is to:

1. demonstrate he knows his letters, and thus

2. gain his teacher's approval.

But what if the child doesn't care? My stepson is a teenager and he has one home (ours) that puts a high priority on education and another home (his mother's) that does not. He wants to be a rock star and travel the world. He can rattle off the names of a bunch of rock stars without high school diplomas. (We can counter with the names of rock stars with long-term success and who have advanced degrees in music, but that has no impact on his perception of the value of education.) He doesn't care to do the work to demonstrate his knowledge. We, however, can place consequences (i.e., the loss of privileges) on him if he does not complete his work. He cares about those consequences. We can also express our pride and satisfaction when he does his work and gets good grades—he cares about that, too.

That strategy doesn't work with Bradley. So, instead of assuming that Bradley struggles with communication and is not motivated consistently to demonstrate his knowledge, his teachers assume that he lacks the knowledge. Within the realm of autism this would not be unheard of. Knowledge and skills that are available one day can be "gone" the next, inaccessible by adult or child. One strategy is to keep drilling, keep practicing until that knowledge or skill is always available to the child.

When do you stop assuming the child doesn't know his letters and start assuming that maybe, just maybe, the child who will not consistently complete your worksheets is thoroughly bored with those worksheets? After *five years* of reading and writing, but not consistently completing alphabet worksheets, do you think it's safe to assume that the child in question knows his letters?

I'm not a teacher and don't know how to teach Bradley what he needs to learn. But I know I can get his interest and teach him various things at home, the way any parent would, from a quick science lesson to how to use a piece of technology, to reading or writing. I know, from how quickly and ably Bradley acquires knowledge that he's interested in, that Bradley does not, in fact, have an intellectual disability. He has a social, communication, and sensory processing disability. And these disabilities definitely impair his ability to learn in a standard teaching environment. But it does not limit the amount or volume of what he can learn, especially if motivated. Maybe he'll show you that he knows something once, but he's not repeating it just to show you that he can, and we cannot make him do it.

What Do I Do Now?

In the last few years, there has been a change in teachers—this time for the better. These new teachers were able to put aside the old assumptions and see a different side of Bradley, reaching new conclusions in the process. This means the urgency of the issue of lower expectations is no longer as intense. However, Bradley is also being bumped up to middle school next year. How will I help those teachers and therapists to find a truly effective way to teach Bradley within his very real constraints? What do I tell them? How do I convince them? What form of documentation or proof should I offer?

Analysis of "The Danger of False Assumptions"

Before the school's IEP process is reviewed, a short summary of the children's disabilities and their mother's learning experiences is in order. Like so many parents, Mrs. Editor experienced what almost every parent in this book has acknowledged. All parents felt that something was different about their child, but were not immediately able to determine what it was or readily to define and describe it. Also, they had difficulty in finding a professional who would diagnose their child's behaviors as a disability, much less recognize the pattern of behaviors to be that of autism.

Additionally, Mrs. Editor described herself as a parent who was perceived as "one of those mothers," the ones who call or visit the doctor with minor issues of concern—as perceived by the professional staff. These are staff who routinely see relatively few infants and toddlers with autism. What they are accustomed to seeing is normal infants' development and first-time parents whose concerns are often a combination of an anxious mother or father, lack of experience in parenting skills, or a developmental skill or behavior found on the edge of the range for expected development, but not low enough (delayed) to warrant a concern. We are talking about the pattern—connecting the dots—of behaviors that are not recognized.

Another important self-observation that Mrs. Editor made was when she admitted that she and her husband were "too immersed in the experience and too ignorant…to recognize what was happening." Although other parents did not state this specifically, many were deeply absorbed with their child's symptoms and behaviors, which, understandably, led to extreme frustration when they felt that they were not "listened to" by the very professionals who they felt should "know."

The issues just raised truly highlight the value of defining and explaining to the medical and educational professionals what you see, so that they can readily picture what you are regularly observing. And you need to do this in the limited office time you are allotted to speak with your physician or pediatrician. Even when the parents were listened to and the boys were found to need special education services through the Birth to Three program, none was initially identified by program staff as having autism.

Reading the scenario, we can see that the Structured Collaborative IEP Process appears to be in effect. It was not due to any efforts on the part of this author or Mrs. Editor. Use of the process does happen at some schools, and, when it does, it is extremely effective. A brief analysis follows to highlight how the school and Mrs. Editor worked collaboratively and took each step in the proper order, not jumping to decisions such as placement before each child's needs were identified and agreed to—the very first step from which every other question is asked and answered.

Where Are We?
What Do We Know?

At the time this scenario was written, and after several years of public education, Mrs. Editor had a very good idea of the boys' needs—as did the school where they were served. There were no issues of what behaviors were observed both at home and at school. Full agreement on each of the children's needs was reached, and those needs were reviewed at each IEP meeting *before* any discussion of goals, services, or program placements. Mrs. Editor even stated that the IEP team would "review what we know" as the first step in the IEP process. This included a review of any formal assessments and a review of the IEP's measurable goals, objectives, and benchmarks to verify where her sons were performing. All of this—in addition to a review of IEP progress over the year and regular teachers' reports—provided a detailed and deep amount of knowledge of each child's progress over time and the child's present levels of performance. The team knew where the boys were, educationally.

What Do We Know?
Where Do We Want to Go?

Again, reviewing the IEP goals and the progress made (or not) greatly assisted the team's efforts to determine where each child's IEP should be moving toward. A clear knowledge of where each child was functioning gave the team the opportunity to revise IEP goals, or to modify the expected levels of achievement or proficiency, or simply to move forward by writing new goals while deleting others. None of this could be accomplished without having answered the first question ("What do we know?"), which this team did in earnest. This important step made making the second question ("Where do you want to go?") relatively easy to answer, because team decisions were based on a wealth of evidence and measurable progress, current data, IEP measured goals, and data on each area of need previously identified. Which direction the IEP should take—that is, the writing of new, measurable IEP goals, objectives, and benchmarks—was unquestionably easier to answer given the team's use of this Structured Collaborative IEP Process, as revealed in this scenario.

How Will We Get There?

Because we now have measurable objectives that are based on a review and identification of each child's needs and present levels of educational performance, determining the required IEP services is a matter of matching the needs and goals statements with services (i.e., speech and language therapies, ABA, etc.) known to result in positive changes to the child's behaviors (i.e., social, academic, motoric, etc.). This was not simply making a selection from a list of possible services, precluding participant discussion—quite the contrary. This step in the process also involved a discussion of what had been used, whether it had been successful, if more or less time should have been devoted to a particular service, or if something else needed to be added or deleted. This open and honest discussion and team agreement are what the Structured Collaborative IEP Process is all about. Again, having proceeded through each step—each one based on the answer(s) to the question before it— collaborative decision-making truly occurred, with the focus always on the child's needs—with one exception.

How Will We Get There?
(The Exception to This Scenario)

Mrs. Editor presented a very detailed explanation of how she approached school staff to try to determine where she "wanted" Bradley to receive his services—the setting for service delivery, found along a typically recognized continuum of settings, based on his needs. To expand just a bit further, we are talking about a gradation of restrictiveness on a continuum of settings, more commonly referred to as the least restrictive environment (LRE). Most clearly stated, we can define the continuum of settings by the degree to which a child with a disability interacts with his or her non-disabled peers (or the amount of time the opportunity to interact is made available to the child).

For example, if a child is thought to be able to access the general curriculum with supports and services—perhaps with accommodations and team teaching—the child will be placed in the traditional classroom. In this instance, there is no apparent need to remove the child to provide the services, because they can be provided successfully in the traditional classroom where the child with the disability is routinely interacting with his or her peers during classroom time. It is the least restrictive placement for him or her.

If, on the other hand, his or her needs warrant more intense or individual services, the team might suggest that the child be pulled from the class to receive services outside of the classroom—say, only for math instruction. The result of that placement is that the amount of time that the child is interacting with his or her non-disabled peers has been reduced, and the setting for service is "more restrictive," but still appropriate for the child's needs. It is still the least restrictive setting given his or her needs.

This is an appropriate place to note a concern with regard to the LRE. Please know that the following example presented will be in the extreme, to make a point. Imagine that a child with a disability has not yet achieved a manner of communication with anyone, that she needs frequent refocusing (on average every five seconds) on any activity that is requested of her. She needs directions repeated, typically three times, and in a one-step-at-a-time manner. Her fine- and gross-motor skills are sufficiently underdeveloped that she needs assistance with fine-motor activities, such as coloring. She also needs numerous modifications to physical education and playground activities to address her gross-motor skills. She will scream or bite, sometimes without an apparent reason. It is obvious that this child requires many supports, services, and individual time with staff for what appears to be all school activities. Where could this child receive her services? What would be her least restrictive setting?

Actually, her needs could be met anywhere on the continuum of settings. She could receive all of her services in the general education classroom or setting. There would likely be a great many service providers entering and exiting the classroom and, perhaps, more than one staff person frequently attending to her educational program. Or, we could provide some of the services in the general education setting, some in a classroom with other children with disabilities, or some in a separate room with no other children in a one-on-one format of service. Or, all services could be provided in a day school or residential school, which only children with disabilities attend, or even a residential setting, where she would see her parents during holidays, vacation time, and when the school is closed. She could be served in any of these settings.

However, looking at the first possible placement—that is, with all her services provided in the general education classroom—we have to ask, how much interaction with her non-disabled peers will occur? The answer is most likely none, because of her needs and the number of constant services that she must receive on an individual basis. By definition, this is the most restrictive setting, because, as presented, she will need one-on-one instruction and assistance implementing her IEP and will have *no interaction with her peers*.

We are not going to debate the degree of impact on the other students caused by the additional number of staff and activities taking place during classroom instruction. There will obviously be a considerable amount. The point is this: when a child with a disability is placed in the "back of the room" to receive her instruction without interaction with her peers, the setting is at the far end of the continuum and by definition is a very restrictive setting. A more appropriate setting might be that of a self-contained classroom or a segregated school. In either case, although the setting appears "restrictive," she would still most likely be receiving one-on-one instruction, but if served in the self-contained setting, this would be the least restrictive setting for *her* needs. What the LRE is for any student is a decision made by an IEP team and is determined based on meeting the child's needs.

This example is included here because, once Mrs. Editor "wanted" (her word) Bradley placed in the general education classroom, she was no longer looking at Bradley's needs, but, rather, her own. When that happens at an IEP meeting, it is important to refocus the conversation on the child's needs, which the school team did. They did not refute Mrs. Editor's desire for the placement; they did not make that the point of the conversation. Typically, this might have been a point of breakdown, where the IEP meeting would dissolve into total disagreement with sides being taken, an atmosphere fraught with emotions, and all aspects of collaboration lost.

What the school staff did was to restate Bradley's present levels of performance (something they had, as a team, discussed), the goals to be met, and the services Bradley needed—all of which they had agreed to. They did this without having mentioned placement for those services. Mrs. Editor truly listened to the team and realized that the appropriate setting for carrying out Bradley's IEP was not at the current school. She also realized that Bradley's needs were different from Tommy's, and that he needed to be provided for differently in terms of services, so a different setting would be appropriate.

(It should not be perceived that every school has to have the full continuum of settings on campus. However, the school system does have to have a continuum of settings available to meet the various needs of all children. Sometimes it is a neighboring school that houses the appropriate setting, sometimes it is a special school within the district, or one located outside of the district. Sometimes the appropriate setting may be out-of-state. The continuum of settings must be available to address the various disabilities and the range of needs of children with disabilities by each school district or system.

Please note that the question of where to provide the services—the placement decision or LRE—is the final decision to be made by the IEP team. Like any other decision in the process, it is to be based on the identified needs, the written goals, objectives, benchmarks, and the required services agreed to by the IEP team. If you attend an IEP meeting during which placement is the first issue of discussion—without first having the answers to the questions used in the Structured Collaborative IEP Process found in this book—then stop the meeting and explain that the meeting will begin with a discussion of the child's needs.)

Mrs. Editor did, however, take the concept of interacting with non-disabled peers (the concept of inclusion) to the new school, where the staff agreed to have Bradley receive his instruction in the general education setting with his peers when appropriate. In essence, by doing so, the school made the location of services "less" restrictive. Mrs. Editor began this process by having non-disabled students come to Bradley's classroom—a reverse inclusion concept that proved to be something both Bradley and his non-disabled peers enjoyed. Mrs. Editor had begun to show school staff that interaction with non-disabled peers could be successfully carried out at his new school.

How Do We Know That We Are Getting There?

True to the team following the steps of structured collaboration, each goal, objective, or benchmark was written with a clearly stated behavior and expected level of performance (behavior) to be achieved by some point in time. If it is a goal, then the timeline is anticipated to be met by the end of the term of the IEP. If it is an objective, then levels of performance are listed as a sequence or order of behaviors to be achieved. If it is a benchmark, there are measurable behavioral statements that are anticipated to be met at a particular point along the timeline of the IEP.

All that remains to answer this question is for the various team members to collect the data (measured results of progress) and to report those to the parent throughout the course of the IEP and school year. Doing so, in this case, resulted in no surprises and a team that met with a very solid understanding of how each child's IEP was being met and the progress made. And this most definitely included Mrs. Editor.

What Do We Do When We Get There?

To avoid redundancy, this question is also answered during the IEP meeting, which may occur at any time, but typically occurs toward the end of the term of the IEP—a year from when the IEP was written—and is typically referred to as an annual review. Once again, this is apparent as Mrs. Editor referenced the decisions to draft new goals or to maintain others if the criterion (level of performance) was met. It could also be that the team decides to modify the degree of performance of the behavior. For example, if the child is to print correctly the letters of the alphabet within ten minutes, the team might decide that the time should be reduced to two minutes, showing an increase in ability to print the letters of the alphabet. This shows that the behavior of printing the alphabet is still important, but that the criterion to change is the time in which to complete the task. This goal will also maintain the skill of printing the alphabet, simply increasing the fluency/speed of doing so.

Key Points

- Mrs. Editor agonized over her decision-making, simply because she did not know what to do for her children. She is more than capable as a parent, but, like so many parents, she suffered from issues of guilt just because she had no background to understand what she was seeing in her children. It did not help that a medical professional recommended institutionalization—when it was not necessary or appropriate—due to ignorance of the field of autism.

- In terms of how IEP meetings were conducted, you will recognize that the school was applying many of the steps of the Structured Collaborative IEP Process. The meetings began with the team determining what they knew by reviewing all available data, including a review of IEP goals, test results, and home observations. The meetings continued with establishing new goals ("Where do we want to go?") and modifying some existing goals to be in line with Mrs. Editor's children's progress.

- Goals were written in measurable terms, but here is also where Mrs. Editor presents a contention with the use of data. (Perhaps it is better said that she had legitimate concerns over how one therapist went about spending an inordinate amount of time reviewing data and preparing for instruction, when actually she should have been providing services.)

- Furthermore, on the one hand, Mrs. Editor stated that much of the IEP meeting discussed progress in terms of qualitative measures and that she did not see the value of quantitative data. But what she appeared to be saying is that she had observed a therapist spending an exorbitant amount of time reviewing previously collected data prior to implementing services. She found it a waste of time. I agree; instructional time is not the time to be reviewing paperwork in order to prepare for the provision of services. It should be done prior to meeting with the child, just as teachers do. I believe this repeated observation made Mrs. Editor resistant to the value of collecting quantitative data.

- On the other hand, when it came to the discussion about Bradley's needs and later placement, it was important that data had been collected to explain in clear measures what Bradley's needs were and the impact of instruction on those needs, i.e., progress and regression. My contention is that measurable data are always important when making programmatic and placement decisions. However, data should not be so complex that they are impossible to collect, and the process of collecting data should never impact instructional time. Collection of data must be relatively easy to do, or it simply will not be done because it can't be done readily. And collecting measures of progress is essential in the Structured Collaborative IEP Process in order to observe changes or meet IEP goals, answering the question of "How do we know that we are getting there?"

- The final comment to be made revolves around the issue of teacher expectations or perceived expectations based on categorical labels. It is true that our thinking can be influenced by words that define *what* a person is (e.g., genius, illiterate, ignorant), but this is not to be confused with *who* the person is. But these are descriptors of "conditions" that do not describe the individual and who that person is (e.g., social, interesting, good at math, enjoys photography). And, being the creatures that we are, and depending on our background of experiences, the perception we might create will vary. Here is where it is important to assess a child's abilities accurately and to use answers to "What do we know?" that are measurable in order to develop IEPs that will accurately measure changes in behaviors (academic, social, motoric, etc.). It is these that will define who the child is in terms of learning within the school structures. Otherwise, our preconceived understanding of words such as "cognitively impaired" can be to our detriment. A classification is necessary to warrant entitlement to special education services. But, once the child has been identified with a classification of disability, you can leave that information in the reports and folders. I say that because determining that a student is eligible as a student with a disability for educational services is like opening a gate to allow the child's needs to dictate which programs and services are to be provided. Descriptive measures of behavior are essential with respect to eligibility, development of the IEP, and defining who the child is in school settings. They go beyond any specific classification and should be the focus, more so than any terms that have been assigned.

Summary

In summary, Mrs. Editor was fortunate to have experienced IEP meetings much as they should be, with a few exceptions. Perhaps the best example is when she wanted Bradley to be in the same placement and receiving the same or similar services as his older brother. Staff did not say "No" to her. Instead, they reviewed what they all knew—where Bradley was functioning, the goals established ("Where do we want to go?"), and the progress made on those goals ("How do we know that we are getting there?"). It was the process that brought the reality of Bradley's needs back to Mrs. Editor, reminding her that her boys were different and, therefore, required different services and programming. As you can see, the Structured Collaborative IEP Process works to the benefit of the child, whether employed by you or the school.

The issue of staff expectations was addressed earlier, and I will only add that, by using the Structured Collaborative IEP Process—in particular, measures of progress—you can point to the degree of progress, or lack of progress, or even regression observed on the IEP goals. If progress is not being made and the intervention or instruction has remained the same, you have the data to question the appropriateness of the goals and, frankly, the methods being used (and to determine lack of progress is due to boredom or simply inappropriate educational demands). Without that information (data), it is nearly impossible to question either the goals, the intervention, or, in this case, the expectations set for your child (e.g., goals, objectives, and benchmarks)—or, to be pleased with your child's program and progress.

Final Note

After learning more about the Structured Collaborative IEP Process and the importance of data in that process, Mrs. Editor was able to apply this information to IEPs for Tommy, Bradley, and Jimmy, with positive results. Since this scenario was written, the IEP team for Bradley has met to plan his transition from elementary school to middle school. While Bradley continues to require a setting that is segregated from his non-disabled peers, Mrs. Editor was successful in her attempts to communicate how his abilities have been underestimated and to develop—

relying on the expertise of IEP team members—new goals and new approaches that would better match his academic potential.

Mrs. Editor also had to contend with an escalation of Jimmy's aggressive behaviors, which resulted in a new placement decision for him. Unfortunately, the placement decision was, in this case, made without relying on the Structured Collaborative IEP Process. Not only was the placement decision made before the team discussed what they knew, where they wanted to go, and how they were going to get there, the placement decision was made by administrative staff without Mrs. Editor's input. During this same meeting, however, Mrs. Editor was able to use the Structured Collaborative IEP Process to modify the expectations implicit in the new IEP developed for Jimmy.

Current evidence suggests that making the placement decision outside the Structured Collaborative IEP Process was doubly unfortunate, because Jimmy has not been successful in his new placement. Despite his making academic progress early in the current school year, the new teacher and therapists seem to have an insufficient understanding of the full range of Jimmy's needs. Jimmy is exhibiting increased aggression at school—while exhibiting low levels of aggression at home—due to unmet sensory needs. Mrs. Editor is using the Structured Collaborative IEP Process, learned through her association with this book, to repair the situation by ensuring that Jimmy's needs are met, even if that means finding a new placement.

Over the summer, Tommy acquired a new diagnosis of epilepsy, which changed his needs in all school settings. At the start of the new school year, Mrs. Editor was able to lead the team through the Structured Collaborative IEP Process to ensure that Tommy's newly identified needs were met, while the team also continued to meet his ongoing needs.

I will conclude this scenario with some final words from Mrs. Editor:

> While the district my boys attend have always tried to follow the Structured Collaborative IEP Process, whether they knew it or not, I've found learning this process to be very empowering when it comes to participating in my boys' IEPs. Knowing what should happen and knowing how to direct the discussion so that it does happen has certainly helped me to help my boys. It's not always easy, especially when my own wants and needs get in the way, but it does result in better outcomes for my boys, which is the whole point of these meetings and these IEPs in the first place.

CHAPTER 3

Physical Impairments and Learning Disabilities

A Child is Better Served at Home

···

This story is about a young boy who was suffering from a variety of physical conditions and, perhaps, trauma to his brain. Careful analysis of the available data would suggest that his disabilities were caused by his difficult and premature birth. The information is limited, so it is only a "best guess," but it seems the most reasonable explanation considering Ellen Huff's descriptions of her son Josh's behaviors. Ellen, a non-educator, decided to take Josh's education into her own hands after the school repeatedly failed to recognize or address his disabilities—disabilities that seem to be a combination of a learning disability, orthopedic impairment, and other health impairments. Regardless of the labels, the school was not meeting his needs. Ellen was determined to do what the school would not. She worked with Josh, homeschooling him using the school's curriculum with the support of a privately paid occupational therapist who recognized and met many of his needs. Together, Ellen and the therapist enabled Josh to return to the public school system—much to the amazement of the school staff.

Determined to Thrive

"He is not on target."

I had a difficult pregnancy with Josh, my second child. I first went into labor when I was only four months along. Placed on bed rest, the contractions didn't stop. I never had a definite due date. They said anywhere from Christmas 1990 to March of 1991. Josh was born January 2, 1991.

Of course he was premature and several hours passed before I was allowed to see him. When they finally let me hold him, I noticed that he had a large welt on his face, running from about midway down the crown to his chin. The nurse said it was a mark from the forceps that would go away in a few hours.

Life was good! I had a three-year-old son and a newborn baby boy! He was an angel and never cried. But, when Josh was seven days old, he would not wake up to feed. It had been seven and a half hours since he last fed, and I was concerned. I tried giving him a bottle. He would suck for about 30 seconds, and then go right back to sleep. I called the doctor, who was on her lunch break. I told the nurse what was going on, and she told me to take Josh to the emergency room. So, of course, I did.

The nurse told the emergency room that we were on our way. When we arrived, we were barraged with questions about the type of appliances we had in the house. They thought he might be suffering from carbon monoxide poisoning. But there were no gas appliances anywhere in our apartment. The doctors took a closer look at Josh and asked questions, no longer focused on just one thing. He tested positive for jaundice, and they said that he would be fine, requiring no treatment. I was relieved to know what was going on. His liver had not yet fully developed. He was just going to be a sleepy baby and quickly recovered.

When Josh was about six weeks old, I noticed that he turned his head to the left no matter which way I held him or laid him down. I called the doctor again and was told that if he didn't scream when I turned his head to the right, I shouldn't worry. At his eight-week check-up, I was told that Josh had tumors in his neck, chest, and upper back muscles and that his hips were "tight." He required a strict exercise regimen for 20 minutes, four times per day. I expressed my concerns over the way the right side of his mouth drooped, making his face asymmetrical. I was told not to worry, but to give him time, that his development might catch up. I watched and I waited, and grew more worried.

As Josh got older, I saw that he didn't hold his head up as expected, based on the development timelines. Actually, he didn't do anything on time. He didn't roll over, crawl, walk, or talk within the window of time suggested by the chart. By the time Josh was 18 months old, he was just starting to pull himself up. When he was 24 months, he started walking. At age three, he had a vocabulary of only 15 one-syllable words. When he marched, his left hand would be doubled up in a fist that he held tightly to his ribs, with his elbow bent and rigid, but he would swing his right arm appropriately. The doctor recommended that we see a neurologist at a nearby children's hospital.

The neurologist said that the crooked smile (asymmetry of his face) was due to being born without the depressor anguli oris muscle (a triangular-shaped muscle in the corner of the mouth), which can also indicate that there may be a hole in the heart. They performed an ultrasound, discovering a murmur but no other abnormalities. The only thing they could do was recheck his heart in a year to see if the murmur was still present. I left without any real answers. They assured me Josh was a normal child and just a little behind in his development. I knew Josh wasn't a "normal child." I knew there was something different about my son.

At three, Josh was enrolled in Head Start, a preschool program for "at risk" children. The first year they offered Josh "homebound" services, because he was too young to attend school with the older kids. The second year he attended a center school program. I kept expressing my concerns about his development, but they would send home quarterly reports saying he was making "great progress." I still knew something was wrong.

I didn't get any confirmation of my concerns from the school until the end of the second year, when the teachers said he was "not on target" with the other kids. As you can imagine, I was angry. He'd been going to "school" for two years, and only now were they telling me he was "not on target!" The next year I enrolled him in kindergarten, and as far as I know, Head Start made no attempt to contact the school about Josh's progress or make them aware of his educational needs.

Again, I received quarterly report cards with nothing indicating Josh was behind. Then, about halfway through the school year, the teacher shared her observations that he was "not on target." She said he did not color appropriately or hold a pair of scissors correctly and that his pencil grip was not appropriate, meaning fine-motor development was delayed. She then expressed her concerns about him falling. She said he would be standing in the playground and fall down, without putting his hands out to catch himself, thereby causing injury.

I had been called to the school about seven times so far that school year because of his falls. I had already taken him to the doctor. School staff asked if he had fainted or lost consciousness. I told them that Josh was just clumsy at home, but never lost consciousness. The doctor had "patched him up" and told me to get more information from the school. When I'd asked, the teacher said that she'd never seen him fall and couldn't be sure. It was all very frustrating.

Josh also experienced a number of ear infections, and the doctor thought his ear infections might be the cause. They treated the ear infection but this did not stop the falls. Following yet another fall, the doctor performed a tympanogram, testing the pressure in the middle ear. The pressure is supposed to be the same as the atmospheric pressure, but his test showed negative pressure. They again provided treatment, but the falls continued.

At home, he would have his hand on the wall, turn around, and then run straight into the wall. At a follow-up check on his ears, the doctor performed another tympanogram. This time it showed that Josh had non-functioning eardrums. I asked if this was caused by yet another ear infection. The doctor said, "Josh is 80 percent deaf in his left ear and probably 80 percent blind in his left eye. He probably has cerebral palsy." Then, he turned and walked out of the room. I was devastated! I didn't know what to do! How could the doctor who had seen Josh so many times be so cruel as to tell a young mother this and then just leave the room? He gave no explanations, no referrals, and no help at all. (As it turned out, he was wrong—Josh wasn't blind in either eye and he didn't have cerebral palsy.)

As I was leaving, I passed the nurse in the hallway. She told me that the doctor was retiring after that day and I should schedule an appointment with another doctor. I did and was referred to an ear, nose, and throat (ENT) specialist.

Meanwhile, I asked the principal of the kindergarten program to test Josh because I knew something was very wrong. She led me down a crowded hallway and said, "We just don't have room for a mentally retarded child in the kindergarten classroom setting." I was furious! I knew that there was something different about Josh, but I didn't think he was mentally retarded. I asked her, "Do you know who my son is?" She replied, "I have to go; we are putting in new playground equipment." This was in 1996, so there were laws that should have been followed—laws to help my son get the kind of services he needed—but I didn't know anything about special education laws then, so I didn't know how to fight for my son's rights. I decided to "wait her out." Josh would go to a different school next year. I would wait until then and speak with the new principal. At least, that was the plan.

The ENT specialist who tested Josh's hearing found that Josh had non-functioning eardrums that made voices sound like the adults' voices on the "Charlie Brown" cartoons. A short while later, his tonsils and adenoids were removed and tubes were placed in his ears in order to improve his hearing. When we were allowed to see him in the recovery room, I bent down beside his bed and he opened his eyes. I said, "Hi, Josh," as I ran my fingers through his hair. He looked directly at me and his eyes opened really wide, and he said, "Mommy, what's wrong with your voice?" I looked at the doctor with what I am sure was a very strange look. He looked back and smiled, saying, "He can hear your voice now." Josh was over five years old when he heard my voice properly for the first time.

Watching him try to understand the new sounds around him was just amazing, but also difficult at times. The hardest thing was watching the confused looks on his face. Just imagine being a child and then suddenly all the people in your life—your parents, your brother and sister, your grandmother, your aunts and uncles, your teachers, everyone you know—are talking in voices very different from what you have always heard. It must have been so scary for him to hear so many new sounds! It was difficult to watch, but amazing just the same.

The operation stopped his falls, too. He was still clumsy, but did not fall and hurt himself all the time. With the falls, the doctor appointments with specialists, the surgery, and follow-up visits, Josh had missed a lot of school. At the end of the year, they told me they didn't feel Josh was ready for first grade. They were going to hold him back for a second year in kindergarten. There went my plans to have him tested at the new school, where he would have attended first grade.

The next year I went back to the same principal to ask to have Josh tested, but she said she didn't have time to speak with me because they were "planting trees in the playground." I knew my son needed more help, but I didn't know how to get him the help he needed. I spent a lot of nights crying myself to sleep. I knew that my child was different from his peers. I knew he wasn't learning like the other kids. I didn't know where to turn for the answers we needed. I had been to doctors and I had pleaded with the school, but it didn't seem to do much good. The ENT surgery had made a breakthrough, but that was only a start. Josh needed more, but at school it seemed everyone was more interested in pointing out Josh's faults and difficulties than providing him with the help he needed. I felt completely alone and completely helpless as another year passed.

Finally, when Josh was in first grade, I learned that the testing that Josh needed was called a "case study evaluation" and that the school was not meant to dismiss my requests. If they were going to refuse, they had to provide a written reason why they would not test him. So, I went right to work. I wrote a letter to the principal of the new school asking for a case study evaluation. They told me that Josh's delay wasn't significant enough to warrant testing. Again, I felt I had nowhere to turn and no one to help me help my son.

I took Josh to another doctor, only to be recommended to another neurologist. I wasn't thrilled about going. Why should we go to yet another doctor in yet another town? This doctor was probably just going to tell us the same thing, "He is just a little behind."

The neurologist's nurse had called and told me to bring all Josh's medical records with me. So, I gathered as much information as I could. I wrote countless pages of things that I saw at home (running into walls, the falls, and everything that had happened in the past). I gathered school records, notes from teachers, and asked for all his medical records from my doctor. This was the first time I had seen them.

Reviewing the medical records, I discovered things that I'd never been told. The "tightness" in his hips the doctors discovered when he was just eight weeks old was due to tumors. According to the records, there were also tumors in his thighs. His very first medical records, the hospital records from his birth in 1991, noted the asymmetry of his face. Scribbled on the side was "birth trauma." I was so angry! The doctors knew all these things, but they'd never told me! As his mother, I felt I had the right to know. I thought they must be covering something up to hide information like that. It was outrageous!

I took everything I had gathered with us to the neurologist's office. She examined him, tested his reflexes and the like, and asked me questions. I felt that she at least listened to what I had to say about my concerns for my son, who was then in the first grade. But we still left the doctor's office empty-handed. I don't recall ever receiving a report, let alone answers. Once again I had tried to get my son the help he needed, and once again it came to nothing.

I had more conferences with Josh's teacher that year and heard the same things that I had been hearing from his teachers all along, that he was "not on target." I asked my sister how she was able to get her school to test her son for special education. She gave me a guidebook that explained the special education laws in our area and that provided some instruction on how to fight for my son's rights. As per the instructions, I wrote another letter to the school and asked for Josh to be evaluated. I think they realized that I was better informed this time around. This time they didn't dismiss my request; instead, I received a letter inviting me to discuss the areas in which Josh would need to be tested. I got the distinct impression that the school still didn't want to test him, but I brought in teachers' notes, past progress reports, and Josh's report cards to help make my case. We actually had a meeting to discuss the information I had gathered, and they reluctantly agreed to evaluate Josh. The evaluations showed that Josh qualified for special education services as a student with learning disabilities. I was right all along, and Josh would finally get the help that he needed!

Writing his first Individualized Education Program (IEP) was a relief. It seemed that the school was finally ready to help Josh. I had just needed to know how to ask for it in the right way, so they couldn't ignore me. The goal was to provide him with supports within the regular classroom. His next year's teacher took charge of the meeting. She used phrases such as, "We can help Josh by providing his spelling words the weekend before they are handed out to the class" and "He will benefit from extra time on tests and classwork." I asked for an occupational therapy (OT) evaluation from the school, but they said that he knew how to hold a pencil, so he would not qualify for OT services or benefit from the service.

I had learned that research indicated that children with dyslexia might benefit from using colored overlays when reading textbooks and that printing their handouts on colored paper helped, too. I thought these techniques would help Josh, so I was happy that the school agreed to have these accommodations in his IEP. I was so excited! I was no longer just a worried mother, comparing my child with his peers. The test proved there was something there. Finally, we would all help Josh together!

Then, when Josh was in second grade, he came home with his handouts printed on white paper. I asked the school why the teacher wasn't using the colored paper as indicated in his IEP. The school said they couldn't afford it. So I purchased the blue paper from an office supply store and gave it to them. They used it occasionally, but only for the first few weeks. I didn't know how to make the school follow his IEP, or even if I could.

Despite that, his general education classroom teacher was amazing and always kept in contact with me. Ironically, this teacher, who was not trained in the field of special education, was a great fit for Josh. She sent home his spelling words on Friday so he would have a little more time to practice them. She created a special folder for extra work that he could do at home. She designated another folder for communication between school and home. She also helped Josh get organized. He brought home A's all year. He was "getting it!"

Once I realized that, I decided not to pursue the colored paper. Maybe he didn't need it after all. I was happy that Josh was learning and catching up. That's what I really wanted. That was such a great year for Josh!

Josh continued to fall and showed other signs of coordination problems, so we returned to see the same neurologist on the advice of Josh's doctor. She determined that Josh had a developmental coordination disorder and wrote a prescription for OT and recommended that we see an ophthalmologist to see if Josh's vision was a factor. I was so excited! Now I had a name for Josh's problem! Maybe we could figure out how to help Josh and "fix it" or, at least, level the playing field for him. I felt like I was finally getting somewhere!

The ophthalmologist confirmed that Josh had visual perception problems. He explained that Josh's falls were caused by the way he saw things. For example, if there was a leaf lying on the grass, it would look to Josh as if it were floating several inches above the ground. He would move his body to maneuver around obstacles that he saw, even though what he saw wasn't accurate (i.e., stepping high to walk over something that was lying flat on the ground). The doctor gave me some exercises to do with Josh, and when I told him that Josh would be getting OT, he said the therapist could address these problems as well.

When I met with the occupational therapist, while I was still filling out the paperwork, he asked if Josh had a diagnosis. I sat up a little straighter and said, "Developmental coordination disorder." The therapist looked at me and said, "Yes, but what is his diagnosis?" I said, "That is his diagnosis. That is what the neurologist said." He said, "Yes, but that is an umbrella description. There are a lot of conditions that could fall under developmental coordination disorder." It was like saying someone had a learning disability: the label itself does not describe the particular condition. It just gives you an idea which "umbrella" the disorder falls under. You have to know what the particular condition is in order to treat it.

So, there I was thinking I had finally gotten somewhere, only to feel lied to by another doctor. It didn't matter in the long run. Josh was still going to get OT, which was what he needed. He blossomed and bloomed! The occupational therapist gave Josh the sensory input training that he needed, and he and Josh did exercises to improve his visual perception. His fine-motor skills improved dramatically. It also gave me something to work on with him at home. I was finally doing something to really help my son!

I received a call from his new general education teacher during the first week of his third-grade year. She had been my first-grade teacher, and my sister married her brother-in-law. So, I guess you could say we were "family," though that didn't seem to help Josh any. She called because she wanted to decrease his spelling words. I asked if she had a copy of his IEP. She retorted, "Of course I do!" in a hateful tone. I said, "Then, you will see that one of his accommodations is that spelling words will be sent home for the upcoming week on Friday, so that he has extra time to practice them."

I told her about my sister, who graduated from this same school district with a regular diploma, and who had been on the honor roll all four years of high school but yet was unable to count to 50. I was not going to let such disregard for a child's progress happen to my son! She said, in the same hateful voice, "Let's get real, Ellen. When is Josh ever going to need to spell *arithmetic* in his life?" I said, "You are not decreasing his spelling words. Have a good day," and I hung up the phone.

Josh received his spelling words on Friday and "arithmetic" was one of the challenge words. The next Friday, when he took the test, he got 105 percent (with extra credit). He even spelled "arithmetic" correctly. The rest of the year would go about as well as predicted by his teacher during that first week. Josh started having behavioral issues at home.

He didn't want to go to school. He was angry all the time and told me that his resource teacher, the special education teacher who was meant to assist him with his academics, had pushed him out of his chair on to the floor on more than one occasion. By the end of that year, I felt like I was up against a brick wall. The teacher said he still didn't have an appropriate pencil grip and his other fine-motor skills were still behind, but I had proof from the occupational therapist that those deficits were improving.

I planned to ask the school at the next IEP meeting if they would provide OT as it had been so successful through the private OT services. Last time I asked, they said he could hold a pencil, so he wouldn't qualify. This time I contacted the Parent Training and Information Center (PTIC)—a service that helps parents of children with disabilities to work with the school by answering questions and assisting parents in obtaining the services required for their child to make progress in school—and arranged for an advocate to attend the IEP meeting with me.

Then it was time to write his IEP for the fourth grade. In the same breath, his teacher told me Josh had attention deficit hyperactivity disorder (ADHD) and that he was lethargic. I asked how someone can be hyper and lethargic at the same time.

Someone accused me of being hostile. The advocate spoke up, saying she was just about to ask the same question and she did not feel I was being hostile at all.

The discussion then turned to placement for the following year. They wanted to place Josh in a self-contained room for all his classes. I said I was not going to let them push Josh to the side and forget about him like they did with my sister. That was not what he needed! They said that was their only offer; they wouldn't consider any other options.

That was unacceptable. I told them that I would homeschool my son. They said I couldn't, but when I asked them to provide a law stating that I couldn't, they all just sat there and looked at each other. I left the meeting. The advocate gave me the phone number and address of the state board of education and advised me to file a complaint, but I was done with them. I wanted nothing to do with the school district any more.

I called the State Department of Education (SDE) to learn how to homeschool Josh. I discovered that Illinois was one of the few states without state-wide regulations on homeschooling and decisions were left up to the Regional Offices of Education (ROE). I contacted my ROE and discovered there were no regulations or criteria to follow. So, I found textbooks at library book sales and teachers' garage sales. My older son even brought home books the school wasn't going to be using. I also found the fourth-grade curriculum online.

During that summer—between his third and fourth grade—Josh's behavioral issues diminished greatly. I taught Josh at home for his fourth and fifth grades. Josh kept his schedule of OT two days per week. His day looked very much like it would if he had attended regular school. We had science, history, spelling, reading, art, music, math, daily oral language, and recess. Josh's day ended with him going to work: he had a paper route, which he did on his own—for the most part.

I started out with the basics. We used hand-over-hand instruction at first. We worked on pencil grasp. We quickly moved to letter formation. His handwriting still isn't very good, but he can do very well if he takes his time; then again, I can't read a doctor's prescription, so I guess it doesn't matter that much.

In math, we started out playing games with dice or cards. I even made up math games. In science we built a gauge out of a paper plate and ribbon. We took it outside and faced north, so when the wind blew we knew what directions it was blowing to and coming from. We did a lot of hands-on things, which is the way that he learned best.

I enrolled Josh in Junior Football League (JFL) the summer before his sixth-grade year. Josh had never played football; he had never played an organized sport. I talked with his coach and expressed my concerns. He assured me that Josh would be fine. By the end of the second week, other kids were looking to Josh, asking him where they were meant to stand and where they were meant to go once the ball was in play.

I was shocked and amazed at what I was seeing in him! Josh had not only memorized his positions, but everyone else's as well. He had the most tackles that year and for the next three years. The original reason I had put Josh in JFL was because I was worried about his social skills suffering by being homeschooled. After the second week, I knew I didn't have to worry about his social skills.

I was so impressed with Josh's leadership skills both on and off the field that I decided, as he would be attending a different school, to enroll him in public school again. I contacted the school district and told them that I was going to enroll him again and that he needed to have another evaluation. They were happy to do so, even though it was summer. I thought that if I wasn't satisfied with what they had to offer, as far as placement and accommodations went, I would just homeschool him for another year or enroll him in a private school.

At the IEP meeting, I was shocked—not only by the evaluation results, but also by what they were offering. They said Josh's IQ was in the upper range (123) and that he would only need one resource class per day. He barely qualified for services and I started to cry. I thought, "Where would he be now if I had not homeschooled him?" I was so proud of Josh! He worked hard and it showed! He went from being told that he belonged in a self-contained classroom to barely qualifying as having a learning disability in just two years. On the first day of school, the teachers all commended me on homeschooling him so well after seeing how far he had come in just two years. I explained that I did not do the work—Josh did.

In junior high, things went pretty smoothly. Part of the difference was that this was a new school, and even though it was the same school district there were different teachers, a new special education coordinator, and a new school superintendent. When I met with his teachers, one told me that she makes the kids take turns reading aloud in class. I had concerns. She said Josh had read aloud in class the first week of school and had no issues.

When I received his graded homework, I saw that he didn't just pass, but scored high grades. I was so pleased! Josh was doing very well. He adjusted to being back in school very fast and very well. He had "outgrown" the falls, and his coordination was no longer an issue, as he proved so well on the football field.

At the next meeting, we went over the IEP goals, and the teachers were noting progress. When we came to the accommodations page in the IEP, the resource teacher described the accommodations Josh used. She said he had not been using the "graphic organizer," because she had no idea what it was. I explained what it was and what it was used for, but I was amazed she didn't know. This was the same resource teacher from when I was in high school, so how could a resource teacher who had taught in the high school for so long not have a clue what a graphic organizer was, let alone how to use it?

Josh, as he did for all his IEP meetings, attended his freshman IEP meeting and said he no longer wanted services. When we got home, he said the resource teacher wasn't helping him. He described how the resource teacher just sat in her chair during the whole period and surfed the Web, never helping any of the students. So, I observed two of his classes.

While at the school, I walked down the short, narrow "special education hallway," which only had special education classes. Not only was the hallway different, but the classrooms were designed differently. Each classroom was about half the size of "regular" classrooms and had a large window facing the hallway. Josh had told me that he felt his dignity stripped away from him every time he had to walk that hallway. It wasn't until I saw the layout that I understood what he meant.

When I walked in, the teacher was sitting in her chair with her hand on the mouse, just as Josh had described. There were no individual desks in this classroom, unlike all the "regular" rooms, just long tables facing the teacher's desk. After about five minutes, she finally noticed I was there. She asked if she could help me. I told her that I was just observing Josh for the day.

Some of the kids were talking about a difficult science test they had to take. Some had already taken the test, but some of the others wouldn't be taking it until later that day. The teacher asked if some of the kids who had taken it could help the ones who had not yet taken it to study. The kids protested. Those who had already taken it said the test was difficult and they didn't think they had done very well, and the kids who hadn't taken it didn't want to rely on their help. The teacher started to squelch the protest, then looked at me and reluctantly took a deep breath and said she would help. She sat with those students, helping them study for the remainder of the period.

The bell rang and the kids gathered their belongings, and we all headed out of the room. Three of the students asked me if I would come back tomorrow, because they were going to have a big history exam. At first I didn't understand why they were asking because I hadn't helped them study. Josh said, "And you thought I was not telling the truth about her not helping us." All eight students agreed. Then I realized that I was the only reason the teacher had helped the students prepare for their science test.

We didn't have another IEP meeting until late spring and Josh no longer qualified for services! I worried that Josh would finish high school without an IEP, and therefore he would not be eligible for any services when he went to college. I let it slide and luckily he didn't need it. Josh got through the rest of high school just fine, and now he's married, has two beautiful children, and is in the Army National Guard.

Analysis of "Determined to Thrive"

Before we dive right into the analysis, let's review some of the background information revealed in this story. If you didn't notice or don't remember, Josh was born in 1991. That may come as a bit of a shock. Reading this scenario, you might have thought it occurred in the 1950s—a time when many students with disabilities were not recognized and were treated in institutional settings.

By the 1990s, many countries had already put into effect laws and regulations far beyond the comments and attitudes demonstrated in this scenario. Programming for students with disabilities had made great strides in the mid-1990s. Schools had moved toward serving children in their home schools, surpassing the simple integration shown in this scenario—where students with disabilities were moved from segregated day schools to typical schools with limited interaction with their non-disabled peers, often placed in self-contained classrooms. School systems had begun actually serving many students with disabilities, who learned with their peers in the general education setting. In both instances, students were receiving appropriate services—educational and related services designed to meet the child's needs—regardless of where they were actually placed for those services.

It is clear from this scenario that this particular school district had *not* shared in these educational advancements!

In fact, changes did not occur until a new superintendent and new special education administrative staff took charge of the school district. It is a perfect example of the importance of good leadership when meeting children's needs. However, even good leadership can face considerable resistance from out-of-date school staff who require extensive retraining.

Ellen inherently knew that something was wrong with her son shortly after his birth, and observed the mounting evidence during his school years. She simply lacked the knowledge necessary to present the information she had and to hold others accountable for carrying out their responsibilities. As Ellen learned what she needed to know, she carried out her own research and taught herself a lot. She learned what the schools were responsible for and how to hold them accountable for meeting Josh's needs.

This scenario also represents a unique situation, as per this book, where the mother, who is not an educator, chose to take her son's education into her own hands for a few years, instead of expending her energy fighting a school that didn't want to teach her son according to his needs. Due to this difference, the analysis below will follow a slightly different flow, but will still apply the Structured Collaborative IEP Process, revolving around the answers to our six key questions.

Where Are We?
What Do We Know?

At the onset (Josh's birth), Ellen didn't receive the medical reports that could have provided her with useful information about what she was seeing in her newborn and that may have helped to explain the "odd feeling" that something was wrong. Lacking those reports, which she would later obtain, she was repeatedly told that Josh, though lagging developmentally, would "catch up," or that Josh's problems were not a cause for concern, that "he might outgrow it," and that "he was a normal child, just a little behind developmentally." She, like so many parents whose scenarios are found in this book, *knew* that what she saw was not "normal" and that something was wrong.

But what do you do when those in the medical field—whom you respect and whom you believe should be concerned by what you've seen—say, "Don't worry?" Clearly, until Ellen located someone who could define and explain the problems she'd observed in Josh's behaviors, she lacked answers to the questions "Where are we?" and "What do we know?"

Where Do We Want to Go?

How could Ellen possibly know where to go if she did not know what she was dealing with? She could not. It is not that she did not seek second opinions, and it was not that she was not persistent in attempting to determine what Josh's problems were, but, despite her consistent efforts, she didn't get the responses she needed. In fact, the responses she received were the problem! These inadequate answers were why she was so frustrated that she was literally asking herself what she should do.

This scenario exemplifies how difficult, or rather impossible, it is to determine a course of action and to know what you want to accomplish if you lack the information for even a basic understanding of the problem. She was stymied, bewildered, and unable to move forward.

Unfortunately, it is not unusual for some parents to approach a school or other professional with a "solution," even though they don't know or fully understand the parameters of the problem they're trying to address. Of course, this kind of behavior is hardly confined to parents. Think back to your work place. You have probably seen bad "solutions" implemented before the problem is understood—and we all know where that leads! This is why it's so essential to answer the first question.

Ellen came to a full stop until Josh entered Head Start at age three, where he first received some programming. Ellen once again heard that Josh was "not on target." His development was lagging, and he'd already fallen behind. Yet, there was no explanation for why that was the case, so we begin the process again.

Where Are We?

What Do We Know?

Because Josh was only three, he received his first year of Head Start programming at home. He attended a center school program for his second year. Head Start didn't reveal that he was "not on target" with his peers until the end of his second year in their program, despite Ellen's repeated attempts to share her concerns about his rate of development over the course of the year. Up to this point, the quarterly progress reports indicated that he was making acceptable progress. This same sequence of events was repeated during Josh's kindergarten year; that is, the school sent home progress reports indicating that he was making progress, but when Ellen spoke with his teacher halfway through the school year, she learned something quite different.

Ellen was told that, in addition to his falling at school, Josh was having fine-motor difficulties. He wasn't coloring appropriately or holding scissors and pencils properly. It would have been fair to ask if there were additional problems that the teacher was seeing, and what was the teacher doing to address those fine-motor concerns—or if she was collecting data about the problems she was seeing with Josh's development. However, the focus quickly turned to his personal safety in relation to his falling which had been observed at school.

The falls continued, even after Josh received repeated treatment for ear infections. Then, during an appointment with a callous and insensitive doctor, Ellen was told that her child was partially deaf and partially blind, and that Josh most likely had cerebral palsy. Fortunately, she soon saw another physician, who recommended an evaluation with an ENT specialist who recognized that many of Josh's difficulties were the result of non-functioning eardrums that had greatly impacted his ability to hear accurately. A wonderful and strange outcome of the procedures for Josh was that he heard his mother's voice correctly for the first time. What is difficult to fathom is why Josh had not received the typical general health screening for children entering school, which should have caught his condition.

Many of Josh's problems were the result of medical issues, so when Ellen was finally able to connect with competent medical professionals, the initial discovery of the tympanic membrane was made. This is why school staff are meant to ask parents if they have presented their concerns to their physician, because there is a chance that a problem in school is related to a treatable medical condition. If this does not occur, parents should volunteer any known medical issues to their physicians and other professionals.

Schools are not going to recommend that a doctor's visit is in order. They cannot make those recommendations any more than they can tell you to get a prescription for medication. What they can and will do is ask if you have met or discussed the concern with your physician. This scenario shows why this question is important and why parents should consider speaking to their physician first to rule out medical issues. Ellen tried that, but she needed to find the right physician, who was willing and able to refer her to an ENT specialist, before she began to understand what might have caused some of Josh's difficulties. This did not magically put Josh "on target," so we still don't know the answer to the question "Where are we?" However, having difficulty hearing certainly did impact Josh's life and educational experiences, and correcting that issue certainly impacted his ability to succeed in school. But that wasn't Josh's only challenge.

Ellen correctly approached the principal once again and was ignored. This was extremely unprofessional and simply intolerable! In order to know more definitively where we are, Ellen and the school needed to carry out a full educational assessment, and her demanding this was appropriate. Furthermore, the school could not legally decline an assessment regardless of their rationale, but Ellen did not know that—then. When Josh was in first grade, she asked for an evaluation for the third time and was told that Josh did not have a sufficient developmental delay to require an evaluation. This, of course, was absurd! She was told year after year that he was "not on target," as the school was well aware, and yet they totally ignored the likelihood that a medical issue caused his delays.

Ellen knows better now, but did not know how to counter the "educational walls" of refusal to evaluate Josh—now three attempts. Had she known, she would have presented all the school information that she had collected over time—including his report cards and teacher reports, medical and any written correspondence showing his not being "on target"—and said, "This is where we are and his needs have not been addressed." If that failed, then she would have put her concerns in writing and forwarded that to the school principal, school coordinator, and district office administrator over special education, and then stated a date by which she wanted a school evaluation conducted and a date whereby she would receive a written reply to the letter—or, now, email. With the large amount of data she had collected and the responses she had received from the school administration, she would have been ready to carry her concerns to the next level—the school superintendent and school board—if she was once again denied an educational assessment.

There simply are times when it is necessary to reach out to the top to be listened to. For Ellen, this was such a time. If she had put her concerns in writing and worked her way up the administrative hierarchy, then she may have gotten the cooperation she needed from the school district. This may seem like a lengthy process, but if you follow the format described above, then your letter of concern will be with the superintendent within ten days, assuming there is another denial. Doing this would have shown her willingness and efforts to work within the system, which would be viewed favorably should she later need to bring a legal suit against the district. Acknowledging the possibility of pursuing a lawsuit should not be seen as a recommendation against attempts to obtain mediation or assistance to facilitate conflicts. Neither is it a recommendation against lodging a complaint to the state or national departments of education. It is only meant to highlight the steps that could be followed prior to taking legal steps, some of which are outside the parameters of this book.

Fortunately, Ellen had maintained all medical records, written correspondences, all school and classroom work samples, and teacher reports and report cards. So, she had all that was necessary to make the demands for an assessment—short of knowing that she could.

In preparing for an initial appointment with another neurologist, Ellen read, for the first time, the medical records outlining the difficulties of Josh's birth and physiological damages to his body—information that had always existed but had not been shared with her, which would have helped answer the question "What do we know?" This time Ellen was totally prepared to present her concerns to the neurologist and state in an understandable (clear) manner with behaviorally stated observations of Josh's behaviors, as one should, regardless of the profession (i.e., medical or educational). She brought all Josh's medical records, a listing of her observations of his behaviors at home, school reports, report cards, and anything else she felt could show the neurologist the length of Josh's problems, timelines, and the pervasiveness of his difficulties—that is, his challenges that could be observed across multiple settings. She was, in a word, *prepared*—only to leave the office with no diagnosis, no recommendations, and essentially no more information than she had when she entered the waiting room. The only conclusion that can be drawn is that the medical staff were unaware and untrained to recognize Josh's conditions, much less provide a recommendation for the school to conduct an educational evaluation.

Despite this experience, we learned that Ellen continued to press the school for an evaluation and eventually prevailed, with the school "reluctantly" agreeing to conduct an evaluation. The results, sadly, confirmed that Josh had a learning disability requiring special education services—I say "sadly" because of the delay in doing what should have been done years ago.

Where Do We Want to Go?
What Do We Want to Accomplish?

Things do get a bit muddled at this point, but we know Ellen met with the school team to develop Josh's IEP, and we learn that Josh was to be provided services in the general education classroom. The only service that she asked for and was refused was OT, because "he knew how to hold his pencil" and OT "would not benefit his education." This is questionable, as the ability to hold a pencil is not the sole criteria for determining the need for OT. And, if you recall, there were other motor issues that Josh exhibited, but Ellen did not know how to pull that information together to contest the school's decision. What she could have done was ask, "What *does* qualify a student for OT?" Had she asked and had they answered her accurately, she would have realized that holding a pencil was not the sole determinant for OT services.

When faced with a "No" to a request, it is reasonable to ask to see the policies or regulations specific to the topic being discussed—politely, of course. Take the time to read them. If they are not clear, request an explanation. You may learn that:

- there is a relevant policy

- there is no policy

- the policy does not relate to the issue at hand, or

- there are exceptions to the application of the policy.

In any case, you will have a copy of the policy as a reference. Another reasonable request is to ask for a copy of all policies or regulations related to students with suspected disabilities and those with confirmed disabilities.

Josh was fortunate to be placed with a general education teacher who recognized his needs and provided multiple accommodations to address those needs, extending the requirements of the IEP in order to teach Josh how to organize his materials and work. Josh actually received no services from a special education teacher and thrived. Remarkably, Josh's needs were met through exceptionally good instruction and the provision of a number of accommodations he needed to be successful in the general education curriculum. All that Ellen wanted (where she wanted to go) for Josh was someone to recognize his problems and provide the necessary programming, and, in this case, he needed a number of accommodations.

How Do We Know That We Are Getting There?

Ellen was no longer told that Josh was "not on target." Instead, he received all A's—earning his grades by receiving appropriate instruction and accommodations that addressed his needs, and by working hard to make the most of the opportunity. This time, Josh's work was accurately reflected in his reports. He was making educational progress!

Where Are We?
What Do We Know?

Unfortunately, Josh continued to fall, and was once again referred to the same neurologist who had failed to provide Ellen with any usable information during the last visit. This time, however, she diagnosed his problem to be a "developmental coordination disorder" and prescribed OT. Additionally, the neurologist referred Josh to an ophthalmologist, who told Ellen that Josh had visual perceptual problems that could also be addressed by an occupational therapist. Now Ellen had sufficient information (data) to take back to the school and have the school provide and pay for OT, but Ellen did not know that. So, she paid for those services.

Third Grade

Josh's third-grade experience was very different from his experience in second grade. His third-grade teacher openly held little hope for Josh's success, and, not surprisingly, he came to hate school. Ellen, for her own reasons, did not complain to the school principal about the teacher's attitude or that of the resource teacher. Josh's teacher noted that his performance showed that he had fine-motor problems. As we know, Ellen had sufficient information from the occupational therapist to show that Josh was making progress. She also had enough data to demand that OT be provided at school and to prove that Josh's IEP was not being met. Instead of taking these steps, she tolerated one more year of public school. Then to paraphrase "The Little Red Hen,"[1] she made the decision to "do it herself." And she did!

Fourth and Fifth Grade: Homeschooling

There is no need to list again the details of what Ellen did for Josh during the two years she homeschooled him. Suffice it to say, she mirrored a regular school day using the school's curriculum, which she found online, to ensure that Josh would keep up with his classmates academically. She also continued with the OT services (which the school did not pay for) and maintained the regimen of exercises that the OT gave her to do with Josh at home.

Before Josh's return to public school for sixth grade, Ellen, on the premise of enhancing his social skills, enrolled him in a summer football program. Through that experience, Josh became a leader who was respected by his peers. He became the "go-to guy" when a team mate needed to know his position or what he was meant to do during a game.

Key Points

- Ellen worked through each of the steps (questions) of the Structured Collaborative IEP Process and in the correct order.

---

1 Muldrow, D. (1954) *The Little Red Hen*. New York: Random House.

- Ellen took the time to learn and understand where Josh was functioning and what his needs were. She obtained this information from the OT assessment, the second neurological evaluation, school reports, and her own observations.

- To determine what she wanted to accomplish, she again referred to the two medical reports and received guidance and direction from the occupational therapist. She also used the school's requirement concerning the district and grade curricula in her goal-setting process, which she located online. With considerable effort on her part, she knew exactly what she wanted to accomplish—that is, to meet the curricular objectives so that, if necessary, Josh could successfully transition back into the school system.

- She also knew that, to accomplish these goals, she would have to continue with the OT services and the home exercises, and she would have to set up Josh's school day to replicate that of the fourth and fifth grades, using the respective curricula.

- We know she continually monitored his growth, making adjustments as necessary, because he was able to return to the public school with the academic skills necessary to succeed in his sixth grade class. In order to accomplish that, we know that she implemented Josh's school program and related services with integrity.

- Because Josh's sixth-grade work was exemplary, he clearly maintained the skills learned and no longer needed special education services to continue through the remainder of his public education career.

Summary

Although these days it might be more difficult to accomplish what Ellen did with homeschooling, given the current "more stringent" educational requirements and demands of students, Josh's return to school was amazingly successful, and eventually he no longer qualified for or needed special education services. Josh clearly had an incredible mother! She did not have a degree in education, but saw his needs and met them with dedicated instruction.

At the time of Josh's schooling, this particular school system was far from being at the cutting-edge of educating students with disabilities. They had neither the understanding necessary nor the desire to use the IEP system to identify a child's needs, use data appropriately, or even willingly provide an assessment for a student with obvious difficulties. Of course, as Ellen pointed out, staff could easily identify his problems, but they did not attempt to meet his needs. With the exception of one very capable and competent teacher, there was little support offered to Ellen and Josh.

Clearly, there was no lack of effort on Ellen's part as she approached both the medical and educational professionals. However, she received little assistance or direction from either. But once the problems were actually defined, Ellen wasted no time in providing OT for her son. Nor did she waste time when it came to approaching the school for the final time to have Josh evaluated. Even though Josh easily qualified for services, the school was still reluctant to test him. The services he eventually received were few and poorly administered. Ellen took the only option left to her: she removed Josh from the adverse and, quite frankly, harmful school environment. The rest, as they say, is history.

There are two important lessons we can learn from Ellen's efforts and approaches to helping her son. First, she continued to seek information in order to learn what recourse she might have so she could approach the school more successfully about how to meet Josh's needs—this includes her attempts to involve medical professionals, asking her sister for information, and approaching the PTIC for assistance. Later, she actually worked with the PTIC to help others. The other lesson, and unbeknown to Ellen, that we take away from this scenario is that Ellen successfully followed the six steps of guided collaboration—she just lacked full collaboration on the part of the school staff, at least until Josh's return to public education. Had she known more about the policies and state and school regulations under which the district was to be operating, it is almost assured that the school would have said "yes" much earlier. As it turned out, without knowing the process of special education, Ellen still managed to provide for her son at home and then successfully "transition" Josh back into the public school system where he was able to graduate.

What this scenario represents is an example of an alternative approach to when a school says "No" and a perfect application of the six questions to ensure a successful educational experience for her son. And she did it herself—with the help of Josh and the occupational therapist, of course!

CHAPTER 4

Three Children with Various Disabilities and Mother Requests an Advocate's Assistance

There are many different service providers in the special education field, all of whom bring their professional expertise and experience to bear in any given situation. Over the course of this book, you will become familiar with many different parents facing many different situations. In this scenario, however, the story is told from an advocate's position. An advocate in the context of special education is someone knowledgeable in national, regional, and local laws and policies as they pertain to the education of children with disabilities. They are not necessarily an expert in a particular disability, but they may be. They assist the parent or guardian when working with the school system in order to ensure that the Indvidualised Education Program (IEP) that is developed abides by all laws and policies under which the school and school district are regulated. The role of the advocate is to assist the parent—sometimes speaking on behalf of the parent—through the special education process.

Good "people skills" are essential in working collaboratively with the school personnel. For an advocate, knowledge and comprehension of the school's systems are an absolute must. Advocates should be skilled communicators, so they can explain the information presented by the school personnel to the parent in a way that the parent understands and can use to make informed decisions. The advocate should *not* make decisions for the parent. The parent remains in control, as a contributing member of the IEP team. The parent must make all final decisions and must be the one who signs all paperwork.

Now, before we delve into this scenario, it's time for some quick introductions. Marion is the director of a Parent Training and Information Center (PTIC), which is a community resource that was established to provide information and training on issues relating to special education to parents of children with disabilities. The center also provides parents with access to qualified advocates. Karen is the person telling this story. She is one of the staff members at the PTIC and is qualified to act as an advocate for parents in this community. Mary, a parent with four children, felt that the school system was not providing her children with the services necessary for them to make educational progress. All four boys had been diagnosed with disabilities and had active IEPs. At the start of this story, Mary has asked for assistance from the PTIC.

An Advocate's Perspective

> *"'Gabe will improve his reading level.' To them, that was an appropriately measurable goal."*

[Marion, the PTIC Director, told me that she had just gotten off the phone with Mary, who had been calling the PTIC for some time. Mary had four boys, all of whom had an IEPS Director, three of whom had significant learning disabilities. I will focus on only two of her children, Joey and Gabe.]

The oldest one, Joey, was legally blind, meaning that his measured degree of vision is 20/200 (he sees at 20 feet what others see at 200 feet) or worse after using corrective lenses. [Being diagnosed as legally blind affects a person's legal status in terms of access to specialized services and determines, for example, whether he or she will be granted a driver's license. It does not mean that Joey is completely blind.]

The family's school district was not able to provide for Joey's educational needs, because it was a very small district. It did what most small districts do: the district paid tuition to another school district for a regional residential placement for the visually impaired. His IEP meeting was coming up, and Mary had concerns about his transition needs and the discussion that would take place to plan for it. "Transition" refers to moving from one age group program to another. A "transition meeting" is held to discuss the child's needs, so that the receiving school will be able to "transition" the child more smoothly into the new school setting without a loss of services.

A major transition is the exiting from the high school to the community. Schools often begin this discussion and transition planning several years before the child leaves high school. Schools do this to ensure that the child's high school experience prepares him or her for post-secondary or adulthood transition, which may involve finding work, receiving post-secondary education, or entering an adult agency program to meet his or her needs during adulthood. This plan is re-evaluated at each

IEP meeting until the child exits the school system. Joey was in the midst of this transition plan, but Mary had concerns that the current plan did not meet his needs.

Marion said that Mary would be coming into the office the following week and assigned me to meet with her, adding that I would be helping her with IEPs for all her boys. Mary felt the schools were not giving any of her boys what they needed to get the full benefit from their education.

Mary's first concern was to get help with Gabe's IEP. She had just had Gabe's IEP meeting but was not satisfied with the results. I pulled out the files on all the boys and reviewed them in preparation for our meeting.

When I met with Mary, she told me that she had severe learning disabilities herself, had a lot of difficulty with reading, and had struggled throughout her school years. She had attended all her boys' IEP meetings and had tried to participate, but she felt that the school was "pulling the wool over her eyes." Due to her learning disabilities, Mary did not completely understand what the school staff were saying nor was she fully able to understand what was written in the IEPs. School staff failed to explain these things in a way that she could understand. She did, however, clearly voice her frustrations with the school. When I started asking her questions, I thought at first that she wasn't familiar with the special education "lingo." Upon further discussion, I realized that she did, in fact, know what most of the special education language meant, but she did not know the laws, regulations, and policies that applied to her children's special education programs.

Mary and I reviewed Gabe's eighth grade IEP together. He attended regular education classes with the exception of one resource period, because the school did not have self-contained classrooms. This was a very small school with few children with disabilities, so they were unable to provide the range of services you might expect in a larger school. If the school felt that a child was not able to learn within the regular education setting or needed more than just a resource period, the district paid tuition to have the child bussed to a neighboring district that could provide more options for programming.

I noticed that Gabe's present levels of performance were vaguely stated, if present at all: for example, "Gabe reads below grade level," which is neither helpful nor measurable. So, it wasn't surprising to discover that the goals in Gabe's IEP weren't stated in measurable terms either. For example, one goal read, "Gabe will improve his vocabulary." I was stunned and found myself sitting there thinking, "If Gabe just sits on a couch and watches television for a year, without going to school at all, and he learns one new word, just one, wouldn't that goal be met?"

Without specific, measurable statements that indicate current levels of performance, and without measurable goals, it is impossible for the school to show progress or to show that students are learning, much less what they are learning. There were no references to the standards of learning, which are essentially the skills to be met by the end of the school year to satisfy the requirements of passing a particular grade, and no efforts to align the goals to those standards within the IEP. Joey's IEP, which was written by the regional school for the visually impaired, was the only one of Mary's boys' IEPs that had cited learning standards showing the relation between the goals and the standards for his grade.

Mary expressed concerns, because she saw that her youngest boy, who was in third grade, was reading within a year's grade level of Gabe, who was in eighth grade. A child who is placed in a regular classroom is given supports that should enable the child to progress with a year's growth during the school year. If done properly, this would help the child keep up with his or her peers. If Gabe was not expected to achieve a year's growth (as noted in his IEP), it suggests that either the placement was inappropriate for Gabe or that the supports Gabe was given were ineffective.

I told Mary she had a couple of options, and I explained what those options were so she could understand and make a decision. She could request another IEP meeting. If she felt that would not solve the issue, she could write a letter of complaint to a number of high-level people in the State Department of Education (SDE). She decided to request another IEP meeting and asked that I attend with her. I drafted a letter for her to sign requesting an IEP meeting and mailed it to the district before she left my office. I also asked if she would be willing to sign a release of information so that I could obtain a copy of Gabe's educational records, including the most recent evaluation results. She agreed to that.

The school district called before the week's end to clarify the information I was requesting. I was pleased to receive the information the following day. Reviewing the most recent evaluation and the IEPs from previous years, I couldn't figure out when Gabe had fallen so far behind. Then I called Mary and we discussed at great length what should be in the IEP (e.g., present levels of educational performance, educational learning standards, measurable goals, specific and measurable objectives, and benchmarks). We also talked about what else she would like to see included in Gabe's IEP.

When we arrived at the meeting, we discovered that the district had requested a representative from the Special Education Cooperative (SEC) to attend the meeting, because of my presence at the meeting and because of my request for records. (Smaller school districts often pool their limited resources to provide shared services they could not afford otherwise. This is not so much to save money, but more to provide needed services in a setting as close to home as feasible. Cooperatives also often invest in oversight for their programs to ensure they meet the legal requirements, and this is why the representative was in attendance.)

At the start of the meeting, Mary told the IEP team that I was there because she felt that the communication between the district and her was not as good as it could be. She felt my presence would help improve communication, which was in Gabe's best interests.

We reviewed the current IEP and discussed Gabe's present levels of educational performance and their absence from the IEP. It was determined that Gabe's present levels in reading, reading comprehension, and math had not been updated since the last school year. Mary requested that Gabe's present levels of performance be determined so that measurable goals could be written based on those levels of performance. A meeting was scheduled for the following week to review the results and revised goals.

After Gabe's present levels of performance were shared, Mary expressed her deep concern that Gabe was so far behind his present grade placement. Current testing showed that, despite being in eighth grade, Gabe was reading at a 3.5 grade level. I presented the school's testing from one and a half years prior to this, which stated that Gabe had been reading at a 2.9 grade level, and pointed out that 3.5 did not represent a year's growth.

I asked the school to write the reading level in the new IEP. I also asked if they were using a research-based curriculum. Staff said they were using a program they'd acquired many years ago, and they didn't know if it met the requirements for a research-based curriculum. Mary asked the school to use a different reading program for Gabe, as the one they were using was not research-based and because he was not making sufficient progress with the current curriculum. The school staff said they would see if they could find a curriculum to fit his needs.

They then said they'd just purchased a new research-based program for the kids in the elementary school, but were afraid that it would set Gabe apart if they used it for him, because he was so far behind. Mary said she did not feel that it would do any good to use a program for kids Gabe's age, because Gabe was not reading at grade level. Reluctantly, the district agreed.

When we started discussing measurable goals for Gabe, I suggested that his reading goal be, "Gabe will improve his reading level to 4.5." I also specified that they would need to use the same test that they had just used to determine his current reading level. They explained that they couldn't use the same program, as that program was only at the elementary school and not in the middle school. In order for Gabe to be tested, he must be at the elementary school. In order to test him for this meeting, the school had allowed Gabe to get off the bus at the elementary school, and then the teacher who tested him drove him back to the junior high school—how odd.

I stated that the goals they had proposed and the ones in previous IEPs were not measurable. The building principal, the special education teacher, and the representative from the SEC assured me that the goals were measurable and that is just how their district wrote them: "Gabe will improve his reading level."

When asked about the learning standards, the district stated that because Gabe was so far behind, they did not want to use the state learning standards. Mary said she could not understand whether the benchmarks and goals were being met, because they were confusing to her, for example "GOAL: Gabe will improve his reading level. BENCHMARK/OBJECTIVE: Gabe will improve his reading skills by 80 percent." The school said that was just how they were written and that Mary really did not need to worry about the percentages. When she saw that the same meaningless descriptions were repeated over and over again, with each area of need (reading comprehension, spelling, math, and vocabulary), Mary became very frustrated.

We talked about the supports that Gabe needed. The school offered reasonable and seemingly appropriate supports and accommodations in the IEP. They offered a graphic organizer, extra time on homework and tests, preferential seating, teacher's notes, multiple choice tests, and only one test in a major subject per day (to allow ample time to concentrate and study for each one). On paper, those supports appeared adequate.

When the meeting was adjourned, Mary said she was not satisfied with the way the IEP was written and wanted to proceed with filing a complaint with the SDE. I drafted a complaint before we met the following week.

Mary and I reviewed the draft letter of complaint that I'd drawn up. It stated that, despite multiple attempts and multiple IEP meetings, the IEP still:

- did not contain present levels of performance that were specific and measurable

- did not contain written goals that were specific and measurable

- did not contain meaningful benchmarks/objectives that were clearly stated

- did not cite any learning standards to be used as reference.

We included the two previous IEPs and the letter I had drawn up to request the IEP meeting for Mary. We sent a copy to the SDE as well as to the school district and SEC.

We received a copy of an information request sent by the SDE to the school district, asking for a current copy of Gabe's IEP. A few weeks passed before we received a copy of the ruling on the complaint. The SDE directed the school district to write a new IEP containing present levels of education performance, measurable goals, learning standards, and clearly stated and measurable benchmarks/objectives.

Within a week, Mary had received a call from the school district to schedule another IEP meeting. At the IEP meeting, the district and the representative from the SEC acted as if Mary and I had "tattled" on them and as if they were being forced to apologize. They agreed to have Gabe's present levels of performance written into the IEP. The SEC's representative presented the state's learning standards, which were written into the IEP. Mary was very pleased, at first, because it seemed as if the district were finally complying.

After the meeting, I explained to Mary what had happened: the school did add the present levels of performance and the state's learning standards, but they did not change the goals and the benchmarks/objectives. Once she understood, she said that she felt it was a step in the right direction, but that she still did not feel that the school had done everything that they were ordered to do, which is what they should have done in the first place. I told her that if she chose to, we could write another letter to the SDE along with a copy of the new IEP. She stated that she wanted to send it to the SDE before the school had a chance to send in their copy, which they were required to do as part of the state's ruling on the complaint. So, I drafted another letter of complaint, which she reviewed and approved, and sent it to the SDE, the SEC, and the school district.

Within three weeks, we received a copy of the ruling on the follow-up complaint. The ruling stated that the school district must attend training on how to write measurable IEP goals and send proof of attendance, after which they also had to write another IEP that contained measurable goals. They had to complete all this and report back to the SDE within 45 days. Thirty days later, Mary received a call from the school district to schedule another IEP meeting. Even after they (presumably) attended this training course, they still had difficulty writing measurable goals. They often looked at me and asked how I would like it written. During a break, Mary told me she was concerned about Gabe making progress and wanted to have another meeting before the end of the school year to check his progress. It took the school district eight hours to produce a complete IEP before the meeting could be adjourned. Mary felt that she was finally on the right track with Gabe's IEP, although she also felt that the school had written the new, adequate IEP reluctantly.

Mary wanted to start concentrating on Joey's upcoming IEP. As you'll probably remember, Joey attended the regional school for the visually impaired, a residential facility, which meant he lived in the school's dorms when school was in session. Joey was having trouble with a couple of boys who came into his dorm room against his wishes. The boys had already been suspended for doing so, but the behavior continued, so Mary wanted to make sure further action was taken.

Mary wanted to discuss the possibility of placing Joey in more independent quarters. This was a way for older students to gain experience living on their own in a somewhat controlled environment, which would help prepare them for living independently in the community after they graduated. She also wanted to work on the services that would be available for him after he graduated from high school the following year, referring to the transition planning that would help him to prepare for life activities after he exited the public school system.

The school that Joey attended was about 60 miles from his home, so Mary usually participated in the IEP meetings by phone. The day of the meeting, Mary came into the office and we used conference calling to participate in the IEP meeting. The school agreed that Joey should be moved to the apartments on campus, not only because it would help him develop his independent living skills, but also because it would eliminate the problems with the other boys.

Mary then expressed her desire to have Joey attend a specific supplementary program over the summer, which was designed to give visually impaired students hands-on-training and vocational experience in a variety of fields of the student's choice. Mary requested that the home district pay for the summer program. The home district wanted to know what other home districts were doing for students who wanted to attend this program. The staff at the school assured them that all other requests for home districts to pay for this program have been "delightfully met." The home district expressed concerns about funding, but eventually granted the request. Mary was pleased with the results of the IEP meeting.

After the meeting, Mary mentioned some issues she'd been having with her car and how she had to borrow someone's vehicle to pick Joey up from the drop-off point about 50 miles away. She said she could not afford to pay for vehicle repairs and the trip to pick up Joey. I asked her if she was getting reimbursed from the school for transportation costs. She said no. I pointed out a law that stated that the home district must pay for or provide transportation when the residential placement required the students not to be present (i.e., during holidays, summer, and any other time that the school was closed).

Not surprisingly, Mary said the home district had never offered either to pay for transportation or to provide it. I told her that we could write a letter requesting reimbursement, which she then asked me to help her write. We sent the letter—including a copy of the relevant laws—requesting reimbursement for the previous and current school years. Mary received a check from the home district for the full amount requested.

The following spring, Mary requested a meeting to review Gabe's progress. We arrived at the meeting to find that the resource person was the only representative the school district had sent to attend the meeting. Mary decided to go ahead with the meeting even though not all the necessary people were in attendance. Although Gabe had not made as much progress as was expected per the IEP, Mary was satisfied that he was beginning to make progress.

Mary asked me to attend Gabe's IEP meeting the following school year. At the IEP meeting, it was revealed that Gabe had made little progress over the previous school year. Mary suggested that the school should try a different research-based program and increase the amount of time Gabe was getting for reading instruction. The school offered to change Gabe's study hall to another resource period.

We then asked if the current program as described in the IEP was being carried out with fidelity, meaning we wanted to know if the district was using the program as described and providing the proper amount of instructional time. We tried to discuss some additional options, such as allowing the use of colored overlays, printing homework on colored paper, allowing Gabe to wear sunglasses in class, and changing reading programs. The district resisted these options, saying that it would draw too much attention to Gabe. They offered to provide Gabe with a one-on-one aide or to send him to another district for services. Mary was afraid that if Gabe were to go to a neighboring district, he would be in a self-contained classroom. She was against this option, but also wanted to get Gabe's opinion before making any decisions.

The school staff provided a room for Mary to talk to Gabe and explain the options. Gabe did not want to change schools or have an aide following him around, but if he had to choose one or the other he would take the aide rather than change schools. Mary went back into the meeting and accepted the offer of the aide as long as they would also change the study hall to another resource period to be used to work on his reading skills. The district agreed.

After the meeting, I explained that we could try to search for different research-based reading programs to find one that would work better for Gabe. When we found an appropriate program, we could present the options to the school district. Mary wanted to wait and see how things progressed over the next year and take it from there. Mary later divorced her children's father and moved away. Gabe stayed with his father and continued his education with the home district.

Analysis of "An Advocate's Perspective"

It is quite evident that Karen was an experienced advocate who—with her knowledge of special education laws, regulations, and policies—competently met Mary's needs. It is equally obvious that Mary—although she had a disability herself—supported her children and paid careful attention to the content of their IEPs, at least to those parts that she understood. She was also knowledgeable of the school's failing to educate her children. The only thing Mary lacked was the legal knowledge that Karen possessed.

We saw that, as the scenario unfolded, Mary became better able to understand what was happening and more confident in her own ability to make sound decisions based on what was presented to her. Karen did not direct Mary to make a particular decision; rather, she presented options—it was Mary who made the choice—which is exactly what an advocate should do. In each case, it is the opinion of this author that Mary made the correct decisions. Because the district had failed to comply fully with the directive forwarded to the district from the SDE (the agency responsible for oversight and governing the school district), Mary could readily show the school and the SDE that the school remained out of compliance.

Where Are We?
What Do We Know?
What Don't We Know?

Looking at Gabe's IEP, Karen learned that it was incomplete. It lacked the present levels of educational performance and the goal statements necessary to understand adequately where Gabe was for each area of need. The school district failed to write the required information in a measurable format, making it impossible to know where we are or to develop plans on where we would want to go. There also was no reference to the learning standards of the eighth grade, in which he was enrolled. And this was true of the IEPs for all Mary's boys, except, of course, Joey, whose IEP was written correctly—with greater detail and clarity—by the regional school for the visually impaired. There is no doubt that this school district had a problem and that Mary was within her rights to access the services of an advocate to resolve the problem.

Now, before we move on, let's take a moment to discuss the issue concerning the learning standards. All students are expected to have genuine access to the general curriculum, which means that the school is required to teach the students the same curriculum that contains the learning standards (local, state, or national standards) associated with the particular grade in which the child is instructed. If these learning standards are not included (referenced) in the IEP documents, then there is no way to compare the goals that are written in the IEP with the learning standards to ensure the child is truly having instruction in, or access to, the general curriculum.

Karen discussed these issues with Mary, who also felt that the school staff had produced a rather vaguely written IEP and thought that it was part of the reason Gabe was not making as much progress as she thought he should, particularly in reading. Mary's beliefs were certainly verified by the lack of measurability within the IEP.

Karen offered suggestions, as options, as to how Mary might want to proceed. Mary felt the first step should be to return to the school and hold another IEP meeting, this time with Karen's assistance. Even then, the school staff could not determine Gabe's reading level with any confidence or substantiated precision; neither could they show his progress or the reasons for his lack of progress. The school did agree to conduct an assessment of Gabe's reading skills and to report those at the next meeting. This is also where a request was made for the district to rewrite the goals in a measurable format. Had the school done so, they would have answered the questions, "Where are we?" and "Where do we want to go?" Had the school administrators done so, they would also have been able to show Mary and their staff incremental measures of progress over the period of the IEP.

At the following IEP meeting, the school did provide a "reading level" obtained from an elementary reading program. However, the IEP goals were not revised. I would also like to point out that Karen knew that the school staff should use the same assessment to evaluate progress as they'd used to assess Gabe's reading level. If a different instrument had been used, then the results might not have been comparable, which means they would have been useless for showing whether change had occurred. The school team members said that the goals were written correctly, meaning that they were (according to the school staff) written in a meaningful and measurable format, so they would not be changed. That, of course, was not true; neither was it acceptable to Mary or Karen.

So, at this point, all that is "answerable" is "Where are we?" and "What do we know?"—although it should be pointed out that, as far as the scenario tells us, we only have these answers for the area of reading. Also note that "answerable" was placed in quotation marks, because we do not know which reading program was used or if the reading score(s) obtained would only be viable if compared with future assessments made using the same reading "test" from the same reading program. We do not know if the reading score(s) would be in agreement with other reading assessments that are not part of the elementary reading program. So, we have to question whether the score(s) obtained are accurate and independent of the reading program. (We may be safe in assuming that there was a math assessment, as math and other academic areas were mentioned as having poorly written goal statements, too.)

A key point to make is that Mary could have, at this point, walked out of the meeting. Wisely, Mary and Karen remained for the entire presentation by the school staff and gathered much more information than they would have had they left prematurely. Furthermore, the school did offer (to Mary and Karen) reasonable and acceptable accommodations to meet Gabe's needs in the general education classes.

Where Do We Want to Go?

"Where do we want to go?" cannot be answered—not with the goals presented in the manner in which they are written. A goal that says "Gabe will improve his reading skills by 80 percent" only begs the question: what, of the many possible reading skills, does 80 percent represent? It could be anything from letter recognition and letter sounds to comprehension when answering inference questions about what he has read. At the conclusion of the IEP meeting, neither Karen nor Mary had enough information to determine where Gabe should be going in terms of writing measurable and meaningful goals based on his identified needs.

Knowing the options available to parents, Karen told Mary that they might, if she wished, forward a letter of complaint to the SDE, which they did. The SDE sent a letter with its findings, directing the school to rewrite the IEP, including Gabe's present levels of educational performance, measurable goals, learning standards, and clearly stated and measurable benchmarks/objectives in the new IEP.

An IEP meeting was conducted and changes were made, which was an improvement, but the district again refused to revise the goals using a measurable format. So, another letter was sent to the SDE, which sided with Mary once again, stating that the school staff needed to attend training to learn how to write proper IEPs, that they had to show proof of attendance, and that they had to rewrite Gabe's IEP—again.

Although the steps taken to resolve these issues were eventually successful, months of time were wasted in the process. This delay may have impacted Gabe's actual education and instruction, because it took so long to draft an appropriate IEP and because those changes would have been reflected in the instruction he was meant to receive. We don't know how Gabe's actual education was impacted by the delay, but we do know that, by the conclusion of this lengthy process, an aide was assigned to assist Gabe.

Mary elected not to invest additional efforts in locating a different research-based reading program for the school to use in Gabe's education. She wanted to see what difference the aide's assistance would make. Unfortunately, we don't know what role the aide was assigned to fill or the relationship of that role to Gabe's reading. We can only hope that the aide's responsibilities were discussed at the IEP meeting, that the person the school hired would assist in answering the question "How will we get there?" and that the aide's services would be part of that answer.

How Will We Get There?

As for Joey's transition programming, Mary successfully made a convincing case for him being moved into an independent living setting that met two needs—ending the "bullying" and offering the opportunity to experience independent living in a monitored setting. Mary was also able to provide him with access to a vocational exploration program during the summer session, with the home district/school paying the tuition for that program. Both of these represent services that support Joey's transition plan, specifically exploring post-high school community living and employment. These activities answer the question "How will we get there?" and aid in his readiness for exiting the public school system and transitioning into the community.

Key Points

- This scenario shows the value in working with a competent advocate. Mary recognized what she did not understand in the IEP process and that she needed assistance. As she put it, she felt "they were pulling the wool over her eyes." In a way, she was correct. Unfortunately, this was a school and possibly a district that were ignorant about how to develop IEPs. As difficult as it might be to imagine a school where the staff were untrained in the purpose and function of an IEP, it is quite possible to run into educators who are unaware of special education laws, regulations, and local policies. As we have seen elsewhere, it is not unusual to find staff referencing policies that do not exist or are misinterpreted. This should serve as a reminder to ask for a copy of the laws or policies when there is a question or concern about a procedure during an IEP meeting.

- Karen was unquestionably a knowledgeable and experienced advocate, who both knew the laws of special education and understood the value of seeking answers to the first question, "What do we know?" The answers to this question (present levels of educational performance or a listing of needs) were not available, and, after explaining the need for this basic information, she requested the school to assess Gabe's present levels of performance.

- A note of caution was referenced in the analysis regarding the reading test score(s) obtained through use of the elementary reading program and bears some repeating. When you are seeking functional performance levels, the assessment used may be a part of a reading program. However, it is important to know that the scores obtained through the reading program's test instrument or assessment could be incompatible with a test instrument from another vendor—one that was developed independently and is not associated with a particular reading program. You need to be certain that any test score is meaningful in another setting, school, or district. Be assured that every program or test instrument has information in the corresponding manuals that will indicate the usefulness of the test scores obtained. A school psychologist can readily tell you the answer to this question, and that is why it is important to have someone at an IEP meeting who is skilled and knowledgeable about any test results so that they can be explained to you. Don't be afraid to ask questions about test data. Once you understand what those numbers (scores) mean, they can be very useful in helping you make informed educational decisions for your child. Ask questions!

- Karen's knowledge of regulations and policies was essential when it came to contesting the school's position on the format of writing the IEP and the other issues of compliance. After lodging letters of complaint that outlined Mary's concerns about the manner in which the IEP was created, the SDE twice directed the school to comply with existing special education laws and regulations. When the school refused to comply fully with the directive, Mary wanted to contact the SDE once again, and, in its reply, the department ordered the school to attend training on developing compliant IEPs.

- We do not know what effects the training and revised IEP had on Gabe's achievement, but we do know that the school is now aware of the requirements for writing compliant IEPs.

- We also do not know what the function and responsibilities of the aide were. It is essential that an IEP includes statements about what an aide's purpose is and which goals will be met through the aide's specific support.

- As written, we saw that Karen did not keep the position as lead on the second IEP meeting for Gabe. She no longer needed to be the spokeswoman, as Mary was making her requests directly to the IEP team and had always been able to make decisions on behalf of Gabe. Mary only needed information on what was to be in an IEP, what the content should look like, and what steps to take to contest how and what the school proposed to provide in terms of IEP content and services.

- Joey's transition planning went very well, and it seems that Mary now had the confidence to make his needs known and to present suggested program changes to the IEP team.

- There will be various times when it is necessary to seek others' advice. Fortunately, Mary recognized when that time arose and found an advocate who enabled her to make informed IEP decisions. She never relinquished her parental rights to make those decisions. This scenario represents an excellent example of a working relationship between a parent and an advocate, where the advocate provides the correct information and options so that the parent can make decisions with confidence.

Summary

There is no reason to summarize the key points in this particular scenario, however, I would share a concern I had regarding the quality of information used in this scenario. Specifically, I would like to address the problem of quantifying progress with the use of grade or age levels. As you might recall, this school measured Gabe's current reading level as being a "3.5 grade level" compared with his previous score of reading at a "2.9 grade level." On face value, there appears to be six month growth in reading over a year. The problem with this conclusion is that it is subject to the particular instrument that was used to measure the child's growth. Simply put, the conclusion is only valid if the same reading series and assessment were used both times, and only shows growth within the limits of a particular reading program.

The scores from one reading program do not necessarily correspond to the scores used in a different reading program. This is why most school psychologists will report standard scores versus grade/age levels. Doing so allows the numbers they use to be compared across different tests, leading to a better understanding of how much progress the child is really making. So, it is extremely important to have someone who can interpret the data that are being discussed at all IEP meetings. If data are not interpreted, and if those interpretations are not recorded in the IEP, then it is impossible for an outsider such as myself to state what reading level the child is actually performing at with any degree of confidence.

CHAPTER 5

A Child with Autism

His Needs Changed, the Program Did Not

Like many of the stories revealed in this book, this is a true, present-day story of the wrongs faced by a mother trying to provide educational services for her child with disabilities. What you are about to read is a phone interview conducted over two days, which has been lightly edited to maintain the clarity and consistency of the original interviews. The goal is to retain the voice and original wording whenever possible, in order to best express Mrs. George's thoughts and intentions. While I have taken great pains to retain the voices of all contributors, the oral form is rather different from the written format, so this story will "read" a bit differently from many of the others.

Mrs. George is a bright woman who continues to take on the challenges posed by a troublesome school system as necessary. You will see that she has learned much from her experiences. She is nearly independent enough to need only the assistance of an attorney if her own efforts fail. She has learned to collect data, to keep meticulous records, and to use both when making her point. I hope you can overlook the less formal presentation style and appreciate what Mrs. George has come to understand and apply when dealing with schools that say "no."

Marcus's Story

"Marcus bad boy! Marcus bad day!"

At four months of age, Marcus had his first ear and upper respiratory infections. At six months, he had his first ear operation and set of ear tubes with two more sets of tubes by age three. I learned that this is a common problem for kids with autism. Because of the number of ear infections, we had to delay his immunization schedule until the age of 15 months, when he received a bolus shot, a combination of six or so different drugs in a single shot. To help Marcus with the side-effects of this shot, he was given an over-the-counter medication which I later learned to be a poison. [The comment here is not to be construed as a warning about the use of over-the-counter medications and was the opinion of Mrs. George. Any medication used should be approved by your child's physician.]

Within 24 hours of receiving the shot, Marcus's bowel movement was bloody and he had become seriously sick, severely dehydrated, and was crying non-stop. We took him to the hospital for a four-day recovery from the shot. We saw immediate changes in Marcus. At the hospital we saw him fix his attention on the overhead lights. They were obviously bothering him because he was crying loudly. The doctor walked in, saw that Marcus was having difficulty with the lights, and flipped off the lights. Marcus stopped crying immediately. He continued fixating at home. For example, he would always focus on the ceiling fan spinning.

We also saw many different behavioral changes. Marcus used to say "Mama" and "Dada." Instead, he had stopped talking altogether. He used to make the effort to pull himself up and scoot along the furniture to get around and follow me. He stopped doing that and was no longer interested in what I was doing.

Because of the language loss, we started wondering if maybe he had a hearing loss. So, we had him tested, but the test results were within the normal range. At this point I didn't know if the problems were because I couldn't breastfeed, because of the ear infections, because of the delay in the new vaccination schedule, or the results of the bolus shot, or from his having the rotavirus. I was totally lost.

Marcus seemed to be continually upset and crying. While I was working in the kitchen, making meals and cleaning up, I found that when I placed him in a small, vibrating chair, he was content to wait until I was finished. But when the chair stopped vibrating, he was no longer happy and could not tolerate the stillness of the chair. He would fuss and cry. I must have run through a fortune's worth of batteries using that chair. Even then he had no interest in what I was doing. In fact, Marcus had very little interest in what any of the family members were doing—including his siblings.

However, he was fascinated with the spinning ceiling fan and any kind of twirling toy, but once the spinning stopped he cried and screamed. He seemed to need the stimulation of the twirling fan or toy or the vibrating chair, but not the bright lights. People held no interest for him. We learned later that he had classic regressive autism. Still, I didn't know what caused any of this. Then I thought, perhaps it was because he was born through induced labor. I really had no idea. I just wanted an answer!

The doctor decided to give Marcus one more vaccination shot, but he immediately became ill. I said that there would be no further vaccinations. At first the doctor agreed, but then he suggested that he could order preservative-free vaccinations. Looking again at Marcus's reaction, he rethought that offer and confirmed that the vaccination was making Marcus ill. The doctor agreed that the schedule of vaccinations would end.

So, here I was, knowing that something was really wrong with my child. I would go to the doctor, and the doctor would say, "If you don't see a change in a month or so, come back." That was the only reply I got each time I went back. Six months later I finally got a referral to the Marshall Institute. It turned out that meant no more than being placed on a waiting list. While waiting, Marcus seemed to be slipping away. He would just lie there, either smiling or screaming. Eventually he was scheduled to be evaluated and was diagnosed with autism. The institute recommended that Marcus receive speech and language, physical, occupational, and Applied Behavior Analysis (ABA) therapies. But it wasn't as if the services were then presented to me. Instead, I was given a list of professional therapists and did the dialing-and-smiling routine, where I called those on the list until I was able to find professionals to provide each of the services recommended.

Eventually, I was able to place Marcus in the William's School's preschool program, a private school—after being placed on another waiting list. The only thing that allowed Marcus to get into the program as soon as he did was because my father paid for the school's playground to be built. Even so, I nearly went broke trying to pay for the program and services Marcus needed. And although I nearly became penniless paying for the program, I felt that Marcus needed the services that he received there. I was pleased with how the staff worked with Marcus and the programs they provided. He stayed for two years of preschool.

The school's basic approach was to use the discrete trial training model along with other services. Marcus was one of three students with autism who received eight hours of training a day from ten different therapists and educators. They made efforts to include Marcus with his non-disabled peers as often as they could. It was a great program.

But it began to take its toll on my other children, because I would not get home from picking him up from school until six or seven at night—it was an hour's drive one way. I knew I was not there when his siblings needed me, and I knew this was not good for them.

Unfortunately, during that same time, Marcus was not a good sleeper, having great difficulty sleeping throughout the night. We were working with a neurologist who recommended several medications for his sleeping condition. This raised a big concern for us.

We decided to seek out a physician of alternative medicine because of all the medications he was already receiving. The doctor found numerous metals in Marcus's system and thought he might be allergic to gluten. She used chelation therapy on his system to remove the "poisons" within him. In a word, I think she was a "quack," who was more interested in selling us her products and making us a part of her lab experiments.

The final straw for me was when the doctor gave me a cream that I was to apply to Marcus's body. She told me that I had to use rubber gloves so that my skin would not come into contact with the cream as I might have a reaction to the cream. I thought this was ridiculous! Besides, how was I ever to keep all the "poisons" out of his system? They were all around him and in all of the foods he ate. By the way, she also prescribed antidepressants and a prescription medication for asthma. Everything she tried seemed to make a difference, but only for a brief time; nothing was a long-term fix. It was time to leave.

I returned to the neurologist only to go through 20 different drugs, including an antipsychotic prescription medication. This time the neurologist diagnosed Marcus with bipolar and obsessive-compulsive disorders, in addition to autism. He also said that Marcus had apraxia [difficulty saying what one wants to say, not as a result of muscle control but due to difficulty with the brain functioning] and echolalia [occurs when a person repeats sounds or words of another person]. Here I was with my five-year-old child, who was now being treated with numerous medications for multiple disorders. They worked initially, but now that he's older, we've had to increase the dosages to have an effect on his mood swings, which can be large.

A side-effect of all the medications was his greatly increased appetite; he was now extremely overweight. You can't imagine the contention that existed, with family members convinced that I was overfeeding Marcus. That was not the case, and I would try to explain the effects of the medication on his system, but it did not stop the accusations. I admit that sometimes I gave in by letting him have extra food because of what he might do if I didn't.

Let me put it this way: I am a single mother and only five feet, two inches tall and 110 pounds. By comparison, Marcus is five feet tall and 160 pounds. He is 11 years old now and entering puberty. With that, he has increased his tendencies to hit me and to break things. Add to this his increase in extreme mood swings, and you begin to see the challenges that I now face. He now demands that I give him food, saying, "Eat, eat, eat," and asks for seconds as I'm handing him his meal. If I do not give him more food, he will swat at me.

In his anger, Marcus recently pushed me into the kitchen stove, demanding more food. My family is concerned now that Marcus will hurt me, or someone else, and my father is worried that something worse might happen. I think his statement was more for effect (to recognize the dangers of his behaviors), and a point well taken. Marcus's behaviors at school have also worsened. I am in the process of getting an updated neurological assessment, with a full review of his medications and behaviors.

In the beginning I really didn't understand a lot and I did not realize that he wasn't going to get "cured." He's going to be 12 soon and is going through a lot of emotional and physical changes. It's kind of like grief acceptance and, at that point, I was still in the anger stage and I was trying to cure him. You don't even think when you're doing it. I think it's a natural process and you have to go through it. I was just being a mom and I wanted the very best for Marcus.

Marcus's Education

Many people had warned me to not even consider public schools, saying they wouldn't have the services Marcus needed. So, before the end of his second year at the preschool, I was searching for other private schools that would provide for his needs. However, Marcus was rejected for one reason or another. Most rejected him because his needs were too severe and because he lacked language skills. I think the private schools only wanted kids who would be more successful in their programs, making their programs look more effective to interest other parents. By connecting with an advocate and a lawyer, I found an acceptable public special education kindergarten program. He spent two years in that program, with three other children and three staff members.

Marcus went to first grade with an aide in the class with him. He and the aide sat in the back of the general education classroom. She also shadowed him wherever he went in order to monitor his behaviors, such as: "stimming" [self-stimulation], flapping [his arms], and vacant staring. Marcus had limited language and no real way of communicating with others. The aide was so poorly trained that she was only able to provide minimal, if any, help to Marcus and the general education teacher.

He was pulled out of his first-grade classroom for speech, adaptive physical education (PE), and occupational therapy. Everything else was carried out in the general education classroom with general education students. For reading, Marcus sat with the other students, and when he acted out, the aide would try to "redirect" his behaviors, but with her limited training, this usually was not successful.

The school did make an effort to provide Marcus's services in a regular classroom setting, because of FAPE and because that is how the programs were set up in the district. I learned that their thinking was that, as a parent, you could sue them for not giving your child an "equal opportunity" in the general education classroom. [FAPE refers to U.S. legislation requiring students with disabilities to have access to a "free and appropriate public education," which requires "the education of each student with a disability with non-disabled students, to the maximum extent appropriate to the needs of the student with a disability." It does not mandate that all students are to be placed and served in the general education setting, but is to be individually determined.]

So, in the general education setting, for reading they would break up into groups where the kids were reading the same book but with different questions to answer. But Marcus couldn't even read at that point; although he knew perhaps 20 words by sight. He got nothing from being in the mainstream classes, because class time was spent attempting to deal with his behaviors.

Recognizing the limited skills of the aide, we worked with the school to find a capable paraprofessional to see if that would help. See, I was young and new to this "autism thing," and I really wanted him mainstreamed. I wanted Marcus to be with other kids, doing the same things they were. But I could not get it to work on my own. I had hired a lawyer who demanded a more highly skilled paraprofessional and more. I mean we went to every avenue and tried everything from A to Z, exhausting every option there was to make the regular classroom successful. Marcus was just not able to function in that setting.

While I was in the "autism-jargon phase"—that is, learning about autism and thinking that whatever I read was what should be—when Marcus was first diagnosed, I was determined he would never attend a self-contained class. But the reality is that the more you learn about this disorder and the older your child gets, you really don't care what people think any more—you just want to do what's best for him—and what's best for your other kids, too. So, I gave up the hopes of mainstreaming Marcus and tried to get him enrolled into a private school. We interviewed at three or four different schools that had special needs programs. He didn't get into any of them, because they said that he didn't have enough language skills.

We then tried the area "autism school," but he didn't get in there because they said that he had too many behavioral problems, which is really ridiculous as the school was set up for children with autism. But it was a very new school, funded by the school parents. It was basically set up for higher-functioning students' success stories, so they could build up their school's reputation. Using their criteria, he didn't "qualify" for the school. Given all of the rejections, we had to go back to the public school system. There was no other choice.

Once we accepted his being in another year of a public school's first grade, we no longer wanted Marcus to be in the regular classroom with an aide. Instead, we wanted a self-contained classroom. Our thinking was that a smaller class and smaller ratio of students to staff would be a better way to address his behaviors and needs. Unfortunately, before the new school year could begin, we moved and Marcus was in a new school. Unfortunately, the staff at the new school insisted that he be placed in the "mainstream" with an aide.

We explained what had happened in the previous school and why we had decided that mainstreaming wasn't working and that we wanted the self-contained program. I guess they're meant to do everything to meet the child's needs in the regular classroom and his home school. If they aren't, then it could cost them a lot of money, because they've either got to pay for a private school or for me to homeschool Marcus. They tried very hard to make everything work in the regular classroom. It didn't.

The paraprofessionals were horrible. I mean they did not have the skills to work with children like Marcus. He regressed a lot, and that's when I again started investigating the self-contained classroom. Again, I saw numerous changes in Marcus's behavior, including screaming, showing much more anger, being less verbal and less intelligible, and he was showing much more "stimming." He was always sick with ear infections and upper-respiratory problems. He was just not a healthy child.

He also had a lot of oral fixation, an issue we still deal with. He would chew his fingers or hands. He would smell things on the floor, but, fortunately, did not eat them. His self-stimulation had just gotten out of control. He would stand against the chair or the wall so he could feel the pressure against his body. He would also do planking. (Planking refers to a behavior where people lie face down on the ground in unusual or inconvenient places with their legs stiff and straight and their arms rigid at their sides.) And all of these were obvious changes that were seen at school and home.

At school they would make attempts just to redirect him, just like they do now, but not work actually to change his behaviors. I didn't think they knew how. They did whatever they could.

It was at this point that I said the regular setting was just not working. So, while I originally wanted him in the regular setting and would have it no other way, now I was bringing in an attorney to help me move Marcus from the regular setting to the smaller, self-contained placement. Of course, other parents were fighting for placement in the regular setting—probably for the same reasons we did in the beginning.

I've learned that it takes a while to deal with all that is going on. It is so different from anything I had experienced. And when I went to the support groups and talked to other parents who have children with autism, I learned what their kids were doing, and I realized that Marcus needed to be in a smaller setting. I know I am repeating this, but the whole joke of it was that my ex-husband and I were fighting to get him into a self-contained classroom a year *after* we had fought to have him placed in the regular classroom. And there they were, not letting us do it, because they were worried about legal issues with the least restrictive environment (LRE) placements. We were looking at Marcus's education and behavioral needs, and the school was looking at a potential lawsuit for not serving Marcus in the general education classroom setting.

It took an attorney and an eight-hour Individualized Education Program (IEP) meeting that cost me $6,000 to make the change. I notified them that I was bringing legal counsel so, of course, they had counsel there, too. There were ten people in the room: my ex-husband, me, my lawyer, their lawyer, *all* of his therapists, the principal, Marcus's teachers, and a school psychologist. That was just one of three meetings we had before we were able to finalize the IEP. I learned much about developing IEPs and IEP meetings.

Our attorney made them account for Marcus's day, minute by minute—making them account for every interaction and every incident that was reported. He wanted to know the antecedent, the behavior, and the response. (I had spent a lot of time with the attorney before the meeting, relaying to him every incident that I had recorded, so there was a lot of preparation.)

We showed how Marcus was not getting his needs met in this current home school and setting, and that he would need the smaller environment and different services. The attorney was using their data and saying, "Look at these behaviors; look at the lack of progress; look at the regression!" He was using the IEP and looking at the goals and using their data to point out that Marcus was regressing. It was obvious that the goals were not even close to being met or even being addressed by the teachers or aides.

Marcus was ultimately placed in a self-contained classroom for his second year of first grade, where he had the best teacher ever. He had another teacher in his second grade and it was an okay year. And then he moved to third grade and then spent two years in fourth grade.

Marcus is currently in the same elementary school, where I wanted him held back for a second year in fifth grade. I was hoping that his behaviors and learning could improve before he moved on to the middle school. In hindsight, that was a mistake that the school and I made. He is now the largest child in the school, and his size and behaviors draw attention. The elementary school is recommending that Marcus be moved to the middle school, even though many of his goals have not been fully achieved.

I decided I should go visit the middle school and was pleasantly surprised by what I saw. I think that Marcus's behaviors stem from boredom in his elementary classroom. Within ten minutes of touring the middle school facility and seeing what the kids were doing, I knew right away he was just wasting away where he is now. It's no wonder he is bored out of his mind! He's just a kid who needs constant activity—it doesn't have to be physical, but it needs to keep his mind working.

After seeing the differences between the two classrooms, I called the school to request a meeting to talk about moving him to the middle school now, before the end of the school year. They want to wait until the fall to move him. I don't think that it's in his best interest to wait. It would really be good for him to move now, because right now he leaves for school at 6:12 a.m. and rides for over an hour. Once at school, he sleeps on the floor because he is so tired from the trip. To get to the middle school, he would leave at 8:30 a.m., would have PE every day and a real curriculum. What he is doing right now is zilch as far as I am concerned.

Looking back, when he first got into the elementary school's first grade program he was seven and a half, and the program was a good match for him at that point. But the program hasn't changed over time; he has. I've known this, but I really didn't think he was ready to move to the middle school, and held him back a year because he was so delayed. However, after going to the middle school program and seeing kids who were just like Marcus sitting at desks with teachers moving around the room, I knew this was where he belonged.

It's a very cool little setup—and at a public school, believe it or not. They have different areas where they rotate the kids. One looks sort of like a house, and students do their own laundry and they learn how to cook. They set up the table and they have an area that looks like a kitchen, and I think that's going to be really good for him to be in that environment and have someone control him more than I can. As I mentioned, it was the kitchen area where Marcus and I often had our difficulties dealing with food limits. I was really excited to see that—all of it.

There are outings twice a week called "community-based interventions." They do that now where he is, but go to fast food restaurants, which Marcus does not need. They do far more things at the middle school and go to places more fitting for him.

One thing that I really liked about my visit to the middle school was that they had the fluorescent lights turned off and had regular incandescent lighting in the classroom. The buzzing of the fluorescent lights bothers Marcus so much that he will enter classrooms and turn the lights off. In fact, the issue of fluorescent lights is written into his IEP, and it's not always being addressed. I asked the social worker, who works at both schools, "Why do you know what to do here and you're not doing it where Marcus is at?" She proceeded to tell me that he's doing fine, that he has good days at school, and that he's usually very happy. She's like a robot, you know.

I also took video footage during a recent visit, because I know what I'm doing this time. Marcus has been handed a really bad hand, so I went in and used my phone to get pictures of the class, so I could explain to them what exists at the middle school that is not at the elementary school. I'm just really glad I went to see the school, and this is after asking for an appointment over and over again. They kept putting me off, and I know why.

I have to say that I originally wanted him in the current behavioral program because a lot of kids will migrate into this program, and many of their behaviors will change and they can return to the regular classroom. I realize now that this just isn't going to happen with Marcus, because his behaviors are really, really extreme and because those behaviors are not being worked on. He comes off the bus now and says, "Marcus bad day. Marcus bad day," and I just know the middle school program is where he needs to be now.

Staff members have a checklist they're meant to check off, letting me know that he did this or that or didn't. I haven't seen it. And there are other problems. For example, I've gone to the school—without them knowing in advance—to observe, from just outside the doorway, what's going on in the classroom. I saw Marcus walking in circles, I saw the teacher sitting at her desk, and I saw Marcus twirling a piece of string for ten minutes before I knocked on the door and said hello. I got the response, "Oh! Oh, hello." And they jumped up and started moving around the classroom, working with the kids. It's nothing more than glorified babysitting right now. Marcus is with one other kid like himself, and he's just bored. He's not being directed toward any activities. He's only being reprimanded and manhandled—I'll explain that in just a moment—for his behaviors. It's just not right, and Marcus is bored and unhappy.

Because Marcus is in a public school, I really don't feel like I get the option of designing his program like I could in the private programs. Private programs provided ABA for an hour each day, and speech therapy each day, and half an hour of occupational therapy (OT) twice a week, and group speech therapy, where all the kids are working together. He received adaptive PE twice a week and went to the cafeteria with all the other kids in the school. Not now.

I'm tired of having him getting off the bus and saying, "Marcus bad boy! Marcus bad day!" It's killing what he has left of his self-esteem, and it is really horrible for the rest of us to hear him say that. He is so unhappy with where he is. He will also say, "No Mrs. Smith, no Mrs. Smith," meaning he does not want to be near his teacher any more. And all of the school year, they're telling me how great he is at school and how he loves school and how they love him.

Because we are questioning what is being done with Marcus in the classroom, my ex-husband and I have monthly meetings to ask them to show us what's being accomplished, and they have little to share. When I first saw that he was bruised and scratched, I went right to that school, asking what was going on, but it did not stop. He continues to come home with scratches and tells us in his own way how unhappy he is.

Right now he is the biggest kid in the elementary school. He's walking around like the giant kid who's misbehaving, who doesn't belong in the elementary school. At first I thought he needed an extra year in fifth grade, but this year has been turning out so badly that I know it was not a good recommendation on their part. It's not totally their fault, because we all sat in the meeting and made the decision to keep him in the elementary school for an additional year. But it is their fault if there's a problem and they don't do something about it!

So, basically, what we have done is to continue to adjust Marcus's medications, trying to address his behaviors and get him through the day at school, and I'm very tired of it. He will always need his medications because he's bipolar, but he probably wouldn't need to go to these drastic levels of medications if he was getting the kind of programming he needs.

We are going to get a full neurological workup, because we haven't had one in a while and to see if I can get the medications changed, because I'm not happy with the amount of psychotropic drugs he's on. He's had about 15 different medications, and right now he's on three, including one that's called a mood stabilizer—I'm not even sure what that actually is. I'm just not happy with all of the medications. He takes Geodon, and he takes Klonopin as needed—and lately we have "as needed" a lot, just to get him through the day.

Right now all the kids who are in the middle school are really calm because they've been there since August and they're settled into their routines. To bring a new kid in right now would upset the routines for everybody. (I understand that, but so what? I don't care! This is my child and he deserves an appropriate program!) And I know some of the parents who have children in the class, and I asked a friend of mine how she would feel about having Marcus move into the class with her child and she said, "You know, you've got to do what's best for Marcus. My kid will be okay." And so will the others!

I'm hoping to get Marcus moved to the middle school without having to call an attorney again, but I'm just not sure at this point. In this district it's very hard to move a behaviorally challenged kid from one location to another, because they set up the system at the beginning of the school year and they really don't want to be bothered with changing it.

To put Marcus in another classroom, they would have to switch everything around to accommodate him and his needs. They'd probably need additional personnel, a one-on-one aide, or a teacher to work with him because of his behaviors. They are not going to want to do that unless they're forced to. So I put a call in to my attorney and I told him I have absolutely no money whatsoever to pay. If he wants to, send an advocate—I am an advocate, but I would not be a good advocate for Marcus in this situation.

It is going to be an interesting next couple of weeks, because I've already put the ball in motion and we'll see how long it takes. I've made it clear that Marcus has had a lot of regression in the areas of his verbal skills and behaviors, and I refuse to let him regress any further.

I am hell-bent on getting him in that middle school program tomorrow. You have to be the squeaky wheel—and I *know* that! I can make a change in placement at any time, and I don't have to wait till next year—especially when I know and have proof that his current program is not working.

Additional Comments

The following three points were made by Mrs. George. Although they are not directly related to the IEP process, they warrant inclusion. They highlight concerns and experiences that many parents have faced or will face. As presented, they speak for themselves as insights and cautions:

1. On Facebook, I have 2,500 connections, and I tried out every group I could find that I thought might be of help to me. Sometimes you run into people who only have one program or one way of doing anything and everything, but I try to keep away from those people. They mean well, but I avoid them.

2. Overall, the Internet is a great source of support and help, and you can find information on any new regulations or laws that might show up that are related to autism. I need to admit that in the beginning I was more angry and frustrated, and so focused on my child's needs that I just couldn't see past the frustration. I found a lot of parents new to the world of autism go through the same process. A lot of parents take on their child's *cause*, but it often gets in the way of their concentrating on their child's *needs*.

3. I want briefly to mention extended school year (ESY) services. This is offered, but it's only for three and a half weeks during the summer, which is too little time to help very much because it is only for the month of June, which gives a lot of time for regression to occur. All the kids are based in one location in the district, and it's really just more babysitting. I do use it, because I've got two other kids who are at crucial points in their lives and I need to spend time with them, because this is a family of three children. Not just one.

Analysis of "Marcus's Story"

At the start of this scenario, Mrs. George was yet another parent struggling to find explanations for her child's behaviors—knowing that something was definitely different very early on, shortly following his birth. She, too, approached the medical professionals and was told to wait. And she, like other parents, returned to hear the same response: "Let's wait and see." Once she had the diagnosis of autism confirmed, she pursued the best educational programs she could locate for Marcus. She was willing to pay for those private services, but her family's budget took a huge hit, and the distance of the programs from her home placed a burden on her other children. As she noted, she was not home when her other children returned from school, because it took so long to pick up Marcus and bring him home. This was something of which she was keenly aware.

Each scenario analysis is presented in a slightly different format. As obvious as this may be, this scenario is not an example of a well-run school system. You may be reading this because you have children who are receiving special education services, or because you have experienced a school saying "No!" or because you are preparing for your first IEP meeting. *Please do not think* that all IEP meetings are conducted like this! *Please do not think* it is commonplace to encounter staff with little training in the field of special education! This scenario is unique and not typical of school systems or staff behaviors. Unfortunately, it can happen.

One thing we can all gain from this scenario is an appreciation for the transformation from Mrs. George's initial thinking—that Marcus should be served only in an inclusive setting—to a preference for a self-contained classroom, as a result of her refocusing on his needs over what she thought his placement should be. You should have noticed the approaches Mrs. George learned to use over Marcus's school years due to her astute observations of her attorney's approach during an IEP meeting, and how she used this knowledge to prepare to deal effectively with the school during the last IEP meeting mentioned in this scenario.

She was totally prepared to show to the IEP team why the current placement ("What do we know?" and "How will we get there?") is not meeting Marcus's needs, which are many ("What do we know?" and "Where do we want to go?" and even "How do we know that we are getting there?"). She is also armed with information about what the middle school program offers, and so is prepared to present why its program and curricular offerings would meet his needs ("Where do we want to go?" and "How are we going to get there?"). In other words, the change in placement would meet his identified needs and the goals of the IEP, which are clearly not being met in his current placement and program. Now, let's begin the analysis.

Where Are We?
What Do We Know?
How Do We Know That We Are Getting There?
In this section, all three questions will be referred to almost concurrently, because we will review both Mrs. George's attorney's approach to the IEP process and how

Mrs. George has prepared for the upcoming IEP meeting. It is difficult to separate out the three questions without losing the sequence and flow of the analysis.

We were informed early in this story that Mrs. George was "warned" by other parents of how poorly the school system would meet Marcus's needs; and, because of that warning, she sought private school programs at every opportunity. During those times, it was unclear whether a completed IEP existed, but we do know what services were provided. We do not begin to get a sense of the IEP content until Marcus's fifth grade. We also learn more of what his program looked like, what staff might be doing when unobserved, what was not provided to Marcus to meet his needs, and some of Marcus's behaviors. Additionally, we learn that restraint was used somewhat routinely, and that Marcus was not happy at school.

Let's first review the process Mrs. George's attorney used during an IEP meeting. At that time, the major issue was Mrs. George's need for assistance in moving Marcus from the general education classroom with an aide to a self-contained setting, which included other changes to the program so that it would actually meet Marcus's needs. If you will recall, the attorney used the current IEP (goals and included services) and the school's data to answer the question, "What do we know?" He also used the same information to evaluate the effectiveness of the program, answering the question, "How do we know that we are getting there?"

He did this by asking three key questions about Marcus's behaviors of concern or those reported as "incidents." Using the behavioral terms, the questions he asked were:

1. What was the antecedent of the behavior?

2. What was the behavior?

3. What were the consequences of his behavior?

In other words, he wanted the staff to describe what Marcus was doing and what was going on around him before the behavior of concern occurred. Then, he wanted them to describe exactly what the behavior looked like. They needed to explain it so others could easily "picture" the behavior. Finally, he asked them to explain exactly what happened following the behavior: What did they do? What happened as a result of the behavior?

If these questions appear familiar, they should. It is the same information you provide to describe your child's behaviors to the medical and educational professionals—just reversed, so they are questions instead of statements. These are also the kinds of secondary questions you can use when you are trying to answer, "Where are we?" and "What do we know?" Remember, these questions work well on all types of behaviors (i.e., academic, social, motoric, etc.).

So, Mrs. George's attorney used a behavioral approach to analyze each behavior by asking three questions to determine, "What do we know?" "Where are we going?" and "How do we know that we are getting there?" This is an excellent approach that can easily be used by parents when you want to have a clear "picture" and understanding of your child's behaviors.

With these questions, he was able to get answers to, "What do we know?" and, concurrently, that "How do we know that we are getting there?" For example, the attorney pointed out that the aide—who was assigned to provide Marcus with individual assistance—was not working with Marcus to prevent him from repeatedly walking out of the bathroom with his pants down. This is exactly how one uses information (data or measures of progress) to answer the questions, "Where are we?" or "What do we know?" and "Are we getting there?" The answers to these questions made it clear that the goals of the IEP ("Where do we want to go?") were not being achieved. As a parent, you have the responsibility to ask these questions, and educators are responsible for providing the answers. Without the answers to these questions, it will be extremely difficult for the IEP team to build an IEP based on your child's needs or to evaluate the IEP's effectiveness.

In this case, it quickly became clear that:

- Marcus's IEP goals were not being worked on

- services (instruction and staff) listed in the IEP were not being implemented or were being implemented incorrectly

- no progress was being made toward reaching the goals established for Marcus.

To summarize, essentially nothing Individualized was taking place to improve his Education in his present Program. To further complicate these problems, Marcus was placed in a general education setting—supposedly to provide him with interaction with his non-disabled peers. Unfortunately, because this placement was implemented so poorly and because the placement was inappropriate for Marcus in the first place, Marcus actually had *fewer* opportunities to interact with his non-disabled peers in positive ways, because he received no specially designed instruction or support from the aide assigned to facilitate positive interactions with his peers. Instead, he was virtually abandoned in the back of the room, with an inadequately trained paraprofessional to meet his social and instructional needs.

Now let's take a look at where Mrs. George is as she prepares for the IEP meeting with the elementary school staff, where she will discuss his lack of progress within the fifth grade program and her recommendation to move Marcus to the middle school, where she feels his IEP could be met. As we are made aware, Mrs. George has, over time, collected a significant amount of information about:

- what is taking place in Marcus's classroom

- how Marcus feels about school and his teacher, Mrs. Smith

- how the school is/is not implementing the IEP

- the results of the monthly meetings with the school staff

- the physical outcomes of Marcus's being restrained

- her informal observations of staff behaviors while Marcus is in the classroom.

She also has records of:

- when homework assignments were and were not made

- reports on daily work/behaviors (when they were and were not provided)

- how his teachers responded to his needs, including the social worker who claimed Marcus was a happy kid at school when it is clear that he was not.

Mrs. George is prepared to use many of the questions revealed in the Structured Collaborative IEP Process—by following the example set by her attorney—during the upcoming IEP meeting.

Pulling It All Together

Mrs. George has choices on how to approach and participate in the IEP meeting. She could come ready literally to yell and scream at the staff for their failure to meet Marcus's needs, and then tell them what they will do for Marcus and make plans to transfer him to the middle school in a week. She could wait until the meeting starts and throw at them all the information she has collected—which will show their failings to meet Marcus's needs—and ask what they are going to do to "fix" it. Or she could implement the Structured Collaborative IEP Process.

What she will do will depend on what she wants as an outcome. If she is hoping to work with the middle school in the future (and a representative from the middle school should be in attendance at the upcoming IEP meeting), there is much to gain from using the Structured Collaborative IEP Process. They will soon learn how she expects future meetings to be held and know how to prepare for future meetings, which is a very good thing. It is certainly not a threatening approach. Rather, they would realize that the IEP holds real meaning for Mrs. George, in that she expects the contents to be carried out.

So, while Mrs. George could vent her frustrations on the school staff by using either of the first two approaches, I highly recommend the last approach. The Structured Collaborative IEP Process revealed in this book is the best tool I've found in my years of experience, to produce positive results that support and provide for the needs of the child.

Although Mrs. George has a great deal of information and has many answers, she should still ask the staff, "What do we know?" or "Where are we?" As per her attorney's example, she will certainly make staff "accountable" for Marcus's day, his school activities, his IEP program, and the services listed in the IEP. We know that, when Marcus's behaviors are discussed, she will ask the same three questions her lawyer did, having the staff explain the antecedent(s) to the behavior, the behavior itself, and the response immediately following each behavior. This way she can clearly understand and picture each behavioral event. And so will the staff.

Once the team agrees that, in overly generalized terms, the IEP was not being met, she can discuss what goals ("Where do we want to go?") should be written into the IEP. (Many will have been established during the discussion of what needs have/have not been met or addressed.) They will be measurably written with specific reporting times to ensure that Mrs. George knows the degree of progress Marcus is making, which will answer the question, "How do we know that we are getting there?" We will also want to discuss what services would be necessary to answer the question, "How will we get there?" Sometimes these two questions are answered concurrently. For example, in very broad terms, if Marcus needs to increase his ability to communicate, so that those unfamiliar with him can understand his needs ("Where do we want to go?"), then we will provide him with speech and language therapy for 20 minutes, five days per week.

Up to this point, the team has not mentioned where the services would be provided. Most likely, the team should agree that, based on the answers and the content of the IEP written so far, the general education setting would not be appropriate. This revelation is important, because, as we've established, Marcus was previously placed in the general education classroom, because it was considered the LRE and would meet his needs, but Mrs. George was able to show why that environment was not the appropriate place for Marcus to receive the services he needed. As this is still the case, services would most likely be provided in a self-contained setting. The team has *not* yet discussed at which school Marcus's agreed needs and services would be met.

The next question would be to discuss school options. Can the elementary school meet the newly developed IEP? Can the middle school meet the newly developed IEP? This would require a review of Marcus's IEP needs and the programming differences between the two schools. It is still a Structured Collaborative IEP Process that is being used, requiring a team discussion. We know that Mrs. George will be able to participate actively in this discussion, because she visited the middle school. She will also be able to participate in defining the difference between the elementary and middle school programs—in particular how Marcus's needs could be met in the middle school program and why they cannot be met at the elementary school.

The team already has the justification for transferring him to the middle school now, instead of waiting for next year. That justification is his failing to be successful where he is presently assigned, the inappropriateness of the elementary program, and the appropriateness of the middle school.

Key Points

- Mrs. George experienced many of the same difficulties other parents have when trying to determine the cause of their child's difficulties. Like many other parents, she was told to "wait and see." Once Marcus was diagnosed with autism, Mrs. George sought private schooling, because the public school system was reputedly unable to meet his needs. She suffered the fiscal impact of private school costs and mentioned her concern with the impact travel time had on Marcus's siblings' needs. She was also concerned because—once Marcus started receiving services in the public school—he was exhausted by the need to get up very early to endure a long bus ride. Lastly, she noted the number of medications Marcus is taking to control his various behaviors, and her suspicion that the need for them might be due, in large part, to his ineffective instruction.

- Mrs. George learned a great deal by observing her attorney as he answered the questions, "What do we know?" and "How do we know that we are getting there?" He may not have asked these specific questions, but he learned the answers to these questions by asking them in a slightly different way. Most likely, Mrs. George will have the school staff describe each of Marcus's behaviors in terms of the antecedent, the exact behavior, and the consequences following Marcus's behaviors.

- She will also ask staff to show measures of instruction and progress on each of the IEP's goals and objectives, and will ask each service provider to show documentation of the provision of services, along with measures of progress.

- Mrs. George will, in essence, use the first three questions of the Structured Collaborative IEP Process and, by doing so, will provide the team with the data she has collected over the school year that will either support their statements of progress or contradict their conclusions. In any case, she will be using information they have or have not provided.

- Mrs. George's contention will be that the present program has failed to meet Marcus's needs and that a new IEP must be written, with new and measurably written goals and objectives or benchmarks. There will be an established structure of reporting to Mrs. George concerning Marcus's progress, using data collected to support claims regarding his progress.

- When the IEP meeting finally reaches the discussion of whether Marcus should be transferred to the middle school, Mrs. George will have a great deal of information to share from her observations of the program. Although her visit was somewhat limited, she saw that Marcus's needs could be met at the middle school program. So, she will not be limited to the information the staff from either the elementary school or the middle school chooses to provide. This will definitely make her an active participant in this area of discussion and not simply an observer.

- There is little doubt that Marcus will not remain in his present classroom once the IEP team reviews his present performance levels and matches those to new, measurably written goals, which will include a listing of services—along with a behavioral plan that will include a modified use of restraints, if they are needed, once he is granted an appropriate program. The list of issues is extensive and need not be repeated.

- However, one final point is worth noting: after reviewing Mrs. George's scenario several times, it is clear that there are multiple and gross systemic problems at the elementary school level.

- Lastly, we can, with a fair degree of confidence, agree that Mrs. George will no longer tolerate an inappropriate program for Marcus.

Summary

By proceeding through the questions used in the Structured Collaborative IEP Process, it would be difficult for the elementary school to refute its own data. By agreeing on Marcus's needs, his present levels of performance, and the effects the implementation of the IEP has had on Marcus's educational progress ("What do we know?"), his present needs can easily be converted to his IEP goals and objectives or benchmarks, which will be stated in measurable terms, specifying when and how progress will be shared with staff and Mrs. George ("Where are we going?" and "How do we know that we are getting there?"). The next question is, "How will we get there?" This is where programming and services will be defined.

After these decisions are made, LRE or appropriate placement where his services are to be delivered should be addressed, and then, finally, whether the appropriate school is at the elementary or middle school. Please understand that the issue of LRE for this case is twofold. First, the IEP team must determine the amount of interaction Marcus will have with his non-disabled peers (general education versus self-contained classroom, or a variation that involves "pull-out" sessions). The next decision is whether the elementary program or middle school program will meet his needs, answering the question, "How will we get there?"

(Of course, issues of assistive technology, lunch, accommodations, or modifications were not presented, but they would be presented during the creation of the IEP and would be based on Marcus's needs.)

We can fairly conclude that—based on the information we have and the assumed use of the Structured Collaborative IEP Process—the IEP team will reach agreement on all questions. The outstanding unknown that remains is whether the school will say "No" to moving Marcus to the middle school now, forcing him to wait until the next school year to have his needs met. It is difficult to believe that the school will be able to justify their preference for waiting, considering that would mean that Marcus would continue to be served inappropriately.

Latest Update: July 2012

Mrs. George contacted me to let me know that Marcus's aggressive behaviors have increased markedly to the point that she had to remove him from the elementary school before the IEP team could meet to discuss transferring him to the middle school. She felt this move was in the best interests of both Marcus and his teachers. Oddly, he was not acting out against his peers, only adults. There is a program one hour from where Mrs. George and her children live that is specifically designed to work with children with autism who have severe aggressive behaviors. This program is particularly suited to meet Marcus's needs due to his use of multiple medications and because the program specializes in autism and severe behavioral conditions like Marcus's. He will attend this program for a minimum of 12 weeks, where both his medications and his behaviors will be evaluated, analyzed, and modified as necessary.

In addition, there is a family component that will involve Mrs. George and her other two children, so that programming at the center and home will be the same. Training family members is an extremely important component in the center's program, and, to assist with this process at the onset of his new placement, Marcus will be assigned a case worker/transition specialist. Finally, when Marcus is preparing for his return to the school system, the transition specialist will also work with staff to improve Marcus's chances of being able to transition successfully from the center to the public school and his peers. The specialist will work with staff, explaining the procedures, techniques, interventions, and reinforcers that were used at the center and home—and how and why they worked. In addition, the specialist will work with school staff so that they can continue using the same successful interventions in the school setting.

It's also worth mentioning that children whose parents cannot afford the center's services are usually put on a waiting list—a *long* waiting list! Mrs. George was persistent, calling almost every day to explain how much more severe Marcus's behaviors were becoming. They escalated almost daily. He had broken all televisions and other electronic equipment in the home, pulled down the refrigerator in an attempt to get to the food that was made inaccessible to him by use of a locking device (recall that eating was a severe problem for Marcus), and he had physically harmed his mother on several occasions. Because of Mrs. George's effective persistence, Marcus moved from the near bottom of the waiting list to entering the program as soon as the first opening became available. This will happen before the beginning of the next school. As the title of this chapter says, Mrs. George knows what she is doing now and she knows how to do it!

CHAPTER 6

Asperger's Syndrome

Negotiating Results in Gains and Losses

···

This story began in the mid-1990s, and although much has changed in the field of special education, most of what we know now existed then. Inclusion programming was well under way. Autism was not novel. The programming needs of children with autism were understood, especially in large school districts. Asperger's syndrome, however, had not gained the same traction and understanding it has today. Still, Wayne's family was dealing with a school district that, irrespective of the name of Wayne's disability, did not appreciate his needs and failed to provide services to meet his needs. The family were, however, adept at seeking outside assistance to explain Wayne's needs—the basic beginning place for the development of a meaningful Individualized Education Program (IEP). Unfortunately, the school staff's resistance to meeting all his needs remained a constant. What this story represents is a parent who was not willing to accept the school's status quo. Furthermore, it will show how Wayne's mother applied what she knew of the Structured Collaborative IEP Process and the results of her skills; and then, I will expand on what she did know and explain what she didn't know, and show how this information could change the results for you.

Focus on the Child's Needs

"I think that guy should just play tennis."

When our third son, Wayne, was two and a half years old, I wrote a letter to his pediatrician expressing some concerns about his development. I highlighted specific behaviors that did not fit the developmental patterns followed by our older sons—then 11 and 13 years old. While his brothers were able, with modest encouragement, to "settle into" adaptive behaviors that balanced their personalities and needs with the requirements of common social situations, Wayne was not.

My letter described a child who, when not focused on a book, a map, or a puzzle, would run in circles, reciting routes to familiar places, dinosaur names, or dialogue from certain favorite videos or stories. He could sit for more than an hour with books on dinosaurs—identifying them, noting their lengths, eating habits, and internal organs—yet, he could not throw a ball, jump, or figure out how to turn a book so that it would fit through the slats of his crib. I also related how our two-year-old son, while trying to exit a lightweight indoor play house, had failed to clear the doorway. He dragged the structure across our playroom floor while pleading, "Get out of here! Get out of here!"

This same letter expressed our perplexity regarding Wayne's extreme contrariness. Although we understood that many of his contrary and uncooperative behaviors were within the normal range for a two-and-a-half-year-old, their frequency seemed to be abnormal. His insistence on routine, sameness, and self-direction was extreme. Wayne didn't really have all-out tantrums—or at least not many. He would cry and plead and resist and refuse, but he didn't throw himself on the floor kicking and screaming.

Whenever Wayne was encouraged to participate in social activities, such as a small play group or an informal "tot" music class, he was noticeably contrary, answering, "I don't know" when asked his name, sitting when asked to run, and running when asked to sit. Most of these responses were accompanied by a smile, and any form of encouragement resulted in his increased resistance. During one music class, while the other kids sat in a circle, Wayne jumped on a mini-trampoline while looking at the group's reflection in a mirror and remarking, "There's one little boy missing from that group!"

Wayne insisted on familiar routines and expressed extreme distress when his expectations were violated. He would drink only from blue cups, accepted no deviation in the routes to familiar destinations, and wanted the same sequence of events to precede and follow daily or weekly events. He became very agitated when he saw us eating or drinking something that he had just refused—even though it was not for him. He tried to force his hand down our throats to retrieve it, all the while sobbing. He did this even after we showed him that his food or drink was still sitting untouched.

Our pediatrician telephoned to say that he believed Wayne had sensory integration disorder, but that there was no point in bringing him in to the office because he probably would not cooperate. (At his two-year checkup, Wayne was very leery of the doctor and did not cooperate with any part of the developmental assessment.

Given that experience and my letter to him, the pediatrician probably did not think it necessary to see Wayne again, assuming that he would be uncooperative.) The doctor recommended lots of interactive play-building on Wayne's interests. He encouraged us to read Jean Ayres' book on sensory integration[1] and implement her suggestions in our play.

So, we took Wayne to community playgrounds more frequently, procured an indoor swing, a trampoline, and an exercise ball, and tried with varying degrees of success to incorporate Ayres' suggestions into Wayne's daily activities. We encouraged climbing, balancing, swinging, and playing with sand, water, finger paints, and clay. However, we found it very challenging to "play" with a child who was so uninterested in playing. Luckily, he did love to be read to, to sing and dance in my arms, and to take very long walks with us. These activities provided many opportunities for positive interaction.

A couple of months later, we initiated an evaluation through the school district's Child Find (a program offering assessment of the school district's population in an attempt to identify children with disabilities and provide special education services), which resulted in Wayne being identified as "developmentally delayed" in January, 1995, when he was three years, one month old. In February 1995, he began attending one of the school district's non-categorical (not restricted to any specific disability) half-day preschool programs located at Milford Elementary School, in which he continued through June 1997.

[When asked how she learned of the Child Find program, Wayne's mother could not recall, but thought it was probably through an acquaintance. She was almost positive that this lead had not come from the pediatrician, she clearly remembers his adomination against placing Wayne into a special educational program, based on the evidence suggesting that kids did better in inclusive environments.]

During Wayne's preschool years we made two significant requests for services. In August 1995, we submitted a request for school-based occupational therapy (OT) services for Wayne, along with a privately obtained OT evaluation. At a special IEP meeting, the school administration readily agreed to approve two one-hour sessions of OT per week. At this time, we also engaged the services of a private occupational therapist for sensory integration treatment. (As I recall, the school district could not explicitly include sensory integration goals because many of the interventions, such as brushing Wayne's skin with a surgical brush and swinging him to music, were not supported by research.)

Then, in March 1996, pragmatic language and articulation goals were added to his IEP, following a language evaluation initiated by his preschool teacher. In both cases, when contrasted with subsequent IEP experiences, the key to these IEP successes was that a professional evaluation clearly and objectively showed a

---

1 Ayres, J. (2005) *Sensory Integration and the Child*, 25th edition. Torrance, CA: Western Services.

need that could be satisfied by trained service providers within the school district. (I should note that the school district then had "limited resources" and would leave it to parents to advocate for "extras." I realize that OT for Wayne should not have been seen as an "extra," but that is the way it was/is.)

To increase Wayne's exposure to more appropriate peer models, we enrolled him in a private preschool two half-days a week in the fall of 1996. He remained in the public school in the non-categorical program on the other three days. However, after the first few months, it was clear that he was not socializing any more in this new classroom than in his special needs classroom.

He was also developing some new behavioral issues in the new setting. Specifically, he was squeezing other children's arms, torsos, or (egad!) necks, when overexcited. This would happen during group activities that required him to stand close to other children while they sang songs or recited poems, with accompanying motions. We decided to withdraw Wayne from this new school rather than invest too much energy advocating for Wayne's needs with a second school.

During the fall of 1996, the school initiated Wayne's transition evaluation. (He was transitioning—really aging out—of the preschool special education environment, and this multi-part evaluation would be to determine the next step.) We decided to obtain an evaluation from a developmental pediatrician to supplement the school district's testing. This doctor diagnosed Wayne with Asperger's syndrome in November 1996, after meeting with us and observing Wayne in her office and in his non-categorical classroom. She noted in her observation summary that "... there was no sense of his participation in the group, as Wayne responded to his own interests and agenda much of the time."

When we began reading the literature on Asperger's and autism, we realized that Wayne, despite his intelligence, would not just outgrow his difficulties (shifting attention, behavioral problems, and social deficits). We became painfully aware that our current interventions were seriously inadequate for meeting Wayne's needs. He was too often allowed to avoid interaction and involvement.

In fairness to the teachers, who worked very hard, the program (with one teacher, one aide, and eight to ten children with a wide range of physical, emotional, language, and cognitive abilities) did not allow for the type of intervention that children with autism require. I would say that staff attempted to encourage socializing, but with minimum success. I just don't think that they were able to implement best practices, given their environment and training.

In December 1996, we hired Anna, a behavioral consultant who had been trained as an Applied Behavior Analysis (ABA) therapist at the University of California, Los Angeles (UCLA), to help us set up a home program to teach Wayne challenging but critical behaviors. Our letter to her, describing Wayne's development up to that point, included the following comments:

Wayne is extremely sensitive to textures, tastes, and smells. His sensitivity to odors seems to cause the most acute responses… He has proven to have an incredibly keen [sense of] smell. Although he is…more receptive to spontaneous and unexpected touch…he still prefers to control the contact, and seeks out firm pressure… [He] loves to act out stories…using videos and books for his scripts. He rarely asks others to join in, although he occasionally assigns a part to one of us, along with our lines. We will observe as he reads a few lines from Roald Dahl's *The BFG*,[2] lays down the book, and bellows out an exclamation while curling his fingers into threatening claws. Wayne's favorite activity, without a doubt, is reading. Although he shows a preference for non-fiction, he often chooses fiction, too. He can easily spend an uninterrupted hour or two with a few good books. Although he will read material that is totally outside his mental grasp…he generally does understand a very high percentage of what he reads… His grasp of straightforward events is much better than his inferential ability, but he is not without the latter.

I have recently begun to use Wayne's love of reading—fiction and nonfiction—to encourage conversational turn-taking and flexibility. While reading—especially a new book, with which he has not developed a rigid routine—I am able to relate story events to our experiences. We have some very pleasant exchanges! I've also been trying to expand the reading experience into short periods (two minutes) of pretend play several times a day. He resists a little, but has acquiesced to talking with the little puppets or dolls that I use. It is not as "free" or elaborate as normal five-year-old play, but it is a big improvement over the endless perseveration [the continuance of verbal or motoric repeated behaviour] that otherwise fills his mind and our ears.

Wayne recently gave me a clue about why reading is so important to him when he remarked that his teachers might help a lower-functioning classmate (not Wayne's description—he named the boy) behave better if they would read books to this boy to help him better understand the behaviors they wanted him to learn. Wayne's comment reflected his own learning needs.

I don't know how Wayne learned to read so early. We read to all our boys from day one—and as they grew, talked about the alphabet and the sounds made by letters—but our other two boys did not read until the age of five. The first time I realized that he could read was when we were walking in the neighborhood and three-year-old Wayne spotted a name etched into the sidewalk, which he actually deciphered as "Dan!" It soon became apparent that he was "hyperlexic," [exceptional ability to read words without prior training] although I found it dismaying that some assumed that he had less comprehension than he actually did.

---

2 Dahl, R. (1982) *The BFG*. London: Penguin.

We wanted our son—then as now, to appreciate life to the fullest extent possible for him. Anna helped us to plan an individual program of discrete-trial learning that broke down behaviors necessary for reciprocal conversation and play, and that gave Wayne positive reinforcement when he demonstrated those behaviors. She visited us weekly to observe or watch videos of our sessions with Wayne, and I often called her with questions in between visits.

Because Wayne had so many skills, we quickly supplemented his table-learning with activity-based and incidental learning. Our program consisted of sessions that lasted several hours most days of the week, although Wayne did continue in the non-categorical preschool for three half-days per week. I would help in the preschool classroom one day a week, during which time I could also observe Wayne. I hoped to facilitate peer interaction during this time, but I did not find this easy to do in the classroom, as I had to be respectful of the teacher's plans and did not have the training needed to ensure success in this environment.

However, it was around this time that the preschool began a program of reverse-inclusion. This resulted in the inclusion of two typically developing little girls who turned out to be quite receptive to facilitated play at our house. They enjoyed it and were very eager to engage Wayne, responding to my suggestions and examples. Wayne genuinely enjoyed their company, liked the activities, and responded well to my facilitation and the girls' persistent efforts to engage him.

And so we began to replace some of his one-on-one learning with this facilitated play, although we continued the individual sessions until September 1997, when Wayne entered kindergarten. During this time, Wayne showed dramatic improvement in sustained attention, flexibility, and turn-taking (although he was still significantly delayed). His repertoire of play skills increased, as did his interests and his explicit imaginary play (as opposed to daydreaming). We saw a marked decrease in his stereotypical behaviors—running in circles, repeating the same phrases, and constant perseveration on his few preferred topics. I did note, however, that although Wayne was very responsive in facilitated, structured play dates and would sometimes initiate appropriate spontaneous play, he was not generalizing this to the classroom setting.

[When asked if she thought any one intervention was more successful than another, Wayne's mother replied, "I think that our practicing social skills with him, combined with planning structured social activities with selected peers in a safe environment, maximized his chances of experiencing natural reinforcement of targeted (and crucial) behaviors."]

In April, we asked staff if Wayne could begin periodically visiting Milford's mainstream kindergarten classroom (in which, we all anticipated, he would be enrolled the following year), in order to reduce his anxieties about the coming year and perhaps identify issues and goals to include in the IEP and in our home learning program. We initially met with resistance, both from the staff and from Wayne's autism resource teacher, Margaret (who came on board shortly after his diagnosis). They felt we were "pushing" him, but, in the end, they agreed to 20- to 30-minute kindergarten visits, several times a week.

Anna and I each accompanied Wayne on one visit, and Margaret or his preschool teacher, Michele, accompanied him on several other visits. Based on our observations of Wayne in his preschool program and our team's collective observations of the kindergarten classroom, Anna and I concluded that Wayne needed supported opportunities to generalize his emerging social behaviors. It was obvious to us that the current program could not provide the necessary support.

I observed the "available" self-contained autism classroom, and while it did provide adequate support and structure, it did not provide anywhere near the intellectual stimulation that Wayne needed. If we had thought that Wayne could learn vital social skills without intellectual stimulation (for a couple of years, anyway), then we would have opted for such a program. Of course, he could always supply his own stimulation, but that was part of the problem. For this reason, we believed that a necessary ingredient of any successful intervention for Wayne was an intellectually stimulating environment.

There was general agreement among IEP team members that Wayne should probably be mainstreamed in kindergarten. There was also a prevailing attitude among many team members that, if he were to be in a mainstream classroom, he could not have extraordinary needs. It was generally not stated exactly this way, but that was the clear message.

However, there was also clear evidence that Wayne had both extraordinary abilities as well as extraordinary challenges. Wayne's preschool teacher noted, in her end-of year comments, that:

> Group participation and peer interaction are more successful [for Wayne] when facilitated by a familiar adult. In play situations Wayne has been observed to be very rigid. He does not take directions from peers, respond to their requests, or make requests of them… In the motor room, Wayne quickly paces the room, often talking to himself and moving/waving his right hand at his side. Verbal and physical prompts are needed to elicit participation in more purposeful activities. Outside, he walks the perimeter of the playground, avoiding group activities. During unstructured play time or transitions, Wayne frequently paces in the middle of the room until prompted by teachers to choose a center or activity. When stressed or anxious, Wayne tends to exhibit more movement and use an unnecessarily loud voice.
>
> …He has demonstrated excellent progress in the areas of sensory processing and fine-motor skill development. He utilizes a variety of playground and gross-motor equipment effectively with adult supervision

and encouragement. With adult prompting he is able to play competently on equipment such as scooter boards, slides, A-frames, balance beams, and swing. When learning new tasks he may need manual prompts in addition to verbal and visual cues. He often takes longer than his peers might to master a new motor skill… He has adequate grasp and release skills when working with a variety of objects. He holds a drawing utensil in a stable tripod grip and utilizes this consistently when working on vertical and flat surfaces…

[I need to add here that Wayne's school occupational therapist said that he had surpassed her most optimistic expectations and that she was quite impressed with his progress. She frequently supported Wayne in classroom activities, but also spent significant one-on-one time with him.]

Academically, Wayne is demonstrating skills significantly above grade level. During recent testing, reading skills appeared to be at the fourth grade level. Science, math, and geography skills were all at or above the fourth grade level.

Wayne's parents report that play skills are significantly improved at home. He is playing independently [at times] with peers and is demonstrating more focused play skills on the playground in the preschool.

[I'm not sure why Michele did not provide examples of this last assessment, as it might seem to conflict with her earlier statement that he often walked the perimeter of the playground.]

Based on team observations and evaluations my husband and I, in consultation with Anna, decided to request the inclusion of a shadow—a trained aide—in Wayne's IEP for his kindergarten year. Prior to the final transitional IEP meeting in June, 1997, we provided the IEP team with two letters (one from me and one from Anna) to support our assertion that this accommodation was a necessary element in an appropriate education for Wayne, at least for a portion of his kindergarten year. We offered to pay for this extra support. My letter listed elements of an effective educational environment for Wayne, including:

- small class size

- appropriate peer models

- intellectual stimulation

- relatively high degree of structure, with rules and routines communicated as unambiguously as possible

- sufficiently flexible and goal-oriented teacher to learn and implement necessary modifications and communicate with parents and support staff

- ongoing, objective, behavioral and environmental assessments

- strategies for behavioral management and social facilitation integrated into the program

- frequent and consistent feedback for Wayne

- shadow to provide a bridge between emerging/inconsistent behaviors and generalized behaviors.

One element on which we were willing to compromise was small class size. To our knowledge the school district's continuum of services did not include a small classroom of eight to ten children that contained appropriate peer models and a stimulating intellectual environment. However, the large class size of our community kindergarten further accentuated Wayne's need for a highly structured environment and a shadow.

We were denied the opportunity to observe mainstream kindergarten classes, other than the one at Milford Elementary School, in order to locate a class that offered more structure for Wayne than we saw in the Milford kindergarten class. The Milford kindergarten's teacher was professional, dedicated, and genuinely caring, but her classroom did not meet Wayne's needs for structure. We were assured this situation could be addressed through the implementation of classroom strategies designed to meet Wayne's needs, but we felt that this was an unrealistic and risky assumption.

We contended that if the classroom modifications obviated the need for shadowing, as had been suggested, then we would be pleased and eager to withdraw the aide upon seeing evidence of this. We did not think the "wait-and-see" philosophy was smart, and preferred to be proactive.

In support of our view that Wayne's IEP should be proactive, we emphasized the fact that both his preschool teacher, Karen, and his autism resource teacher, Margaret, insisted that Wayne's needs would be best met by retaining him in the preschool setting for all but 30 minutes a day (which were being spent in kindergarten) until year's end. They were adamantly opposed to the idea of gradually increasing Wayne's kindergarten time to prepare him for the coming year. If this need for the restrictive setting of the non-categorical preschool outweighed his need to be eased into a new socially and behaviorally challenging environment, then how could staff argue that he'd do just fine next year with very little direct support in those areas which are the most challenging for him?

The most objective, if not strongest, argument for providing Wayne with a shadow for his kindergarten year was his preschool testing results, which revealed that he had made virtually no progress in the areas of social skills in the preschool program. He tested at 27 months in this area in May 1995, and at only 31 months in January 1997. These data seemed to indicate that Wayne's preschool program was ineffective in fostering his personal/social development and that he was obviously not able to meet these developmental needs through his own resources or the other resources that were made available to him. Unless we assumed that these results reflected an inability, as opposed to an impaired ability, to learn appropriate social behaviors, we had to conclude that Wayne needed a different type of intervention in order to achieve progress in this area.

Anna's letter explained how a classroom shadow would help to meet Wayne's IEP goals. The functions she listed included:

- helping him to follow the teacher's directions, if for some reason (e.g., class is very noisy) he is unable to do so on his own

- prompting him to do independent work by utilizing visual cues provided by the shadow

- prompting him to respond to peers

- providing reinforcement and encouragement as necessary to help him maintain his gains (our intention was to withdraw the shadow as Wayne showed competence, but we realized he might need support even after he began showing progress)

- fostering social interaction as often as possible—the most important responsibility of the aide. Anna stressed that the trained aide would be temporary, and gradually phased out as Wayne progressed. We planned to hire an aide through the Education or Psychology Department of our local university or community college. We would have provided both initial and ongoing training through Anna. Unfortunately neither we nor the school had any experience in this area.

My husband and I, along with Anna, Milford's principal, present and future classroom teachers, autism resource teacher, and therapists attended Wayne's transitional IEP meetings to determine support services for his transition to kindergarten. In those two meetings I stressed that Wayne showed clear ability and interest in peer interaction, but that his positive experiences with facilitated and (rarer) spontaneous peer play were not yet sufficient to motivate him to generalize these behaviors.

We strongly asserted that these inconsistent social behaviors should guide the development of his IEP goals, as these behaviors reflected his potential. We had no reason to believe that Wayne was ready for a sudden withdrawal of facilitated interaction at such a critical time. He needed a shadow to help him to capitalize on opportunities presented during the school day. He did not passively acquire social learning, as did his neurotypical peers.

Finally, I assured the team that our desire to provide a shadow for Wayne (at our expense) did not reflect a distrust of school staff, but rather, it reflected the sometimes-conflicting realities of Wayne's needs and the limited resources available for one child's special education needs.

[When I asked why the family was willing to pay for the services of the aide, Wayne's mother said, "I thought that if we could bear the cost risk and demonstrate a benefit, we would be in a better position to ask for county funding, later. I don't think we would have fared any better if we had requested funding for this intervention in the beginning."]

The IEP team members responded to our request to accommodate a shadow for Wayne with the following comments: "We don't do that. If he needs that much individual attention, he should probably be in a self-contained classroom. If we have a non-school district person on the team, it could impede the smooth functioning of the team." These comments were all made before Wayne's need for a shadow was even considered.

When I pointed this out, the responses were, "He might become too dependent on the aide," and "We wouldn't want him to think he couldn't do it by himself." At some point, the remark, "Well, this is something they don't outgrow," was made. This latter remark competed with the following statement for the most unforgettable comment of the entire meeting: "We are going to be the boss; we are going to have the final word."

Wayne did not receive the requested social facilitation for his kindergarten year. We were denied the aide for shadowing services. When I observed Wayne at school—where I often volunteered in various capacities, including helping out in his classroom—he did not interact with the other children and kept to himself in the playground.

During the year, when I asked for a more consistent, systematic approach to fostering Wayne's social participation, his resource teacher replied, "This meeting is simply to discuss goals. It is our job to develop strategies. You can give suggestions, but we will decide what is best."

Various staff members said to us, "If Wayne doesn't enjoy playing with kids, why do you want to force him to be something he is not?" and "I don't know how much of the way Wayne is can be helped and how much is part of his condition."

I think we were seen by many of the team members as parents who could not accept their child's limitations. We saw their view as similar to believing that a child with dyslexia should not be given more intensive interventions, because he was just not meant to read. It seems to me this conflicting estimation of our son's potential is what lay at the foundation of our disagreement with the school.

Afterword

Throughout the year, we requested some quantifiable data about Wayne's progress in social learning and language pragmatics. After promising us the data, several times, his autism resource teacher, Margaret, eventually lost it in a computer crash the night before his final IEP meeting of the year. Toward the end of Wayne's kindergarten year, we began looking at other possible placements for him, public and private. During this time, the Milford kindergarten principal approached me on one occasion and asked me how I thought Wayne was doing. I noted several areas in which I thought Wayne was doing well, but expressed my concern about his lack of socialization and the need for more facilitation in this area. She replied that it was probably good that we were looking at other programs, because Milford Elementary did not have the resources available to provide such facilitation.

In late spring, when we requested that Wayne be placed in Landmoor Elementary School, which was piloting the Coordinated Services Model, this same principal denied our request. [I cannot help but note that again we have a single person, in lieu of a team, making IEP decisions.] I learned of this model when I heard the Landmoor principal speak at a monthly school district meeting which I regularly attended as the Milford's principal's representative. Here is the website school description and why we felt that Wayne's needs would have been better met:

> The Landmoor Elementary is a school of 600 students, where 150 of the students receive special education services (learning disabilities, mental retardation, visually impaired, emotional disabilities, autism). The philosophy of the school is that all children can achieve when given appropriate adaptations and accommodations to meet their unique learning style and needs. Using a collaborative approach, all the school staff and parents are involved in planning for the success of the students. All students with IEPs are included in general education classrooms. Students complete the regular education curriculum with accommodations, as necessary. The school uses a school-based staff development model to build the capacity of individual staff members and the school as a whole. Administrative vision and support provide guidance to the staff as they actively plan and implement educational practices that are responsive to the needs of all students.

After I observed Landmoor's first-grade classroom and talked with the vice-principal, I contacted both principals to request a pupil placement for Wayne. The Landmoor principal responded that she would accept Wayne if the Milford principal agreed to it. The Milford principal stated the reason for denying my request was that she believed Milford *could* meet Wayne's needs.

We hired an advocate in the summer of 1998, who told us that if we really wanted Wayne at Landmoor, we could make it happen. She advised us to think carefully about it, however, because a neighborhood school might offer Wayne more opportunities for peer relationships outside of school. We decided not to pursue our transfer request.

We did foster several peer relationships for Wayne over the next three years, although the after-school play dates were always structured and facilitated by myself or his private speech therapist. After getting off to a shaky start, involving a very negative IEP meeting at the beginning of Wayne's first-grade year, we hired a behavioral consultant to develop a few classroom behavioral strategies.

Although the principal told me, privately, that they couldn't include specifics in the IEP because the school would then be obligated to provide them, various resource teachers did facilitate social interaction between Wayne and two or three other students in twice-weekly pull-out sessions, increasing to thrice-weekly during the last quarter. My concern, which came across to some school personnel as lack of appreciation (even though I frequently expressed appreciation for their efforts), was that these interventions were not part of a planned, coordinated approach tied to specific, measurable goals. The concern of certain school personnel was that we expected too much from Wayne and from them.

We discussed Wayne's diagnosis with him at the beginning of his first-grade year. More importantly, we talked about what it meant in terms of his strengths and challenges. He has always been pretty perceptive about his own abilities. Once, before learning of his diagnosis, he remarked, "I'm good at learning about things, but not at learning to do things," which was quite accurate.

I was surprised one day when he remarked, "Mom, I think I should tell Mrs. Karter [his teacher] that I have Asperger's syndrome because she expects us to do a lot of group work and this is very hard for me." I reinforced Wayne's instinct to advocate for himself, acknowledging that sometimes people will expect too much, too soon, from him, without giving him the help and practice that he needs. I encouraged him to ask for this help. But, I also suggested that he practice his social skills frequently so that they would become easier for him.

I illustrated the power of determination and practice by telling him the story of Jim Abbot, the one-handed major league pitcher. He listened attentively and then remarked, "I think that guy should just play tennis." I wished that Wayne either didn't have to work so hard to learn basic social skills or that there would be fewer consequences if he did not.

When Wayne wondered why anyone would knock themselves out learning something that doesn't come naturally, he also unknowingly defined the crux of our disagreement with the school, and, increasingly, with him. The decision of whether or not to learn basic social behaviors is not the same as the decision of whether to play baseball or tennis, of course. There is no healthy alternative for learning social behavior and, without intensive community intervention, there is little real opportunity for a person with autism to achieve the basic social competence that offers many options for building a rewarding life.

As Wayne's fears and anxieties have intensified, he has embraced his isolation as "just another lifestyle." Our hope, when he was young, was to help him find motivation through structured interaction with built-in rewards (not simple). I think it was tempting for some to equate Wayne's understandable deficit in motivation with a lack of ability, or perhaps they assumed that his motivation would "kick in" as Wayne matured. I have to admit, there was a part of us that also hoped the latter was true.

Analysis of "Focus on the Child's Needs"

Relatively speaking, this scenario took place quite some time ago. However, the concept of providing services to children with disabilities was far from novel, even in the early 1990s. Terms such as inclusion, where students with disabilities were receiving their services and programming in the general education classroom setting, were quite commonplace in vernacular usage and programming. Furthermore, inclusion was replacing integration—where students had simply been moved from segregated settings to typical school settings, and then were often placed in self-contained classrooms with no interaction with their school peers.

Autism was certainly not a new disability, nor was there a complete lack of programs and services across the country. Yet, the idea of meeting a child's needs—a child who just happens to have autism—was still a foreign concept at this school, so Wayne's needs would not be met without the parents' determination and persistence. Even then, the logical and obvious connection of Wayne's needs with the provision of applicable services did not guarantee that the school would provide those appropriate services and programming in the least restrictive setting.

Strangely, this was a district that, in spite of the mentioned "concern for money," is very large and served in a community of significant state affluence and legislative knowledge.

So, just how can a well-to-do school district surrounded with educational resources not provide the necessary services in the face of data clearly identifying a child's educational needs? The answer is twofold: by ignoring the answers to the six questions of the Structured Collaborative IEP Process, and by dismissing the value of collaboration (i.e., "We are going to be the boss; we are going to have the final word.").

Where Are We?

What Do We Know?

Wayne's mother provided the school—and us—with a great deal of information about him, including his social behaviors, skills, and academic levels. She also implemented various home training interventions and was in a position to explain the intervention and outcomes. She is an excellent observer of her son's behavior and is quite adept at explaining Wayne and his characteristics in explicit behavioral terms. Moreover, she is capable of explaining when the behaviors will be observable and which specific conditions will prompt his particular actions. As we have learned in other parts of the book, being able to describe your child in such detail (e.g., condition, behavior, consequence, and frequency) enables others (medical and educational professionals) to visualize the behaviors that you routinely observe.

Wayne's mother was willing to allow the school system to conduct educational assessments, but she also employed independent evaluators to assess Wayne's needs, to supplement the testing conducted by school staff, which she then readily shared with the school staff. She sought assistance from a developmental pediatrician, a private speech and language pathologist, and an occupational therapist. The parents also sought the assistance of a special education advocate to advise them about the steps that could or might be taken.

There is something that this particular developmental pediatrician did that needs highlighting. She conducted an interview with Wayne's parents and also took the time to observe him in her office. Additionally, and frankly this is a rarity, she observed Wayne in his educational setting. The value of this is twofold: first, by observing Wayne's behaviors across multiple settings, the pediatrician gained a much more expansive understanding of how Wayne reacted to a variety of settings and environments. This informed her recommendations much more than simply interviewing only the parents, or Wayne, or the educational providers. Second, it added considerable credibility to her report, because school staff knew that the professional writing the report and making the recommendations had actually seen Wayne in the school setting where his education was being provided.

This is worth mentioning, because often schools see evaluations with determinations of a disability, without having, for example, an understanding of what regulations and laws schools must adhere to; and a list of recommendations, without the evaluator having made contact with the educational staff, much less having observed the child in the environments/settings of concern.

Frankly, there was never a lack of data from formal assessments that could be used to determine Wayne's needs. That was not the issue. Nor was there ever an issue with having information on Wayne's disability or behavioral and academic skills. All this information was readily available in various forms—but there were two issues at stake.

The first was a missing piece of evidence, mentioned in the scenario: the classroom teacher's documentation on Wayne's classroom progress in the areas of social learning and "language pragmatics." The parents had requested this information several times during the school year, and the teacher promised to deliver it. However, if you recall, those data were lost due to a "computer crash" the day before the IEP meeting. This, of course, would have been valuable information to have in order to know what kind and how much progress had taken place over the course of the school year. This is especially true because social skills and pragmatic language usage were two major areas of concern where the family wanted to see progress made.

The second issue was the level of understanding, or rather lack of understanding, of autism, which was highlighted when staff and the parents were talking about Wayne's avoidance of social interaction with his peers and others. According to his mother, "Various staff members [said to me and my husband] 'If Wayne doesn't enjoy playing with kids, why do you want to force him to be something he is not?' and 'I don't know how much of the way Wayne is can be helped and how much is part of his condition.'" More than a few warning bells should be going off, in particular, with regard to these last two statements—bells ringing and one growing question: "Just how knowledgeable are these program staff regarding children with autism and Asperger's?"

In spite of the lost data, there remained a great deal of other information from which to establish Wayne's needs and from which to develop measurable goals, benchmarks, and objectives for inclusion in Wayne's IEP. We are left, however, wondering how skilled the school staff are with children with autism and Asperger's.

These issues will be addressed in the next two sections.

Where Do We Want to Go?
What Is It We Want to Accomplish?

We have established that this is, unfortunately, where the school and family diverged more widely in their thinking. Perhaps the difference is subtle in terms of what areas needed to be addressed, where there seemed to be agreement, but what was needed to accomplish the goals involved intense differences (the answer, as we noted under the previous question, would directly affect the *degree* of accomplishment).

The school appeared to recognize and agree that the basic behaviors that Wayne exhibited and his preference for solitary activities and disregard for social opportunities and activities were major deficits. There seemed, as well, to be agreement that his academic skills surpassed his peers' and that he would need to have instruction at a level that would ensure a continued increase in those skills. So, to some major degree, there was agreement on Wayne's needs.

Jumping a bit ahead, the differences surfaced when the discussion moved to how the school would achieve his IEP goals of social skills training and pragmatic language development. In fact, you will recall that when the conversation moved to increasing the frequency of social interactions, his placement in a self-contained classroom is strongly suggested by the school staff without regard to the availability of academic instruction at his level. By making that proposal, the school had already put a limit on how much Wayne's social skills and pragmatic language skills could be practiced. That, in effect, put immediate limits on what could be accomplished, which would have to be accounted for by reducing expectations regarding his measured skills of verbal interaction with his peers, staff, and family as written in his goal statement. Does this seem absurd to you? By limiting the interventions used, the school staff were also limiting the possibility for success, and they acknowledged this by lowering their expectations for success instead of developing appropriate interventions that could better meet the child's needs. Of course this seems absurd, because it is absurd!

You can see how that statement and thinking impacted the establishment of measurable goals, benchmarks, or objectives, because it impacted the answer to the next questions ("How will we get there?" and "What do we need to get there?"). By answering the questions out of order, the school devalued the IEP's ability to meet Wayne's needs. Remember, too, that placement(s) for services was the last decision to be made.

How Will We Get There?
What Do We Need to Get There?

In order to answer these questions in a collaborative manner, the IEP team needs to discuss what services are going to be needed to meet the needs and goals the team has already agreed to. However, in this scenario, discrepancies quickly surfaced with respect to the settings for services, the degree of educational challenges to provide, interventions for Wayne's sensory disorder treatment, and the degree of support (a shadow) to provide to facilitate social learning and language pragmatics. These decisions had essentially been made already by the school team, or at least by certain individuals who showed, through their comments, that they were not open to genuine discussion.

And we already have staff admitting, "I don't know how much of the way Wayne is can be helped and how much is part of his condition." It is extremely difficult to know what instruction or intervention(s) are needed or what to do, if you do not understand a child's needs and abilities—specifically, in this case, Wayne's preference for isolation. There is a strong sense that the school did know that facilitated social interaction was an appropriate intervention, but they did not seem to know how to provide the opportunities and instruction necessary for change to occur.

And here it becomes exceedingly evident that it was not this school's practice or policty to make collaboration part of the process when conducting IEP meetings. Whereas the school appeared to agree with Wayne's needs, they literally balked when faced with a discussion of how services were to be provided, what services were to be provided, and how decisions for programming and settings of services were to be made.

In essence, here is where the school says, "No!" When Wayne's mother asked for a more consistent, systematic approach to fostering Wayne's social participation, his resource teacher replied, "This meeting is simply to discuss goals. It is our job to develop strategies. You can give suggestions, but we will decide what is best." That's a pretty clear "No!"

In response to Wayne's mother's request for a shadow (whom the family was willing to pay for) for Wayne, the school staff replied, "We don't do that. If he needs that much individual attention, he should probably be in a self-contained classroom." They then added, "If we have a non-school district person on the team, it could impede the smooth functioning of the team." Wayne's mother noted, "…these comments were all made before Wayne's need for a shadow was even considered."

The school was making a placement decision prior to having fully discussed Wayne's need for services to enhance his social interaction, and to accommodate for his deficits in that area. In other words, independent of how his needs could be met, the recommended decision for a self-contained placement had already been made. Because the school refused to consider alternative services to what they had in mind, they simply "passed Go" and went straight to a placement decision. When Wayne's mother pointed out this fact to the school staff, she received the following response: "He might become too dependent on the aide," and "We wouldn't want him to think he couldn't do it by himself." At some point, the remark "Well, this is something they don't outgrow" was made. This competed with the following statement for the most unforgettable comment of the entire meeting: "We are going to be the boss; we are going to have the final word."

And we need to recall that, in the past, throughout the year, when Wayne's mother asked for a more consistent, systematic, approach to fostering Wayne's social participation, his resource teacher replied, "This meeting is simply to discuss goals. It is our job to develop strategies. You can give suggestions, but we will decide what is best."

And finally, at this planning meeting various staff members also said "If Wayne doesn't enjoy playing with kids, why do you want to force him to be something he is not?" and "I don't know how much of the way Wayne is can be helped and how much is part of his condition."

Truly, this is painful to read as it typifies their attitude toward, and understanding of, children with Wayne's challenges at that time. What's worse is that this was *not* one of the worst school systems in the country. So, one can conclude that this attitude was systemic, and that the school staff needed a great deal more training to work effectively with children with autism/Asperger's syndrome. Even for the mid-1990s, the school's approach to programming was immature with respect to the common practices that were generated in legislation and put into practice decades ago, including parents' input in the IEP decision-making process and having properly trained, knowledgeable staff providing the services needed.

We are told that, while much of Wayne's program needs were included in the IEP, he did not receive a trained aide to assist with his social skills development. This forced Wayne's parents to make a difficult choice. They could agree to place him in a self-contained classroom, where he'd get the support he needed to develop his social skills further, or they could agree to place him in a general education classroom, where he would be denied the support he needed to interact with his peers. The parents opted to focus on Wayne's academic needs and agreed to place him in the general education classroom, where he was afforded the opportunity to be instructed academically (by an aide, not by the classroom teacher), but he was not afforded the opportunity to interact successfully with his peers. This shows why negotiation is such a weak approach when trying to meet a child's needs. The parents, in this case, negotiated to get one need while giving up services to meet another need.

A Different Approach

We all recognize that the development of social skills and pragmatic language usage is essential as a framework from which children, as individuals, are empowered to interact successfully with school-age peers, family members, and—later—adult peers in the community and the work place. You may well run into similar situations, given the parameters of this particular point of disagreement; and because you might, it is worth looking at an alternative approach to dealing with this situation or a similar one. There is, of course, more than one approach, but the example on p.144 will follow the collaborative process and show how, by using its sequential framework, you can bring the discussion and solution back to your child's needs.

Remember that any time you find the team lost for an answer or simply unsure, you can return to the previous question and the answer the team developed. You can ask if the team missed something during the discussion, or if the answer still seems correct. If it is correct (and it most likely is), the team might then ask what they do not know in order to answer the question they are having difficulty with. They may need further information from someone else (i.e., another team person is needed) or something else (i.e., a different kind of assessment is needed).

Another time when you may need to back up to a previous answer/decision is when you are presented with statements similar to those given to the parents. That is a clear indication that the focus is no longer on the child, but on the service providers and their needs.

Let's look at this scenario in a slightly different way, putting *yourself* in the position of the parent. Read each instruction below carefully and try to carry it out in your head. (What would you say and *how* would you say it? You can say your statements out loud or even write them down if you prefer.) But, let's assume you actually had to do the following:

1. make the case that one of Wayne's greatest weaknesses is the lack of social interaction

2. present recommendations developed by you and an expert

3. make multiple requests for a shadow

4. offer to pay for the trained aide (shadow).

After doing all of that, imagine you were still told "No" in various forms, as was Wayne's mother. Do you feel frustrated, not only with the answers, but with the clear understanding that *you* are not a full participant in the school's decision-making activities? This is not the time to walk out or become angry. Remember, the process gives you a structure to work from—a plan. The reason it is called the "Structured Collaborative IEP Process" is because you are structuring the conversation and leading the team through the process.

Let's now approach this by asking the following questions of the school staff. Keep in mind we already know the answers to each of these questions. That is why they are being asked—the IEP team has already agreed on the answers, except for the last question, number seven:

1. Could we return to the issue of Wayne's limited social-interaction skills?

2. I think we agreed that one of his greater weaknesses is his preference to remain in solitary activities, am I right?

3. I think we also agreed that with prompts and facilitated activities, Wayne will interact with one or two other children. We have seen facilitated peer interaction working both at home and here at school. Isn't that what you have seen (looking at Wayne's classroom teacher)?

4. I believe you had a concern about including the specific strategies that I presented in Wayne's IEP, right? I am wondering, did you have an issue with any of the suggestions in particular? I mean, did you see any that you feel

would not be of benefit to Wayne if they were practiced in the classroom? Maybe we could discuss those that would be least likely to help Wayne increase his social skills. Could we do that?

5. So, we have agreed pretty much that one of Wayne's biggest needs is to develop social skills and we recognize that having those skills is important for interacting with you (looking at his classroom teacher), his peers, and, in the future, his adult peers. We agreed that we have seen that, with guidance, Wayne can interact with a very small group of his peers and that, without it, he will be quite satisfied with solitary activities. We agreed that academically he is quite ahead of his peers. Am I correct?

6. I have one more point: you mentioned that you had some concerns about our paying for a trained aide because you felt that having a non-school staff person could create some problems with working relationships. Am I correct? And you were concerned that Wayne would become reliant on the aide's services; but we know that, like any service, the goal is to phase out the supports as he gains the skills to interact with his peers independently. Agreed?

7. So, we agree that socialization is a need that can be addressed through facilitated peer interaction and that Wayne is academically functioning above his peers. If that is the case, and the issue is that, although an individual is needed to guide him into social interactions, we cannot hire a staff person to meet his needs, then I believe it would be your responsibility to do so. Otherwise, the IEP will not be providing the services he needs to meet his needs. And I am sure we agree that that is not right. Am I correct?

Notice that you only ask questions and that you make no statements without asking if there was agreement. You restate all the points of agreement, enabling the team to refocus on Wayne's needs and his receiving some form of dedicated support to increase his social skills and pragmatic language usage.

The questions guide the school team into agreeing to one of Wayne's problems and ask them to confirm that facilitated social interaction has been successful and observed. Next, you give the school an opportunity again to review the recommended interventions suggested by Wayne's mother and to indicate which ones are not appropriate to address his needs. Finally, you confirm that a non-school staff person might create some internal team problems. So, by using the Structured Collaborative IEP Process, you establish agreement on the known information, which sets up the discussion of what is not yet known.

This moves the school back to Wayne's identified needs and to what should be accomplished. So, now you can agree on how to meet these needs, with the final conclusion being that without such support (a shadow, in this case) his needs will not be met. Furthermore, you establish that the responsibility for providing the support personnel belongs with the school system. It is not a trick or a "gotcha" approach. Instead, it is a process of collaboration among IEP team members that is based on Wayne's agreed upon needs, and that ends with a written IEP of goals and services developed to meet those needs, which is agreed to by the members of the team.

Finally, if the issue of placing Wayne in the self-contained setting arose again, you would remind the team that they agreed that:

- his academic skills far surpassed those students in the self-contained setting

- he would need individual assistance for academic training

- the teacher/aide in the self-contained classroom would still have to establish regular and frequent appropriate social skills opportunities to ensure that his social skills would also progress.

The question you would then ask the team is, "Can you provide the individualized academic instruction and facilitated social skills training in the self-contained classroom without jeopardizing the other students' needs?"

So, that is how you would use the process: asking questions, restating decisions already agreed upon, asking for reaffirmation of those earlier decisions, and moving to the next question. You guide the team through the process.

Returning to this scenario, the remaining questions will be briefly discussed.

How Do We Know That We Are Getting There?

Recalling that Wayne's teacher lost all progress data to a computer crash, it is essential to state directly in the IEP when school staff should send progress reports home to the parents. In this case, with the history of lost computer data, it is also essential to state explicitly what data you want to receive. This is partially determined by the goal statement—the reports should measure growth in each "general area" covered by the IEP. But, considering there should be a number of specific objectives and benchmarks under each general area, you should also receive progress reports concerning each identified need under each goal statement. As a parent, these are the data you want to be provided to you, because they will give you a much more specific measure of growth on particular behaviors. They will be far more informative than the progress made on overall goals. Therefore, if your IEP is written with goals, objectives, or benchmarks, measures of growth should be reported on each of these, and not just the overall goals.

How Do We Know When We Have Arrived?

We don't know what progress Wayne made toward reaching his goals, because the data that would provide us with this essential information were supposedly lost to a computer crash. While losing data to a computer crash is unfortunate, it would be worse if the data had never been collected in the first place. If the data had been collected, the teacher could still provide a verbal summary from memory to provide some clues as to Wayne's progress. If the data had not been collected, then there would be no way of knowing if we had achieved the goals, benchmarks, and/or objectives stated in the IEP.

So, we have reason to doubt the reported computer crash, because we do not know whether the goals, benchmarks, and/or objectives were reached, which is essential information to have in order to move forward. After all, how can we decide where to go next if we don't know whether we've arrived at our planned destination? Of course, the IEP team could still review the IEP and establish revised goals to determine whether or not Wayne had "arrived" at his goals. However, without these data, we are not as well informed as we should be regarding how to modify Wayne's goals, benchmarks, or objectives. This lack of data truly inhibits the successful development of the next IEP, regardless of whether the data were lost or never collected.

How Do We Keep What We Have?

Sometimes, our children truly master a skill and can move on to new activities. Other times, they reach mastery level, but without continued reinforcement there is a strong possibility they will lose the skill. Extended school year (ESY) is based on that concept. (That is, ESY is programming typically offered during the summer, when the regular school programs are not in session. It is intended to provide continued services in areas where the child's skills and competencies may be lost without continuance of services. Those areas are determined by the IEP team during the IEP meeting.) Other times, we need to continue with the same services to maintain a skill. What we do not want is for the child to lose skills he or she has learned, and that is why we ask the question, "How do we keep what we have?"

For example, Wayne might master multiplication of six digits by six digits with 100 percent accuracy. But if we move on to fractions, we might discover that Wayne is now struggling with multiplication. This is always a possibility for any of us. Without review or practice, we can all get a bit "rusty;" but there is a difference between being "rusty" and truly losing a skill. Periodically, we have to check to make sure learned skills have remained mastered and have not been forgotten. The point to remember is that *mastery is not an event; it is a skill that is learned for the long term.*

Key Points

- If a school says "No," parents must remain vigilant and consistent with the issues of concern. If the concern is important, you need to continue making it an issue—not by whining or complaining, but through the use of the Structured Collaborative IEP Process. Wayne's parents did so—they also provided supplemental programming and supports at home and in their neighborhood community. Had it not been for those efforts, Wayne would certainly have experienced an even greater delay in developing the competencies he needed when interacting with others in his community.

- The Structured Collaborative IEP Process is a set of questions that you can use to guide a team through the development of an IEP.

- If the team drifts from the child's needs, you can use the Structured Collaborative IEP Process to return the team to those needs.

- IEP teams and schools do not always have all the answers.

- Schools do not always have or want to provide a needed service.

- This particular elementary school staff and leadership exemplify deficits under the above two points.

- There is never a need to negotiate away a child's needs. If the team has identified that the need exists, then the programming to provide instruction or accommodations should not be traded away for something that does *not* increase, reduce, or maintain the target behavior!

- Having data, either informal or formal, is essential in defining a need or behavior and for measuring a change in behavior.

- An advocate the parents hired made an incorrect recommendation. This advocate told Wayne's parents that they could pursue and obtain placement at the Landmoor School, where Wayne's needs would more likely be met, but she felt that Wayne would have more opportunities to build peer relationships outside of school if he remained in his neighborhood school. This would only have made sense had Wayne been able to receive an appropriate program at his home school, where, in fact, development of social skills was built around a planned program of interaction with his non-disabled peers. Without this, the Landmoor School would have been the better choice, because that is where the opportunity for developing a social interaction program was far more likely. The school highlighted its commitment to collaboratively based, individual programming and the provision of needed accommodations, which is exactly what was missing at the home school. The Landmoor School should have been investigated further regarding, and focusing on, the differences and similarities between programs, with an onsite discussion with the school staff. Placing Wayne in the first grade at his home school guaranteed that Wayne would not be provided with the services required to achieve the goals he needed to be successful.

- Recall that after Wayne began first grade, his parents hired a behavioral consultant to develop a few classroom behavioral strategies, but that the principal told Wayne's mother (in private) that if they included any specifics in the IEP (i.e., recommendations from outside the school system) "…the school would then be obligated to provide them…"

  » Not all schools would have made the statement the principal did, and it was inappropriate for the principal to have said it outside of the IEP meeting. Those recommendations should have been a part of the IEP discussion.

  » Although specific programs need not be included in an IEP (e.g., specific reading programs are not usually listed in an IEP), if the school recognized that particular behaviors might benefit from particular language development strategies, those could have been built into the IEP under language goals, as behaviors to be changed, and as objectives and benchmarks to achieve, and they could have been stated so that the behaviors would be addressed across school settings.

  » Lastly, a behavior intervention plan (BIP) is not limited only to negative behaviors, but can be used to shape desired behaviors as well. This concept might well appear to give the BIP a different purpose from that originally intended, but the concept behind this plan is to prevent, increase, or maintain a particular behavior(s). Given that, a BIP could have been written that included the behaviors to be addressed, the interventions to put into place and under what circumstances or conditions they were to be employed.

Summary

Wayne's parents did a great deal to obtain the needed services for their son and unknowingly implemented many of the steps of the Structured Collaborative IEP Process. We can learn a lot from their approach, but there are two issues where the process was not used. Although they were prepared for the IEP meetings (with or without an advocate), they sought outside support when they felt it necessary to validate their observations. That way they could present the IEP team with clearly stated needs and complementary goals. Unfortunately, Wayne's parents passed on three opportunities to strengthen his program.

The school staff repeatedly showed that they did not fully understand Wayne's needs or his disability. Wayne's parents thought that by having an outside assessment conducted and by having recommendations provided that would assist Wayne, the IEP team would, in fact, understand more of Wayne's needs and implement the recommendations noted in the report. The school did not. At this point, the parents could have pursued or demanded an independent educational evaluation, but they did not—perhaps because they did not know that they could, or perhaps because they did not understand how this step could help them persuade the school to meet all of Wayne's needs.

When one member of the IEP team said, "I don't know how much of the way Wayne is can be helped and how much is part of his condition," that was a clear indication that an independent educational evaluation should be requested. The school staff (whether the statement is made by one person or the whole group) is admitting that they are unsure of both his needs and the impact his disability has on his needs—two essential pieces of information, without which appropriate goals cannot be established.

The second area of concern was when the parents were "given" two choices of programming: they could either accept the IEP the school recommended, where his academic goals could be met, or they could place him in a setting where, to some extent, his social skills could be improved. I call this negotiating your child's rights away, and this is exactly why I do not support negotiators. Ask yourself this question: which rights (your child's needs) are you willing to give up in order to obtain (or satisfy) another? Perhaps it seems Wayne's parents made the best choice possible, but the reality is that the two options the school presented were never the only choices available. Don't negotiate, as Wayne's parents did, because when you do you're giving up something to get something else. You do *not* have to do that!

In addressing both these issues, Wayne's parents were unaware of all the options they had available. With or without regulations in place to support you, if the school staff admit they do not understand your child's needs or how your child's disability impacts his learning, it is time to stop the IEP process. It is impossible to build a program without knowing the child's needs! You should never feel that you are negotiating your child's program. There is no reason to give up one service to obtain another! If both are needed, both are to be provided; that determination would be made when defining the child's needs, answering the questions, "What do we know?" and "What don't we know?"

Beyond these two issues, the story is well worth reviewing to see how the parents implemented much of the Structured Collaborative IEP Process and the manner in which they did so. They did their best to put emotion aside and deal with facts and data. The school simply lacked sufficient knowledge and understanding of Wayne's disability and skills to appreciate the parents' contributions and to develop and implement appropriate programming to meet Wayne's needs.

Finally, it became quite clear that the school lacked an understanding of the purpose of having parents as part of the IEP team when school staff dismissed the information presented by Wayne's mother by stating, "You can give suggestions, but we will decide what is best." This is not acceptable! It reveals a systemic problem in the school staff's comprehension of the purpose of an IEP meeting.

Any of these three points exemplify when you can (and should!) bring the meeting to a stop and seek an audience with the district or county director of special education to explain what has transpired. Of course, be certain to maintain records and a paper or email trail of conversations you might have.

Your second choice would be to make a note of the issue, but continue with the IEP meeting to see if other issues arise that you might also wish to share with the director of special education services. Politely tell the team where you disagree during and at the close of the meeting, adding that you will await a copy of the IEP, but will not sign your agreement to it because of the issues you presented. This is the documentation you will need to share with the school system's director of special education services and anyone else with whom you might wish to share it (e.g., school district superintendent).

Is it easy to maintain self-control and hold on to your emotions? No, not always. But, if you want the meeting to reconvene in a collaborative manner at a later time—remember, you are building collaboration—then, you will do your best to control your emotions, make your points of disagreement *and* agreement understood, and state clearly what you do/do not intend to do as a next step.

Final Note

Wayne lives at home with his parents. He is currently investigating the possibility of applying to the local community college. His mother is attempting to have Wayne visit the college to develop familiarity and comfort with the college setting. However, Wayne's preference is to remain at home and complete his coursework online. He remains a delightful and insightful young man who still loves to read and learn.

CHAPTER 7

Parents' Solutions for a Child with High-Functioning Autism and High Anxiety

This story is about Libby and Walter Wolverton and their son, Jman, who is a bright and introspective young man. Mrs. Wolverton felt it important for Jman to be able to advocate for himself—not in terms of demands, but to be able to explain his disability and what school accommodations he felt would enable him to be successful in school. This story is about two parents who would advocate for their son, but who knew when they should stop to allow and teach their son to advocate for himself. The focus of this story, written by Mrs. Wolverton, is a family who knew how to prepare for an Individualized Education Program (IEP) and who attempted to work with a school that repeatedly failed to grasp Jman's disability and needs.

Getting Down to the Specifics

"Do you think he is playing you?…
Because he seems fine at school."

Our son, Jman, has autism. Some would say he has high-functioning autism, which is an interesting concept that depends on your perspective and the depth to which autism affects your child. He has verbal skills, is funny, kind, friendly and a diligent, hard worker. He loves to read and watch movies. He is also naive to the point of being at risk when he is out in the "real world."

All these attributes are part of what makes Jman an exceptional person who you would truly enjoy knowing. However, sometimes these same attributes can contribute toward masking his disability, for those who are not familiar with autism, which can lead to social isolation and confusion.

Jman has a high level of anxiety. He is very sensitive to noise and wears custom-made noise buffers whenever he leaves our home (they look like hearing aids). When he is anxious or excited he will "stim" and bounce. His diet is extremely limited, and he has sensory issues related to foods and clothing. His fine-motor skills are weak—his writing and drawing ability is comparable to that of a five- or six-year-old and he is unable to tie his shoes. Academically, he understands and processes work that is four to five grade levels below his chronological age of 15.

Jman was diagnosed with autism at age eight. Prior to this, he had other diagnoses, such as pragmatic language disorder, benign congenital hypertonia, and others that did not fit him. Because Jman is unique in his skills and deficits, getting to the right diagnosis for him was a challenge.

Today, Jman accurately fits the current criteria of an autism-spectrum disorder diagnosis. We feel that our family has been paving the way for school and community services to learn what is needed to support children with autism—a very frustrating place for us to be.

The nurturing and inclusive environment of elementary school did not prepare me for how difficult the transition to middle school would be. In fact, "difficult" is much too weak an adjective to describe this experience for us. The words "crippling, excruciating, and painful" are more accurate.

The increase in academic and social demands was beyond my son's ability to cope with—not to mention the lack of an inclusive atmosphere and the bullying behavior adopted by his peers. It took every ounce of Jman's being just to walk into the school building. I would have to unbuckle Jman and gently push him out of the car door. He would say, every day, "I'm not going in there!" And I would say, "You need to try." And he did try, but the cost of that trying was just too much.

By the end of sixth grade, he was in daily agony; he had stomach pain and vomited every morning before school. I often cried as I drove away—unable to hold in the pain of seeing my child in such distress. I would call the school to see how he was coping and knew, if he were still upset at school, I would bring him home. The feeling of that daily drop-off was akin to putting Jman in front of a firing squad. He was getting a lot of support at school, but it just wasn't working.

When I picked him up at the end of the school day, he would completely fall apart. The cost of holding it together during the school day was taking a physical toll on his body. At my son's annual physical, the pediatrician told me that Jman would develop an ulcer if there wasn't some sort of change.

When I left the doctor's office, I immediately called the school to request an IEP meeting. The team convened in May 2009 and included the following people:

- my husband and me

- the school adjustment counselor, a licensed clinical social worker who works with students who have issues to do with anxiety

- the school principal

- the general education teacher from the inclusive classroom (our son also required extra assistance in areas of existing or potential noise that could trigger fear, such as the cafeteria, where Jman sat at a small group table to eat)

- the special education teacher from Jman's self-contained class program (our son received instruction in English language arts, science, math, and related services including, for example, group social skills).

There was also an extensive plan in place to assist him with fire drills—Jman's worst fear at school. The adjustment counselor was his safe go-to person during the day if Jman needed assistance in any of these areas.

My husband and I voiced our concerns regarding our son's physical well-being and shared a letter from our pediatrician. We discussed the current supports in place to help him cope with his anxiety. The supports included the following:

- Jman would arrive at school 20 minutes early every day and wait in the adjustment counselor's office until locker time. The counselor led a small social skills group during this time.

- The counselor accompanied Jman to his locker and classroom to assist with the anxiety caused by the noise level and large crowds of people in the hallways. It was also to assist with bully prevention, as there had been incidents of bullying in the locker area. (We did address bullying, due to incidents where our son was targeted. The school had a student-led committee, facilitated by the assistant principal, where "bullying situations" were looked into and consequences were assigned, if appropriate. Jman was the first special-needs student invited to participate on the committee.)

- He kept "comfort items" from home in his pencil case and backpack (a photograph of our family, a small angel figure to remind him that he was loved—things that he could look at or touch that helped him cope with stress and anxiety).

- To deal with the noise and number of people, the counselor would walk Jman out the door for afternoon pick-up by me.

We asked the school staff for ideas on what else could be done to help. Sadly, we were met with blank stares and a comment from the adjustment counselor, who asked, "Do you think he is playing you? You know, maybe faking it at home? Because he seems fine at school."

At this point, I realized my child with special needs was not someone the school understood—and his needs were not being met. They didn't have a "category" for him, because they didn't have any prior experience with a student like him. Ultimately, they were at a loss for how best to support him.

We did not know what more the school could do for Jman. We left that meeting, and I drafted a letter informing the school that I would "homeschool" Jman for his seventh grade year. At home, he could heal his body, rest his mind from the anxieties brought on by the middle school, and learn and grow in his favorite environment—home.

Although homeschooling was a successful endeavor, I knew that this was not the long-term solution for Jman's educational needs. To make this work, we used an online school program called K-12, which, at that time, provided an approved homeschool curriculum for all 50 states in the U.S.

I was required to provide documentation to the middle school with regard to the homeschool plan; K-12 assisted with this process. I was also required to meet with the principal of the middle school to provide evidence that Jman was making progress.

The K-12 program has assessments organized to identify and target where your child is academically and will not allow a student to advance until he or she has achieved a level of successful progress based on student work and testing scores submitted online.

In addition to the online educational materials, hands-on materials were provided. These included textbooks, teaching manuals, science experiment kits, and, generally, everything you needed to teach any child using the child's particular learning style. It matched Jman's needs very well. However, even though the program was exceptional, there was a challenging learning curve going from mother/son to educator/student.

Once we got the hang of it, we enjoyed the program. I absolutely noticed physical changes in Jman. He spent less time feeling anxious, and his ability to focus, without fear and worry filling his mind, was obvious. He was well rested, and it helped that we did not have to start our day on the same schedule as public school. Because the teaching was one-on-one, our school day was not as long as public school, and this helped to reduce his stress.

Jman no longer suffered from stomach pain and vomiting in the morning, and did not exhibit tantrums or meltdowns. He stopped complaining about how hard the school day was. He was physically more relaxed and a truly happy child—everyone noticed the difference, including his pediatrician.

Although the K-12 program was exceptional, I knew we needed to have a strong focus on Jman's social skills development—a major part of his disability. He needed peer interaction experiences so that he could develop his social skills. And, honestly, I felt he needed his academics to be taught by special education staff. I needed to find a way to make him feel safe and comfortable while in the middle school building. I needed help.

In August 2009, I contacted the school principal to request a meeting, and asked that my son be allowed to attend physical education (PE) classes at the middle school—it was his favorite class. I shared what accommodations would need to be provided so that Jman's educational needs could be met. I also explained to our son that, although we were "homeschooling," it was important that he stayed physically active and involved in the public school in some way. We knew that he needed same age friends to socialize with and this was not something easily accomplished outside of middle school.

We told Jman how important it would be to talk to the school administrators about what he needed to be comfortable in PE and how homeschooling with PE classes at school could be of benefit. The principal agreed and twice per week Jman attended PE class. (This experience was the start on the road to self-advocacy.)

We told Jman that he was responsible for consulting (self-advocating) with his PE teacher before class to see what activities were scheduled. If Jman was nervous or anxious about any of them (and he is the only one who would know this information, unless he shared it verbally), then it was his responsibility to advise his PE teacher, so that the teacher could make adjustments that would make him comfortable with the class activities.

I wanted Jman to know that our family would always do what was best for him, but that he played an important role in making sure that happened. He needed to learn how to communicate with the school staff (as well as with us) about what worked and what did not.

We stayed active at the school, volunteering at the book fairs, and we timed our participation so that Jman would see his peers from his previous self-contained classroom. Teachers who knew my son would approach and tell him how much they missed him and that they were hoping to have him back soon. These were all positive experiences and I considered our homeschool year a great success, academically and socially. To expand on his social opportunities, we participated in a homeschool book club at the local library and a homeschool bowling league.

As much as we wanted Jman to explore developing new friendships with other children his age, and as much as we tried, this lovable kid would only occasionally interact with friends on weekends. His theory was that he had two friends and did not need any more.

I contacted the school principal in August 2010 to meet and discuss Jman's continued participation in PE and to make a request that he be allowed to take math (his most challenging subject) with a special education teacher. I was met with a resounding, "No!" The law in our state allows for homeschool students to participate in PE and after-school activities, but it makes no requirements for academic classes.

The principal told me our son was "either a homeschool student or a public school student." We began the path of transitioning Jman back to his home school, but with a focus on the accommodations he would need to make his school experiences successful, academically and socially. To prepare for the transition, we completed a private neuropsychological evaluation so that we could best address our son's current needs.

We used the findings and recommendations from that evaluation to identify the types of supports that would be needed. Bullying was addressed in the neuropsychological evaluation, determining that Jman had all the characteristics that would make him a potential victim of bullying. Our state had just passed anti-bullying legislation requiring each school district to develop district anti-bullying policies which would help support our son.

We started the transition process slowly. We continued to homeschool until November, when we requested a team meeting to discuss Jman's return to the school. The school was in receipt of the neuropsychological report.

The IEP team that convened included:

- my husband and me

- the IEP team chairperson

- the special education teacher

- the general education teacher (the PE teacher who had been working with him)

- the student services coordinator (a sort of school ombudsman)

- the newly appointed district special education director.

The special education director began the meeting by stating that she was willing to work with us to make the transition back to the school the best that it could be for Jman. Our major concern was to make sure that staff would help our son continue to develop his self-advocacy skills, teaching him how to identify his stress (and stressors), and how to seek help when he needed it.

This all sounded very helpful and promising, but it was difficult to put this request (needs) into a measurable goal statement. We've always found it easier to make meaningful measurable goals and objectives for academics. That has not been our experience with social and emotional goals—what our son needed most.

The neuropsychological report identified what our son's needs were and what accommodations and services should be provided for him. It was up to the team to develop and implement an IEP that met and supported those needs.

We agreed that Jman would start transitioning back to the school slowly: first he would attend PE; then he would go to his special education classroom for math instruction; and then he would return home. After a few weeks, when he appeared comfortable, we would add another class. We would continue in this way until he was at the school full-time again. The only exception to full regular attendance would be for him to arrive and begin school 15 minutes later than the regular start time, thereby avoiding the noise and commotion of the students, in order to address the issues of stress.

We also discussed the upcoming transition to the high school. The high school was twice the size of the middle school, with twice the population. We were advised to visit the high school with our son at an upcoming family event to be held at the school during the evening. (In addition, I made arrangements with a family friend, who worked at the high school, for us to take our son on a private tour of the school. We scheduled the tour for after school hours, so that there would be fewer students present.)

The meeting ended with the understanding that I would receive a proposed IEP within ten days. Due to "technical computer problems," I did not actually receive the proposed IEP until 35 days later. It is important to note that at each IEP meeting my husband and I were prepared with a list of our concerns, our long-term goals, Jman's concerns, and a list of questions we had.

Once we had the neuropsychological report completed, we consulted with the psychologist who completed our son's evaluation for assistance prior to the IEP meeting. Her advice was significant, including requesting a behavior consultant—a Board Certified Behavior Analyst (BCBA)—to become part of the IEP team.

When we received the proposed IEP in January 2010, we were very disappointed. Many of the issues we discussed were not addressed in the IEP. It was fairly clear that the findings and recommendations from the neuropsychological report had not been considered at all. Our son was reading between the fourth and fifth grade level, but there were no reading goals.

There were so many issues raised at the IEP meeting that were not addressed in the document that we did not sign it. I knew the school was willing to work with me, but in this environment it seemed like they were saying, "Okay, you tell us what you need, and we will consider getting it." We needed school staff with some expertise to help identify and provide the necessary supports for Jman.

To do that, we decided to hire an advocate and then requested another IEP meeting. We shared all the documentation we had collected with the advocate in preparation for the next meeting. Due to many requests from the school to reschedule the IEP meeting, the meeting did not take place until March 2, 2010—almost three months since the initial IEP meeting had taken place. In the weeks leading up to the meeting, we consulted with the advocate to ensure that we had a clear understanding of what we were going to ask the school for. Our requirements were greatly based on the neuropsychological report, which provided a list of recommended strategies. We had a clear outline for the discussion:

- The IEP needs to incorporate reading, science, and social studies goals. In addition, math and writing goals need to be modified, based on the results of the neuropsychological report. Goals need to be developmentally based versus grade level modified.

- Pragmatic social language with peer mentoring and social emotional goals need to be included in the IEP. Lunch time: Is anyone transitioning from the classroom to the lunch room with Jman? Is there an adult to facilitate the social opportunities in the lunch room?

- We would like an autism specialist to review our son's progress toward meeting the IEP goals and objectives on a monthly basis.

- We would like to have extra textbooks or recorded readings of texts at home.

- Due to his later start time, Jman does not have a "homeroom" class and does not receive regular school notices or memos. A plan needs to be put in place so that Jman receives homeroom notices and to be offered the opportunity to participate in all school activities.

- Ways of increasing Jman's stamina and ways of staff and Jman recognizing his fatigue need to be discussed.

- Executive functioning skills (i.e., organization skills) need to be discussed. What supports or services can be put in place to assist with this?

- Extended school year needs to be discussed.

- We have made a previous request to include a behavioral consultant on the IEP team. What is the status of this request?

- Assistive technology (AT) needs to be discussed.

- Transition to high school needs to be discussed.

As you can see, we brought a lengthy list of topics we wanted to address. But we had an unexpected glitch. When I informed the school that we would be bringing an advocate to the meeting, I learned that she had worked with our school district previously and did not have a good working relationship with them. (I had found out through some parent detective work that she was considered argumentative, belligerent, and unprofessional.) Ugh!

I did not want that type of person representing our family in a meeting with the school that we had worked so hard to foster a good relationship with. Having had to pay a hefty retainer in advance, I decided to utilize the advocate outside of the IEP meetings. (The school personnel indicated to me just how thankful they were for that decision.) However, we still didn't have an appropriate IEP in place. The proposed IEP remained insufficient with regard to transitioning to the high school, so this time we rejected it.

I consulted our neuropsychologist, asking for her advice. She recommended that we consult with an educational consultant and an AT consultant and provided us with referrals. The educational consultant we hired held multiple credentials as an educator.

The AT specialist had earned an education specialist degree in assistive special education technology and a master's degree in creative arts and learning. She had completed undergraduate work in elementary education and moderate special needs education. She held positions as a regular educator, special educator (moderate special needs), special educator (intensive special needs), technology curriculum specialist, and AT specialist. As an adjunct faculty member at a local university, she developed and taught graduate-level courses in AT that included designing curriculum modifications for diverse learners. She "rocked" at IEP meetings! Staff members at the IEP meetings would actually ask for her contact information, so that they could email her questions they had regarding other students! They responded well to her exceptional knowledge and professional demeanor.

The AT specialist was to review all the testing reports for Jman, review the proposed IEP, observe the program options at the high school, and identify how, and what kinds of, AT would benefit our son.

She would also identify how AT should be incorporated into the IEP goals. Because it was so late in the school year, the plan was for her to observe our son in his classroom setting when high school began in September 2011. She would then issue her report, and we would discuss it at a team meeting in the fall.

Jman was due for his three-year re-evaluation from the school system in November 2011. This would lead to another team meeting to discuss the results of the evaluation, which we hoped would also assist in the preparation and implementation of an appropriate IEP for him.

In advance of high school starting, we had taken Jman on several tours, and in May and June of 2011 he took a bus to the high school from his middle school once a week to participate in a social skills group at the high school. This was a small group of freshmen and sophomores who were experiencing social issues.

I suspected that most of these students were on the autism spectrum, but I did not know for sure.

The adjustment counselor worked on many different areas of social skills, depending on the students' particular issues. There was not a "social curriculum" in use, so I provided her with a resource that I thought might help her develop such a curriculum.

All of this helped Jman to acclimate to the building and greatly assisted his transition to the high school. Prior to the first day of school, we had set up a meeting between our son and his special education teacher, so that they could meet each other and he could visit his classroom. In preparation for that meeting, I developed a written introduction of our son that described who he was beyond his IEP. Here is what I gave to his teacher:

> Our son, Jman, is an amazing person who you will very much enjoy having in your classroom. He is kind, funny, respectful, and very hard working. As you may know from reading Jman's IEP, he has autism, but as autism is such a broad spectrum we wanted to give you some insight into some of his non-academic needs. Jman is extremely sensitive to unexpected noise. His biggest trigger is the anticipation of fire drills. Although he is able to follow procedure for a fire drill, he has high anxiety around the anticipation of when a drill will happen. He worries about this frequently and sometimes has difficulty entering the school building because of it.
>
> He is also someone who does not respond well to angry voices or yelling. Even if the anger is not directed toward him (I can think of no time that it was), he will be afraid of the person who is yelling. He will think that someday that person will yell at him and he will not know what to do about that.
>
> Jman struggles with executive functioning skills and has trouble with keeping things organized. Also, when he is nervous he will have trouble remembering things. For example, one time when I gave Jman a check to put money in his lunch account, he did not realize that he could use his lunch account each day. He ate lunch the first day and went hungry the next because he did not realize there was enough money in the account for a month's worth of lunches. It also takes Jman a long time to remember the names of people who interact with him.
>
> It will take a long time for Jman to trust and confide in teachers and aides who are new to him. Fear and anxiety are in the forefront of his mind while at school, and when he has a problem or needs help he may never ask for it. We are working with him on self-advocating, but he will need assistance in learning this skill.

Our goals for Jman are:

- to make friends and be involved in school activities with friends as well as activities outside of school

- the ability to participate in school without such high levels of anxiety so that he can fully access academics and social opportunities

- that the supports put in place for Jman at school will work, and he won't fall through the cracks. That the people who are employed to support Jman will do their jobs to the best of their ability, see all his potential and help him meet it in a positive and caring way

- the ability to self-advocate for himself

- that he not give into depression and self-loathing

- that he will grow up to be a positive contributor to society—that he will grow to be a confident and successful independent adult.

Although the beginning of school was off to a good start, we felt as though the educational program designed to meet the IEP was not the best fit for our son. Specifically, we felt that the level of instruction was below his potential. I observed him in the program and concluded two things: I felt that the pace of instruction and activities was too slow academically—so slow that one might be tempted to nap. On the other hand, the program seemed well suited for our son socially/emotionally.

The greatest concern we had was that students in this program did not take the regular state-mandated assessment test in tenth grade, which was a requirement for high school graduation and a diploma. The curriculum that students in the classroom worked on was an alternative version of the regular program. This meant that these students would not be qualified to attend a college or university.

I learned that students in this class did not navigate the building independently. There was an aide with them at all times and these same students were together all day. There was no exposure to any other students in the school or opportunity to interact with them. On the other hand, the program did include life skills training, which is something our son would need.

I also viewed a program at the school called the Language Based Program, which was considered the next "step up," but I thought that it was too fast-paced and perhaps beyond Jman's academic ability. Students in this program, however, do take the state-mandated assessment in tenth grade, which yields a standard high school diploma. The students navigated the building independently, but did not work on any life skills training.

In September 2011, the educational consultant observed Jman in the high school and then issued a report. We had a brief IEP team meeting on September 19 to review any concerns and to agree to initiate the process of the three-year re-evaluation. The educational observation report was issued on October 21. It contained a full review of all the previous academic testing done by the school system, as well as the most recent neuropsychological report we had completed outside the school system. The educational consultant made suggestions that Jman should look for social opportunities during lunch time, and that staff should see if and how those opportunities took place.

The consultant also interviewed our son's academic teachers and reviewed the school district's description of the program in which Jman was placed. She observed the AT that was put in place (a laptop computer) and how Jman was using it to access the curriculum. She then issued her report noting five specific recommendations.

The following is one example of a reading recommendation from her report:

> Jman should receive a comprehensive literacy assessment by a literacy specialist for the purpose of documenting his current independent and instructional reading levels and qualifying his capacity to identify sight words, apply phonics to read/spell words, and make use of a variety of comprehension strategies. The information gleaned from this assessment should be utilized to develop a program of individualized instruction in the area of literacy that incorporates components of specialized instruction and guided practice in decoding/encoding, vocabulary, and comprehension, expanding his goals and benchmarks beyond the present focus on the elements of fiction. The literacy specialist, special educator, and AT specialist should collaborate on the development of a plan that defines which tools and strategies are best applied to specific academic tasks to ensure that Jman is provided with sufficient opportunities to continue to develop skills in this area while being appropriately supported in accessing the curriculum across content areas.

The copy of the report was shared with the school and a meeting to discuss it was scheduled following the school's completion of all of the testing associated with the three-year re-evaluation. The IEP meeting was set for early December 2011.

The meeting attendees included:

- me (my husband was unable to join us)

- our educational consultant (it is important to note that neither my husband nor I will attend IEP meetings alone, because we feel that an IEP meeting is too difficult to navigate individually; so we either both go or we have a hired consultant attend with us)

- the student services coordinator

- the adjustment counselor

- a special education teacher

- the school psychologist

- the school academic testing/assessment person [this is not a school psychologist. It is someone trained to administer and interpret academic tests, i.e., reading, math]

- a guidance counselor (the person who helps students with post-secondary goals through career and vocational testing)

- a BCBA (you might recall that we had made requests to have this person join our IEP team many times before, and we were very happy to see her on the attendance sheet!)

- an occupational therapist

- Jman. (We planned to have Jman attend at least a portion of all meetings.)

The meeting began with Jman reading information that we had prepared in advance. He listed what he liked best about school, what he found difficult about school, and what he flat out did not like about school. Next, I read a statement that is part of the IEP and is called "Parent Concerns," which, in a letter format, listed our concerns—most of these have already been presented in this scenario. We also provided our vision statement as follows:

> The team would like Jman to transition successfully to a high school placement that provides him with the academic and social supports he needs in order to meet his IEP goals and allows him to earn a standard high school diploma. Jman would like to attend community college after high school. The team would like Jman to become a more independent learner and for him to learn self-determination and self-advocacy skills. The goal of the self-advocacy training is to make sure that Jman has as much input as he is capable of providing regarding his thoughts and dreams for his future. The team would like Jman to identify post-secondary and occupational interests. Further, the team would like Jman to receive skills training and academic supports based on the identified interests. The team would like for Jman to develop functional life and problem-solving skills. The team would like Jman to develop positive social interactions and connections within a community of his peers in after-school and extracurricular activities with special education support. The team would like for Jman to participate equally to the best of his abilities in all

areas of school life. The team would like for Jman to be prepared for further education, employment, and independent living with the means to provide himself with economic self-sufficiency.

The results of the three-year re-evaluation assessments by the school staff were presented. (Personal note: when the clock hit the regularly scheduled lunch time for our son, he was out of there—no way was he missing a meal!) It is important to mention that the educational consultant took notes and kept track of all the information presented by the school in a more meaningful way than I ever could.

Here is an excerpt of the written results of the reading assessment:

Letter-word identification measures Jman's ability to identify sight words. Jman's word identification skills are not automatic. He requires increased time and attention to phoneme-grapheme relationships to determine the correct response. The standard score from the WIAT-III [Wechsler Individual Achievement Test—Third Edition] for word reading was 83. Passage Comprehension measures Jman's ability to understand what he reads. The items require Jman to read a short passage and identify a missing key word that is logical in the context of the passage. Jman's ability to comprehend written passages while he is actively reading is challenging; however, after referring to the text to determine information, Jman's overall reading comprehension skills are typical for an individual at his age.

The results went on and on, but I shared this section to show how the educational consultant took this information and shared her interpretation with the team. First, it is important to note that she had reviewed all Jman's previous testing results (for the same test) and had them with her to reference. Second, she had her own observational report and recommendations from the classroom. Finally, she had a clear understanding of how the curriculum needed to be targeted and taught to a student with special needs who needed to take and pass a state standardized test in order to get a diploma.

She also advised the school on how to incorporate the AT piece into the IEP—something the school admitted they did not know how to do. She questioned the testing protocol for the WIAT-III, indicating that protocol should not have allowed our son to refer back to the written text to obtain his answer. She also noted that the last statement, "Jman's overall reading comprehension skills are typical for an individual at his age," is fundamentally wrong—our son, unfortunately, was not able to read and comprehend at the level of a 15-year-old typical student. Why would he need special education reading goals if that were the case? Simply stated, the statement was incorrect and the school was advised to reissue the report with the correct statement.

As a team we came to an agreement that, due to Jman's unique skills and struggles, further testing was needed to identify his present levels of performance more accurately.

The educational consultant also made many recommendations with regard to how the IEP goals and benchmark objectives needed to be written. Specifically, they needed to be meaningfully based on our son's present levels of performance and written in measurable terms.

The team chairperson was to draft the proposed IEP and email it to us to review. Once we had received it, we shared it with our educational consultant, who provided her feedback and suggestions. The following is what was originally developed in Jman's IEP:

The proposed English language arts goal:

Jman will improve independence in English language arts skills to better access his curriculum by meeting six out of six objectives.

Decoding current performance level:

Currently, Jman is labored when orally reading; oftentimes he struggles with unfamiliar words. He has more difficulty with words that are multisyllabic and relies on teacher assistance to help with decoding unfamiliar words.

The educational consultant's comments and suggested changes on the English language arts (ELA) goals are as follows:

The problem with this description of Jman's current ability to demonstrate accuracy in decoding words is that it is vague…it does not qualify precisely what he can do now (how labored, how often, how much difficulty, how much and what type of teacher assistance, and how accurate (percentage)) and as such makes it impossible to appreciate what the decoding benchmark's targeted performance level of 25 percent improvement is being compared to (25 percent beyond what?). As written, this current performance level statement and benchmark will make it impossible to determine if he is making "effective progress."

Objective 1. Decoding:

Jman will improve speed and accuracy with phonemic awareness/decoding by improving the amount read of known phonemes/graphemes/chunks accurately in one minute's time by 25 percent above baseline levels across five work sessions.

A running record of known and unknown graphemes/phonemes/chunks will be utilized for this objective.

A portion of the final agreed IEP goal and objectives for ELA is as follows:

Measurable annual goal:

Jman will improve independence in his reading and writing skills in order to better access his curriculum by meeting six out of his six benchmarks/objectives.

Benchmark/objectives:

1. Jman will improve speed and accuracy with phonemic awareness/decoding by improving the amount read of known phonemes/graphemes/chunks accurately in one minute's time by 25 percent above baseline levels across five work sessions.

2. Jman will spell regularly and irregularly spelled sight words/high frequency words with 100 percent accuracy and 80 percent independence across five teaching sessions.

3. Jman will demonstrate the ability to use a word processor with text to speech and word prediction capabilities to independently generate a response to a multi-step question about a reading selection at his independent reading level that is at least 80 percent accurate, without referencing the text, across five teaching sessions.

4. After reading a passage at his independent reading level, Jman will independently answer a multi-step question without referencing the passage through multiple-choice with 75 percent accuracy across five teaching sessions...

This took quite a bit of time and effort and this was just one small component of the IEP. We spent just as much time working on appropriate goals for math, written expression, social/emotional issues, and transition.

I also sent a letter noting my concerns about the transition plan and will only note that I worked hard at keeping all my communications professionally stated and my interactions collaborative, which I think is the key to getting what you want/need. I also feel that if you are met with a "No," then you must keep asking until you get to the "Yes." I received this advice from many people within the school system itself: "Just keep asking."

After sending the letter about my concerns about Jman's transition plan, I requested a meeting with the special education director. Interestingly, she also included the BCBA in our meeting. I came with a printout summary of what had taken place and what action items we felt were still open and in need of resolution.

I showed data that clearly emphasized how critical it was to create and implement appropriate programming to meet Jman's needs. The high school had an obligation and a duty to meet his needs effectively and appropriately. His future quality of life depended on it.

This meeting proved to be very productive, and soon afterwards we received a proposed IEP that was acceptable to us and that we signed, indicating our agreement—finally.

Analysis of "Getting Down to the Specifics"

Jman's parents certainly demonstrated a great deal of persistence to make certain that Jman's educational program and services were provided explicitly for meeting his identified needs. Jman's mother credits her success only to this persistence, but she did much more.

Unknowingly, she implemented many of the steps of the Structured Collaborative IEP Process, specifically asking the key questions of the team and expanding the team until she could get appropriate answers. Because she did, she was successful in pointing out Jman's needs and the services he required to be successful in the school setting—which, in itself, was an area of concern that had to be addressed. Having said that, let's begin the analysis of Jman's parents' meeting with the school IEP team.

It might have crossed your mind that the word "led" could be used in lieu of the word "structured" in the phrase "structured collaboration," and you would be correct. The questions do, in fact, lead the team to seek the answer(s) together, and that is collaboration. It is very much the technique Jman's mother was using. So, as much as she might believe it was all due to being persistent, it was her persistence and her use of the Structured Collaborative IEP Process to obtain the "Yes!" from the school. And she had to do this multiple times!

Where Are We?

What Do We Know?

What Don't We Know?

Mrs. Wolverton was quite articulate in defining Jman's school problems to us ("What do we know?") and readily shared with us what was in place ("How will we get there?") to meet his needs ("Where are we going?")—that is, those of which the IEP team was aware. However, Mr. and Mrs. Wolverton realized that staff didn't *really* understand Jman's needs when the school's adjustment counselor asked her, "Do you think he is playing you?… Because he seems fine at school." So, staff did not really know Jman's needs or why the things that were in place did or did not work. Worse, when Mrs. Wolverton asked what else the school could do to assist

Jman (remember, he was extremely reluctant to enter the school building and was sick to his stomach), she was faced with blank stares from the school team—no answers, no suggestions; nothing was proposed.

In essence, the school had unmistakably admitted they did not have a firm understanding of Jman's needs. This would have been the perfect opportunity to request the district to pay for independent educational evaluations (IEEs) or to conduct outside (independent) evaluations that could ascertain Jman's needs and provide recommendations as to what to implement in his school classes. However, Mr. and Mrs. Wolverton did not pursue this course of action. Instead of arguing the point or suggesting that the school complete a full evaluation to determine his needs, Mr. and Mrs. Wolverton elected to remove Jman from the school and provide "homeschooling."

Sadly, the school team faltered with the initial and very basic question, "What do we know?" Unfortunately, and worse, they had no idea of what they didn't know and just barely understood what they thought they knew. This is a dilemma that could end with severe consequences for an IEP team and especially for Jman.

Where Do We Want to Go?
How Will We Get There?

Mrs. Wolverton located an approved online home school program ("How will we get there?") that would enable Jman to stay on course for a high school diploma ("Where do we want to go?") on her own. (She recognized from the onset that this would not be a long-term solution.) It did, however, work well for Jman, because it compensated (or accommodated) for his stressors. As a result, his work and task-pace improved, reducing the stress that accompanied strict timelines in the school setting. He experienced a more "relaxed" atmosphere, because of a reduction in the anxieties he had experienced in an environment of overstimulation. Instead, homeschooling afforded Jman with:

- a more placid environment

- structure (consistency) to the day's events and environment

- flexible scheduling and timelines

- elimination of anxiety-producing crowds and noises

- removal of social anxiety

- withdrawal from the intimidation imposed on him by the bullying

- termination of social reactions by his peers to his unique and disability-related behaviors.

For the most part, these were his social/emotional needs, but, sadly, the school staff had not recognized the associations between these events and situations and his anxiety, or how to address them in his IEP. They appeared barely to recognize that, when the stressors were reduced or removed, Jman was more able to cope with the school environment. But that may have been why the school adjustment counselor thought things were fine, because, with the interventions in place, the counselor did not see any issues. It is a narrow framework to work in when you have only one individual's perspective—hence, the value of a team where more people have more information. It is hoped that it is accurate information.

Where Do We Want to Go?
How Will We Get There?
How Do We Know That We Are Getting There?

Mrs. Wolverton recognized that she was not accomplishing what she had hoped for with only homeschooling. Although Jman was making educational progress "How do we know that we are getting there?") through the homeschool program, he was not meeting two additional needs ("How will we get there?") that would ultimately enable him to be successful in the general community (which is where she wanted him to go/what she wanted him to do). One issue ("What do we know?") was that Jman needed interaction with his peer group, which would be limited, at best, if left to his own accord. (Remember, he had two "friends" and did not see a need for more than those). A second issue ("What do we know?") was that Mrs. Wolverton felt that Jman would be better instructed with trained and certified special education teachers ("How will we get there?").

Her first decision ("How will we get there?") was to have Jman return to the PE class (his favorite class), and she broached this with the school principal, who agreed. Mrs. Wolverton explained that Jman would have to explain to the PE teacher what his needs were on any given day, should he be experiencing stress, and then discuss with the teacher a way to address it ("How will we get there?"). For Jman, this was the beginning of his practicing self-advocacy, a necessary skill that he needed now and would continue to need in the future. Mrs. Wolverton also made concerted plans to have Jman "run into" his former teachers at school activities, who said they missed him, and she got him involved in bowling with peers who were also homeschooled. She realized that these efforts were not producing the results she wanted ("How do we know that we are getting there?").

Mrs. Wolverton wanted to improve Jman's socialization skills, but her success was limited by the activities she could arrange, which were not helping him to expand his relationships with his peers. To achieve that goal ("Where do we want to go?") and to have her son taught by teachers of special education, she approached the principal to see if Jman could take part in the school's math class, in addition to the PE class that he was already attending ("How will we get there?"). She received a resounding "No" that was based on regulations. In order to accomplish her goals for Jman, she realized that she had to transition him back to the school ("How will we get there?"), but with a thought-out plan and in a slow manner to ensure successful re-entering into the school ("Where do we want to go?"). She had hoped to begin by adding just one class, and, when Jman became comfortable, they could add another, and then another ("How will we get there?").

But, since the last IEP team replied to her question, "What can you do to help?," with blank stares, she knew she needed to backtrack and obtain information to explain Jman's needs to everyone ("What do we know?"), in order to make the plan successful and fully understood. Again, it was a great opportunity for Mrs. Wolverton to have requested the district either to conduct specific educational evaluations or to have them cover the costs of an IEE. In this case, as the team had already admitted they had no idea of what to do, it would have dictated the seeking of IEEs to be conducted at the cost of the school.

However, Mrs. Wolverton did not ask the district to pay for the IEEs; neither did she request additional internal assessments to be conducted. Instead, she hired a neuropsychologist to carry out an assessment, in order "to identify…the types of supports that would be needed both academically and socially/emotionally." A neuropsychologist typically studies brain functions and the relationship to psychological processes and behaviors. The selection of the neuropsychologist and the areas of study certainly would address the major issues facing Jman, which the school did not understand. That is, the test results would help to explain why Jman might be feeling and acting the way he did at school.

The report identified Jman's needs and provided a number of recommendations and accommodations to be made that would increase his chances of being successful in the school setting. The findings also noted that Jman's behavioral characteristics would "make him a potential bully victim." The report essentially provided insights and conclusions necessary to answer a number of questions: "What do we know?" "Where do we want to go?" and "How will we get there?"

To condense and summarize, Mrs. Wolverton met with the team to review and discuss Jman's needs and the neuropsychological report. Mrs. Wolverton also provided a list of her and her husband's concerns with Jman's transition to the high school. After an extensive 35-day delay due to a "technical computer problem," the parents eventually received the school's proposed IEP. It did not include any reference to or apparent understanding of the neuropsychological report's recommendations about Jman's social/emotional needs. It also excluded, for example, IEP goals to improve his reading skills.

This was completely unsatisfactory to Mr. and Mrs. Wolverton, who then hired an advocate to assist them in representing what they wanted for Jman. Two interesting notes should be made here: first, the advocate, as was later learned by the parent, was perceived as antagonistic by the school. Mrs. Wolverton had a "good" relationship with the school, so she decided to continue using the advocate's services only outside of the school meetings. Second, Mrs. Wolverton stated that the school operated in an environment of "Okay, you tell us what you need and we will consider getting it." Knowing this and the weak credibility of the advocate, Mrs. Wolverton returned to the neuropsychologist, who recommended that the Wolvertons work with an AT specialist and an educational consultant. In essence, Mr. and Mrs. Wolverton were returning to the first step and obtaining information to answer the question "What do we know?" Or, perhaps in this case, "What else should we know?" or "What don't we know?"

The consultant analyzed all available paperwork, school work, and test results (actually noting computational errors in the administration of the school conducted assessment and noting the effects on the results), and, in addition to providing a report of her findings, assisted the team in writing (i.e., wrote) IEP goals and objectives for Jman.

As Mrs. Wolverton put it, the AT specialist "rocked." It became apparent that the school was limited in their understanding of the area of AT, and the AT specialist became an asset, assisting staff by answering questions about other students in addition to Jman. She was to observe Jman across various school settings at the beginning of his high school freshman year to collect information in order to answer the question "What do we know about Jman's needs?" and to determine what AT services would be needed ("How will we get there?") in order to achieve his IEP goals and objectives ("Where do we want to go?"). An IEP meeting at the high school was to take place after the completion of the evaluation, and the IEP was amended accordingly.

Key Points

- It is worth noting that, as with all parents who submitted scenarios, there were exchanges of emails and phone conversations—and with these interactions a lot of unwritten emotions, struggles, and successes were conveyed. This scenario, as the reader can see, took place over a long period of time. Sometimes this is the case. While the parents could have "charged" ahead with an attorney, they elected to find ways to work with the school instead. They took the lead when it was necessary and provided IEE providers (experts in their fields), who also knew how to work with school staff. The experts understood the need to show, not just tell, the school team Jman's needs (conducting numerous assessments and providing written reports); the experts explained to the IEP team how to implement solutions (via reports and onsite presentations). They also consulted on how to write measurable IEP goals and benchmarks/objectives that addressed Jman's needs and service implementation.

- When a school team concludes that they do not understand a problem, or they have no suggestions when asked for ideas (as happened in this scenario), it means that evaluations conducted by experts outside of the school system are warranted. It also means that you have the responsibility to ask the district to pay for those services. The request and expectation of payment are most reasonable when the needs of the child have been identified but the school team is unsure of how to address them. It is appropriate when the team states that they are uncertain of the child's needs.

  This does not mean that you simply locate anyone to do just any sort of assessment. It means that you and the district agree on what information needs to be sought. You discuss the necessary credentials required of the individual and state clearly what you expect to be provided (i.e., a written report and its content, presentation in person or over the phone, recommendations, etc.).

  You and the school team make an agreement, together with their promise to make payment to the "vendor" through a contract. This process may take longer than if you pursued this on your own, but the value of waiting is that it saves you personal expenses.

- Achieving an IEP that met Jman's needs was successfully accomplished using the Structured Collaborative IEP Process, though it was not identified as such at the time. It was accomplished through collaboration—allowing those who could to lead, while seeking input from everyone to define Jman's needs, set goals to meet them, and determine the services and programming necessary to achieve the goals. Because the goals and benchmarks/objectives were written in measurable terms, the team could observe Jman's progress toward meeting the goals over time and readily report growth to the team and parents.

- Considering the samples provided, with respect to format, detail, and structure of the goals and benchmark/objectives, there is an important point that needs to be made. Although the items under the goals (in the examples) were described as "benchmarks/objectives," they were, in fact, objectives. Benchmarks would have indicated a time by which a particular behavior would have been achieved.

Suffice it to say, as objectives, there is sufficient detail in each, so that if staff from another school were to receive the IEP, they would have a very good idea of Jman's needs and the expectations to be met by the end of the term of the IEP. If you had a concern about present levels of education performance not being included, please note that there is a reference to baseline data, regarding present levels of academic achievement and functional performance (FLAAFP), which could be found elsewhere. These data simply were not included in this scenario. They were not forgotten; instead, they were included elsewhere in the IEP.

- The greatest key point is that this scenario represents an excellent example of how to carry out the Structured Collaborative IEP Process, even when faced with a school team that was reluctant to take the lead, which is one of the greatest values in this process. *You* are empowered to lead this process.

Summary

It is unnecessary to review each of the many steps and issues resolved in this section. What is important to note is that the Wolvertons spent a considerable amount of time obtaining information to answer the basic questions, "Where are we?" "Where do we want to go?" and "How will we get there?" The school team was literally led through the Structured Collaborative IEP Process by the parents (and supported by the consultants), in order for the school staff to understand Jman's needs and what services were required to meet those needs.

Additionally, the team needed assistance in writing the IEP, including measurable goals and objectives that would address all of Jman's needs—even those related to his social goals. What is extremely important to note is that Mr. and Mrs. Wolverton and their consultants were patient with the school team. To be otherwise would have led to conflict and a dysfunctional IEP team.

Mr. and Mrs. Wolverton clearly implemented the Structured Collaborative IEP Process, yet they thought their success was due only to their persistence. The persistence certainly helped, but success was really down to the Structured Collaborative IEP Process, with each step carried out in the correct order, while working *with* the team to accomplish the writing of the IEP *and* obtaining a supported "Yes!" from the school.

You, too, may find that your school team is somewhat lost about what to do or how to proceed—either by design or truly due to a lack of knowledge and experience. This scenario is an excellent example of how you can take the lead, while maintaining a collaborative atmosphere. Intuitively, Mr. and Mrs. Wolverton knew how to approach the school and not take "No" for an answer, in a way that enabled the entire team to develop the IEP that was focused on Jman's needs—and they did this together.

It is worth repeating: persistence means not giving up, because you are your child's greatest advocate. And, with all happy endings, we saw that Jman was on his way to advocating for himself!

A Parent Faces a District with the Wrong Concept of the Least Restrictive Environment for a Child with Autism

As you will see, this is another story where the school district felt that least restrictive environment (LRE) meant inclusion. Ariel's mother, Giselle, came to feel differently and experienced a great deal of resistance from her daughter's school district when she tried to focus the services on Ariel's needs. The school staff were so committed to their perception of LRE, however, that even after finally moving Ariel from the general education class, the district's director recommended just a few days later that the next year Ariel could return to the general education class to receive services similar to those that had failed her in the past. You will see how persistence was Giselle's forte. As you read this scenario, which is admittedly a bit longer than most, you will realize that had Giselle not been the strong advocate she'd become, then Ariel would have had another year without academic and social growth.

Part 1: A Parent's Long Road to Success

"We don't do feeding programs in grade school. That happens at the preschool level."

Although I had some concerns, it was not until Ariel was 16 months old that I approached my pediatrician with them. I was told it was too early to be too concerned about my daughter's development. I wasn't convinced of that, but I had no way to know otherwise, so I did not question the doctor's judgment. I was pregnant with

Ariel's brother, who was due soon, and troubled how Ariel might react to my being gone while I was at the hospital. Oddly enough, she never noticed my absence!

When her father brought Ariel to see me and meet her new brother, she was far too interested in the balloons that decorated the hospital room to pay attention to me. I described Ariel's behaviors to my family and friends. They all said, "Oh, she must just be jealous." But my husband and I thought she was too young to be jealous; we believed there must be something else wrong. Then, at Ariel's 18-month appointment, I asked the doctor to refer her to the county Early Intervention Program (EIP), where children are screened for possible learning difficulties. (The EIP was contracted by the county, but was not under the auspices of the public education system.) Unfortunately, her pediatrician repeated that Ariel was too young for us to be so concerned with her behaviors, or to be referred to the EIP. We should just wait and see.

By Ariel's second birthday, I noticed she wasn't interested in playing with other children at play groups. She wouldn't even play beside them. Instead, she would go off and chase the family dog or whatever pet the family hosting the play group might have. I brought this to the pediatrician's attention, but with the same reply: It was still too early to refer Ariel for an evaluation. But I knew better, and this time I went straight home and called the county EIP.

A representative came to my home to conduct an intake interview and a brief observation of Ariel, which resulted in a decision to conduct an evaluation. It started with a speech/language evaluation. I prepared a list of the exact words that Ariel used and gave it to the therapist. The therapist determined that Ariel's speech was delayed, and we began speech therapy. It was a nightmare! Ariel couldn't seem to pay attention to, or interact with, the therapist. Ariel was completely incapable of engaging and would totally ignore the therapist by looking away and moving her chair from the work area.

After about a month of this, the therapist thought Ariel should have an occupational therapy (OT) evaluation. She thought that OT services would help Ariel to attend to tasks, and that the evaluation would determine if there were any sensory issues.

The OT evaluation was fairly extensive and had even picked up on Ariel's toe-walking—something I'd never noticed. The occupational therapist also noted that Ariel had difficulty with crossing the midline as well as a variety of other issues. However, the therapist refused to work with Ariel, because she had never dealt with a child who had so many tantrums and crying fits. She suggested we seek the assistance of a play therapist. The "play therapist" was a social worker, but after seeing Ariel felt that she could do more good by supporting me than by playing with my daughter.

(Please understand that I had never raised the issue of autism at this stage of Ariel's development, neither had anyone else from the EIP. I was aware of autism, but I didn't really know much about it and I had not researched autism spectrum disorder to see if it might help me understand my child. Following each EIP evaluation, after noting that the term autism had not been raised by the professionals, I felt relief, because "we dodged that bullet." By that I meant she was not diagnosed with autism.)

I became involved with an online group for children in EIPs. One night I posted that I really didn't understand why a "play therapist" was called in as a service, or what was going on. Another mother replied, "I'm not really saying your child has autism, but I'm telling you, you need to take her to get an evaluation. Because even if your child is on the spectrum of autism, the EIP will not say that she has autism." (This turned out to be one of several reasons why I later brought a lawsuit against the county.) I stayed up all night reading—and then I knew that my child was going to be diagnosed with autism.

The next morning—early in the morning—I called my service coordinator at the EIP and asked if it was true, that even if my child was suspected of being on the autism spectrum she would not tell me so. She replied, "Yes, that's true." I asked, "Would you say anything to me at any point?" She said, "Oh, if after eight months she's not making any progress, we might tell you, off the record, that maybe you should have her evaluated." When I asked why, she said, to the best of my recollection, that it was a scheduling issue. But it turned out that it was a staffing and program issue, not a scheduling problem. If my daughter were diagnosed with autism, then they would be required to make a psychologist available as part of their staff, but they didn't have a psychologist on staff.

I immediately started trying to get an appointment with a developmental pediatrician, but I quickly learned that the waiting lists were at least six months long. I knew that we needed a diagnosis to get Ariel appropriate services, and we couldn't wait. Ariel couldn't wait.

Finally, I was able to get an appointment with a neurologist. We were to see the neurologist on December 26, 2006, when Ariel was just under two and a half years old. Making the appointment, I explained to the woman on the phone exactly what the problems were, but when I got there the neurologist said he didn't deal with behaviors, which was extremely disappointing. He did, however, recommend someone else who could see her—a pediatric psychiatrist who worked at the local hospital.

[The reader should note that these assessments were paid for by the family. They were not funded by the EIP or by the county, neither were these expenses made an issue during the lawsuit.]

On January 16, 2007, the psychiatrist diagnosed Ariel with autism and recommended she receive Applied Behavior Analysis (ABA) therapy. So, at age two and a half, the battle to get Ariel appropriate services began, starting with the county.

The state of New York recommended 20 hours of ABA in its "best practices" booklet on serving children with autism in EIPs. I could only get eight of the ten hours of services that were already written into our Individual Family Services Plan (IFSP). [The IFSP is developed to provide the family with services that would benefit both the child and family as necessary. It is different from an Individualized Education Program (IEP) in that the Individualized Education Program is developed to deliver services specifically addressing the child's needs.] Although we were told that we had the "best" ABA person in the county, the therapist continued to tell me, "More is not better."

The team leader at the IFSP meeting was also the owner of the program (it was a private program contracted to provide services by the county), and was always too busy, never getting things done on time. I met her for the first time when she came to my house to meet my daughter and me and to explain the program. The service team would consist of the ABA therapist, a speech-language pathologist, an occupational therapist, and a social worker. We were to have monthly meetings that would begin shortly after we started to receive services.

After reading books all night for weeks straight, I realized my daughter's ABA program was a farce. I think the first time I had an inkling that something was wrong was when the ABA therapist came to the house and immediately tried to extinguish some of Ariel's behaviors, without having spent any time getting to know her—much less, without having yet observed her.

She had me observe what she was doing with Ariel, and then asked me to take over. I had no idea what was going on! And then I knew nothing about "extinction," so I let what was happening, happen. All that resulted from this "work" was that Ariel screamed for two hours.

I looked more closely through their program booklet after that. I realized it was all "smoke and mirrors." They were just re-teaching her things she could already do! If they introduced something new—something that they had a difficult time teaching her—then, that part of the program was scrapped.

I sat down with the ABA "expert" and questioned her on what she meant by "More is not better." Her explanation was not at all satisfying, and I felt that it simply meant that they did not have the staff to provide enough services. At the end of the conversation, I fired her and brought in a team from another county. (The county EIP allowed us to determine whether to continue with a particular service provider or not.) It was the right decision, but the part that infuriated me most was that I was continually told that the original expert was the best ABA coach there was.

I continued to fight the county to get my daughter the hours and services she needed. I also tried to get a list of other early intervention providers in the county, but they would not make that available. My husband had to use the Freedom of Information Act (FOIA)—a piece of legislation that forces public organizations to provide/release public information following a written request—to get what I was entitled to. I used it to contact other service providers. I was extremely dissatisfied with the county program.

[When asked how Giselle had acquired all this information, she said, "I learned as I went along, and thank God for the Internet! In my previous career I had to problem-solve, and 'No' was not an option, and getting something from one place to another had to be accomplished. You could not say, 'No, it cannot be done.' I learned to do! I learned to research and figure things out and problem-solve."]

I took it upon myself and learned about what Board Certified Behavior Analysts (BCBAs) do, as I did with the IFSP policies and procedures. I needed to know what was taking place in the program. I would observe sessions on a closed-circuit camera, and I saw that the therapist would write her notes indicating something different from what I observed in those sessions—more red flags.

The team leader ended up being a "Floortime person." [Floortime play therapy uses interactions and relationships to reach children with autism. It is also known as the Developmental, Individual-difference, Relationship-based model—or DIR/Floortime, for short. Floortime is based on the theory that autism is caused by problems with brain processing that affect a child's relationships and senses, among other things.]

Although the person assigned to floor therapy was not yet fully certified, she worked with others on the team who were. Ariel did not do well with the ABA program, but did much better with the Floortime therapist. She started to open up and blossom during her Floortime sessions. We saw Ariel begin noticing and interacting with other people. There had been a baby brother in the house for more than a year whom she never looked at, and, suddenly, she was looking at him! We did a lot of videotaping of her and her brother, and Ariel suddenly discovered she was a "girl." And the Floortime therapist really brought out the "girly-girl" in her. The therapist learned what appealed to Ariel and, using those interests, was able to increase her interaction with others.

(At about the time Ariel was ready to transition to preschool, I joined a group of parents in a class-action federal lawsuit against our county EIP—something I mentioned earlier. The county filed a motion to have the suit dropped, but the federal judge ruled in our favor because the county was so far out of compliance with the national disabilities education law. As a result, some changes came about in the county. Sadly, many parents dropped out of the suit because they were afraid of retaliations and of what might happen to services for their children. We had already gotten what we needed, but I did not want to see another family go through what we had. I did not want to see a less knowledgeable/resourceful family, or a family with English as their second language, not get appropriate services for their child simply because they did not know how or what to ask for.)

As I picked the second team of service providers from around the county, I was thinking ahead to the preschool program and wanted to make sure that the team I picked was going to be able to provide preschool services. (Preschool services, which begin when a child exits the EIP at age three, is a program that falls under the responsibility of the public school education system.) Ariel had tested socially/emotionally as a child of six months. My intuition was not to send a child functioning as a six-month-old outside of the home all day—the public school program format. When I raised this with the team leader, I was shocked when she agreed with me.

Because we were transitioning into a three-year-olds program, the team that I had selected would now come under the direction of the public school system—that is, if the school system agreed to continue with the existing program. Before we had our first Committee for Preschool Special Education (CPSE) meeting—another term used for an IEP meeting—with the public school system and the EIP team, I met with the chairperson of the public school system. I brought Ariel with me.

I wanted the public school chairperson to see my daughter in all her "glory." I wanted Ariel to be more than just a list of needs on a piece of paper at this big meeting. I think parents should routinely do this, and, as it turned out, the school system agreed that Ariel should be served at home, continuing with the existing program, and that it would pay for the services to be provided.

I had also checked with the other programs in the school system to see what was available for Ariel, but I wasn't happy with any that I saw. I knew why: I knew what Ariel needed and what was working.

I was even able to get the CPSE chairperson to agree to increase speech services from three days a week to five, as Ariel's speech was not progressing, and to expand on opportunities for social interaction by having Ariel attend a typical preschool for two and a half hours, two times a week. I offered to drive (a half-hour each way) in order to get OT services before going to school, so that she would be "regulated." (Ariel received therapy to aid her ability to focus and to attend to a task.)

That meeting was a turning point in my life. I knew what I wanted and had developed a game plan, but I'd always been a really quiet person. I hadn't even planned on speaking at that meeting, but instead planned to have my husband do all the talking. The meeting started, and I just started talking about what Ariel needed and who she really was—my husband never spoke a word. When we left the meeting, he complimented me for the way I handled myself and how I had put Ariel's needs first to the group. He said, "Wow! You really blew me away in there. You sounded like a doctor!"

Besides having introduced the chairperson to Ariel, I had the data to show that she was socially and emotionally at the six- to eight-month-old level, and I explained, as a mother, that I did not want her going out into a full-time program and why. I pointed out that we were having a meeting in the spring, that she had not been diagnosed for that long a time, and that we had not been doing the home program long enough to make any significant changes. Because of that, I felt that continuation of the home program was necessary. Ariel's whole team (Floortime teacher, speech therapist, occupational therapist, and social worker) was at the meeting. They gave examples of the kinds of behaviors I was talking about, and were able to explain her social and language behaviors and needs.

My daughter thrived that year, with the help of a great team that met her needs. Ariel was not yet speaking or interacting with the other children she had begun tolerating being around—those at the preschool (a non-special education program). (Although I paid for this, I really hadn't given much thought to who should pay.)

Ariel had also started taking swimming lessons, and her classroom teacher had asked the students to draw a picture of something that they liked to do. She gave the teacher a piece of paper that was all blue and said "swimming" (written in her own spelling). She was beginning to make connections outside of home, understanding her world, and communicating in her own way. It still brings tears to my eyes to have been there for that experience.

Several legislators were holding town hall meetings about autism. After the presentation ended, I was approached by the director of a school for autism in another county and invited to go to visit the school, which I did. That school had a very long waiting list, but my daughter was accepted because they wanted to have students with parents who were committed to following through. (I also had a list of the words Ariel knew and other information that provided concrete data. I took that with me, and that went a long way toward having Ariel accepted at the program.)

She spent two amazing years at this school. She began speaking, became toilet-trained, and started learning some academics. My daughter's whole person was being educated including and beyond her IEP. Her classroom was set up in the Training and Education of Autistic and Related Communication Handicapped Children (TEACCH) style (a holistic program out of North Carolina that addresses the child and family). They used Verbal Behavior Analysis (VBA) based on ABA to do one-on-one teaching. Extended school year (ESY)—services and programming provided during the time when the traditional school is not in session—was based on Ariel's needs and her IEP. She was really showing an interest in other children and at the end of kindergarten (the second year at this school), the team felt she was ready to return to the district. (I forgot to mention that the school system had agreed to this program.)

I think one of the other things that helped gain approval by the school district was that I had come prepared for the IEP meeting. I visited the special school and asked a number of questions, as I had done with all other programs. I discovered that other schools relied on an aide to provide the ABA, and that it was hard to keep them on staff because they could make more money at any fast-food restaurant. I would advise you to research other programs before approaching the school district, as I did. It will make your presentation so much stronger to be able to compare one program to another.

For example, several schools did not have an ABA program. In fact, one of the schools I looked at was providing services by the first EIP team I had earlier rejected as a service provider for Ariel. I was again ready with more information than even the school staff had.

Because we all felt that Ariel was ready, she was enrolled into the public school's first grade. Because of the experience I had had at the special school, I was expecting the same of her first grade. However, I learned that the teachers and related staff personnel worked only on what was listed in the IEP. I will explain more in the following paragraphs.

My daughter started first grade in September 2010 in a self-contained class with a six-to-one/two ratio. IEP reports were provided to parents three times a year, and, until I received the first progress report on her IEP goals, I was told by staff that she was doing "great." However, when I went to the school for the first parent-teacher conference and I was handed Ariel's report card, I was completely shocked to see how poorly she was doing academically. I was appalled to see that her "reading level" was below state standards as were her "applied learned phonics skills." Then I was told to ignore the report card and only to focus on her IEP. Honestly, as I thought about it later, I had not seen growth at home that would have warranted their saying she was doing great. What was going on?

I called a Committee for Special Education (CSE) meeting in which I fought to get Ariel auditory processing assistance, a feeding program (she was down to eating only three foods), and one-on-one reading with the teacher.

I wanted auditory processing in the IEP, because I observed her watching a TV program where the character would say things and Ariel would repeat back what the character was saying. However, what she said was not what I heard. I told them at the meeting and they said, "Oh, yes, she does do that and we see it, too." An auditory processing goal was added to her IEP.

Ariel had a very limited diet and would get sick often and missed a lot of school. I would bring up her feeding issues to anyone and everyone who would listen to me. The head of speech pathology said, "Well, she doesn't look emaciated to me. Don't worry about it." And then she said, "We don't do feeding programs in grade school. That happens at the preschool level." I did not get the feeding program then, but at the annual review, I did. (I think what made the difference was that I was looking at other programs on my own and learned that you get a feeding program at the elementary, middle, and high school levels. They provided a feeding program with a BCBA that they hired for Ariel.) I also got her one-on-one reading assistance. I continued stressing how well she worked one-on-one at the other school and that she was a very visual child.

At that meeting, staff said she was doing great with her behaviors, being responsible (e.g., using materials responsibly), working cooperatively, working independently, following directions, and following classroom rules. But my concern was with her academics and this was the first time I had to face something called "state standards." The teacher again said, "I wished I didn't even have to give you this report card." She told me, "Just look at the IEP. Focus on the IEP. She's in special education, so don't worry about the report card." I realized, then, that the IEP needed to be improved in order to make the report cards better.

The school said that Ariel had made a year's growth in reading, but she had only made five months of progress in reading, according to the graph I made. (I had attended an advocacy course and was given the Fountas and Pinnell Benchmark Assessment System [BAS] chart,[1] which I used to measure her growth. It listed what skills should have been reached by a particular time [benchmarks] in the school year.) The school insisted that she had made a year's progress, meaning she was beginning to learn letter sounds.

Interestingly, as the school mentioned a weakness in social development, they tried to drop her counseling services from twice to once a week. Every single annual report from each of her therapists and her teachers mentioned problems with social interactions, and problems with language skills involving social interaction. I pointed that out and did not allow the service to be reduced.

What I learned from this annual review was that, instead of reviewing each of the goals and discussing progress on every one, the school provided a summary report of the school year. Goals, which were poorly stated, were not necessarily addressed in the reports. More time was spent discussing what services were to be provided and what they were to address. I was not given an IEP at the end of the meeting. I left, and then the goals were mailed to me. I was not consulted when they wrote the goals or when they wrote the rest of the IEP. Yes, I learned much from this first year's experience. I would not allow this to happen again!

Later I was faced with the ESY summer program. It was horrible! She received two and a half hours a day, four days per week, with programming that was not related to the IEP or Ariel's needs. Although Ariel had received ESY previously at the special school, program staff there would fight with the district to make

---

1 Fountas, I. and Pinnell, G.S. (2010) *The Benchmark Assessment System (BAS)*. Portsmouth, NH: Heinemann.

sure none of the services was dropped during the summer. (At that point, the district agreed.)

Neither the elementary school nor the county directly provided ESY services. Children with disabilities were sent to SECS (Special Education Cooperation Services) programs for the summer. SECS is a cooperative program shared across several school districts and is contracted to provide specifically agreed-upon services for the school districts. The SECS program the school offered was basically babysitting. I learned later through a conversation with another mother that she was going to teach special education classes at the SECS ESY program. I asked what kind of classes she was going to teach, and she said a class of students with autism. I asked if she was a special education teacher, and she said, "No." I ended up giving her lots of tips on how to work with students with autism. I then let all the other parents know that this was the way the program was being run. Parents went to the district and complained about the program at SECS. The district decided to develop a program just for children identified with special education needs.

My daughter started second grade (September 2011) and was still reviewing previously known words at the end of October, while staff insisted that she had not regressed—but, obviously, she had. Ariel's reading was far behind her peers' and grade level, and she had difficulty with writing. Speech evaluations pointed to average speech abilities, but she had a huge expressive language problem and was not able to formulate concise narratives.

I wrote to the teacher and speech therapist and asked them to explain how a child's expressive delay would impact the ability to write. My common sense asked, "If she can't clearly formulate a sentence in her head, how can she write one?" I asked them to look at the homework, because the sentences Ariel was writing were so fractured, with some making no sense to me—but they did make my daughter laugh. The return note ignored my question totally, saying they thought that Ariel needed to work on punctuation. It seemed like the most bizarre response, and then I realized that they were referencing what her IEP goal stated for writing—punctuation. This caused me to examine all her speech evaluations with a fine-toothed comb, spending a full day researching them. I realized that the speech evaluations had not captured her obvious and easily observable problems noted on the standardized tests she had been given. In addition, IEP goals only addressed some of the testing results and not those observations made by other staff and included in their reports.

I had to figure out how to get an appropriate evaluation to show how the speech issues would lead to or cause problems with learning to read and write. I felt I needed to get Ariel evaluated for central auditory processing disorder (CAPD), as the issues she had a year before had not improved with the 15 minutes of the

Earobics™ programming per week that she had received. (Earobics™ is a program that assists in phonemic awareness, auditory processing, and phonics skills.[2])

When you first hear "central auditory processing disorder," you might think that it has to do with a hearing disorder, but actually it does not. It is when the brain doesn't process or understand what the ears hear. The school would have to pay for this evaluation, and I was searching for assessments to suggest to the speech pathologist. An audiologist, who was working out of a local cerebral palsy center in the county, would conduct this assessment.

Earobics™, I learned, is a remedial reading program. The school system used it for 15 minutes a week, but I went on the company's website and found that they also had a program for use by parents in addition to the school program. I was getting the runaround about getting the district to pay for that, so I considered just buying it myself; it only cost $60. The district's Information Technology (IT) department said they couldn't install Earobics™ on a parent's computer because of concerns with the computer having difficulties or crashing. I said I would sign a waiver, but they dropped the conversation without committing to or rejecting its purchase. I learned that the school uses the DIBELS (Dynamic Indicators of Basic Early Literacy Skills) program[3] to assess the Earobics™ program, but I didn't know if DIBELS actually measured what Earobics™ instructs.

The teacher was using the Orton-Gillingham program. (The Orton-Gillingham website states that it is a reading program that is phonetically based.[4]) I read about the program and found that the teacher wasn't really using it with Ariel. I realized that the way Ariel had to do her homework had nothing to do with the Orton-Gillingham program and she was so frustrated with her homework. I requested that the school change the way Ariel had to do her homework—to make it more interesting for her—and they agreed.

One task Ariel was asked to do was to create sentences using her sight words. From working with Ariel I realized that she did not know the meaning of the sight words. So, how could she possibly have written a sentence using them? She couldn't, and so she would write "sentences" that made no sense. Again, I asked the school staff if her expressive language problem was going to impact her writing. They agreed that it would, and now Ariel receives expressive language services.

By reviewing the assessments and the IEPs, I discovered that if a need was not found in the evaluation, then the need was not going to be addressed in the IEP. This made no sense, as there were a number of behaviors that Ariel exhibited in all classes. They needed to be addressed in her IEP!

---

2 Available at www.earobics.com, accessed on June 30, 2013.

3 Available at http://dibels.uoregon.edu, accessed on June 30, 2013.

4 Available at www.orton-gillingham.com, accessed on June 30, 2013.

There were also issues with her activities of daily living (ADL), but the school said they couldn't, for example, go to the bathroom with her. However, I knew there were other children with physical impairments in that school who had bathroom needs. The school said, "The law prohibits us from being in the bathroom." I thought that was an odd law.

I suggested that maybe Ariel needed a reading specialist. The school said that because she was in special education she wouldn't get a reading specialist or access to the remedial reading program (called the Academic Intervention Services [AIS]) used in the school. I said to them that the law doesn't prohibit her from getting a reading specialist, and the chairperson said, "Oh yeah, we know, we know. We just meant it's a school thing and we have to check with the school principal."

Another problem Ariel faced was that her class consisted of all boys. It had been a problem, because it was hard to find a social skills program or setting where there were girls to interact with. The speech therapist finally said one day, "I really feel bad for Ariel; she has no friends." So, they decided to move her into general education class settings for lunch, recess, and specials (i.e., music, art). In the meantime, I pushed for peer-to-peer programming and peer relations development in the school.

After receiving the IEP, I had to go back and listen to the recording that I had made of the IEP meeting, because I'd discovered that the list of things that we had agreed upon weren't all included in the IEP. I called another meeting to have the IEP corrected, sending a letter listing each issue. At that follow-up meeting, I went over each and every point in the letter. I went prepared.

At this meeting, where the IEP needed to be corrected, there was a long-term substitute standing in for Ariel's special education teacher, who said, "You know, I don't think she needs to be in this class [special homeroom class for students with disabilities] anymore. She could go to a regular homeroom class." This teacher had not succumbed to the school philosophy. I again asked if Ariel could have a reading specialist. The substitute teacher agreed that it would be the right thing to do.

(I know they used to have goals *and* objectives in her IEP, but by this time they just had goals, claiming that the regulations had been changed on what needed to be in an IEP. Quite frankly, the goals they included still were not measurable.)

But the school had placed Ariel in more typical classes for specials and morning meetings (much like a homeroom) and lunch. She loved that and responded well. And, although my daughter did fairly well during the school day and followed the classroom rules and routine, she did not generalize those skills in the community or at home.

Ariel was coming to a point in her life where she knew who she was and wanted to be like all the kids around her, and I wanted to see that happen. I felt that once I was able to "educate" the district about what my daughter needed, then they would address it, but they would not take the initiative to get to the root of a problem on their own. I wonder, was this a common practice? It drove me crazy!

Part 2: A Journey of Two Months

The following supplement captures some of the major activities that took place after the first segment of this scenario was written. It spans two months in second grade, February and March 2011. Ariel's mother explored in earnest several of the key questions with the school district. She also realized that she might need advocacy assistance, because she had reached a point where she was beginning to question whether she was right with what she was seeing, hearing, and doing for Ariel. Giselle was wondering if what she wanted for Ariel was what was best for Ariel. In the end, she adhered to what she believed and made the school accountable for their actions—in spite of advice given by both an advocate and lawyer, both of whom were not focusing on Ariel's needs, but, rather, their own preferences not to confront the district. So, instead of helping Giselle advocate for Ariel, they wanted to make compromises. Giselle did not accept the limitations presented in their advice, neither did she wish to compromise on Ariel's education; instead, she maintained her focus on Ariel and her needs.

I have condensed this portion of the scenario into a series of linear key points, to better enable you to follow the multitude of activities and interactions that took place between Ariel's mother and the various school staff. I have highlighted important actions that occurred within the timeline, including supportive examples or quotes from Giselle, her advocates/attorney, and the school staff.

February 12

Giselle met with school staff, taking a friend and advocate, so that there would be two extra sets of "ears" to hear what was said. Prior to the meeting, she had met with an attorney, who gave general advice and had previously said to return after the meeting that took place prior to February 12 and to be certain to take good notes. He felt that the district was committing gross errors and was out of compliance with the court order that came about because of his previous suit against the district, but he needed more information.

The key district contact called Giselle prior to the meeting to say that even though Giselle disagreed with Ariel's IEP and placement, the contact had been told by the regional special education administration that Ariel had to stay in the LRE—which was neither accurate nor true. She told Giselle that she "was told that Ariel could make it" and "was making it in the regular class." Giselle told the district coordinator that this did not make sense, that she did not agree with the IEP, and that the IEP, Ariel's program, and her placement needed to be changed.

Giselle returned to her collected medical and educational reports, evaluations, previous IEPs, teacher reports, email correspondences, and samples of Ariel's classwork. She wanted to be ready for the next IEP meeting, having all past and current information readily available for presentation and discussion. (You will notice that these steps prepared Giselle to address our first set of questions, "Where are we?" and "What do we know?") The following is from Giselle:

> The three-hour IEP meeting was like beating a dead horse. The general education teacher, who told me Ariel was misplaced and was not doing well in class, changed her position stating that Ariel was "accessing the curriculum and writing on her own, without the aide." I asked why the communication book was not being used, and learned that the general education teacher knew nothing about it and had not seen Ariel's IEP. The special education teacher said she was "in touch with the general education teacher," but I corrected her, reminding her of what she had said that contradicted that statement the previous week. The school was opposed to providing Ariel with a consultant teacher in her general education classes, because, according to the district administrator, "it would put too many people in the classroom." The school finally agreed to an internal evaluation of Ariel's reading skills and would meet with me in five weeks. They also said that a consultant teacher would be made available to Ariel "as needed."

Although Giselle had taken an advocate and a friend with her, she realized that the advocate was of no use, only interjecting with what had been done to meet her own child's needs regarding accommodations for spelling. Later, Giselle learned that the advocate had a strong relationship with the coordinator. Regardless, her friend was more helpful with the questions she asked. The advocate was released. Giselle also realized the school had failed to capture Ariel's skills accurately, and lacked the answers to the questions "Where are we?" and "What do we know?" despite Giselle's attempts to provide this information.

February 21

After having reviewed the most recent speech and language assessment, Giselle said, "I realized that the area of language had not been evaluated and yet communication is one of Ariel's greatest needs." She had also observed that Ariel's home behaviors were changing—she was becoming more defiant and appeared sad—the changes were impacting her at school, too. To Giselle, this was further evidence that the general education classroom was inappropriate. Giselle was prepared to ask the district to allow her to have IEEs conducted that included AT. When Giselle had previously asked the school to conduct an AT evaluation, she was told that AT "would make her go backwards" and decided not to conduct an AT evaluation, saying Ariel does not need AT.

Giselle was beginning to doubt her own decisions. Her friend had suggested that she not "press the district too far" and that she should be willing to accept some minor modifications. "I considered placing Ariel in a small private school, but knew that the defiant behaviors I was now seeing would prevent Ariel from being accepted," Giselle said. Instead, she decided to write to the coordinator and remind her that she had yet to receive a copy of the IEP. She also included the procedures for bringing a lawsuit to the district in that email, due to the many issues that had surfaced regarding the inappropriate placement and services that were negatively affecting Ariel's progress.

Giselle began regular correspondence with Ariel's teachers and shared her concerns about Ariel's behaviors and a number of other issues. She received polite emails from the teachers, but little changed in terms of Ariel's behaviors.

February 24

Giselle called another attorney, recommended by another parent, who initially found that the school was out of compliance, but also noted how difficult the school district's attorney could be. Pleased that the attorney spoke in a relaxed manner and made her feel better, Giselle returned home and gathered all the documentation that she had in preparation for meeting with the attorney.

In the interim, the school had sent a summary of the meeting which listed the changes that were discussed and those that were to be implemented. However, it was missing several points of agreement. Giselle emailed the coordinator with her concerns and again asked for a copy of Ariel's IEP. She also noted her concern with the consultant's time expressed in terms of "as needed" and wanted it to be specific with regard to the length of time and the number of times the teacher would be in the classroom. Yet again, the goals were not written in measurable terms and in her email, Giselle requested they be reworked and returned.

February 25

Ariel's teachers and Giselle continued to exchange emails, with Giselle initiating each communication. All correspondences, copies of IEPs, and assessments were sent to the attorney. Additionally, she received a letter from the school board, stating that they had approved Ariel's IEP. This was the IEP the district coordinator had referred to in her email to Giselle—the very one that Giselle was contesting.

February 27 and 28

Giselle received an email from the consultant teacher, who described her services as flexible ("as needed"), based on Ariel's needs, and that they could be "direct or indirect." The consultant thought that there should be at least one day per week that she met with Ariel, and had asked Ariel which day she would prefer. Giselle didn't agree, because, during the meeting, staff had agreed that the consultant was to provide direct services to Ariel, not consultant services. Giselle also felt it was inappropriate to ask Ariel—who had no concept of time—what day would be best to miss class to receive these services. With this information, Giselle realized that the consultant was going to remove Ariel from the regular classroom. That was not what had been discussed and not what Giselle wanted.

March 2

Giselle met with the attorney to whom she had sent her extensive collection of documents. The attorney told Giselle that she did not think that the district had done anything wrong, that Giselle should stop sending emails requesting a copy of the IEP, and that she should stop sending emails quoting federal regulations where Giselle felt the district were out of compliance. She should, in essence, stop challenging their decisions. (Giselle questioned the logic of these suggestions.)

Giselle also received an email from the coordinator, who said that if Giselle thought Ariel needed more support, they would move her into a co-teaching class. This was a classroom with both a general education and a special education teacher, who would instruct their students—children with and without disabilities—as a team.

At this point, Giselle was overwhelmed and totally discouraged by the attorney's thinking. She recognized that the district were neither collaborating nor following through on discussions and agreements. She was now considering moving to another district. Several days later, Giselle decided that the district was not going to scare her away from her home.

March 13

Giselle wrote an email to the district contact, outlining a number of issues that needed to be addressed, including the fact that she had not received a copy of Ariel's IEP. Her email was very detailed, asking for timelines for the completion of some activities while setting timelines for actions to be completed by the school.

Ariel's behaviors at the center where she was to be tested for an CAPD were totally non-compliant and the assessment could not be conducted. It was, however, recommended that Ariel have a different kind of CAPD assessment from the one used by the school. Giselle was also told that the school could help do this. Giselle was brought to tears, knowing how difficult it was to work with the school district.

The same day, Giselle received an email from Ariel's teacher, expressing how well Ariel was doing in class.

Giselle was now considering bringing court proceedings against the district.

March 16

Giselle volunteered to read to Ariel's class at school and her offer was welcomed. She was aware of the questions the children were asking and the attention that the students were giving her. However, when Ariel attempted to contribute, Giselle said, "Her language was so disordered and broken down that I could barely understand her. The class and teacher never responded, as they just sat looking blankly at her. It was very disheartening to me." Later, she learned from a friend who has a child in the same class that Ariel often spoke out; she was just as often redirected and was usually paired up with another child for almost all activities.

Giselle determined that there were too many discrepancies between the school's evaluation reports, the needs identified by the school, and the corresponding services Ariel was receiving to have the school conduct additional assessments. She decided that she would pursue having IEEs conducted by someone else, but paid for by the school district. So, Giselle called the center school Ariel had once attended to ask about the programming there and if the IEEs could be conducted at the center. They said they could and offered to act as paid consultants to the district. They also said they could place Ariel in a class with much higher functioning children with autism, if Giselle wished.

March 19: Regularly Scheduled Parent–Teacher Conference

Giselle reported that the substitute special education teacher (the one who was substituting for the teacher on maternity leave) "…is providing *miracles*," because she noted in her last email to Giselle "how far Ariel has come since the last goal report." Giselle attended a regularly scheduled parent-teacher conference as part of the school's regularly scheduled activities. The meeting was tense. The general education teacher explained Ariel's morning activities to her, where she would put her materials away, and how Ariel "does not follow morning routines and throws her stuff on the floor." The teacher would then ask Ariel why she threw her "stuff" on the floor. Ariel did not know, and the teacher said that she would "tell her to pick up her stuff." Giselle noted that there was no effort to teach Ariel to do this routinely, neither was any sort of reinforcement used.

The rest of the meeting was about what Ariel could not do, how she complained when asked to read or write, but that the teacher would ask her to try and she did— all by herself. At the end of the day, the general education teacher would tell the whole class to go to the homework baskets and pick up their work and she would tell the aide—who was assigned to work with Ariel, but "not to help" Ariel—that she had to get her own work. But when it was time to pack up materials to go home, she then had the aide assist Ariel.

Giselle said that "the majority of the meeting was a listing of what else the other children are asked to do that Ariel cannot, and…it became clear that there were few accommodation or modifications provided to her. It is no wonder Ariel was not happy with school!" The IEP meeting was not scheduled until March 23, and as Giselle recalls, "So, I mostly listened and could not believe what the school staff were now saying. They were contradicting their own earlier reports, what they had previously said across all areas of Ariel's IEP and program. And, not surprisingly, they were placing blame on the substitute teacher."

March 23: The IEP Meeting

Giselle's friend, who had attended previous meetings, was unable to attend this meeting; however, Ariel's Medicaid service coordinator joined her. (The coordinator represented a federal program established to provide medical services to children with disabilities who met an extensive set of conditions, requiring both the child and the family to be able to demonstrate significant needs.) Giselle started by asking for a copy of the IEP, and was told that it has been mailed to her home (they did this the day before the meeting). Giselle said she would wait for them to find and provide a copy for her before they continued the IEP meeting. They did so.

The IEP team concluded that Ariel continued to qualify as a child with autism and remained in need of special education services. The speech and language therapist led the first area of discussion, but she referenced the wrong area of Ariel's needs, recommending the use of graphic organizers. Giselle "…pointed out that graphic organizers were insufficient, because Ariel still had to get her thoughts out of her head and into boxes using writing, which she cannot do. I showed them an example of a graphic organizer that I found on the Internet that could be made using photos. I brought an example that I made for Ariel, using photos that I took with us when we visited the planetarium recently." Giselle felt that "it went over their heads."

The rate of Ariel's speech and its unintelligibility were also addressed, and Giselle argued that they should make an effort in all of her classes to work to slow Ariel down, so that she could be understood. And if they refused to do that, then it was an example of why the general education classroom was inappropriate. Furthermore, the requirement should actually be written in the IEP, so that, as Giselle said, it "had to be addressed." Giselle also pointed out that Ariel's speech was regressing, even though they had "insisted by being in a class with typical peers her speech would improve." But it had not. "In fact, it had gotten worse."

The team began saying how well Ariel was doing and the kind of progress she was making, but Giselle "confronted them and questioned [how they could come to those conclusions] a lot." Giselle had videotaped Ariel attempting to phonetically decode the word "transformation," and asked if they wanted to watch it. She noted to the team that "this was one of the words that Ariel was sent home to learn from her list of words that I was to work with her on." They declined the offer, and Giselle asked how that word "was selected as something Ariel should be able to decode." No answer was provided.

Giselle took the opportunity to explain to the team how decoding training for Ariel should be carried out and continued without interruption. She explained that it was clear to her "…that Ariel could not identify the difference between a short and long vowel, and that they were incorrect to expect her to be applying higher levels of phonetic skills when she has not mastered even the lowest." She added that "Ariel has processing difficulties, yet those were being ignored." Finally, one of the teachers admitted that Ariel only knew about half of the letter sounds.

When the general education teacher was due to make her presentation, the school called the school psychologist on the phone to participate. Giselle described how "the teacher nervously explained that if Ariel was interested in continuing a project/activity that the class was to cease work on, she would let Ariel continue." Giselle pointed out that she "appreciated that the teacher would allow Ariel to feel successful and that I hoped my son would have her as his teacher next year." However, she also pointed out that the teacher "was actually doing a disservice to Ariel, because Ariel needs clear and consistent boundaries and limitations." Giselle again stated that Ariel's classroom, the general education setting, was the wrong placement for her.

Giselle requested that Ariel be placed in a self-contained classroom, stating the reasons just presented, as well as others. The reply was that the make-up of that classroom had changed since Ariel was moved from there, and that Giselle should consider a co-taught classroom. Giselle said, "I refused, because Ariel is already stressed out, and shame on them for suggesting it."

The Medicaid coordinator raised the point that the report cards were not accurately reflecting what Ariel could do, and "told the team that they had not been truthful to them." The result was a bit of "ugliness," with the district coordinator eventually saying "We need to move forward and fix whatever it is that has gone wrong." With that, Giselle provided her with her written request for the various IEEs, including speech and language and AT. The coordinator "agreed without looking at the letter." Although the meeting might have ended with the Medicaid coordinator's comment as the last straw, Giselle recognized that "those things all needed to be said."

Giselle said that the school team then tried to "fix" current issues, but she said, "Stop! We cannot build a program around a bad placement." She had to repeat her statement several times before adding that the school did not have a proper placement at this time. Giselle added, "I think I made my point when I told them how I was walking on clouds for days when Ariel was moved into the general education classroom and I have been a wreck since, because of Ariel's regressing. I started crying and said, 'Don't you think I wanted to be the parent with a child that is indistinguishable from her peers? Do you have any idea how horrible this has been?'"

The social worker had to leave, but commented that "this had become a big mess and that she had hoped it would be resolved soon." This was totally the opposite of her previous comments and behaviors where she "seemed so disconnected from Ariel and had suggested that counseling services for Ariel be ended in spite of her increased behavioral changes."

After the meeting, the coordinator said "it was a building-level problem that they never wanted to see happen again, and that they saw Ariel as a child with a lot of strengths and potential."

Giselle had to wait and see if anything changed, but, at that point, she had used the data she had—the school's own information—and made the IEP meeting about Ariel's needs. She had also made it clear that without additional assessments and a review of those results, the team could not develop an appropriate program for Ariel. As Giselle put it, "I still do not trust them any further than I can throw them, but it is a start."

Closer to Success

A number of things took place following this last IEP meeting. The school system finally agreed to move Ariel back to the self-contained class she'd been at during the beginning of the school year. The teacher of that classroom had returned from leave and was happy to have Ariel return. Ariel was happy, too.

When Giselle received the preliminary findings from the clinic's language evaluation, stating that Ariel had severe receptive and expressive language deficits, she immediately shared this information with the district coordinator, who agreed that Ariel would receive additional speech and language therapy. Once the evaluations required to be completed by the independent educational evaluators were concluded, Giselle planned on having a representative from the center attend the IEP meeting to share the results with the school staff. She would make sure these results were used as the basis for rewriting Ariel's IEP, to ensure that the program and services would meet Ariel's needs and that staff who worked with Ariel would implement the IEP consistently.

After the IEP was concluded, Giselle was contacted by the same attorney who had led the original lawsuit against the district, saying that he had contacted the school district's attorney to discuss Giselle's experiences and dissatisfaction with the school for ignoring Ariel's needs. Though this conversation was not the singular reason that the district had become more cooperative, it certainly helped. More importantly, the district and school staff had realized from the previous IEP meeting that Giselle was gathering data she could use to prove the inappropriateness of Ariel's program, services, and placement in the general education class, even before the attorney called. This may also be why the district agreed to pay for the IEEs, to be conducted by the assessment team of Giselle's choice, before the conversations with the attorney had taken place.

So, the discussion between the attorneys was just the final touch. Giselle had already done the real heavy-lifting, because she had put the school staff on notice that these issues existed within the district and that she would not tolerate their damaging effects on her daughter's education. There's reason to hope that the example Giselle has set will result in some positive, district-wide changes that will ensure that staff "never [have] to see [this sort of thing] happen again, and that they [see other children as having] a lot of strengths and potential."

Analysis 1: From EIP to the End of Kindergarten

As you'll recall, this scenario is broken up into two parts. Part 1 is told in a style similar to many of the other scenarios in this book, and through Giselle's story we learn a lot about Ariel and the long road Giselle was forced to travel to provide her daughter with appropriate services. We also get a glimpse of the difficulties still to come as we see the repeated resistance to Giselle's choice to focus on Ariel's needs. We know now that Giselle eventually succeeds, but at the close of Part 1 we are less than satisfied with the results of Giselle's hard work.

In the first portion of this scenario, we get to see how Giselle was able to achieve the "Yes" Ariel deserved, by working with different programs and staffs until she found one that worked, whereas in the second portion of this scenario, Giselle is forced to deal with similar destructive attitudes expressed in very different ways. Due to these differences, my analysis will be divided into two parts. Part 1 will focus on everything up to the end of Ariel's kindergarten year. Part 2 will include the interactions and activities that shaped Ariel's first and second grades.

Under the first section of the scenario, Giselle effectively applied the first four questions of the Structured Collaborative IEP Process. This, of course, was after she faced several major challenges in her efforts to have Ariel's problems recognized by various professionals. We cannot be sure how much of the difficulty Giselle had when trying to convince the professionals that she saw a real problem was due to the manner in which she explained Ariel's behaviors, and how much was due to the professionals' lack of knowledge and experience with regard to the behaviors of a child with autism—particularly a *girl* with autism.

Certainly, Giselle is to be credited with her persistence in wanting to understand what Ariel's behaviors represented in terms of a diagnosis. She "knew" that there was something unusual with Ariel's development, but at that time had less knowledge of autism than the professionals she approached. This was true until she began receiving services from the county EIP that served children from birth to three years of age.

What Do We Know?

Giselle provided us with a great deal of information that she had documented since the time Ariel was two years old. We know that Ariel has a severe language deficit and that, in the most general of terms, her social skills are significantly underdeveloped. We also know Ariel's environmental and social surroundings are of little importance to her. She has many classic symptoms of a child with autism, and you, the reader, may think that it is so obvious. Why didn't Ariel's pediatrician recognize these behaviors—or, at least, agree they might be worthy of further investigation?

First, you are more likely, as a reader of this book, to be acutely aware of and attuned to the behaviors of children with disabilities, because you are likely to have experienced some of these behaviors yourself. Second, pediatricians are faced with "new" parents who have many questions and concerns that to them, the pediatricians, seem routine. Typically, an issue or question posed by parents does not warrant further investigation. Many doctors respond by dismissing the concern as insignificant, even though it is important to the parent. So, it becomes the parents' responsibility to present their concerns in behavioral terms, so that the professional can (in a very few moments) visualize what the parents see routinely. And that's what is required just to get the attention of the physician or other professional! A diagnosis, or even a referral, may require even more effort on the part of the parents.

If you will recall from an earlier scenario, Brint's parents videotaped him using the DynaVox®, and, because they did so, staff who watched the video could readily see his behaviors and could better understand the benefits of the AT device. Parents could easily do the same, by using the video capabilities found in so many cell phones, to show doctors and other professionals the behaviors that concern them. Lacking that, the words used to describe the behavior(s)—explaining when and where the behavior occurs, as well as how often it occurs or how long it continues—go a long way in enabling the professional to "see" what you see, and increase the likelihood that you'll receive a referral to a specialist for an evaluation. Just be sure to give the doctor salient details. After all, if you suspected you needed to have your appendix removed, you wouldn't just say, "I hurt." You've got to be specific.

In this case, even with persistence, it took Giselle a significant amount of time before she finally received a medical referral to assess Ariel's condition. In the interim, Giselle decided to take Ariel to the county EIP for assistance and perhaps a diagnosis. To prepare for the home visit by the EIP representative, Giselle had compiled a list of words that Ariel used to help the representative understand Giselle's concerns. This list, along with her observations of Ariel's behaviors, should have enabled the representative to provide the appropriate staff to conduct the necessary assessments to "diagnose" what Ariel's behaviors represented.

Where Are We?
What Do We Know?
Where Do We Want to Go?
How Will We Get There?
How Do We Know That We Are Getting There?

Following the evaluation conducted by the speech-language pathologist (SLP), the EIP staff determined that Ariel qualified for speech and language services. So, a preliminary direction was determined. However, following a month of failed attempts to provide those services due to Ariel's inability to pay attention to the therapist, the SLP suggested she be evaluated by an occupational therapist to:

1. investigate possible therapy to increase Ariel's ability to attend to tasks

2. determine if a sensory issue might be part of Ariel's problems with focusing.

The occupational therapist had a great deal of difficulty assessing Ariel. She suggested that Ariel might benefit from a play therapist, who turned out to be a social worker whose skills were better suited to providing parental support than play therapy for Ariel. The entire process resulted in Giselle's learning that the EIP was unable to conduct an assessment of Ariel's needs, much less provide services that would be of benefit to Ariel.

So, up to this point, although a general direction was set (to have Ariel evaluated for appropriate programming), those whose role it was to identify children with disabilities and provide applicable services could not do so. The program did not have staff who could work with children with, as we learned later, autism. Giselle realized that she still lacked sufficient information to know what the appropriate direction should be, so she returned to the task of obtaining a diagnosis in order to determine the appropriate programming for Ariel.

A short time later, Giselle returned to the EIP with a physician's diagnosis of autism, along with the recommendation of ABA and speech and language therapies. Another team—still under the direction of the EIP—was established to provide support to Giselle and therapies to Ariel, but Giselle was not finished learning. She soon realized that the programming provided was not appropriately implemented and "fired" the ABA therapist.

As you'll recall, around this time a class action lawsuit was brought against the county EIP due to their failure to comply with government regulations. Is it any wonder? Regardless of any national or local laws that the program failed to meet, the program was incapable of providing staff who were sufficiently competent to evaluate children with developmental delays, let alone diagnose the nature of those delays. If they could not perform these necessary actions, imagine how inadequate the services and programming they provided were with regard to meeting children's needs! Clearly, a systemic problem of this nature would not simply impact one child, but would affect all the children under their care. And so, a class action lawsuit—which doesn't serve to confront the unmet needs of a specific individual, but uses the experiences of specific individuals to address the unmet needs of a class or population of people—was brought against the county EIP. A lawsuit of this nature also empowers the individuals listed in the lawsuit to challenge the status quo, even before the courts reach their decision.

So, Giselle was able to fire the staff who had repeatedly failed to meet Ariel's needs. Though she struggled to locate a new team, she succeeded. She soon saw how the new team and different therapies began to change Ariel's behaviors and help her progress in the areas of language development and social awareness.

Keep in mind that Ariel had just begun receiving services from the county EIP in the spring, and that Giselle and the staff would soon need to develop an IEP for next year's programming—covering Ariel's first year in the three-to-five preschool program, which would be under the auspices of the public school system. Thinking ahead, Giselle built her team very carefully around the idea of continuing the existing services and program at home, instead of transitioning to the school's preschool program located in the school building. This proved to be a valuable victory for Giselle and an essential strategy for successfully meeting Ariel's needs.

Key Points

- Clearly, it is essential to be persistent when you find that a professional—in this case, several medical professionals—is not attending to your concerns. Like Giselle, if you are dissatisfied with the response or lack of a reasonable response by your medical professional, you have an obligation to seek someone else's opinion. Should you ultimately learn that nothing is wrong and there is no need to worry, having an assessment conducted to provide you with that level of comfort could well be worth the time and cost invested.

- Unfortunately, the only program that offered services was incapable of carrying out a proper assessment to identify Ariel's needs; and the staff were unable to answer the question, "What do we know?" As a result, all other questions could not be answered.

- Giselle did something that all parents, as well as program staff, should do: She evaluated how the program was being implemented and what effect it had on her child's educational progress. It is because Giselle sought to learn about ABA therapy and how it should be applied—and then secretly watched how her daughter's program was implemented—that she knew there was little integrity to the program. It is appropriate to ask why you are not seeing your child making progress. It is important to keep in mind that progress might not occur for any number of reasons. For example, the IEP team may have decided on the wrong program or incorrectly identified or stated the goal or benchmarks for the particular child's need. Don't first assume that it is due to the teacher's inability to instruct. This particular scenario was unique. It was an unusually bad situation that is not typical of educational programs.

- Fortunately, Giselle was persistent, which is what you have to be when using the Structured Collaborative IEP Process, because you or the team can fall prey to developing a program before you understand your child's needs ("What do we know?"). It is not unusual for a team to begin by discussing services and setting(s), which should be the final discussion and decision in the IEP process. Without asking each question in the order presented, you, too, could find yourself going in circles—putting, as they say, the cart before the horse—and left wondering why you are not making progress.

- Giselle continued to seek a professional evaluation to explain Ariel's behaviors. Because she did, she was able to obtain a medical diagnosis ("What do we know?"), which helped her to determine what Ariel needed in terms of services and programming ("Where are we going?" and "How will we get there?"). Furthermore, she had created a team of professionals who were able to carry out the program of services—effectively answering "How will we get there?" and "How do we know that we are getting there?"

- As you will see in the analysis of Part 2, Giselle applied all that she learned from these experiences and exercised the Structured Collaborative IEP Process—again, effectively. She needed to if Ariel were to have her needs identified and an IEP written that would meet them.

Analysis 2a: Early Interactions with Public School Staff

Analysis 2a covers Giselle's early interactions with the public school staff. In one instance, Giselle was able to carry over what she had learned with the second EIP team and apply it to Ariel's preschool program, which was overseen by the school district. However, once Ariel moved into first grade, Giselle found the school system to be far less cooperative and much less focused on discovering Ariel's needs or her present levels of performance. As you read earlier, Giselle had begun to wonder whether her decisions were right for Ariel. It could be said that pulling back to the Structured Collaborative IEP Process helped her retain a bit of sanity. It gave her a base from which to work, and helped guide her with the steps necessary to bring order back to the development of Ariel's IEP.

Let us look first at where Giselle takes the lead in transferring Ariel from the EIP to the preschool. Here she unknowingly used many steps from the Structured Collaborative IEP Process.

Where Are We?
What Do We Know?

Giselle began by making sure the preschool program staff knew just who Ariel was by taking Ariel with her to meet informally with the public school chairperson, who would lead the IEP team in developing Ariel's IEP. As part of answering "What do we know?" Ariel's presence helped the chairperson to "picture" some of the behaviors that could be anticipated once she began the program in the fall. (Giselle recommended that all parents do this. It is why, when appropriate, the student should also attend the IEP meeting.)

This, of course, is another approach to presenting parental concerns to a professional and will often help clarify those concerns, because the professional gets to observe the child's behaviors first-hand. It will also provide some of the answers to the question "What do we know?" for the staff who will be developing the IEP. Of course, there are times when it is not beneficial for the child to attend an IEP meeting. For example, it will not be appropriate to have the child attend when the conversation is likely to be above the child's level of comprehension. Neither will it be appropriate when the child's behaviors will only serve to disrupt the flow of the meeting. Like so much of special education, it depends on the individual child and the purpose of the meeting.

Giselle, knowing a number of Ariel's needs, also investigated other "neighboring" programs to compare what services were provided and to determine if there were viable options beyond Ariel's continued receipt of programming at home. None provided all the services that Ariel was currently receiving.

Giselle's rationale for remaining in the home program was quite sensible, given the short time since Ariel had been identified as having autism and had begun receiving appropriate EIP services. She correctly pointed out that there were little data yet available to warrant a change in placement. In fact, changing the setting for service (from home to a preschool setting) at that point was not warranted, based on the information that was available at the time the IEP was written.

This brings us to an important point: When there is insufficient information (data) to make a change in programming or placement, don't make one—the rationale is simply not there. Furthermore, when there is more that we *don't* know than that which we do know, it is not the time to make any modifications.

Where Do We Want to Go?
How Will We Get There?

Giselle shared what information she had with the IEP team, including what she had learned from her efforts to locate alternative programs. She had the foresight to bring the staff who were working with Ariel to the meeting, so they could answer any questions that might arise regarding the therapies provided, the manner of implementation, their observations of her behaviors, and the few measures of progress that were available. The public school preschool staff agreed that—given the evidence of Ariel's present levels of performance, the placement rationale, and recognizing that she would not be able to socialize well with other children—the home setting and continuance of present services would be written into the IEP. Both questions—"Where do we want to go?" (presumably, we want to improve Ariel's language and socializations skills) and "How will we get there?" (continuation of current services)—were answered at the IEP meeting.

How Do We Know That We Are Getting There?

Giselle reported that Ariel had a wonderful year at the preschool. Although she did not provide us with measurable or specific data, she noted that she observed Ariel's growth in the area of language, and that Ariel had become tolerant of other children in the typical preschool where there were children without disabilities.

Unfortunately, services in the typical preschool, where Ariel could interact with non-disabled peers, were something that Giselle had paid for. She had not requested payment for the services by the school nor their inclusion in the IEP—something I feel should have been discussed, offered, and provided as part of the placement-of-services decision. Some countries refer to this as inclusion, while others refer to it as the LRE. The point to be made is that *all* services found in a child's IEP do *not* have to be provided in the same setting. Therefore, some children might require and benefit from—as defined by their needs—receiving services that are provided in a self-contained setting. Other children might be provided with services in a setting that includes children without disabilities. Some children will need support, others will succeed independent of supports or accommodations, and some might benefit from a combination of settings—self-contained for some services and the traditional setting for others.

"How do we know that we are getting there?" could not be answered with the information provided, and the answer was not made available to Giselle. However, she learned the value of this question and the need for monitoring Ariel's program relatively soon after her daughter was transferred to first grade.

We saw that Giselle used an approach (a form of structured collaboration) similar to the one she unknowingly used in developing Ariel's preschool IEP when she met for the second and third years of preschool. This time, and for two full school years, Ariel was placed at a special school for children with autism, and it was paid for by the school system. Giselle reported that Ariel continued to grow in the areas of language and social development. We also learned that Giselle continued to seek more information and training in the areas of autism that included, for example, training on the use of VBA from a national leader in the field—something she paid for and attended independent of the school district.

Analysis 2b: Interactions with Public School Staff on Grades 1 and 2

Where Are We?

What Do We Know?

After two "successful" years in a school designed for children with autism—where Giselle was confident that Ariel's needs were being met—Ariel was placed in a self-contained kindergarten class, where she received services similar to those provided at the school for children with autism. This was a decision that Giselle and Ariel's school team felt was appropriate for Ariel, as she had made "so much progress" in the areas of language development and socialization.

Giselle received pleasant, supporting comments of Ariel's success in school, noting that "Ariel is doing great." But then Giselle attended a regularly scheduled parent-teacher conference that was provided to all parents at the school and saw Ariel's first report card. It did not correlate with the words "doing great." The teacher went to great efforts to explain that there was no relationship between the report card and Ariel's IEP, claiming that Giselle should ignore the report card and focus only on the IEP.

This was also the first time Giselle had heard about "standards" of education. These standards represent the skills selected for first grade; therefore, they are the skills that all first-graders are expected to achieve by the end of the school year. Giselle learned that Ariel was "significantly below [the] standards [of education]." And, for the first time, she reflected on Ariel's home behaviors (language and social skills development), realizing that she had not seen changes warranting her being told that Ariel was "doing great." Giselle, now monitoring Ariel's growth or lack thereof, called for a meeting to learn the answers to, "What do we know about Ariel's present levels of performance?" and "What do we know about her growth since entering first grade?"

Giselle had enough information just from the report card to ask for assistance in reading and to have the IEP include goals on auditory processing. She did this because she learned that the teacher agreed that Ariel appeared not to process teacher directions or commands and couldn't repeat back what she was told—she agreed to it, because Giselle raised the very same issue that she had observed at home. So, a need was identified and a related goal was established. This is the way it is meant to happen at IEP meetings! Thus, they answered "What do we know?" and then "Where are we going?" along with "How will we get there?" (the provision of services).

However, when Giselle raised concerns about Ariel's poor eating and the need for a "feeding program," she was told that it was not offered for children in first grade. Of course, this was not true, but it meant that the need was not met at the school, because the staff declined to provide it. Obviously, this is not the way it is meant to happen at an IEP meeting. What was missing was a discussion of whether the school observed this to be a problem area, which they may not have noticed. But to respond by saying that, in essence, "We don't do that here," was not a collaborative reply and lacked a behavioral rationale.

Giselle should have pursued this reply by politely asking for a written copy of the school's policy basis for their decision not to provide the feeding program. Never hesitate to ask for documentation of a policy with which you are unfamiliar, especially if it sounds in any way unlikely. It may or may not exist, but, in either case, you need to know and should feel comfortable asking. However, the feeding program was written into the IEP during the spring IEP meeting. Giselle attributed that to the school's learning that she'd found out that other schools did, in fact, have feeding program services in place—not because they recognized Ariel's needs. There was no policy as stated by the school team.

At the spring IEP meeting, she was again shown the discrepancy between Ariel's needs, her progress, and the information found on her report card. Once again, she was told to ignore the report card and to focus only on progress related to her IEP. Furthermore, the school had reported that Ariel had made a "year's growth" in the area of reading. Giselle contested that, showing on a graph she had made (using a system of measurement that she had been trained on earlier in the school year) that

Ariel had only made five months' growth. The school replied that Ariel had made a year's growth, referencing that she was now beginning to learn letter sounds, and that represented a year's growth in reading. One immediately has to question what program of assessment would reflect a year's growth in reading with the behavior of "beginning to learn letter sounds." At this point, Giselle could have appropriately requested a reading evaluation to be conducted, so that there was a standardized measure of her reading—clearly none existed.

This is the year that Giselle admits that she "learned about IEPs." She learned that the only things instructed were those that were specifically written into the IEP—even if other areas of concern were observed by staff. She also realized that the IEP goals were not written in a measurable format. She began to doubt if the school really understood Ariel's skill levels, and, because they actually didn't, it made it very difficult for them to answer the question "Where are we going?" much less "What do we know?" Again, it would have been quite reasonable to ask for a formal assessment of Ariel's skills. This is especially true as "beginning to learn letter sounds" was considered a year's growth without having or referring to a baseline (a beginning reading level at the time the IEP was written).

Giselle explained that the ESY program—an extension of the IEP services that are in effect for the period of time that schools are typically closed for summer—did not address Ariel's IEP or her needs. (All of these issues bring to light a systemic problem, extending beyond Ariel's IEP and the school. It is also at this point that Giselle and the author began conversing and where she first learned about the Structured Collaborative IEP Process, which she started using soon after we began our correspondence.)

During Ariel's second grade, Giselle became even more keenly aware that her daughter's reading and writing skills were uniformly behind grade level. In a note to the school staff, Giselle raised the issue, saying that the speech evaluation indicated that Ariel's speech abilities were average, but that she had difficulties in the area of expressive language. Giselle also asked whether this deficit would impact her ability to formulate thoughts (processing sounds, reading, and comprehension) and written expression (using her study words in complete sentences). Giselle received a reply stating that Ariel needed work on punctuation, but failing to address the issues she had raised.

This was another opportunity rightfully to request a full language assessment in order to ascertain what Ariel's skills actually were with respect to her receptive and expressive language and the effects on her reading and writing skills. If such an evaluation had occurred, the problem could have been identified along with how it impacted her learning—at least in the two areas noted and most likely others. This, in effect, is what is commonly done when attempting to define what disability a child might have and *its relation to learning*. It is the same as identifying a child's needs ("What do we know?") and their impact on learning ("What do we know?"), and writing goals ("Where are we going?") and objectives ("How will we get there?") in a measurable format ("How do we know that we are getting there?"), which will be worked on through the provision of various services ("How will we get there?") throughout the life of the IEP.

Instead, recognizing that the school was not responsive to her query, Giselle sought out a specialist to conduct an evaluation for a suspected CAPD. She again paid for a service that the school should have been responsible for. At this point, however, you can feel Giselle's frustration with the responses of the school and district staff, and you can easily understand why she simply did it herself.

Giselle continued evaluating Ariel's program, discovering that the Earobics™ program that the school was using for reading could be augmented with a home version. In spite of Giselle's willingness to have the program loaded onto her home computer, the school would not purchase the modestly priced home-program version, because the IT department said that they did not want the responsibility if something detrimental happened to her home computer because of its installation. Giselle offered to sign a waiver for any issues related to its installation, but the offer was ignored and she dropped the matter. What we do not know was whether the program was working and how the home version might have impacted what was being taught at school—which is what should have been investigated, but only after the effectiveness of the school program was determined. Again, we are talking about how we are going to get there before determining what we know—rather, we are talking about providing a service before we know what the need is or if the service would appropriately address the need.

Similarly, Giselle discovered that the Orton-Gillingham program, which is designed to increase reading fluency, was not being implemented with instructional integrity—that is, it was not implemented in the manner in which it was designed. Furthermore, she realized that homework assignments were (in addition to being incorrectly assigned) not of interest to Ariel. The likely reason for this was that Ariel was being asked to write sentences using sight words that she did not understand. As a result of these discoveries, Giselle requested a reading specialist to assist Ariel; she was turned down, because Ariel was "already in special education" and "did not need the services" of a reading specialist or assistance from the remedial reading program located at the elementary school.

The list of issues continues, but, ultimately, the school rejected all Giselle's requests, except to place Ariel in more regular classrooms to increase the opportunities to develop her social skills. As we know from Giselle's record-keeping, this only created additional problems, because the school also expected Ariel to work alongside non-disabled students with very few of the accommodations or modifications that may have enabled her to access the regular curriculum. The result was a very frustrated and upset second-grader who was unable to adjust to the classroom demands, and who received limited and questionable support from the classroom aide, as directed by the classroom teacher, who also held very low expectations for Ariel's success.

It is impossible to move to "Where do we want to go?" when so little is known that could answer "What do we know?" And, given the school's responses to reasonable requests, Giselle reached out to advocates and attorneys for assistance. If you find that, like Giselle, you're still not making progress with a school or school system—even after making reasonable personal efforts—then it is necessary to seek assistance. When you choose to do so will depend on your personal threshold for frustration. When you have reached an impasse, seeking an advocate or attorney to intercede on your behalf might be the only way to reassess where you are. The goal of a worthy advocate or attorney is not to take the school to court, or to "beat them up," but instead is to seek a way to reinstate a conversation that is collaborative in nature and focused on your child's needs. They can provide a sort of "rebooting" of your interactions with the school.

Unfortunately, Giselle's experiences with one advocate and one attorney were such that it became clear that their services did not fit her needs—in a word, they were ineffectual. Instead of addressing Ariel's needs, they were more concerned with their own needs and their concern over the difficulty of working with the school system. Fortunately, Giselle, although in the midst of questioning her decisions and wondering whether simply to move to another district, decided to remain and hold firm to her choices/decisions for Ariel. For Ariel's sake, it is good that she did.

You will see in the next section that Giselle learned more about the Structured Collaborative IEP Process taught in this book and was able to implement the process fully. She did this by holding the district accountable for making decisions based on information that she had obtained and that the educators had provided via emails, IEP meetings, parent-teacher meetings, and Ariel's work that was sent home. She began by providing the IEP team with some of the answers to the question "Where are we?"

Where Are We?

What Do We Know?

This time, Giselle was determined to apply what she had learned from past experiences and from our discussions about how to apply the Structured Collaborative IEP Process. And it was her persistence in applying many of the same steps she'd used previously that helped her to succeed.

It takes persistence to apply the Structured Collaborative IEP Process. You can easily get led astray because of a comment someone makes—or a comment someone doesn't make. You can end up listening to or providing irrelevant points of conversation at an IEP meeting that only serve to distract team members from answering a particular question.

It is also easy to jump to or be pushed to providing a service before the team has a sound understanding of your child's needs, obtained by answering the first question first. Anyone on the team can become defensive when an innocent question is asked—for example, "What evidence do you have supporting that last conclusion?" People are not, in general, asked to defend their statements, but—in the Structured Collaborative IEP Process—justification is required for all decisions. And that justification is based on the answers to the questions!

The team has to justify the answer to each question. You are a part of the team, and everyone attending the IEP meeting, including you, is expected to participate in answering each question. Sometimes, however, a question is asked and there is *no* information, too little information, or questionable information (e.g., too old, gathered using the wrong testing instrument) available to answer it. That is acceptable, because it then becomes the team's responsibility to obtain the information (or ask for help to obtain the information) necessary to arrive at the answer.

A number of correspondences between the school staff and Giselle were presented in Parts 2a and b of this scenario, showing how Giselle adhered to her points regarding the program's failure to result in Ariel's growth. If you have read the previous scenarios and analyses in this book, you are, by now, very familiar with the Structured Collaborative IEP Process, so comments will not be made on each email. Instead, the remainder of this section will summarize and highlight key points, covering how Giselle used the Structured Collaborative IEP Process to get the "Yes!" her daughter needed.

Giselle pointed to the inappropriateness and ineffectiveness of Ariel's placement in the traditional classroom: where, under the direction of the teacher, the aide offered very limited assistance to Ariel. She noted that the services that were agreed upon in the IEP were not in place, including the provision of assistance in reading and direct contact between Ariel and the consultant teacher, who elected to provide indirect services instead of direct services to Ariel.

Further, Giselle stated that the services from the consultant teacher were provided outside of the regular classroom; these were unmistakably segregated services and not inclusive instruction. This strengthened her rationale for disputing the appropriateness of Ariel's placement in the regular class. By her own observations in Ariel's class, Giselle saw the degree of assistance that Ariel needed during class time and during transitioning from one activity to another—when a peer was assigned to help Ariel move to each new task. And finally, when reading to Ariel's class, Giselle saw the degree of difficulty that Ariel experienced when attempting to tell her own mother something about the story just read. She used these observations, plus the recent report identifying Ariel's significant weaknesses in expressive and receptive language, as the basis for discussing the development of Ariel's IEP.

Using the data she had acquired—consisting mainly of observations and comments made by the school staff, plus the preliminary language report—Giselle "guided" the school into understanding Ariel's needs and partially answered the question "What do we know?" and then moved toward developing a preliminary plan to change Ariel's program and setting for services. That is, she used the information (data) to determine the answer to "Where are we going?" She would immediately receive reading support and a change of placement into the self-contained classroom. Just a few days later, the district director asked Giselle to consider the regular classroom placement for Ariel's third grade school year. Giselle stood firm, using the same rationale she used during the IEP to discuss Ariel's removal from the regular classroom and her placement in the self-contained program. The director agreed to Giselle's reasoning for Ariel's placement a short time later.

Giselle obtained a major "Yes!" from the school staff, yet she still felt that the school team and she did not have all the information necessary to know where Ariel was functioning in many areas, including AT. She asked and the school agreed to pay for IEEs to ascertain Ariel's skill levels. And so, we can only look at Ariel's last program and placement change as temporary, because the IEP program will continue to be incomplete until these new data become available.

We know that Giselle will bring the independent educational evaluation reports back to the school for review. We also know that she will be bringing at least one representative from the center, where the IEEs will be conducted, to be part of the IEP team that will then continue to answer the question "What do we know?" After sharing the evaluation findings, discussing them, and reaching agreement, the team will be able to answer the question "What do we know?" The IEP team can then confidently answer the question "Where do we want to go?" by developing goals for the IEP. "How will we get there?" will be answered by the team's determining the appropriate programming, modifications, accommodations, AT, related services, and placement for the delivery of Ariel's IEP, which will be based on her needs. "How do we know that we are getting there?" will answer "when" and "how much" of Ariel's progress on each goal will be evaluated and shared with Giselle, which will also be written as part of the IEP.

There are two more questions to be answered: "How do we know when we have arrived?" and "How do we keep what we have?" The team may modify the IEP whenever a goal is achieved, and could do so throughout the school year, but—minimally—these modifications should occur at the time of the annual review. Modifications can consist of writing new goals and/or objectives; however, it is *not* necessary to rewrite the IEP because a goal has been achieved. Good instruction would dictate that the teacher would simply move forward by either working on the next step in the learning process or amending the criteria to a higher level.

This time, however, Giselle will not be surprised with how Ariel is doing with her program and services when she reviews the IEP and Ariel's report cards. She will have regularly scheduled reports on Ariel's IEP progress. She will have made certain that all Ariel's needs are reflected in the IEP and that the setting(s) in which Ariel receives those services will benefit her.

We also know that Giselle is going to give the director and the school a chance to make sure nothing like this happens again. The best way to accomplish this very worthwhile goal is for them to follow Giselle's lead by using the Structured Collaborative IEP Process to develop an IEP for every child under their care that is based on the individual child's needs—not on the needs and habits of the school district or those of the school staff.

Key Points

- When teams work collaboratively, information is shared from all participants, and all IEP participants have a voice during the meeting. In Part 1, for the first three years, the IEP team relied on data (information or "What do we know?") that Giselle, the preschool program, or the special school for children with autism provided for programming decisions and the writing of Ariel's IEPs. No issues on the IEP content, the program, or Ariel's progress were presented. However, there was a significant change with respect to the interactions between Giselle and the elementary school. That is a summary, but the specifics of what Giselle did were in line with many of the steps of the Structured Collaborative IEP Process.

- Giselle and Ariel met with the IEP chair in advance of the scheduled IEP meeting to help the preschool chairperson understand Ariel better. By doing so, the chair literally saw the behaviors that Ariel presented, providing the chair with partial answers to the first and most important questions: "What do we know?" and "Where are we?" Giselle expanded on this approach by bringing her birth-to-three service team with her to the IEP meeting, resulting in the IEP team members having a deep understanding of Ariel's needs, programming, setting of services, and progress (which was limited, given the short time of services after receiving an accurate diagnosis).

- Due to this detailed presentation, answering the remaining questions was relatively easy for the IEP team, and they agreed with Giselle's proposal for Ariel's services to be provided in the home setting. This process continued for the full three-year preschool program. Questions one, two, and three were clearly answered.

- Unfortunately, Giselle did not ask the school to pay for time in the traditional preschool program that she felt was appropriate to enhance Ariel's socialization skills. This would have been a reasonable request and expectation, because weak socialization skills were recognized as one of Ariel's major difficulties. The preschool setting would have provided Ariel with the opportunity to become accustomed to other children and to begin to interact with them. This service would most definitely have fit into answering the question "How do we get there?"

- Giselle faced an entirely different situation with the elementary school staff and later the district director, who were unwilling to recognize that Ariel was not being successful—especially in the second grade. Even when data were presented to the school team, including their own data, Giselle faced a great deal of resistance to requests to change Ariel's program or placement. She received the dreaded "No."

- Giselle persistently pursued appropriate services and placement for Ariel, forcing the school and district staff to focus on how the existing data showed the program's failure to meet Ariel's needs. Eventual success was not only due to Giselle's personal persistence, but also the continual effort she made to use the Structured Collaborative IEP Process in spite of the many refusals she received from school personnel. (When I asked if knowing about the steps and questions of the Structured Collaborative IEP Process was helpful, Giselle said that, after she had been provided the information on structured collaboration, she did use it.)

- Giselle's consistency in application and the resulting outcomes are proof that the structured collaboration system can get the school to say "Yes!"

Persistence is Key

Persistence is essential for all parents of children with disabilities. When facing an uncooperative school district, this trait can be even more important. Regardless, a level of persistence is required even when working cooperatively with a school district. Asking and answering the questions posed by the Structured Collaborative IEP Process in the correct order can be difficult—even if you have practiced this method of conducting an IEP meeting. Persistently applying this method will enable you to ensure, for example, that the IEP team does not develop programs or services before you have discussed and agreed what your child needs. The list of questions is your guide. You should share them with the team and let them know that the first question must be answered before the fourth question is, and that you will expect the team to answer each question in order. It helps if you also make sure they understand that if the team answers the first question, then the next question becomes much easier to answer.

Update

After school closed for the year, Giselle was asked two more times to meet with district staff. The first time was before she'd received all of the IEEs; the second time was after she'd received all three. The assessments used by the independent occupational therapist were to be discussed with the school psychologist and the certified occupational therapist assistant (COTA), who had written the end of year summary. (A COTA may administer assessments, but is under the supervision of a fully certified occupational therapist, who must review and sign off any reports written by the COTA.) The summary was signed by both the COTA and the occupational therapist. The summary was a quick review of previously administered assessments, in addition to two other short, quickly administered assessments. A fully certified occupational therapist was not in attendance at the meeting. The school psychologist stated that neither he nor the COTA were familiar with the assessments used in the IEE and they were not in a position to comment or interpret the results.

This was problematic for two reasons. As the correct personnel were not present to interpret the IEE, then:

1. it was impossible for the IEP team appropriately to review, discuss, or even "consider" the report

2. this meant it was an inappropriately constituted IEP team.

The psychologist added that they had just received the report from the district contact the day before. This was especially disturbing to Giselle, as she had forwarded the report to the school in advance of the meeting, giving the school ample time to review the report, so that they would be prepared to discuss it.

Needless to say, the meeting did not go smoothly, but Giselle was able to have the school pay for Ariel's enrollment in a private school program in lieu of the ESY program offered by the school district. Transportation to and from the program was to be paid for by the district. Ariel would receive the necessary OT, speech and language, and reading assistance appropriate to her needs, which the school had failed to provide during the school year. Her services would also address her sensory defensiveness and feeding issues. Furthermore, she would receive individualized instruction and, at the end of the ESY program, would have current levels of educational performance in the areas of concern noted in the IEEs.

Giselle would then have the necessary information to identify Ariel's current needs ("Where are we?" and "What do we know?"), enabling an IEP team to develop corresponding goals ("Where do we want to go?") for her IEP and the services needed ("How will we get there?") to meet Ariel's measurable goals ("How will we know that we are getting there?").

Once the IEP—which was developed by the school over the course of the meetings held at the end of the school year and after school closed—was finally received by the private program, the ESY staff found the goals to be improperly written and difficult to understand in terms of what was to be accomplished through the implementation of the IEP. So, clearly, the school staff still need to improve their skills and procedures in order to serve their students appropriately.

Summary

Ultimately, Giselle, although finally achieving what Ariel much needed during the school year, decided to move to another district. As she shared with me, "I just can't go through this every year, even though I now know how to get the services and program Ariel needs."

I followed up a month later and asked how registration went with Ariel. Giselle told me that the school registrar asked if "Ariel would also be in need of an instructional assistant with her classwork." She added further, with relief and satisfaction, that she felt that, unlike the previous school district, the new school system cared for their children's needs, and she has a very positive outlook for Ariel's upcoming school year.

Just prior to finalizing this scenario, I received the following email from Giselle. I include the emails exchanged between Giselle and Ariel's new teacher before the first day of school. I think you will agree that these emails say it all:

Wow, I just had to share. Ariel so deserves this!! Is this what the real world is like?

Begin forwarded message:

From: Giselle

Sent: Friday, August 31, 2012 2:39 PM

To: MM

Subject: Ariel/New Student

Dear Mr. MM

My daughter, Ariel (third grade) was just assigned to your class on Wednesday and we had the opportunity to visit the school for a tour with Mr. Peters as we are brand new to the district. I am very excited to learn that you are Ariel's teacher as Ariel attended a special program until she started first grade. We are close with Audrey LeBar and she said that Ariel will thrive with you as her teacher!!!

I do not know if you will have time to review Ariel's IEP by the time she starts but I thought I would just give you a heads up on a few things for her first day as a couple of issues are new this summer and would not even be on the IEP. Please feel free to share this email with her team.

- Ariel is classified as a student with autism and has a medical diagnosis of autism and a reading disability. Ariel is verbal but she has significant expressive and receptive delays and she may be very quiet with new people. When excited, or nervous, or trying to tell a story, Ariel's rate of speech can become very rapid and she may not be understood. It took her a long time to warm up during her new summer program at Castle Grove in Newtown and she was never able to answer any questions I asked, such as: What is your teacher's name? What is your aide's name? Can you tell me any names of other kids at camp? Once she gets comfortable she will not stop talking or trying to boss everyone around!!

- Ariel just got glasses in the spring for farsightedness and convergence issues but the dog chewed on them and we hope to have them back by the first day of school.

- Ariel wears AFOs [ankle-foot orthotics] for tight heel cords due to toe walking but they do not interfere with her ability on the playground or in PE [physical education]. The AFOs even help regulate her and her rate of speech slowed down when she began wearing them.

- Ariel needs support and encouragement at lunch to eat as her sensory issues impact her eating and her diet is extremely limited. Most days I will send in items that she eats, and she likes to buy chocolate milk. I would like her to try the school chicken nuggets on the first day and will also send something she likes in case she does not like the nuggets. Smells, colors, taste, and control issues all contribute to her eating preferences.

- Ariel exhibits central auditory processing issues and is stronger in math than ELA [English Language Arts] as she struggles greatly with letter sounds, sounding out words and spelling, and her reading success has come from memorization as she is an extremely visual learner. Ariel will complain if noise bothers her by saying it is "annoying" and as the Gordon School is a smaller school than her old school, I am hoping these issues will be minimized.

- Ariel *loves* space and her favorite planet is Saturn. She also loves maps and learning about other cultures. She also still loves her Disney Princess and I can send items in if you need motivators for her. Computer time is a big motivator and she is the queen of Google. She also creates a lot of animated stories at home on the computer and iPad.

- Ariel has never acted out physically at school but she can be very direct with her words to students and staff and perseverate on topics that she is bothered by. You may hear her complain about kindergartners in the building and the fact that there are no lockers. The school she was to attend in our old district was grades 3–5 so she was excited to be an older student and have a locker!

- Ariel does not crash around for sensory input but she will mouth items still (I have ordered a pencil topper for her; she has chewed up the rubber on my cell phone case) and the AFOs help. At her preschool program she had a pressure vest but her old district took it away and said she did not need it. Ariel will internalize everything and cry if the frustration becomes too high if she is not understood; or if she becomes anxious, she will pick at some scabs on her arm till they bleed.

- This summer with the move, Ariel has regressed in her toileting and has been holding until the last possible minute even when prompted to go use the bathroom, so I am sending in some extra clothes as she has had to change a few times a day. I am hoping this will self-correct as she will not want this to happen at school. If you see her rocking or squirming, she needs to go!!

- Ariel started a social skills group a few weeks ago at her summer program. She almost did not make it in as she was extremely "rude" during the intake (and picking at her arm) and it was then revealed that a girl was mean to her at her summer program and she was too scared of telling me or anyone—she thought the girl would become more mean with her. So I think that she had anxiety about joining the group and meeting new kids. I hope that she can learn to communicate appropriately if someone is bothering her.

- I did not know what you need for her to have for school supplies so I have purchased what was requested for her brother, including wipes and tissues for the classroom. I am also sending in a couple of notebooks for communication. Please let me know if there is anything else that you need.

Dr. Harris from the summer program did a psychoeducational IEE on Ariel this past May and I would be happy to share it with you and her team as it is very informative. I am not sure how much of her file gets distributed as we are new to the district.

I am sorry, this turned out to be much longer than I expected!!! My hopes for Ariel this year are for her reading/language skills to increase along with her social skills so that she can be mainstreamed next year.

Ariel is fun, creative, imaginative, and will bring everyone a lot of joy as they get to know her (this is Ariel and her brother Cason, he will be attending first grade at Brenda Hills). I have also included a link to a video Ariel made of the story "Three Billy Goats Gruff" that she learned for a Read A Loud last year.

Thank you and I am looking forward to a great year! I hope you enjoy your last weekend of summer!!

With kind regards,

Giselle

From: MM

Date: September 1, 2012 9:49:40 PM EDT

To: Giselle

Subject: RE: Ariel/New Student

Giselle,

Thank you for reaching out to me in regards to your daughter Ariel. I am very grateful for parents like you who are involved with their child's academic and social needs. It really does improve the likelihood of a child succeeding in all facets of life. I would like first to state that I am looking forward to meeting and working with you and your daughter this school year. To give you a brief background about myself, I have been in the special education field for almost 15 years now. I originally started at The Annex Program, which is now the Center Program, as a Behavior Specialist and finally as a special educator. I am very familiar with the autism spectrum disorder, working with children of ages from 3 to 15 years old. Along with working at the Annex Program, I am entering my fifth year in the public setting as a special educator.

My main goal for all my students, which includes Ariel, is to include them with their general education peers based on their academic strengths. I also love to implement opportunities for my students to share social and interactive activities with their peers throughout the day. I have a wonderful TA [teaching assistant] who assists me with our centers in the classroom. I usually divide the students into centers based on their academic levels, especially ELA. These small group or cooperative learning centers provide my students a comfortable balance of success and challenge to do better to stay with their group. I do focus on phonics and sight words daily to practice and to promote confidence to reading.

Well I hope this helps you to introduce me to your daughter, as you did for me learning about Ariel. I could provide a photo if needed for I know that some children within the spectrum do feel more accepting to the change with some headlining. Again thank you for helping me know more about your daughter and her needs. Oh the toontube video was priceless.

Kindest regards,

MM

....

CHAPTER 9

Parents versus District/District versus Parents

A Broken Relationship

....

This scenario is the result of multiple conversations, emails, and Skype™ interviews that took place over six months. Mr. LeBar provided the foundation of the first part, with Mrs. LeBar adding and modifying information during an interview I conducted with her via Skype™. Two additional Skype™ interviews with Mrs. LeBar continued the saga, with the last update beginning with input from Mrs. LeBar and ending with Mr. LeBar's clarifications. The LeBars devoted a great deal of time to ensure the accuracy of this story, so others could benefit from their experiences with a school that said "No."

(The following is the result of culling over 100 pages of transcripts. As one parent shared with me—after I shared that scenarios have typically been, at a minimum, 25 single space pages and often more—that "our stories are not short ones." Her point has not been forgotten.)

The School Said "No, No, and No!"

> *"At our first IEP meeting, all that we heard was 'Jane can't do this' and 'Jane can't do that.'"*

Mrs. LeBar: Jane, our 11-year-old daughter, has a diagnosis of regressive autism. My pregnancy was normal. We celebrated her birth and relished our beautiful newborn girl—we were and are proud parents of our daughter. Life was wonderful until Jane was about 20 months old—although we had noticed that she seemed extremely cautious walking. Often, babies will just try to walk, fall, then get up and try again, but Jane was far more careful in how she moved. It was oddly apparent to us that she was overly guarded compared with other children's first walking.

Over a relatively short time, we observed an initial reduction of her language and other skills, beginning at about 24 months. Within six months, she had lost nearly all language. She stopped responding to her name and lost interest in us and others. She showed no interest in participating with us or playing, but would rather be alone. Jane also had begun putting everything into her mouth and repeating physical movements. Prior to that, Jane was able to count to 20 in English and in French and could recite the alphabet in both languages. [Mrs. LeBar's first language is French.] Jane was quite active—a happy little girl. I persistently tried to determine what the problem was and to find the solution for what Jane was experiencing.

Between ages 24–30 months I was quite concerned and cried in front of my pediatrician, saying things were not right. We saw other developmental pediatricians, but all they would suggest was that she had a developmental delay. They did not recommend for us to enroll Jane in a special program—I wish they had. They gave no suggestions.

We took Jane to a speech-language pathologist (SLP), who, after extensive efforts to work with Jane, totally misdiagnosed her. She couldn't control Jane or convince Jane to attend to the instructions. She said that, because we had a bilingual family, we were not providing sufficient socializing opportunities for Jane to increase her (English) language skills. Yet, on the form, she recorded "mental disorder" as the reason for treatment.

Jane also had a visual disorder (polyopia) that involved seeing multiple images, but she could not have the operation to correct that until she was about 30 months old. It was thought that perhaps she would not look at either of us because of her distorted vision and that she was simply too young to explain any of that to us. The surgery was successful; however, this did not impact on her lost skills or increase her attention toward us.

As we wanted to increase Jane's exposure to the English language, at 31 months of age we enrolled her in a private preschool program modeled after the Montessori system. She had a tremendous amount of anxiety the first day at the school, so I stayed with her. After two days, we decided that Jane should attend alone, thinking her discomfort might pass without my presence.

The director called and said that Jane had a serious problem: "She cannot process information. We will have to discontinue the program for her." The director said Jane needed a full psychoeducational assessment and suggested that we go to the local First Steps program—a program for children aged birth to three who may have a disability—for a full assessment. If Jane qualified, the family would receive supportive services.

We contacted the program's intake person, who scheduled an observation in the home. The coordinator made a total of six visits to our home to observe Jane and asked many questions. The administrator said, "I hate to tell you this, but I think your daughter may have autism," then added something to the effect that there was no cure for autism. I thought that was a harsh way of presenting this information to a parent.

As she continued to talk about expected outcomes for children with autism, I received a clear message that they did not expect her really to achieve much. They did not even list Jane as having autism, but said she had a pervasive developmental disorder, which was a generic classification for all children in the program. I think they avoided classifying her as having autism because they did not want to have to provide any additional special services due to extra costs. I am not even certain they had staff trained to provide the right kind of services. In any case, the administrator said one thing, but did not list autism as the diagnosis on the official paperwork.

["Pervasive developmental disorder" is the umbrella category under which autism and a variety of other developmental disabilities fall. It is unlikely that the administrator in question had the necessary qualifications to make a diagnosis of autism.]

I felt like I was just hit square in the face and knocked down. When I got up there was no one there to help me. As parents, there is a mourning period, a need to adjust, after hearing that your child has a disability. You just have to get back up and do something for yourself and focus on helping your child.

Jane remained in the First Steps program for about a year, where she received services at the preschool and some at home (i.e., speech and physical therapy). When Jane turned three, she was transferred from the First Steps program to the local school district's preschool program, where she then received all her services at the preschool program. I spent the first three months with Jane while she was there each day, to help her adjust to the new setting and program. After about three months, we [Mr. and Mrs. LeBar] felt that I could finally allow Jane to continue with her services in my absence. She did not have a diagnosis of autism, and I was told that, without this classification, Jane's services would be limited.

We were not warned that Jane's services ended with the end of the regular school year. There was no extended school year (ESY) (summer program services) available for Jane or any other children with similar needs. However, we knew that to continue developing her socialization, language, and other skills we would have to provide our own services. So, I hired someone to work with Jane during the summer months using play therapy, which would address both her language development and socialization skills.

When Jane was about four years old, we scheduled a medical appointment to conduct an assessment to determine if Jane did have autism. Part of the intake process required we provide the facility with a full health and developmental history. After the assessment process was completed, the facility confirmed Jane's condition as autism, stating further that she manifested the "classic symptoms of autism." At that time, her behaviors included "stimming" (self-stimulation), language deficits, a lack of social skills, and other body movements typical of autism. However, they also added that she had mental retardation. We were told that when a child is as low functioning as Jane was, it was not unusual to add the diagnosis of mental retardation at the early ages, because it can sometimes be difficult to be certain.

Jane showed the same biomedical issues, autistic behaviors, and language problems as do children with autism. She had tremendous gut (gastro-intestinal) problems, with difficulties digesting foods, and numerous allergies. Because of the extent of her difficulties, it has been challenging to treat her. She is a child with very complex needs. I should add that we approached the school district, asking if they would pay for the evaluation; however, the school district said they would not pay for a medical assessment, so we paid for one privately. It was expensive, but quite enlightening.

Mr. LeBar: As an aside, we were somewhat fortunate, because our neighborhood area had a very active advocacy group that provided a great deal of information to parents of children with autism. We were, as you can imagine, actively seeking as much information on autism as we could. I personally became very active in the local group. As it turned out, it was also an excellent social and support group, where you could talk about the effects of autism on the family and other issues that arise when attempting to raise a child with autism. The group members became excellent sources for sharing useful websites and other resources that could help answer many of the questions we had—we had many.

Jane remained in the district's preschool program for children with autism from the time she was three and a half to five years old. Unfortunately, we found the staff to have limited training in the treatment of autism.

We continually searched for information that would help Jane, learning that it takes 30–40 hours a week of Applied Behavior Analysis (ABA) therapy—one-on-one instruction by an individual who holds expertise in ABA—to have a positive effect on a child's learning. To reach that amount of time and the type of instruction necessary, we had worked with the school to establish a program with ABA for Jane—later adding a verbal behavior (VB) component. We had looked at other programs (e.g., the Lovaas program) but determined they wouldn't be appropriate for Jane. We knew, too, that we needed to address Jane's language development and that the VB model would accomplish that—fortunately, the school had made the same selection.

[ABA is one of many programs used to provide behavioral re-training therapy for children with autism and is not an educational program. The claim that 30–40 hours of therapy per week is required, which is made by some ABA providers, has not yet been independently verified by research scientists, neither do all ABA providers agree on the amount of therapy required. Most state that it, like many interventions, is dependent on the child and the child's specific needs.]

In order to supplement the language and social development interventions that were being provided at school, we learned how to carry out play therapy at home. I had even gone to a workshop presented by Dr. Solomon[1] to learn how to implement play therapy.

At the end of the second school year, we were prepared for ESY programming so that Jane would continue with her education and not lose what was learned during the school year (experience regression). We realized that it would be necessary to hire our own home team of aides for Jane. The school was only providing a few hours a week of one-on-one ABA therapy, and we knew that wasn't enough. The school had one teaching assistant and one teacher with special education credentials running a class of 12 kids, which certainly wasn't enough staff to work with that many children. So, to supplement the school's program, we hired, at our own expense, our own aides and a professional Board Certified Behavior Analyst (BCBA) to train them. We tried to schedule the aides to provide enough hours to get the recommended 30–40 hours of instruction a week.

To accomplish this, we hired a married couple—both had Ph.D.s in behavioral therapy—to supervise our team of aides. They were expensive, as you can imagine, and we simply could not afford to have them work with us and the aides as much as we wanted; so, we arranged for them to coordinate the services between the school and home. Otherwise, we might have ended up with two distinctly different programs with different goals. This seemed to be the best use of their services.

At one point, we learned that once the kids exit the preschool kindergarten program at age five, the public school district didn't really have anything for children with autism. Instead, Jane would have been placed in a classroom with children with various disabilities, because the school lacked teachers trained in autism. Given that, we opted to pay for Jane to attend a private school for the first couple of grades. The school was not really set up for working with children with autism, but staff agreed to have Jane accompanied by an aide (whom we provided and paid for). This person was one of the aides whom we had trained for Jane's home services, and the arrangement seemed to work out fairly well.

We continued to learn about local policies and educational laws, as we had to deal with them—sometimes after the fact. Advocacy groups were certainly helpful, sending messages about related activities and inviting us to trainings with organizations and individuals. For example, the first presentation was about being

---

1   Richard Solomon, M.D., is the Medical Director at the P.L.A.Y. Project (www.playproject.org, accessed on July 1, 2013).

certain that your child had a diagnosis/classification of autism, because it would determine the services your child would receive and would mean that you would also receive one-on-one services.

[Parents should know that this contradicts the concept, proposed in this book, that your child is to receive the necessary program and services based on identified needs and not based on your child's diagnosis. This is why the Structured Collaborative Individualized Education Program (IEP) Process begins with identifying the child's needs and answering the question, "What do we know?" Determination of the child's disability and matching that to "a program of services" is *not* answering the questions "What do we know?" or "Where are we going?" The disability should not automatically determine either the program of services or "How will we get there?" Furthermore, one-on-one aides are not provided everywhere.]

In addition, I would attend workshops, seminars, and meetings where information was shared about national or local school laws and policies related to special education.

Jane's second grade school was meant to be designed to educate children with autism, having staff trained in the area of autism; but we had a mixed bag of experiences in terms of the quality of staff. We saw very slow progress, given the amount of program time provided by the private schools—three to four hours a day, and her home program, another two to three hours a day. When the experts were brought in, we saw her learning skills improve much more quickly. But the cost of $200 or more an hour made it that much more problematic to afford. It also made it difficult to provide the aides with enough training, so that they could apply the ABA/VB as easily and effectively as the experts could.

To help staff become more adept at implementing the ABA/VB, we set up video cameras at home to tape what our experts were doing with Jane. We sent the tapes into the schools, allowing staff to observe the experts' techniques with Jane and her response.

What we did see, as a result of the combined efforts and intense services, was a very slow and gradual growth in Jane's receptive language skills (her expressive language skills remained weak, however). We saw that she was better able to follow an increase in the number of two-step directions. Her motor skills were also slow to improve, with most of her development limited to that above her waist.

We had to insist on having allergies written into her IEP, so the school knew the things she needed to avoid. For example, other kids would be eating peanut butter sandwiches. That in itself was not the issue, but Jane would then pick up the crumbs and, of course, eat them. She had reached a point in her life when she would eat anything that she saw that appealed to her. But getting the school to pay attention to that took a lot of work on our part, so that she wouldn't be near other kids who were eating food. And, if she had to be near another child, there had to be someone next to her to make sure that she wasn't picking up or eating any of the other child's food—or anything else (non-food items) that might be within her reach.

We also tried a number of therapies with Jane, including sensory integration therapy. It consisted of the therapist placing a gently vibrating table in a very dark room, which Jane would touch (to feel the vibrations). Then, headphones playing music were placed on Jane's head, and she was meant to follow, with her eyes, a white dot that moved across the ceiling while the table rocked back and forth. The combination of auditory, visual, and tactile stimuli was meant to improve her eye coordination. Following that session, we saw more improvement in her eye coordination and language than we had seen as a result of all that we had tried before. We went to a couple of "refresher" sessions on this therapy, but they did not have the kind of impact on Jane that we had seen on the first day. We believe that the initial impact indicated a kind of rewiring of her brain. She really enjoyed the experience—so much so that at subsequent sessions she was more than happy to go directly to the table and sit down. Jane knows what's good for her, and this was good for her.

We had tried sensory integration training when Jane was younger and felt we might find this approach to be helpful again. We have since rented the equipment, and my wife is now administering most of her treatments. As before, Jane is more than willing to take part in the treatments. After several sessions, her eye gaze improved, and she is much calmer. Although we see benefits, it is costing a great deal. It is still a relatively new thing for Jane, having had 25 sessions with a doctor and another ten with her mother.

Another approach that we tried was neuro-feedback therapy. The purpose of this was to have portions of the brain communicate more effectively. Electrodes were placed on the sides of Jane's head while she watched videos, like cartoons. She started with ten-minute sessions and has since moved up to 30. When Jane arrived, she would try to put on the electrodes herself, showing us how comfortable she was with the therapy. She has better eye gaze and is much calmer. The whole idea is that the therapy calms the right side of her brain.

Eventually, the cost caught up with us and we decided that we could no longer afford private schools and would have to look to the public schools for Jane's fourth grade. This was also the school year that we moved to another state. It's important to know that, even while she was in the private schools, Jane had IEPs and that we had created an IEP for her fourth grade, for the 2008–2009 school year, prior to moving.

The first program Jane experienced in the new school system was 15 miles from our home. The program was simply a classroom in an elementary school for children with autism. At our first IEP meeting, all that we heard was "Jane can't do this," and "Jane can't do that." We questioned the staff's observations and knew this wasn't the Jane we knew; she was a great deal more competent than they would give her credit for. They held very low expectations of Jane, anticipating very simple kinds of learning from her. They had low expectations in terms of reaching her IEP goals and approached instruction in a manner that would accomplish the minimum and just get by.

This attitude is pretty much what we've experienced throughout our time in this school system. Our impression is that schools simply do not have appropriately trained staff who know what they are meant to do with children with autism. We get more accomplished with Jane after school, with the help of untrained respite caregivers whose wages are one-quarter of what the school providers make.

At the start of Jane's fourth grade year, we no longer had the home program that we had in the previous state. Combining that with the failing school program, we saw our daughter no longer happy to go to school. This is a child who was generally happy, but we saw no more smiles on her face. Jane was also increasingly having more tantrums at home and school, showing us that the program was not working. So we requested mediation through the school system and explained why the program was not working and that, among other things, there was a strong need for ABA therapy to enable her to learn.

Mediation involved meeting with the director of special education and a large number of other people to try to get outside services to provide ABA therapy, because the school was not willing to hire a person with those skills. As I remember, that first summer, we wanted Jane to have ESY services. She was to be served in a program very close to home for just a few weeks of the summer. But, in the IEP we actually had ESY services stated for a much longer period of time. We had requested another three weeks added to the five-week ESY program to ensure Jane would not regress (lose any progress made during the school year).

We explained that we simply hadn't seen any progress; we said that we did not see Jane enjoying school and this was a big change. We looked at the school day and the little data that existed. I pointed out that the school's data indicated Jane was making minimal progress.

We also brought in independent evaluations that showed that Jane was making very limited progress and that any noted progress was more due to maturation than it was on her actually learning anything. Again, we knew that somewhere between 30 and 40 hours of individual instruction (ABA) were required for a child with Jane's needs. The school said that they were not prepared to provide that, but they would give her 12 hours of service. They did not feel she needed the 30 to 40 hours of training.

I told them that the evidence indicated that you don't get half the results if you give half the time of services; you get zero progress. Of course, we were hoping that something would be better than nothing and that, if the school trained the staff, maybe it would work. The aide who would then be trained by the beginning of school would be good enough—the whole idea was to get an aide trained "good enough"—so that Jane could have the one-on-one instruction.

(My problem with the school district is they do things half way, doing just enough to say they're doing something. My thinking is that this is the way it is done all over the country. They want to spend as little as possible—at least in this particular school system. And we knew we couldn't afford private school programming any longer, so we were going to try to work with the school system as best we could.)

So, for ESY, Jane was placed in the school, which had younger staff who were not trained in ABA but were willing to try to work with her. So we had some positives. But, on the negative side, the staff didn't have the ABA training.

Then, at the end of the summer, we went to mediation to get the extra time that was originally in the IEP. We wanted somebody with ABA experience, because we saw that Jane had clearly regressed during the summer months, in spite of the few weeks of ESY. The regional supervisor, who really seemed to care, "turned us on" to a teaching assistant who was really good with "tough" kids. As a result of the mediation with the district, Jane had six sessions with that assistant that lasted two hours each.

In those 12 hours, the aide had gotten more completed than had been accomplished during the whole summer program. We saw differences in Jane's learning, happiness, and engagement with this woman, who had really connected with Jane. We learned that she had actually been trained by a local expert and consultant in ABA programming.

The following fall, as part of the mediation agreement, the teacher at that elementary school was to be trained in ABA by a local expert, who had been contracted to work with staff who were working with children with autism. Jane was to receive 12 hours a week of one-on-one instruction. The district had also agreed to have a full-time aide assigned to Jane when school began in the fall. Before the aide would be allowed to work independently with Jane, she would get 30 days of observation by the local experts and intensive training from these experts in ABA/VB. But when school started, no aide had been hired.

We asked why there was no aide and we were told that they had hired somebody, but that she had just declined the position. I said to them, "You know where I'm coming from, because the connection with Jane is so important." I added that I thought that parents would be involved in the interview of these prospective teachers and aides. Then, I added, "We've never been invited to do that." They replied that it was not their policy to involve parents in the interview process of aides. I asked to see that policy, but they could not show me one. I told them that it's important to have a teacher who has energy and who was willing to be trained and learn new methods to work with children like Jane.

[Teachers and IEP participants are not likely to have ready access to such an interview policy, because it would be the policy of the district's human resources department. However, it could be obtained easily enough via a request of the department.]

As the school district had failed to meet the mediation agreement—that of having a trained aide, in particular, which was also reflected in Jane's revised IEP—we decided to file a complaint with the state Department of Education. The state found the district at fault for not having provided the aide, who might have bolstered Jane's school progress. I asked the state representative what the district would do to correct the deficiency—specifically, I wanted to know what kind of compensatory services the state was going to direct the district to provide. The state responded, saying they cannot tell the district what kind of compensatory services to provide, but that the district had to meet with my wife and me to determine what the compensatory services were to be.

When we did have the meeting with the district, they said that they didn't feel that Jane required any compensatory services—end of conversation. Yet, we had prepared a whole list of possible services that could have been provided and chosen from but they didn't want to hear them. [The family did not continue to pursue this issue with the district or state.] We did, however, finally get a full-time aide assigned, who was given training, but less than originally planned for.

Jumping ahead to the following year, ESY once again was addressed as part of the IEP discussion. The district said that now that we had a trained aide who had worked with Jane the previous year, Jane wouldn't need ESY services. We said she wasn't yet a trained aide, as it required many more months of training than the four to five months she had with Jane, the first of which she merely observed Jane in the classroom with her teacher during the school day.

The aide had only worked with one child, and that was not sufficient to say that she was trained. She needed more experience and, as Vince Carbone said at a presentation, "Bad ABA is worse than nothing," because it takes years to unlearn what bad ABA teaches. [Dr. Vince Carbone, a BCBA-Doctoral, has more than 35 years of experience designing learning environments for persons with autism and development disabilities.] When the aide was originally trained, the expert trainer's staff would monitor, support, and guide the aide, often for hours over several days a week, but that time had been reduced greatly to only four hours a week, and the aide still needed more support and training.

Nonetheless, we finally worked out the ESY program without the need for mediation, and Jane had a reasonably good summer in 2011. Jane went to the site where the contracted ABA/VB provider held their "summer camp." Until the aide and her family went on their own vacation, the aide instructed Jane at this site under the supervision of staff from the contracted provider. Jane received some socialization experiences with the help of the aide's daughters, who accompanied their mother (our aide) to the site and who "took a shine" to Jane. Sometimes the children of camp staff also socialized with Jane.

The last two weeks of the eight-week summer program were provided by a long-time paraprofessional of the district, who had instructed Jane for six sessions the previous summer. To date, she was the only district ABA/VB provider who has helped Jane make significant gains. She loved working with Jane, and Jane loved going to school when this lady was her instructor. It is too bad we couldn't get her more often.

This school year (2012–2013) is Jane's first year in the middle school, and has been a disaster. For example, my wife observed the interaction between the aide and Jane in classes away from the teachers and saw that Jane wanted to escape and appeared to have no idea of what she was meant to do—the aide had very little control over Jane's behaviors. We have asked to make a video of Jane and her school behaviors and were told, even though *they* have videos, they would not share them with us. Neither would the school allow us to observe with a video camera.

At a recent meeting, the school showed us a small picture book that contained photographs of the food Jane eats. This was the same thing they showed us early in the school year, and you have to wonder what Jane had been working on. She already knew the food names in the book. They were teaching the same lessons over and over; there was no growth. They broke up the day into 15–30-minute segments, and even if Jane was in the middle of learning something, they had to stop and move on to the next segment instead of taking the extra time to continue working on the task in hand. Their data misrepresented Jane's actual abilities. She could do things at home that the school said were not within her capabilities. They said she knew 95 sight words in October, and then, in February, she knew 105. This was insufficient progress for this period of time.

The school stays on the same goal, partially meets the goals, but then keeps the same goals year after year. Some IEP objectives change but they use data from previous years and count them toward the current year's progress. Is there growth? Yes, there is, but, Jane isn't even halfway through first-grade reading, and she has no math skills, even at the most basic level.

Although the school records IEP progress data, the district doesn't record statistics for the autism program as a whole. As a result, they cannot tell us whether their programs are working at all, let alone whether they are getting better or worse from one year to the next. After our recent experiences, we think that school is doing her harm.

Continuing Concerns: Key Issues

A month and a half after obtaining the initial information from Mr. LeBar and some from Mrs. LeBar, the author had the opportunity to interview Mrs. LeBar again. This is a summary of the key issues from that interview.

A number of difficulties that Mr. and Mrs. LeBar raised in the original scenario continued between the district and the family. More difficulties arose when the LeBars made additional requests that the district denied. The LeBars have determined that they can no longer take the lead on Jane's behalf and have sought and located an educational advocate to assist them and to work on their behalf. They made this decision because they felt that they had reached an impasse with the district and that no matter how they approached district staff, they would be told "No" in one form or another.

Although the LeBars had considered requesting a due process hearing, they learned, from speaking with others, that often an advocate can open new avenues to resolve old issues. Although there are times where a due process hearing is the only recourse, it can often result in a long-term state of animosity between the district and parents, with IEP meetings becoming very tense and uncomfortable. The LeBars did not want Jane to suffer from such a situation and, therefore, elected to hire an advocate to assist them.

(A due process hearing is a procedure where the complaints of the parents are heard by an independent panel or individual, who then determines if the district is or is not out of compliance with national laws in the relevant procedural regulations and the provision of services to a child with disabilities. If the district are found to have followed all laws and regulations, then the complaint is dismissed. If, however, the district are found to be out of compliance [i.e. they did not comply with the national laws or regulations] then the panel or hearing officer will dictate the corrective action to be taken by the district.)

What follows are brief descriptions of a few of the recurring problems and new issues encountered by the LeBars:

- Due to the discrepancies between what staff see at school and what the LeBars see at home, the LeBars want to have Jane's program assessed by an independent evaluator.

- Unfortunately, the district imposes below-market restrictions on the cost they will pay for independent educational evaluations, among other unnecessary policy limits.

- Furthermore, the LeBars had previously requested a music therapy assessment, which was conducted and then reviewed by the district, and for which the district paid. Then, at the IEP meeting, just as the music therapist began to speak, the IEP team leader said that the report did not meet their requirements and would not be used in the IEP meeting.

- At the same IEP meeting, the LeBars expressed their concern about Jane going to the cafeteria, where there is loud music playing constantly. This is an issue, because the music provides unnecessary stimulation—in addition to the general noise of the cafeteria and the students' movements—that surpasses Jane's level of sensory tolerance. The director, indicating a failure to understand Jane's conditions, said, "Jane has to learn to deal with the real world."

- The LeBars are troubled that Jane's programming addresses a limited set of real-world activities, and those few experiences that are real-life activities are not preparing her to live in the community.

- Finally, and most recently, Jane was supposedly overheard at school using inappropriate language and, possibly, directing it at another student. She had apparently referenced her breasts in some manner, using terms other than the word "breasts." As a result of this incident, a state officer from Services for Children was sent to the home to investigate the parents, the home environment, and their behaviors and language usage, among other things. Following the visit from the officer, the speech and language therapist who works with Jane at home performed an experiment to determine the body parts Jane could identify. Jane could touch her ears upon request. This was repeated for four or five body parts, with Jane accurately touching the requested body part. When asked to touch her breasts, she did not respond. When asked to touch her chest and various other words that Jane had allegedly used, she did not respond. The therapist and Mrs. LeBar concluded that Jane had no idea what the words meant, and it was unlikely that she had used them.

What made this incident even more disturbing was that when the LeBars contacted the staff about it, they were told that the staff could not talk about certain issues of Jane's behaviors. They added that they were specifically prohibited to speak about Jane's behaviors by the district director.

Mr. and Mrs. LeBar believe that the school is acting in a vindictive manner. Mrs. LeBar added that now the district will offer a single option for any problem presented. Worse, they feel that the option is presented in a way that they are left with the decision either to "take it or leave it." Holding meetings with district personnel is simply no longer effective.

As noted earlier, the LeBars have realized that they have reached a point of standoff with the district and recognize the need for an advocate to speak on their behalf. They also realized that emotional play of both the district and the parents is interfering with collaborative efforts. They stated that, recognizing this, there is value in having an advocate speak for them and with them, instead of bringing these issues to a court or hearing. By using an advocate, they are likely to accomplish a great deal more, because conversations can be reopened, which cannot occur in a court setting.

Analysis of "The School Said 'No, No, and No!'"

What Do We Know?

Where Are We?

Putting Jane's needs aside for the moment, it is abundantly clear that communication between the school and parents has reached an impasse. In fact, given the last experience with the unwarranted claims of neglect, staff are no longer at liberty to discuss particular issues, and the district is now using their attorney to make decisions on parental requests. It appears that the district is preparing for a legal action that may be brought by the parents—especially when topics related to Jane's behaviors are no longer open to discussion and the district's attorney is involved in issues that would normally be determined "in-house"—that is, by school and district staff.

At present, it is unclear as to what the school or family is certain of with respect to Jane's needs and measurable progress on the goals and objectives of her IEP, or to what degree the IEP is being implemented. There is a great deal of uncertainty regarding what skills Jane actually possesses. It is unknown if the home services are producing results, in what area the results might be observed, and to what degree progress is being made. Another question is whether the services requested or provided are actually necessary or of benefit to Jane.

Unknown, as well, is how closely and how well the home SLT is working with the school speech and language therapist. Less is known about the integrity of the implementation of the IEP across settings, by all staff. In other words, do all staff who work with Jane carry out the same procedures and instructions (i.e., ABA/VA, language interaction/communication, etc.)? Were these procedures and instructions put in place as a result of the written IEP, including services provided at school that were enriched at home?

The degree of decay in the relationship between the parents and the school system did not occur over a single incident, event, misstatement, or IEP meeting. We may draw a number of conclusions as to how this situation came to be, and are likely correct for a multitude of reasons. First, the current predicament developed over time and is likely due to a historical repetition of actions and responses by both parties. Second, to ferret out, investigate, or analyze who, what, when, where, and why would be an unwarranted waste of time. Blame will certainly be placed on both parties, but to spend time rehashing every nuance would likely further ramp up an ongoing "dispute," to put it mildly. This is not to say that emotions can be ignored—no matter what steps are taken toward enacting a resolution, the lead person must recognize the existence of emotional discord and approach the solution accordingly.

We are unsure of what Jane's needs are; therefore, the most reasonable and useful approach would be to start from the beginning and to have a full behavioral, communication, academic, sensory, and motoric set of assessments conducted. Although the school and parents have a number of evaluation and assessment reports, the most judicious manner of determining "Where is Jane functioning?" would be for the district to put aside the district policies regarding independent education evaluations (IEEs)—because these policies hinder more than they help—and have a full battery of assessments carried out by independent evaluators. For example, it would be most logical not to limit the area from which "evaluators" may be sought to a 50-mile radius. Furthermore, it would not be unjustifiable to look at neighboring states for licensed evaluators. In this case, there are several states and large cities within 100 miles of the school system.

Granted, no school system is going to support flying in an expert who lives 3,000 miles away when there is another qualified individual within a 100-mile radius of the school system. A guideline might be that the distance and time to travel should not require an overnight stay at the cost of the district. But it is also important to be reasonable, which may include an overnight stay if the evaluation is going to take more than one day. The point is that the 50-mile rule is unduly restrictive, as are the capped costs for services. The team must first agree upon what areas of assessment are necessary and prioritize those in order of which is needed most first ("Where do we want to go?"). Next, the team must lay out what specific information in that area is expected within the report ("How will we get there?"), and then compare costs of several possible vendors to determine which will be contracted to carry out the assessment within the requirements of the district policies, to which the team would need to agree. This would be an incredible beginning and give the team a chance to begin re-establishing a collaborative relationship.

Where Do We Want to Go?
What Do We Want to Accomplish?

These questions cannot be answered, much less discussed, until all of the IEE reports are received, and each is presented and discussed with the appropriate personnel—those who are qualified to interpret the assessment reports—and, of course the parents. In addition to the assessments, teacher records, samples of Jane's classroom work, parental input, records of program implementation, and measures of progress would need to be discussed. In total, this should clarify Jane's needs and answer the first question, "What do we know?" Once the team has identified Jane's needs, the team could answer the question, "Where do we want to go?" And, following the above IEE presentations and the question-and-answer discussions, the team can begin the development of measurable goals, objectives, and benchmarks that need to be written into the IEP.

How Will We Get There?
What Do We Need to Get There?

Once the team has established the goals and benchmarks, the team can then discuss what programming and services would be required to achieve the goals, how often the services should be provided, and where the programming and services will be provided.

Then, the remaining questions can be answered as the last part of the Structured Collaborative IEP Process, including "How do we know that we are getting there?" and "How do we know we are there?" However, there is no need to continue with a discussion of the remaining questions of the Structured Collaborative IEP Process, because the school and parents have not yet achieved the answer to the first question.

A Difference in Approach

In no way should the reader perceive that bringing a due process or legal action against the district is necessary or even recommended. The Structured Collaborative IEP Process can still be conducted successfully. However, due to the condition of the present relationships among the school, district staff, and Mr. and Mrs. LeBar, this process will need to be carried out differently. Simply asking and answering the structured collaborative questions will not work in this case.

Conducting a Structured Collaborative IEP meeting characteristically requires the participation of the parents, the relevant IEP school staff, and, of course, the child when appropriate. This process can work very well most of the time. But when the relationships between the family and the school system reach the level of dysfunction seen in this case, then a slightly different approach is necessary.

It is easy to agree that the term "dysfunctional," at its most basic of denotations, means that there exists a failure of the members of a group to act in a constructive manner. Given that definition, it would not be difficult to accept further that the following descriptions define the mutual dynamics that are actively in play among the parents and various district personnel and that have led to the dysfunctional relationship between the LeBars and the school staff:

- district and parent animosity

- general distrust or disbelief

- general blame

- difficulty in expressing points of view without intense affect or emotion

- loss of a feeling of a safe environment

- feelings of not being listened to

- feelings of not being able to participate equally

- different values and levels of concern about Jane and her program

- overly criticized

- and more…

The IEP Facilitator and Dispute Resolution

Because so much resentment and emotions—real and perceived—are at the forefront in this particular situation, the manner in which a resolution may be reached will need to be carried out in a slightly different fashion. Actually, it is not so much in a different manner, but with a different meeting leader—someone called an IEP facilitator. This person has expertise in group dynamics and a deep knowledge of the regulations and process of special education, and in the development of an IEP and other related documents.

The IEP facilitator is not a lawyer, a mediator, an arbitrator, or even a negotiator. Each of these aforementioned professionals' function is to reach a final decision and—in most, if not all cases—the final decisions are made by those individuals leading the meeting. As a result, the decisions and decision-making process are taken away from the participants—the intent and purpose of a group of individuals making a team (collaborative) decision based on a child's needs are diminished.

Furthermore, by definition alone, to negotiate means to give up something for something else. Why would you possibly want to give away a needed program or service to obtain something else that is also necessary for the child to make educational progress? Shouldn't the child receive all the services that are needed? Or do we really want to act on the premise that something is better than nothing? To bring this sharply home, what would you be willing to give up so that you could receive 50 percent of your air supply, when you need 100 percent of that air to function?

That is not the purpose of an IEP team or an IEP facilitator. The IEP facilitator conducts an IEP meeting using some of the components of the Structured Collaborative IEP Process. The skills of the IEP facilitator are used to aid the team in working together. The facilitator in no way represents the parent or the school district. The facilitator is a true "third party" and acts independently of everyone's concerns, acting only on the child's behalf. And the facilitator maintains that position throughout the IEP meeting.

The scope of this book is not sufficient to cover the entirety of the facilitated IEP process, but it is sufficient to note that such professionals do exist and are excellent alternatives to lawyers, mediators, or negotiators. Their services are preferred, because they are skilled at helping to bring people who have reached high levels of discord and impasse—as exemplified in this scenario—back together to refocus on the needs of the child, so that true parent and school collaboration can occur.

(A reminder: Most often, and under "normal" and "typical" circumstances, parents or school staff can successfully conduct the Structured Collaborative IEP Process and still have the school say, "Yes!" This is simply not the case in this scenario—not at this point.)

Key Points

- I felt it important to include this scenario in this book, because it represents how parent–staff relationships (and the subsequent IEPs that result) can go completely wrong, even when both parties have the best of intentions. Jane was originally the focus of both the parents and the school, but somewhere along the process distrust began to build. Requests became demands, and both sides felt backed into a corner. Their experience illustrates how the right statement can be misunderstood, an unintended meaning may be read into an email, or personalities simply become the issue. In any case, the original issue—Jane's needs—became secondary or tertiary for both groups of people.

- This scenario is also included so that the reader can understand that situations like this can occur, though they are not the norm. It is included because it shows how a child's needs could be lost in the turmoil when either side tries to be heard or to be in control to the point that results in a full breakdown in communication; where intent and purpose are absent and where lines are literally drawn and "sides" are readied for legal recourse. It is a discouraging situation, needing—much like a computer that locks up—a "reboot" by an expert experienced in relationships and group dynamics.

- There is little doubt that Mr. and Mrs. LeBar want the best for Jane. There is no doubt that they love and care for Jane and are willing to spend the time and finances to provide Jane with the services they feel might improve her life. They are certainly willing to sacrifice their time—although they would never think of it as a sacrifice—to do their best to enable Jane to be successful at home, at school, and in the community.

- We should assume that the school district wanted to do their best for all children with disabilities as individuals—including Jane. We should assume that, initially, they felt that they were providing Jane with an appropriate program of services. Most likely, they would have continued in the same manner, but they were challenged by Mr. and Mrs. LeBar, who had different prior experiences and were more accustomed to working with a school district that was open to parental suggestions. The LeBars told us that even the prior school system did not have staff with sufficient credentials or experience for them to feel that they could carry out the programs Jane needed.

- In simple terms, the family and the school began to press each other and disagree and request and deny almost every idea presented. Perhaps this is more familiarly known as butting heads. Granted, with the district putting caps on the amount of money they were willing to spend on an IEE, plus placing limits on the distance an evaluator would need to travel from or where he or she could be licensed, they were "drawing lines in the sand." This author believes that few—if any—courts or hearing panels would accept the restrictions put into place by the school district. There is value in having policies in place, but they must also be reasonable; these were not.

- Jane does have educational needs that include language, behavioral, and academics. She is a child whose needs border between moderate and severe, and there are reasons to question whether those needs are being met. However, it remains unclear what Jane's real needs are, and even if there is agreement on what those needs are, questions would remain as to the services to be provided as well as the manner in which the district is collecting data on Jane's progress. The latter two (services and data collection) are barely provable as being appropriate and, in some cases, existent, at least as portrayed in this scenario.

- For example, music therapy itself was not the issue of contention. The issue was that the district paid for and allowed the music therapy assessment to be conducted, and then said that they did not have to review or consider it because the requirements of the IEE were not met. The action taken by the district was not carried out in good faith.

- The school has worsened the situation by bringing in child protective services, instead of dealing directly with the parents.

- The major learning to take away from this scenario is that, had the district or parents stepped in early and taken the lead in the Structured Collaborative

IEP Process, then perhaps the present situation could have been avoided. Given the disintegration of collaboration, and no longer having cooperation between the parents and school personnel, the most reasonable and promising recommendation is to bring in a third party whose purpose is not to negotiate a child's needs and services away, but to focus on meeting the child's needs by helping parents and staff to use the Structured Collaborative IEP Process.

• The professional who is most likely to help the IEP group to collaborate effectively is one whose expertise is deeply rooted in group dynamics and social interactions. The IEP facilitator is also one who has extremely strong knowledge and field practice in the application and understanding of the laws and regulations of special education. Dissecting or analyzing the breakdown of the IEP team would be of no benefit. Many of the issues leading to this unstable situation between the LeBars and the school district are self-evident and cumulative. Reliving those interactions would only reinforce their differences and further remove the focus from Jane's needs.

Summary

Several additional meetings between the LeBars and the school staff have taken place. Distrust and animosity continued. The LeBars recorded all the meetings, and the district repeatedly stated that Jane was "continuing to make educational progress." This was in total contradiction to the LeBars' observations, and Mrs. LeBar felt it was part of the district's preparation for a possible due process lodged by the LeBars. And the district knows that the words "continuing to make educational progress" are important to have on record, should the proceedings result in a court hearing. The LeBars recognized the legal wording and its repetitive use, although they knew it was not true.

At each of the meetings, the school staff continued to refuse to address the issue that brought child services to the LeBar home. As mentioned earlier, Mrs. LeBar's native language is French, and Jane will often mix the two languages; the word *petite*, given Jane's enunciation, could have led the staff to misunderstand and believe that Jane was referencing ("saying") "tit" (a slang term for breast). Another factor that was realized after the visit from the child services personnel, and not known at that specific time, was that Jane was also suffering with a severe urinary tract infection, which irritated her genital area. Because of this, she was also repeatedly observed touching her genitals. It appears that the school put the two unrelated events together and drew the conclusion that Jane might be experiencing some form of sexual abuse.

Additionally, and unknown by the LeBars, the school had recently assigned two staff to be with Jane at all times, who would monitor her "every move." Jane, when touched by the staff, began to slap the arms of the aides. This was a brand-new behavior and drew more concern from the school staff, who failed to share that with the LeBars directly. They would, however, make notations in Jane's daily notebook that was completed by staff, reporting any progress or issues each day. The LeBars found this unacceptable, wishing to be notified immediately should such behaviors arise. The LeBars also emailed staff, making that request; however, staff reported that they never received the emails.

The situation now is that we have a child with limited language and enunciation skills, who:

1. will, on occasion, mix English and French words and who might well have used the word "petite," misunderstood by the school staff to be referencing the female breast

2. is suffering from a urinary tract infection and, not knowing how to express that problem, did what any child of her abilities might do (rubbing the irritated area)

3. when in close proximity to the two adults who would guide her by the arms, reached out and slapped their arms in an attempt to make them move away.

In short, Jane had become an extremely unhappy child and was acting out both at school and at home.

However, once the LeBars realized that Jane was suffering from the urinary tract infection, they removed her from school and immediately brought her to a physician, who prescribed several medications. Two months later, she was still at home, not yet having fully recovered from the infection. This, according to Mrs. LeBar, was not unusual given Jane's general health. Mrs. LeBar felt that between the pain that Jane was in and the constant monitoring by staff, her daughter had become frustrated enough to slap staff's arms as her way of expressing herself.

At the last IEP meeting, the district refused to provide either homebound services (for children who are expected to be out of school for an extended period of time) or home instruction (an optional special education programming at home under certain conditions, usually related to behavioral issues in school, but that can also be provided under other agreed-upon circumstances). The rationale for refusal of home instruction was that, even when Jane was not feeling well in school, she would "make educational progress." (Again, the school used key wording they could use to "defend" the programming provided, should there be a court action.)

Jane is currently receiving ESY services from an exceptional instructional aide for three hours, three times per week. The LeBars report that Jane is a happier young lady, "much more like herself," with no slapping. She is making significant and observable progress with the instructional assistant, and, given the magnitude of differences from that in the school, the LeBars have decided the best approach to take will be homeschooling. They are presently investigating the laws and regulations related to the homeschooling of children with disabilities, to ensure that they are all followed. They are certain that Jane's needs are finally going to be met. According to the instructional assistant, "Jane has such good manners."

For now, this may be the best placement for Jane. The LeBars are video-recording Jane's instruction to show her academic, social, and behavioral growth. This is an excellent way of collecting academic and behavioral data. It is hoped that the LeBars will be able to use this information, should they wish to return to public education, to develop an appropriate IEP that will meet Jane's needs. Certainly, the videos will provide documentation to answer the first question, "What do we know?" If the videos do assist in showing visual measures of the skills and behaviors Jane exhibits, the recommendation remains that they and the school work with an IEP facilitator.

Addendum

Just prior to completion of this book, Mr. LeBar contacted me to ask if I knew any sources to locate caregivers or graduate students who were familiar with ABA to work with Jane. Mr. LeBar explained that he made his final attempt to request home services for Jane, because she has a medical prescription to remain at home due to gastro-intestinal problems that have yet to be resolved in spite of various medical treatments. To his surprise, the district director approved after-school ABA services from an instructional assistant who is well-versed in the program and who has also been able to obtain "significant" growth, having worked with Jane in the past. To my surprise, the director also approved the very music therapy report that, in an earlier IEP meeting, she had claimed failed the criteria established by the district for independent educational evaluations.

The only explanation that Mr. LeBar could conceive was that, should the LeBars elect to remove Jane from the district special education count, the district would lose some amount of funding that would normally be allotted to the school program had Jane been included in that count. At this point, we simply do not know the district's rationale, but I do know that the family is seeking additional caregivers to support Jane at home.

CHAPTER 10

When a School Should Say "No" to an Attorney

As we've discussed, an Individualized Education Program (IEP) functioning at its best is the result of a collaborative meeting of parents, teachers, and other professionals that focuses on the needs of the child by asking and answering key questions:

1. What do we know? What don't we know?

2. Where do we want to go?

3. How will we get there?

4. How do we know that we are getting there?

5. Who is responsible for this plan?

6. How do we know when we have arrived?

7. How do we keep what we have?

8. When is it time to move on?

Unfortunately, this ideal is not always achieved. Sometimes a teacher or a school district has an agenda, goal, or plan that conflicts with the needs of the child. Sometimes the individual with a personal agenda is the parent. When the IEP team veers off the course set by these specific questions, then—even with the best of intentions—the child's needs can become a secondary focus. When this happens, what is best for the child is often lost to a diverted agenda-oriented discussion, with decisions being made that are not related to the child's needs. Determination and advocacy are always important, but neither the wishes of the parents nor those of the school team should ever take priority over the needs of the child.

Mrs. Torney and Dane's Story

"…It was much quicker for me to pay for the doctor's reports and get exactly what I wanted than to wait for the school to schedule them."

I am the dedicated, devoted, unstoppable mother of Dane, a nine-year-old little boy with severe autism. I will do whatever it takes to make sure he has the best life possible. When it comes to advocacy, I have an advantage. While I don't have the influence of a celebrity, I do have a juris doctor of law. I'm not some high-powered attorney, but I can work my way through the legal jargon to understand what the laws say about my son's rights. I'm determined that he receives everything he is entitled to by law.

Many parents are at a disadvantage when it comes to advocating for their child. You hear all sorts of stories about parents who are denied services, because they don't know how to demand them. They need to learn how the special education legal system works, and work the system to their advantage. I can do that, because I bring the weight of my legal expertise to every IEP meeting. I do the research and the preparation necessary to make a solid case for my son's needs.

It's up to the parents to make certain their child's individual needs are met. I have always been treated as an equal with Dane's IEP team, but I believe it's because I have "Esq." [meaning that she is an attorney or barrister] at the end of my name. I don't believe all parents are treated as equals, which is quite wrong. What I do for a living has had a huge impact on what I am able to get for my son.

I believe that parents should make sure their child is placed in the school environment where he or she has the greatest opportunity to interact with children who do not have a disability and to participate in the general education curriculum. And I have a voice—it is a very loud voice that will always be there to speak up for Dane. This is my passion! Once I set my mind to do something, there is no turning back. "Can't" isn't in my vocabulary. It is this strong attitude that's helped me throughout this journey with Dane's autism and his IEP.

It started when Dane, my older son, was diagnosed with classic infantile autism at age two. Dane is at the severe end of the autism spectrum, which, for him, means he cannot use words to communicate, use the toilet by himself, or take care of his personal care needs. He's constantly running around the house and requires 24-hour care and special education services.

Before he turned three, he was also diagnosed with severe sensory integration disorder. This affects his ability to organize and process information captured by his senses the way another person would. A child with sensory integration disorder can experience hypersensitive or hyposensitive symptoms, meaning the child may avoid certain sensory inputs or may seek out certain sensory inputs. Dane is hyposensitive, and craves constant sensory input, especially touch. This is why he is in constant motion, never sitting still. Dane is unable to sense where his body is in relation to the space around him, so he runs around and crashes into things to get enough input to understand where he is in his environment.

When he was four, Dane was diagnosed with severe verbal apraxia of speech, a disorder that seems to affect the brain's ability properly to send signals to move the muscles involved in speech. Dane was also diagnosed with epilepsy when he was seven, which was an adventure in itself. Dane has been on anti-seizure medication for the past two years, but could still have a seizure at any time. So, Dane has a lot of challenges, and it's my job to make sure he has the best services possible, so he can overcome these challenges and make the kind of progress I expect to see.

Dane's services started with early intervention services provided by the state, which included Applied Behavior Analysis (ABA) and speech therapy. Every aspect of this intervention is customized to each learner's skills, needs, interests, preferences, and family situation in order to train the learner to use desired behaviors, instead of undesired behaviors. This would become Dane's most effective therapy, but, when he turned three, things needed changing.

My First IEP

At three, Dane was meant to start attending the school's pre-kindergarten ABA program for children with autism. Before that would happen, I needed to make sure everything would be in place to meet his needs. All of that was to be determined at my first IEP meeting, which I expected to be a fight. Others told me, "You won't get anything you need at your IEP meetings—the school district will fight you on everything." But they were wrong!

Dane's child study team was made up of some of the best professionals I have ever met. After working with this team for the past six years, I can say they have been nothing but accommodating, supportive, and caring of Dane's needs. Of course, I didn't know that going in. All I knew was that preparation would make all the difference in the world.

I started preparing months ahead of time. I read up on all the services that Dane would be entitled to. I scheduled appointments with doctors, and I paid for any appointments the insurance company wouldn't cover. At each appointment, I told the doctors specifically what the medical reports needed to state (i.e., needed therapies) so that the school would provide the services Dane needed for each of his diagnoses.

I suppose I could have waited for the school district to do their own analyses, but it was much quicker for me to pay for the doctors' reports and get exactly what I wanted than to wait for the school to do so. The quicker I got the reports, the quicker Dane got the services he needed. When I arrived at the IEP meeting, I had my paperwork in a tabbed binder along with a list of my concerns.

I was ready to fight for my son. I was determined to get everything that Dane needed at that meeting. I brought my sister-in-law with me for moral support and as a second set of ears to listen to what the child study team would say.

To my surprise, the meeting was conducted in a very congenial atmosphere. The focus was where it ought to be—on Dane's best interests. The case manager started the meeting by sharing all the information they had received. The school had read the doctors' reports and agreed with their recommendations. I got everything I wanted for my son, because it was all stated in the reports. I was very lucky to get such a great team! Later, when differences of opinion did arise, we were able to work through them amicably.

Preparation really does make a difference. I had that binder with a picture of Dane on the front cover, showing that picture to everyone in attendance. I told them, "I am here to get what is best for this beautiful little boy."

Starting School

That first year at Jetson, Dane received occupational therapy (OT) for his sensory integration disorder, physical therapy for his low muscle tone and balance issues, and speech therapy for his communication skills, particularly speaking. The school used ABA throughout the day. Dane had a one-on-one paraprofessional, his classroom teacher, and the head behaviorist of the school working with him. All of these things are specifically stated in his IEP.

The first few months were a difficult transitional period for Dane. He screamed and threw tantrums at school, but he was always happy and content in his own house, where he had no demands placed on him. The school, however, placed demands on Dane (e.g., sharing, attending to instructions, etc.). He did not want to sit for them. Eventually he would, and would start to do his programs, but it was a very long process. Everything has to be broken down into little bits and pieces when teaching Dane. Progress comes very, very slowly. This was something I had to realize.

I was also able to have the school pay for Dane to receive ABA therapy at home every Saturday for two hours. Without this extra therapy time, he would have a very difficult time going back to school on Mondays. So, Sunday was the only day he didn't receive therapy.

I learned how to continue Dane's ABA program myself. I would do whatever the school was doing at home. I attended training sessions the school provided for parents of children on the autism spectrum. I had to learn a whole new way of raising my son. It wasn't just me; my husband, my mom, my dad, and my stepmom all had to learn these new ways to handle Dane's behaviors.

I would also do Floortime, with Dane at home. I wanted Dane to take an interest in his little brother, who does not have autism, and this proved to be a great way to get Dane and Dale to play together. We would follow Dane's lead in trying to have him interact with us. We did this almost every night for about a half-hour.

So my homework was to continue all the therapies Dane was doing at school while he was at home. Even then, with everything the school and I did, it just wasn't enough to see the gains I wanted.

Lack of Progress

By May 2007, all these therapies had been going on for a year. Dane was four, and he was still not talking. We would meet with our child study team every month to review Dane's progress. He just wasn't making progress with his speech teacher. This wasn't what I wanted, and it wasn't what Dane needed. I didn't wait for the school to come up with a plan. I scheduled an appointment with a speech pathologist, whom a friend had recommended, and that's when Dane was diagnosed with severe verbal apraxia of speech. The evaluation cost $2,500, and I knew the school district were not going to pay for this. I didn't ask; I just did it.

The evaluation itself was a horrible experience. Dane cried and threw tantrums. It was all so very stressful. The new diagnosis had shocked me. So, now I had to learn what this new thing was. I learned that verbal apraxia of speech is present from birth, so even though it was news to me, it wasn't new for my son. Some believe it is a neurological disorder that affects the brain's ability to send the signals necessary for the muscles to make speech properly. Children with this disorder generally can understand language much better that they are able to produce it. This is my Dane, and the disorder is severe.

The specialist said that Dane's speech therapy services should be provided by a PROMPT-certified speech therapist. PROMPT stands for Prompts for Restructuring Oral-Muscular Phonetic Targets. In simple terms, the therapist puts his or her hand on certain areas of the child's head—his or her face, jaw, or under the chin—to help the child say a specific type of sound or word. But, even with PROMPT therapy, severe cases like Dane's often require the use of alternative forms of communication. The specialist recommended we teach Dane to use the Picture Exchange Communication System (PECS™), which is a communication tool that uses generic pictures of items or actions to help a nonverbal child communicate basic wants and needs.

Luckily, the child study team understood and implemented it immediately. My strategy worked. Dane received PROMPT speech therapy from his speech pathologist—a half-hour each day. We hoped we would see progress with both his verbal development and his ability to use PECS™. It takes Dane a very long time to grasp new concepts and then use them. I never in a million years would have thought the ability to talk and speak was so complicated, but I was beginning to understand what that meant to Dane's learning.

I Got What I Wanted, But…

By February 2008, it was clear that—despite getting everything I wanted from the school district—Dane was not making the progress we'd hoped to see. We had hoped that Dane would have started talking. The IEP was being implemented exactly as it was meant to be, but it wasn't enough. The increased therapies were not helping Dane make progress with his language development. I had even asked for speech therapy at home and received it. Schools usually do not want to pay for speech therapy at home, but they did for Dane.

We got everything we knew to ask for, and it wasn't enough, so we started looking at other schools. This was one of the hardest things we had to do, because we didn't want Dane to leave our school district, but I firmly believed he needed a new speech therapist to get him to talk and communicate with us. I honestly believed that Dane's speech therapist was totally responsible for getting Dane to talk. If she couldn't, we'd find someone who could. What I didn't realize was that speech therapy was only a small part of Dane's overall program, and that the whole program affected his development in communication. In my mind, it was all about the speech therapist, and if this one wasn't going to work, then we needed to find a new one—which meant a new school.

I was very particular about what I wanted in a school. I wanted one with a strong staff of qualified speech therapists—the more the better. I wanted a school that could accommodate my son's needs until he was 21, which our current school couldn't do. So, I looked for a new school for my Dane. When I found a school I thought would work, we took Dane on a tour. I had done my research on this school, and I had a list of about 20 questions that I wanted answered at the meeting. I was satisfied with the answers. They had nine speech therapists, and I hoped one of them could make a breakthrough with our son.

Escalating Behaviors

In September 2008, aged five, Dane started at his new out-of-district school. At first, all appeared well, but staff used group teaching more than the previously more helpful one-on-one instruction. Within the first six months, we saw behavioral changes occur. By June 2009, Dane would not sit or attend to his work. He was attacking the staff—biting, pulling hair, scratching, pinching, and kicking. It worsened over summer. Staff said they needed three or four people just to calm him down. Dane regressed, losing the few words he had. After this regression, communication was limited to sounds and hand gestures. This was intolerable!

Through another service provider, we received a recommendation to the Carbone Clinic, an ABA program in New York. I set up an appointment, hoping the evaluation would determine the best teaching method for Dane. Despite the cost, I wouldn't ask the school district, because I didn't want to wait for their lengthy decision. We needed answers now!

We didn't have the money, so I hung up and told my husband. He said, "What if this is the one specialist that can help our son? What if this evaluation will make a difference for Dane?" He was absolutely right! I called and made that appointment. We sold some things to pay for the appointment, but it was worth it. After all, those were just things—things can be replaced. This was an opportunity to help my son and that's all that really mattered.

It turned out to be one of the best things we could ever have done. The results were surprising. We learned that Dane's current program's level of difficulty made the entire experience far more frustrating than he could handle. Even more surprising was that the clinic recommended the exact kind of environment and programming that Dane had been receiving at Jetson.

The out-of-district school couldn't, or wouldn't, provide Dane with what he needed. We realized it was time to return to our home school. I had gotten so caught up on the fact that this out-of-district school had nine speech therapists and had believed so strongly that at least one of them would make the breakthrough Dane needed to talk, that I lost sight of the other things our home school provided that had worked so well for Dane.

Returning to Our Local School

It took until January 2010 to complete the transfer to his home school. It worked out well as this would occur after the winter break, making for a clean break between schools. All things considered, Dane adapted extremely well. The violent behaviors stopped. He no longer needed to be restrained in order to calm down and he stopped attacking staff. It was like he became a completely different child. I could see in his eyes how happy he was to return to the school that better met his needs.

Progress remained slow. Dane would still run around in circles when he was to sit, or cry to get his way. But these behaviors were nothing like the aggression we saw at the other school. We were much happier with the changes. Thanks to the programs we'd developed and recommendations made by the Carbone Clinic, Dane was getting the services he needed at home and at school.

Everything seemed to be going well until May 20, 2010. It happened about five minutes before Dane was meant to get on the bus. His teacher noticed a glazed look in his eyes. His face turned white and his lips went blue. He started to drool. She picked him up and rushed him to the principal, who called an ambulance to take Dane to the hospital. Then, Dane just fell asleep and remained asleep all the way to the hospital.

Around 3 p.m. my cell phone rang. I was at work, so I didn't answer it, but I did listen to the voicemail message. When I called back, the school secretary told me they were taking Dane to the hospital, because they thought he'd had a seizure. By the time we arrived at the hospital, Dane had woken up and was crying hysterically. I was so thankful to see that he was okay. For the next hour he was attacking us and crying. He wanted to leave the hospital, but he couldn't. Dane was admitted for an overnight observation and a video electroencephalogram (EEG). At some point the neurologist told me that Dane did have a seizure and that autistic children have a 25 to 33 percent chance of developing epilepsy, which is a seizure disorder. The chances were even higher, because Dane's father had epilepsy when he was young.

Dane didn't have another seizure right away, but the after-effects of that first seizure were horrible. His behaviors were out of control. For two weeks, Dane was constantly upset—seeming uncomfortable. He attacked us, and nothing would appease him. The neurologist told me it can take children up to two weeks to recover from a seizure and that during this time their behavior can be affected. After those horrible two weeks, Dane was almost back to being himself.

Then, almost three weeks after his first seizure, Dane had his second. Again, it happened at school, at the same time, in the exact same way. I was prepared and knew what needed to be done this time. The neurologist put him on anti-seizure medication and upped his dose of Risperdal. Dane officially had epilepsy.

These two seizures greatly affected his behavior at school. He did not want to sit and work anymore. All his achievements were gone. He would no longer sit and work for his teacher any more than five minutes at a time. Before the seizures, he'd been working through all 20-plus programs throughout the day, every day, without any major catastrophes or problems. He had regressed yet again. It was time for a change.

Another New School

If Jetson could no longer meet Dane's needs and help him progress, then he needed a new school. I would not tolerate regression. So, once again, I began the search for the right school.

This time I wanted to make sure we found one that could accommodate his needs until he turned 21. I printed out a list of over 150 autism schools in the area and called every single school that was in or around the area we lived. I described Dane to them to see if they could accommodate his needs. Out of 150 schools, only six were worth touring. Two of the six survived that list. One of the remaining two schools said they couldn't provide Dane with anything more than he was already getting, so that left one.

Unfortunately, the school I liked best, the one that felt right in my gut, told us they did not have an opening for Dane, but could put him on a waiting list. It had taken five months to get this far and it appeared that Dane would have to wait for the next several years for an opening.

Luckily, we discovered that Dane was making progress at Jetson after all. It was slow, but progress was progress. Unfortunately, Jetson could not accommodate Dane's needs through age 21, so we still needed to search for a school that could. Until then, we were content to stay with Jetson, or so I thought.

Then, just to prove that he really didn't want to be at Jetson anymore, Dane started throwing up at school. As per school policies, Dane was sent home every time he threw up. We took him to the doctor, but nothing was physically wrong. It was a new behavior. I thought he wasn't connecting with school staff any more and this was his way of telling. He knew if he threw up, Mommy or Daddy would come pick him up and take him home. The school did a functional behavior assessment (FBA) and agreed that he was throwing up to escape from school. So, we decided, as a team, that Dane needed to get into another school right away that could meet his needs and had an opening.

In the end, we didn't find the right school; the right school found us. We had placed some video footage of Dane and his behaviors on YouTube. About a week later, I received an email from someone who had seen my video. She was truly touched by my video and wanted me to come to her school to do a parent presentation. I called, and we ended up talking about how Dane needed a new school to accommodate his needs. By the end of the conversation, we determined that her school would be a great fit for him and conducted an intake the following week. This time Dane didn't throw a tantrum as we walked through the door. He had a smile on his face! We took our tour, and I liked what I saw. I knew this was the right place for my child.

Dane could start during the summer program in July 2011. I am happy to tell you that since my Dane started full-time in September 2011, he has been making tremendous progress! He has been able to learn how to use Picture Exchange Communication System (PECS™) to communicate, and that's a huge, huge accomplishment! He is also being potty trained again and it seems to be working. I am hopeful he will be fully potty trained within the next year. He sits and attends to his programs again, sitting at his desk for 30–40 minutes without getting up, which is another huge accomplishment for him! I am hopeful that the 2012 school year will be Dane's best year yet.

Analysis of "Mrs. Torney and Dane's Story"

This scenario illustrates an important lesson for us all. Regardless of the mother's occupation or the child's disability, the actions taken by Dane's mother and educators could easily happen to any child with a disability. The lesson applies whether you have a law degree or any other form of exceptional influence. The lesson applies whether your child has autism or any other disability, regardless of its severity. There is a problem any time an individual or institutional need outweighs the needs of the child, and this needs to be addressed and resolved. This analysis will look back on the information presented throughout the scenario and recall the specific data that indicated Dane's levels of performance and functioning. This information (or lack thereof) will be important as we attempt to answer the six key questions that make up the analysis.

Where Are We?

What Do We Know?

The first thing we learn is that Dane's mother is determined to advocate for her son and will use every resource available to her to ensure that he is placed in the best environment. Mrs. Torney is certainly *not* to be faulted for this or her approach in any way. She also adds, "Once I set my mind to do something, there is no turning back." We learn that Dane has a complex set of disabilities that include autism, sensory integration disorder, severe verbal apraxia, and epilepsy. We learn he received early intervention services that included speech therapy and ABA therapy, both delivered at home. We do not learn what these services were intended to address or anything about the progress he did or did not make while receiving these therapies, though we do get a general assessment of the language and behavioral delays associated with his disabilities. We know these services continued, with variations in time and in combination with some additional services, over the course of the entire timeline of this scenario. We know that Dane's mother came into her first IEP meeting expecting an adversarial relationship.

From the start, we know Dane has developmental issues that include behavior and language delays. Keep in mind that these scenarios could not and need not provide all the details that would be necessary in an IEP meeting. We learn enough to know these delays are historical and continue throughout the scenario and after its conclusion. Dane's mother came to her first IEP meeting well prepared, with documentation that included medical and therapist reports that contained recommendations pertinent to the IEP plan under discussion. We also know that this level of preparation continues throughout the scenario. We can assume that these reports provided sufficient detail about Dane's abilities, at least for the initial IEP meeting, to answer the first questions, "What do we know?" and "Where are we?"

Perhaps most important, we learn that Dane's mother is prepared to present this wealth of information to the IEP team in order to "get" everything she wants for her son. She is not disappointed, which changes the relationship from a potentially adversarial one to one of cooperation and collaboration—from the perspective of Dane's mother. We do not know if a representative from the early intervention program (EIP) attended the meeting, and we do not get a sense that staff at the preschool program had previously observed Dane. While we do not know how the discussion unfolded at this meeting, we do know that the team members agreed to the recommendations presented in the various reports, and that Mrs. Torney "gets" everything she wanted. So, we see that answering "What do we know?" and "Where are we?" is key to a successful meeting.

We learn later on in the scenario that it is extremely important, even urgent, for Mrs. Torney to have her son evaluated as quickly as possible, because, as she says, "Time is of the essence." As Mrs. Torney undoubtedly realized, the school's procedures are not designed to satisfy her sense of urgency. Her commitment and resourcefulness is laudable, but I can't help but point out that by paying for and overseeing these assessments and the reports they produced, she had a great degree of influence on the reports' recommendations.

Mrs. Torney readily admits that her status as an attorney influenced how she was treated by the school team (e.g., cordially and with respect). She notes, with full candor, that she does not feel all parents are treated in a similar fashion and that her position as an attorney influenced Dane's program development. This may have been a satisfying position for Mrs. Torney, but, as we will see in the analysis, this level of influence did not always work in Dane's favor with regards to the development of his programming.

Where Do We Want to Go?
What Is It We Want to Accomplish?

Mrs. Torney's preparations included more than just the reports she gathered for the team to review. She spent considerable time generating key questions that would, with the team's agreement, answer the question "Where are we going?" More than anything, Mrs. Torney wanted to hear Dane "call me 'Mommy.'" Despite the hopeful culmination of her story, she is still waiting to hear those words from Dane, and this desire became the driving force in the development of Dane's programming.

Now, looking at this scenario from an outsider's perspective, we have to ask, "Was this driving force based on Dane's needs or his mother's?" "Was the cooperation Mrs. Torney received from the school based on a shared vision of Dane's needs, or was it based on the institution's need to comply with Mrs. Torney's requests?"

The answers to these questions become increasingly important as we proceed with this analysis.

Mrs. Torney came into that first meeting with a list of concerns that she wanted addressed. Overall, she had fairly specific concerns that focused more on how the school was going to do something rather than the objective of what they were going to do. We can also assume—though no specific data were provided in the scenario—that the assessment reports provided measurements of Dane's current functioning and performance levels, from which the initial measurable goals and objectives or benchmarks could be developed. We do not, however, know how these measurements were used to develop goals, objectives, and benchmarks that would set the course for Dane's programming.

Let's take a brief break from the analysis to explore the differences among goals, objectives, and benchmarks:

1. Measurable goals are statements—based on the child's needs as identified through assessments, tests, observations, etc.—that describe what is expected to be accomplished over the life of the school plan. They are measurable, because they describe a change in behavior that represents growth or progress; for example: "To increase the time Dane remains in his seat from zero minutes to ten minutes." But this only begins to describe what will be changed. So, we add objectives or benchmarks that are typically written sequentially.

2. An objective specifies the conditions under which we expect to see the change and begins to describe a pattern of improvement. For example, we might specify that we want Dane to remain in his seat for two minutes during instructional time, followed by another objective that increases the time to five minutes, and then increases it again to ten minutes. So, we know that the condition is instructional time, that we will measure progress in minutes, and that there is an expectation of slow growth over the course of the school year.

3. To change these objectives into benchmarks, we add an anticipated time when each objective will be achieved. For example, we could write that Dane will remain in his seat during story time for two minutes by the end of October. So, we know that we will be observing the length of time Dane stays in his seat during story time, and that a measure of two minutes is expected by the end of October, demonstrating learning through the change in behavior.

As you see in these examples, the components of each provide a different set of details. In many countries, goal statements are sufficient to meet the legal requirements, but it is important to use the added details provided by objectives and benchmarks when developing programming for children with more complex, basic-functional needs. If objectives and benchmarks had been used when developing

Dane's programming, then Mrs. Torney would have had a written statement on which to base her expectations of growth. It's apparent that this was not the case. Mrs. Torney was very well organized and thoroughly prepared. She presented her concerns, making good use of supporting assessments to make her case to the team. Due to Mrs. Torney's underlying desire to hear her son call her "Mommy," the pertinent question might have been stated as, "Where do we want to go immediately?" Certainly, language development was a priority for Mrs. Torney, but neither the school nor the reports indicated the degree of progress Dane could be expected to make given his various diagnoses.

In summary, we were not provided with a description of what exactly they wanted to accomplish or how these accomplishments were to be measured. For example, was saying "Mommy" sufficient to signify appropriate language development? As we proceed through this analysis, it will become more and more apparent that these objectives were not clearly defined as a team, and that this ambiguity created problems that were still not, at the conclusion of the scenario, resolved.

How Will We Get There?

Mrs. Torney was very specific about the services that were to be provided: speech therapy for language development; OT for motoric development, sensory integration, and spatial orientation; and ABA for behavioral training and reducing "autistic-like" behaviors. On the surface, these specifications answer "How will we get there?" But they could only do so if the team had clearly stated where they wanted to go.

How Do We Know That We Are Getting There?

Under normal circumstances, we would assume that the team had developed reasonable and measurable annual goals, objectives, and benchmarks when they answered the question "Where do we want to go?" These expectations would be based on what could be accomplished over the period of the plan, based on the teacher's and therapists' professional experience and training, as they reviewed the information found in the reports provided. We would also assume that the staff would be the first to recognize whether Dane was making the expected progress described in those goals, objectives, and benchmarks. We might also assume that this information was communicated in a format that all parties could understand and interpret, so that all parties knew what to expect in terms of Dane's rate of progress.

This, of course, does not mean that each benchmark would be met at precisely the time indicated in the goals. But it does mean that the teacher and therapists, based on their professional judgment and the measurements they took, could demonstrate the present levels of performance, which would answer the questions

"What do we know?" and "Where are we?" at future meetings. It would give the entire team a guide as to what to expect and when.

Unfortunately, it's clear from how the scenario progresses that this probably wasn't the case. It seems that Mrs. Torney—an intelligent and informed woman— had inaccurate expectations regarding the rate of progress she was likely to see, which led to her frustration and her determination to seek services through a program that she presumed would be better and more able to provide the results she wanted.

If the team had agreed on the progress they expected to see and tracked the results of their efforts, then they could have effectively answered the question "How do we know that we are getting there?" during their monthly meetings. Furthermore, because the staff were monitoring Dane's progress, they could have identified areas of minimal or exceptional growth, and the team could have invited Mrs. Torney to come in to discuss the direction Dane's progress was taking and possible revisions to the plan. Instead, at least after a certain point, Mrs. Torney was leading the team to make other programmatic and placement decisions based on *her* needs and expectations.

Was it wrong for Mrs. Torney to seek the very best for her child? Absolutely not! The problem, however, comes from defining "the very best" based on her needs and her expectations, instead of basing the definition on Dane's needs and the informed expectations of professional staff. So, for the remainder of this analysis, we will focus on the breakdown of "perceived" collaboration—just saying "Yes" to Mrs. Torney—between the parent and the school staff versus what should have taken place. Essentially, we will explore why the school staff should have said "No," and what parents can do to ensure they do not displace their child's needs with their own needs and expectations.

How Do We Know When We Have Arrived?
How Do We Keep What We Have?
Where Do We Want to Go from Here?

It should be perfectly clear that Mrs. Torney was not satisfied with Dane's growth, particularly in the area of language development. We know she ultimately paid for another outside evaluation, which provided an additional diagnosis of verbal apraxia. So, these questions ("How do we know when we have arrived?" "How do we keep what we have?" "Where do we want to go from here?") cannot be answered. All we know with any certainty is that Mrs. Torney observed growth that was much slower than she wanted. Eventually, Mrs. Torney realized that this was part of Dane's learning process, though she had difficulty accepting this; subsequently, she needed to adjust her expectations. Had the school made the effort to explain that Dane was progressing at his own pace, and had Mrs. Torney accepted their explanation, then several problems could have been avoided.

Programming at Home

Mrs. Torney requested and obtained ABA therapy at home. She and the school staff noticed that over the course of a weekend, Dane would lose some of the behavioral progress he made during the week, because of the time he was away from school. As Mrs. Torney insisted, parents should watch for regression—which is a loss or deterioration of previously acquired skills—and should bring these observations to the attention of program staff. Mrs. Torney also took advantage of training provided by the school in order to learn how to carry out ABA therapies at home and made certain that her very caring and supportive family worked with Dane in the same way, recognizing his need for consistency.

Mrs. Torney genuinely devotes an incredible amount of her home time to Dane and his language development. More to the point, despite these efforts, she had yet to hear Dane call her "Mommy" and had, in general, not seen sufficient progress in language development to satisfy her expectations. Unfortunately, at that time, she held the speech and language therapist personally responsible for the lack of language development.

A Decision Point for Mrs. Torney

It is at that point—due to her dissatisfaction with Dane's rate of progress despite the services received at school and at home—that Mrs. Torney became determined to find the person, intervention, and program that would enable Dane to reach her goal. In the process, she narrowed her focus from the scope of Dane's needs to a set of criteria dominated by speech therapy. To meet her need for change, she sought out a costly language evaluation to help determine what type of programming Dane should receive, which she paid for herself, noting that immediacy was her primary motivation and that she never requested the school system to conduct such an evaluation.

While many parents may applaud this decision and Mrs. Torney's willingness to assume this cost, I must point out that many parents simply cannot afford to pursue this avenue of investigation independent of the school system. It is precisely for this reason, and because they recognize the need for reliable information, that the school system has resources to investigate and assess the needs of children with disabilities, which is available regardless of a family's ability to pay. Therefore, Mrs. Torney could have asked the school system to pay for the evaluation.

If the school system refused, and if the results of the independent evaluation differed from the evaluation that had been used in the initial programming—

meaning that there were differences in conclusions, recommendations, *and* programming—then the school could have been held accountable for the payment. On the other hand, the school could have intervened and offered to conduct an assessment of its own. This is a moot point for this scenario, because the school staff were not asked, and we don't know if they were aware that Mrs. Torney was seeking an independent evaluation. I bring this up only to reassure readers who may think they would have to pay for this kind of evaluation themselves; Mrs. Torney's urgency aside, there are opportunities through the school system to conduct in-house assessments and to fund independent assessments when necessary.

My purpose is not to criticize Mrs. Torney but to point out other steps that could have been taken, which is particularly important in light of the financial difficulties the family faced later in the scenario. Of course, this represents a real dilemma for many families with children with disabilities, especially when so many parents are warned that school assessments are biased in the school's favor, which is, unfortunately, sometimes true, though the practice is perhaps not as prevalent as some families are led to believe.

Parents often face similar questions: Do I pay for something that might actually tell me what the problem is and might help me to get more appropriate interventions in place more quickly? Or do I try to convince the school system that an independent assessment is reasonable because the present interventions are not producing the results that I want? What if the professional educators tell me that the present interventions are appropriate for my child, and I still have to pay for the independent evaluation? What if they're wrong? What if they're right?

It's very difficult to know what the best approach to take would be in such a situation. I can, however, propose a set of steps that could have and should have been taken that may have accomplished Mrs. Torney's goals without costing her any money.

A Better Approach for Mrs. Torney

Before deciding to pursue and pay for an evaluation independent of the school system, Mrs. Torney should have called the staff together and clearly stated her concerns regarding Dane's progress in the area of language. The next step would have been to ask the team, "Why has progress not taken place?" This would bring the entire team back to the questions "What do we know?" and "Where are we?" These answers would have led to the questions "Why are we here?" and, ultimately, "Why are we not further along?" This is the very first step in the Structured Collaborative IEP Process.

It is the team's responsibility to answer these questions. The team should have compared earlier assessments and the related goals, objectives, and benchmarks with current classroom behavioral and work samples in order to determine what progress has been made. Through this process, they would have determined whether Dane was making the degree of progress expected when the plan was first written. If the team had had shared expectations and if the team felt insufficient progress had been made in meeting these expectations, then they would have asked, "What don't we know?" This would have led to further research—either by conducting another evaluation or by trying a different intervention, depending on whether the data were sufficient to indicate if the current interventions were inappropriate for Dane's needs. But these questions were not asked.

There may well have been other staff within the school system who could have carried out the assessment. The team may have had access to other people within the school system who had unique skills or knowledge—staff they could have invited to observe Dane and his teacher/therapists and then sit in on the meeting to advise the team. As a result of such a meeting, the school system may have selected to pay for an independent assessor. They may even have paid for the assessment that Mrs. Torney had previously had conducted.

The question then becomes: Why didn't this happen? At this point, it's fair to conclude that Mrs. Torney's degree overshadowed the effectiveness of the team, because the team developed a routine simply to comply with her wishes rather than risk a legal entanglement.

Cost is a very real issue for all parents, and the time for legal intervention may come despite our best efforts to avoid it, but parents should work with the school first by using the process of guided collaboration and by answering the six questions posed throughout this book to ensure that the services provided meet their child's needs. Remember, the purpose of special education services is to meet the child's needs—not the school system's needs or the parent's needs, which was what had happened in this scenario.

Another Decision Point for Mrs. Torney

Through the independent assessment, Dane was diagnosed with severe verbal apraxia. As a result of the independent assessment, the school immediately implemented a new therapy, PROMPT. Approximately eight months later, Mrs. Torney reported that "they [still] did not see the results they were hoping for…" in Dane's language development—he still was not talking. She continued to blame the speech therapist for this lack of progress, and so she sought a different placement for her son.

Ultimately, and quite some time later, Mrs. Torney realized that it was not the therapist who failed to make the kind of progress she was hoping for, but rather the result of the severity of Dane's apraxia and the fact that speech therapy is only "a small part of his overall therapies…[to enable Dane]…to communicate." This is another critical realization, which the school had not made clear to Mrs. Torney.

Developing communication skills is not something that happens in isolation due to a single therapy. Perhaps they had tried to explain this, and she was not prepared to accept it, but the opportunity to do so had come and gone twice while "they" searched for another program for Dane.

The team ultimately agreed upon another program, one that had many more speech pathologists than the existing program, stirring Mrs. Torney's hopes that one of them would make a "breakthrough" that would empower Dane to talk to her. This program was located outside of the existing school system, but was paid for by the school district.

Yet Another Decision Point for Mrs. Torney

Shortly after beginning the program, Mrs. Torney and the new school staff saw a number of negative behavioral changes. Rather than address each behavioral change, I'll just point out that, again, Mrs. Torney did not choose to take her concerns to the school system and did not ask them to explain the reasons why the new program was not working, what options might remain, or if it was time to reassess Dane's program and needs. Instead, Mrs. Torney sought another assessment to determine the best method of instruction for Dane, which she also paid for, though she and her husband did not have the money readily available.

To quote Yogi Berra, a famous baseball coach who was known for his statements of the obvious, "It's déjà vu, all over again." The new evaluation revealed that Dane's behaviors had deteriorated because the new program did not, in fact, meet his needs. *The programming that would best address Dane's needs was, in fact, the programming provided by the original school that had only the one speech therapist.*

It is unmistakably clear that, when it came to shifting Dane from program to program, his mother being an attorney worked against him. According to Mrs. Torney, the school team was always ready to comply with her wishes and readily supported Dane's move from program to program. It is also apparent that the team, including Mrs. Torney, had failed to match the program of services to Dane's needs. The result was months of lost opportunity for Dane, time that would have been put to much better use with Dane continuing his progress in the original school environment.

Even after these experiences, we know that Mrs. Torney continued to look for other programs that would be "better" for Dane, and we can assume that the school system continued to agree with the parent. We can also assume that the team did not actively participate in the review of questions one through four. This begs the question: How can you possibly "get there," if you don't know where you are or where you are trying to go?

Wrapping Up the Analysis

Mrs. Torney is an incredibly dedicated mother. She is a champion for her son, Dane, and an advocate for children with autism. She is a brilliant and articulate person who can motivate others to her cause. She sacrificed much to provide her son with what she deemed was the best possible program for him. In the process, she lost sight of Dane's needs in favor of her own expectations, and—because the school did not say "No" and return the focus to identifying Dane's needs and evaluating his progress—she spent an exorbitant amount of time chasing her own tail. In the end, she was trying to meet her own needs, instead of Dane's.

There are five key issues within this scenario and the subsequent analysis with regards to Mrs. Torney's desires for Dane:

1. Mrs. Torney wanted to provide Dane with what she thought was the very best staff and programming available. As a result, she repeatedly sought a better/different program.

2. Mrs. Torney sought immediate action, whether it was an assessment or a programmatic change. The worst consequence of this urgency was the first change in school and program, which provoked Dane's aggressive behaviors—only to be followed by a costly evaluation that stated that Dane had been receiving the type of programming he needed prior to the change.

3. Mrs. Torney's sense of urgency also resulted in her choosing to incur the cost of multiple evaluations, which may have been conducted or funded by the school system.

4. Mrs. Torney's educational and career status—which should have been irrelevant during these proceedings—may have caused complications with regards to the way the school system responded to and interacted with Mrs. Torney, and may have caused the school staff to defer to Mrs. Torney's wishes in order to avoid litigation.

5. As a clear and formidable strength, Mrs. Torney is very thorough, organized, and articulate. She is able to gather the evidence required by the team to understand Dane's needs and to make very precise presentations. These are skills all parents would do well to learn and practice.

The school team did go through the first three steps of the Structured Collaborative IEP Process—that is, *they followed the parent's lead*. This raises five additional issues:

1. According to the scenario Mrs. Torney presented to us, the school staff did not lead the IEP team through the Structured Collaborative IEP Process, neither did they seem to add any information based on their own

observations or assessments. However, at the first meeting, the IEP team did answer the questions "Where are we?" and "What do we know?" They did so, because Mrs. Torney:

a. presented Dane's needs

b. explained Dane's levels of functioning

c. described his behaviors

d. shared supporting documentation that answered these questions.

2. Mrs. Torney then led the staff through the next question, "Where do we want to go?" Based on the information she had available, she was unable to answer this question beyond a general desire to improve (ability to attend and remain seated, interest in events and people around him, speaking and language development, among others) the areas identified above. At this point, the school should have made a clear case for where they could and would want to go within the limits of a single school year and a reasonable rate of expected progress. Had the school presented Mrs. Torney with clear, measurable goals, objectives, and benchmarks based on the evidence Mrs. Torney presented that established Dane's needs, they could have helped establish and express a reasonable expectation of growth shared by the team. Instead, Mrs. Torney retained her own set of expectations, which were not fulfilled by the plan the team created.

3. Once again, the school staff abdicated their responsibility to lead the IEP meeting in answering the question "How will we get there?" Mrs. Torney specified what therapies were to be provided and the amount of time and the frequency of those therapies. The school agreed without qualification or clarification, and this served as the answer to "How will we get there?" despite the lack of a clear "there" to get to.

4. According to the scenario, the team did not answer the question "How do we know that we are getting there?" Again, the answers to this question would have provided Mrs. Torney with some guided expectations regarding Dane's progress over the course of the school year. Additionally, regular reports would have communicated the progress he was making with her. Remember, it was eight months after implementing the new speech intervention that Mrs. Torney decided to look for another program. The school may have provided progress reports during this time period, but we have no indication that the school reviewed Dane's progress with her or explained why the

services he received were appropriate when they learned she wanted to seek another program.

5. They never reached the questions "How do we keep what we have?" or "Where do we go from here?"

We can draw a simple conclusion from these events: the school simply became a rubber stamp for Mrs. Torney's requests. Had they applied the Structured Collaborative IEP Process and appropriately addressed the second question— "Where do we want to go?"—it's quite likely that the outcome of this scenario would have been different. The problem is that no one stated what Dane was expected to achieve over the course of the IEP. If they had done so, Mrs. Torney would have learned more about Dane's disability, established realistic expectations for her son, and received and understood the school's reports concerning Dane's progress. If they had done so, then it is highly probable that Dane would have continued to make his slow, steady progress without being derailed by changing programs and having unmet needs.

Following the Structured Collaborative IEP Process isn't necessarily easy, but the process itself is simple and straightforward. It is important to address each step thoroughly and in order. You can't move forward successfully until you provide an appropriate answer to each question. We all want to see improvement and we all want to provide children with the best we have available, but these are abstract desires that do not make for appropriate educational goals. The IEP team needs specific, measurable goals—like a target on a dart board. That doesn't mean the team will always achieve the goals in the time allotted, but it does mean that the team will be able to recognize whether they are achieving those goals. If they're not achieving specific, measurable goals, then they need to go back to "What do we know?" in order to figure out why. These decisions are urgent, but it is also both urgent and important to base these decisions on data (information), not simply a want.

When Should the School Say "No"?
How Should Parents Respond?

First, to be clear, Mrs. Torney did what she felt was best for her son within the boundaries of her limited understanding of Dane's disability and needs. Despite these best intentions, it is undoubtedly clear that the school system should have said "No" to Mrs. Torney's demands on at least one occasion. It can also be assumed that Mrs. Torney's status as a legal professional and the school's strong desire to avoid a legal battle led the school system to abdicate their responsibility to lead the Structured Collaborative IEP Process.

What got lost in the process were Dane's needs. By not applying the six questions of the decision-making process, the team lost sight of Dane's needs, which resulted in a program that failed to meet his needs. Obviously, we can't go back and change the outcome for Dane, though we can hope that both Mrs. Torney and the school system learn from these experiences and make better choices for Dane in the future. Perhaps most importantly, we can learn from the experience. So, let's take a step back and reflect on what you can do to avoid a similar outcome.

At first glance, it can seem like the best approach to obtaining the services you want is to bring reports generated by medical and therapeutic specialists with you to your IEP meetings, especially if you pay for these reports and stipulate the programming recommendations they should contain. What better way to get what you want than to walk in with experts claiming to know exactly what your child needs? After reading this scenario, however, the problem should be obvious. What you want may not be what your child needs. If, whether you intend to or not, you ask for and receive what you want instead of what your child needs, then the contents of the reports will be flawed and will not help your child to succeed. So, the first thing we can learn from this scenario is that, as a parent, you must take care not to influence unduly any private specialists or consultants you use to help your child. Keep the focus on your child and on your child's needs, not on what you want for your child.

In addition to this obvious problem, however, there is another problem that pertains directly to the issue of collaboration. When a parent seeks recommendations from an expert, he or she often doesn't know whether that expert is qualified to work with the school system. The medical and therapeutic communities have their own standards, regulations, ethics, and legal obligations to uphold. The school has a different set of standards, regulations, ethics, and legal obligations to satisfy. Sometimes these different rules overlap, but sometimes they don't. The expert you choose to consult with may not be familiar with the school system or the requirements and regulations under which schools must operate.

Schools operate under a set of rules that are determined by governmental bodies, ranging from national to local governments, and judicial rulings. Rules like these influence or even dictate certain procedures and activities that must be followed within the confines of a school day. If the recommendations you bring with you ask for more time than is available in your child's day or ask for services that the school is not legally allowed to provide, then the school must refuse.

From a collaboration standpoint, it may seem to you that the school is simply being uncooperative. However, it is important that you realize that the school has its own standards, requirements, and regulations to follow. The school should review and consider the reports you bring in, but they do not have to accept the conclusions or recommendations found in the reports.

Furthermore, they have personnel who may interpret the findings and test results within the reports. "Interpret," in this case, means that the school personnel can understand the results of the assessment and interpret or "translate" those results into statements that are useful for program development and instruction. So, even without the kind of specific recommendations Mrs. Torney insisted on having, outside reports can be useful to school staff, because they do provide valuable information that answers the questions "What do we know?" and "Where are we?" Now, it's important to point out that their conclusions may agree or disagree with the interpretations of the expert; results are not necessarily definitive. Furthermore, the way you understood what the specialist said and wrote may be different from the way the school staff understood the same material. The school's professionals should even be able to explain things to you that you did not understand.

As a parent, you are not expected to be an expert in the various assessments or readily understand what the scores mean. You do not need to be able to "translate" these results in order to determine what type of service should be provided, if any, during the school day to address the needs identified in any of the reports provided, whether you bring the reports or whether the school performs the assessment. The team members are there to explain the scores to you so that they make sense. It is *your* responsibility to ask as many questions as you need in order to understand what the school personnel are saying. The intent of this discussion is to begin answering the first question, "What do we know?"

So, let's assume you want to follow Mrs. Torney's lead and come thoroughly prepared to your first (or next) IEP meeting. That's fine! Keep in mind, though, even assuming you do not influence the reports unduly, you may still arrive with a report that includes recommendations that are unreasonable, unnecessary, or overly specific without addressing the possibility of appropriate alternatives. Every school system has finite resources and abilities. A law-abiding school system will ensure those resources and abilities are invested in such a way that they meet students' needs. However, that does not mean you can or should demand whatever you *want* and expect to get it.

The outside specialist or consultant isn't going to be familiar with the resources available at your specific school. The school staff may realize that the school can meet your child's needs successfully, but in a way that differs from the recommendations you received. If you come to the meeting with a very narrow focus, ready to insist that the recommendations be carried out, you may close off the opportunity to collaborate successfully.

You do not start a successful Structured Collaborative IEP Process with "How will we get there?" You start the discussion with "What do we know?" Then, if you know enough to move forward, you ask, "Where do we want to go?" You can only determine how you are going to get there after you know where you are and where you want to go. That "how" is best answered by the team. You know your child best, so you are an important part of that team. But the school knows what they can reasonably achieve and what resources would be the best fit for your child's needs and the school's abilities. So, the school staff are equally essential for a successful team. You'll notice, however, that outside specialists aren't part of the team. They're outside of the team, and their results and interpretations are influenced by the resources they have available, which may differ considerably from those the school has available.

In the end, the school team may, after discussion, come to the same conclusions as the specialist. But if you skip that discussion, you might also find that your expectations for progress are not realistic. You might end up fighting for program changes and school changes simply because you are not pleased with your child's progress, only to discover that the progress your child was making was wholly reasonable within your child's limitations—that it was your expectations, not the program or the school, that were unsuitable.

The way to avoid being in this position is to ask each of the six questions and have the team answer those questions, interjecting with the information you have, but forcing the team to present the answers. By doing so, you will be facilitating a discussion in a collaborative manner, where the team (including you) will reach an agreement. If you don't ask the questions, you fail to create an environment that invites full participation, and you exclude alternative ideas and solutions that might otherwise arise from the discussion process.

Summary

In short, by skipping the Structured Collaborative IEP Process, you create a frustrating environment that limits the input you receive; by following the Structured Collaborative IEP Process, you increase the chances that the team will develop an IEP designed to benefit your child. By using the questions that make up the Structured Collaborative IEP Process described in this book, you will enhance the cooperation among team members, generate more ideas, and increase the likelihood of a successfully written plan that is based on your child's needs. The process protects you, your child, and the school from developing a plan that will fail, because it actively encourages the team to focus on meeting the child's needs.

CHAPTER 11

The Physical Education Conundrum and Solution for a Child with Physical Impairments

In this chapter, we have the opportunity to see the same scenario told from two different perspectives. I was fortunate to find a parent, Kathy, and a department chair of special education, Margaret, who were willing to share the story of how they worked together to provide a child with cerebral palsy with the physical education (PE) credits he needed to graduate by trying something new.

Kathy actually has two children with disabilities, and both are now in high school. Xavier, the eldest, is set to graduate this year. Margaret was appointed as the special education department chairperson only a year ago. Although she had 20 years' experience in teaching and private school administration, she received little training concerning the policies of this new position and relatively new school district and state. While federal legislation is intended to be applied consistently in each state or province, we all know that each state, school district, and school has its own procedural nuances that do not always transfer well from state to state or district to district. Regardless, Kathy and Margaret bravely agreed to write their portions of this story independently, knowing that both would share a different version of the same story.

Unlike most other scenarios in this book, this scenario revolves around a single, specific issue: should Xavier take a PE course "in class" with his peers, or could he take a more rigorous online course that could be adapted to his physical abilities?

This scenario demonstrates the importance of challenging the status quo in order to meet a child's needs. I also think it is interesting to see the different perspectives in terms of the two individuals' personal interactions and how they went about collecting information to answer the questions "What do we know?," "Where do we want to go?," and "How will we get there?" The last of these was the ultimate decision to be made. You will also see how and what each learned as a result of the decision-making process.

And, in case you are wondering, yes, Kathy and Margaret will be reading each other's version of this scenario for the first time when they receive their copies of this book.

Part 1: Can Physical Education Be Taught Online? A Mother's Perspective

"Before I decided if a battle was to ensue…"

Of all the courses to be online, PE is one of the last ones you may think of. After all, isn't PE meant to be active and not passively sitting in front of a computer? Most parents would think this is a contradiction in purpose. "An easy way out of taking PE," would be the next thought. Well, to me, as a parent of a child with cerebral palsy, I immediately thought this to be a *perfect* solution, but not for the reasons some may think.

My son, Xavier, is an Eagle Scout with the Boy Scouts of America; he hikes, he camps, he pitches tents, he rock-climbs, but high school PE classes simply weren't his "thing." Some of you might remember the horror stories of your own high school PE experiences. Perhaps you were always picked last for the teams, or you were made fun of for being a slow runner, or were just intimidated by all the sports jocks. As difficult as it might be for general education students trying hard just to "fit in," students with special needs struggle even more so. My son was no exception.

I was planning Xavier's tenth grade year, which is the last year PE classes were required to meet graduation requirements. As you can imagine, he was not looking forward to another year of PE. So, when I heard of an online PE course, I was ecstatic! I was not just thinking of his physical well-being (the demands on his system), although that was a factor; more importantly, I was reflecting on his emotional welfare. His self-esteem would really benefit if he could only escape that atmosphere of unfair demands, peer competition, and the fear of ridicule.

I was extremely excited, and, truthfully, my son was excited as well. This was *the* solution. We knew this would work for him for the very reasons just mentioned. Then came the wall—a big wall. The school said "No." They said it loudly. I was crushed—online PE would be such a great option for kids with similar needs to his. "Are you kidding me?" I thought, "Here we go again! Yet another battle with the school district. Sigh." (I am being polite using this word.)

Truly, I wondered if getting an online PE class was worth fighting for. I knew that it would involve finding the right laws, regulations, and any local policies.

It would mean finding the right people with the right answers, followed by a number of Individualized Education Program (IEP) meetings and the inevitable paperwork. Was it really worth all that work just so my son didn't have to do archery, weightlifting, or whatever else they had planned for him, which he couldn't do with his one useful hand? So, like so many decisions that we faced, I had to decide whether I wanted to fight this issue or save my energy, perhaps for a later fight on class schedules or something more important. I dreaded another round of battles.

The reasons the school denied our requests were clear to them: Xavier really didn't need the online class; besides, it was harder. Actually, the online class required him to monitor and keep a particular heart rate for a certain amount of time, then document it—electronically. It meant that a computer had to be made available to him, along with special computer connections meeting some sort of technical specifications. It meant that, because it was an online course, his classes would have to be hand-scheduled, so he could have a period freed up to take this course.

Before I decided if a battle was to ensue, I called the school division in charge of the online courses and asked some very basic questions. I was very careful not to give too much information, particularly about who I was or who my son was, during the conversation. (I thought this would help me to get truthful answers.) I asked, "How do the online courses work? What is the objective of the course? Have they ever worked with students with special needs in the online PE course? What did they do to make it work?" I chatted with the contact person, made notes, and then it hit me: *I can win this!*

Here is how I did it: the general objective of PE is to get the students actually to see and understand the benefits of an active lifestyle—or something close to that. The question was, "Just how active is my child in regular PE?" For example, for one quarter (half a semester) the sport activity is archery. Which meant, the question was, "How can a one-handed person participate in archery?" Of course, the answer was, "He couldn't."

So, the next question was, "What was the school's plan for him for that unit of instruction?" Well, he could be a score keeper or he could retrieve arrows. But, would my son's heart rate be raised? Would he be what most people would call "active," doing these things? Not at all!

So this was my rationale: Xavier would not actually be meeting the goals of the PE program if he were to "participate" within the general education PE curriculum. With the online PE course, he would be forced to exercise three times a week in a sport or activity that he could do, which would raise his heart rate for 30 minutes to a designated level. The sport activity (archery) being offered in the general education PE course would not do that for my son.

I poked and prodded different people, calling and talking to them, and I began to build my case for replacing the regular PE class with the online course. I started with my son's case manager, with whom I have an excellent relationship, and told her why we, as a family, thought the online PE class would work. I told the case manager that we would put in the extra effort to "scout out" and get the technical specifications, computer software, and whatever else we needed.

I called the high school counselor, who helps make class schedules and makes sure students meet graduation requirements. My approach with her was, "As my son is a tenth grader and this is his last year of required PE, could we try online PE? If it doesn't work, then he would still have his eleventh and twelfth grade years to do another year of the general education PE class in order to graduate." I stated that this class would actually make him more active than the general education class. It was a more personalized program for him that would allow him to do what he could do, unlike the general education class that would remove him from what he could not do.

A few more calls to the counselor and the case manager, and I could tell the tide was turning a bit. But they were not the final decision makers. I again called the school contact for online courses and asked, "Who makes the final decision if a student can take an online course?" The person told me, and I sent off an email to the director of student services (DSS) stating my case.

In the email, I stated my reasons and explained why we wanted to try this approach and I copied the guidance counselor, case manager, the "final decision maker," and now Margaret, the special education chair of the school. (She was my initial wall builder, the one who had said "No" so loudly a few months back.)

I waited. And then I waited some more. Finally, it was time for the annual review of my son's IEP, and time to select his classes for the next year. This was crucial timing for me, so I took on his IEP first.

The first step: I made sure the IEP team knew my son—his limitations, but also what a hard worker he was. He was on the honor roll and he was an Eagle Scout. They all agreed he was a conscientious student. No arguments there.

The next step: After the IEP was finished, I asked if we could take a moment to discuss the best choices for class selections (i.e., team taught, self-contained, or the general education classroom settings). We spoke a bit, made some decisions, and then I cautiously brought up the online PE course. The answer was still "No." The attitude was: "*We already told you this!*"

My heart sank. I asked nicely, "Can you just hear my reasons why we as a family think it can work?" Margaret sat down—I knew her time schedule was ticking and she wasn't going to hear me out for long.

I built my case, starting with the course objective, and explained how my son could meet that objective. I spoke about the importance of lifetime fitness goals, not just meeting a graduation requirement. I spoke about how, without online PE, my son would not be active at all within the general education curriculum. And I spoke about my son's self-esteem and how working in the online PE course would remove him from the ridicule he would receive when "participating" in the competitive piece of team sports in the general education PE class.

All I heard was, "OK, I'll approve it." Margaret was not thrilled, but she would support me by getting the administrative decision maker to sign off on the class change. I knew it meant more work for her, as my son's schedule would now have to be hand-scheduled to allow for the last period of the day to be freed for the online course. I hoped my case came across as "being worth the time." My son needed this course.

Well, after the summer, my son started the course, and in most respects we hated it. How we hated it! The heart monitor he needed to wear to document his workouts constantly didn't work. The computer programs did not work on our home operating systems. The quarterly in-person exercise tests were an hour away and took most of our family Saturday.

The work was far more than a usual PE class. He had report after report to do—all for PE! The good thing was that my son worked out—he really did! He got into the habit of, three or four times a week, going to the gym or getting on our equipment at home. He would put on his music and work out. I could not have been more pleased! Here he was doing something within his capabilities, at his own pace, not competing against anyone else, and being happy about it! It wasn't a race. It wasn't a contest. It was about his personal level of fitness.

Okay, I admit in some ways the school was right—the class was indeed more work. But I was right as well—it did help his self-esteem. It did remove him from the social aspects of the PE competition, and it helped him to think about himself, his own fitness goals, his own personal levels of fitness, and his own lifetime health. He earned a grade of "A" for the course. But he gained so much more in terms of personal fitness and self-esteem! The hassle of the class was worth it!

Part 2: Can Physical Education Be Taught Online? A Special Education Department Chair's Perspective

"But I do recall thinking that she was making some very good points and justifications for something other than what was typically offered…"

I must preface my account by saying that I met Xavier and his mother at the end of my first year as the high school special education department chair. I had no training, assistance, or support when I moved from a special education teacher into this position. Unfortunately, almost everything I learned about my position, I learned "on the job." As I recount this story, I can look back and see where I should have done things differently. But I can also reflect about what I have learned. I know why I acted the way I did then (because that's the way it had *always* been done, or because I didn't know any differently, or because that's what I had been told), but I now know that I can question what I'm told (just because someone answers my question doesn't mean it's the correct answer) and that, just because something is the "way it's always been done," doesn't mean that it's the correct way or that there aren't other, different ways to approach a situation.

So, now to the scenario: I met Xavier and his mother, Kathy, in his transition IEP meeting from eighth to ninth grade. Xavier had cerebral palsy that affected his left side. Academically, he was performing slightly below grade level, with goals for reading, writing, and self-advocacy. Given his physical disability, he required accommodations to compensate for his gross- and fine-motor skills. He needed extended time on assignments, as it took him longer to get materials out, to put them away, and to complete assignments. He was capable of the work—it just took him a little longer.

Xavier needed extra time between classes. He could navigate his way around the building, but he walked more slowly than most students and, in a school of close to 3,000 students, leaving class a few minutes early to get ahead of the crowd was critical. Xavier also needed push-button locks for both his school locker and his PE locker, because he was unable to operate a regular dial-combination lock. Push-button locks are not a typical accommodation, but we only had a small number of students who needed them. Several such locks were available, so providing this accommodation was easily feasible.

Transition IEP meetings (meetings to discuss high school differences and expectation, as well as accommodations provided in the middle school and required at the high school) are cordial meetings where I learn a bit about the student, and the parents learn how high school experiences are different from those at middle school. My meeting with Kathy at the middle school transition IEP meeting was not any different from the typical meetings that I had attended in the past.

However, her "other self" arrived at the beginning of Xavier's ninth grade year. First, there was Kathy's angry email to Xavier's case manager, complaining about Xavier's first experience in a high school PE class. Xavier had been late for PE class because he couldn't use the dial-combination lock on his PE locker, and his PE teacher told him that this was no excuse for him being late to class. Xavier's case manager was a new teacher who wasn't sure how to handle this email, so she forwarded it to me.

I have no idea why the PE teacher didn't know about Xavier's disability—all teachers had access to the IEPs of the students they had in their classes. I have no idea why the push-button locks hadn't yet been given to Xavier. But I found Xavier the next day and gave him his two push-button locks and their combinations (one for his school locker and one for his PE locker). I showed him where his school locker was (one without a combination lock built into it) and emailed his PE teacher to let her know that Xavier needed a new locker (one without a combination lock on it) for his push-button lock and preferably an end locker, where he wouldn't be crowded by classmates on both sides of him.

I understood that it was the very beginning of the year and that the PE teacher likely hadn't yet memorized all students' IEPs and accommodations. I felt that a "gentle" email to the PE teacher would adequately address the issue. But I also emailed the PE department chair to keep her in the loop, just in case Xavier's PE teacher (or his mother) voiced concerns to her.

I also replied to Kathy's email with the steps I had taken. Bases covered! I got a "thank you" email from Kathy a few hours later. I liked that she was such a strong advocate for her son, and that, if there was a problem, I heard from her immediately. However, her emails tended to have the overtones of a "bull in a china shop" and could easily be interpreted as a reprimand. Yes, it was a problem that a teacher did not know Xavier's accommodations, but it was one that could have been easily remedied—and done so without such an adversely phrased email. Needless to say, Xavier's case manager was on edge following that email, wanting to make sure that she was doing the right thing.

A month later, I was copied on an email from Xavier's mother to his English teacher, this time accusing the English teacher of assigning timed tests that were "in violation of his IEP." She stated that his IEP "...dictates *no* timed tests are to be given...and a scribe [should] be made available to him if need be." Actually, his IEP had not stated this.

Xavier did not have the accommodations of extended time or opportunity to respond orally, when fatigued, written in his IEP. I was quite certain, however, that, when this IEP was written for Xavier in eighth grade, his teachers were simply not giving him timed tests and were scribing for him because they knew Xavier and his needs and just provided him with these accommodations outside of the IEP. In fact, after further investigation, it seemed that his middle school teachers had been providing Xavier with accommodations beyond those that were written in his IEP. However, it can be problematic if a student comes to rely on accommodations that are "just provided," because, under most circumstances, only accommodations that are written into the IEP are allowed during state testing. [This is an example of why it is important to make sure the accommodations written into the IEP match the student's needs and that those accommodations are provided in the classroom.] If accommodations are needed, then the rationale for those accommodations needs to be documented in the IEP and implemented in the classroom. Here, because the middle school went beyond stated needs, Xavier's mother assumed that he would receive no timed tests and could provide oral answers when he was tired, neither of which were documented in his IEP.

The email to Xavier's English teacher continued with veiled (and not-so-veiled) accusations of incompetence. Statements such as, "I'm not sure what has been happening in English class but my son has been very frustrated lately…" and "I'm not really sure his IEP is being followed or understood by many East Side staff especially as he is very upset…"

While I know that a "tone" can be read (or misread) into emails, Kathy's words left no question as to hers. So, in response to his mother's accusatory email, Xavier's English teacher sent a simple and professional email, stating that there had been only one timed writing assignment to assess students' independent writing skills. She had offered Xavier the accommodation of working on the assignment at home and turning it in later. She explained that she had also given Xavier copies of notes, where he only had to fill in key words, instead of copying all of the notes. His teacher ended the email by cutting and pasting the accommodations (verbatim) from Xavier's IEP. She suggested that if Xavier's mother had concerns about the content of Xavier's IEP, then she could contact his case manager (who was copied on the email) for further assistance.

A month later (November), another email was sent to Xavier's case manager and copied to me. This email complained about the progress check (this is a report sent to parents mid-semester, indicating a student's progress in each of his or her classes) Kathy had received. She stated that Xavier's progress toward his IEP goals was marked for second quarter (we had just started the second quarter) and there was no indication of Xavier's progress for the first quarter. Kathy wrote, "Even if a true mistake on someone's part, it is just another way I have been shown that hardly a care or concern is given to my son's IEP, progress, or accommodations, which I have been discussing with you since basically September. Truly all these IEP problems are not the standard I have hoped for with the [high school's] reputation." (Our high school is one of the newest in the county and has a reputation of being a first-rate school of high academic standards, champion sports teams, and award-winning music, theater, and publications. No doubt these "slights" toward Xavier were tarnishing our reputation in her eyes.)

As it turned out, the progress report that had been sent home was from the second quarter of the previous year. An error, yes, but it was easily fixed. The correct quarter's progress report was printed and sent home to Xavier's mother. Although this "crisis" was resolved, it was not without its share of drama. Again, Kathy was not one who was hesitant to share her concerns—or her criticisms. The tone of her emails really set the case manager on edge. So far, there hadn't been a problem that couldn't easily be resolved. I understand that Xavier's mother had concerns, and I was glad that she let us know. But the issue of concern to staff was more the continual and "cumulative" delivery (tone) of the messages than the particular content.

In February, we were preparing for Xavier's triennial re-evaluation—the law requires the school team to review, every three years, the results of an evaluation to determine if the child still qualifies as a child with a disability—and annual IEP meeting. Kathy sent an email to Xavier's case manager requesting that Xavier take PE online for tenth grade. She felt that it would better accommodate Xavier's unique skills. His case manager forwarded the email to me, not knowing how to respond to her.

At the time, I knew very little about online classes, and what I knew was limited to what I had heard from our guidance counselors—that online classes were difficult and required a great amount of dedication and commitment from the student. And all I ever heard from the guidance counselors was that few students finished or passed the courses. But, knowing Kathy, I knew that was not enough information to present to her, so I contacted our PE department chair. She said the same thing—online classes were a lot of work, and most students didn't do well. Well, that confirmed in my mind that this would be a point to be stressed during the IEP meeting.

There seems to be a general perception that online classes are easy and do not require *nearly* as much work as in-school classes; however, this is a *mis*perception. For the online PE class, students are required to keep a regular log of their physical activities, monitor their heart rate, log into the "online class" via computer at specified times to check in with the instructor, complete various related online activities, and more. I could not speak in detail about the types of activities the course included, but I did report what I was told.

The IEP meeting was held with the required team members: Xavier's case manager (special education teacher), his math teacher (general education teacher), and me (principal designee). [The minimum requirements for an IEP meeting include at least one of the child's classroom teachers, a general education teacher familiar with the general education curriculum, and an administrator, or designee, who has the authority to approve IEP services.] We discussed the idea of Xavier taking the online PE class. I asked Kathy questions, including: "Why do you wish for Xavier to take an online PE class? How do you see this as being more beneficial for Xavier?"

Kathy had done her research. She knew what was included in the tenth grade PE curriculum—bowling and archery were the two examples she gave. Our students walked two "blocks" down a country road to the bowling alley, bowled, and then walked back. Given Xavier's physical impairment on his left side, he walked more slowly than his peers. Kathy expressed her concern that bowling was not a practical (from a life-skill perspective) physical activity for Xavier. Given his physical impairment, bowling would not be a leisure activity in which he would ever participate.

Additionally, Xavier would not be able to hold a bow for the archery unit of the PE course. His mother argued that even attempting to go through the motions of archery would have no meaningful benefit to Xavier, as, once again, it was another leisure activity in which he could not physically participate now or in the future. She proposed the following: have Xavier take his PE course online, giving him a reduced day with no seventh period so that he could take the online PE course then.

It is important to note here that, at our school, students were scheduled for seven classes. Seventh period met every day for 50 minutes. The other six periods met every other day for 90 minutes. So, Kathy was proposing that he would leave 50 minutes before the end of every day. Xavier's parents would pick him up each day and drive him to the local recreation center. There he could engage in the required PE course physical activities that would "provide him with a fitness program for life," such as swimming, treadmills, and stationary bike for cardio activities, and free weights and machines for strength building.

I explained what I knew about the online PE class—that students were required to use heartrate monitors and keep logs of their activities to be reported to the online PE teacher. I said that many students (both general and special education) found it hard to keep up with the pace and the expectations, after thinking an online class was going to be easy.

(I had not included the PE department chair in this meeting, because I thought I had enough information to dissuade Xavier's mother. Xavier's counselor was also not in attendance. This was, at that time, because we were "doing what we had always done"—that is, not invite the counselors, because they were too busy to attend IEP meetings.)

My concerns about online PE were dismissed as Kathy told me that she or her husband would pick Xavier up each day and take him to the recreation center. They would also make sure he did what he was meant to do. I still had my concerns, and I honestly didn't know if it would be approved by our DSS (guidance department chair). At that time, requests for a reduced day were approved by him and, having never been through this process, I wasn't sure how this would work. But I do recall thinking that Kathy was making some very good points and justifications for something other than what was typically offered, which just might better meet Xavier's needs than what he was expected to take. So, I decided to pursue the next steps to learn if this could actually be done.

I emailed our DSS, who would need to sign off on the online course form, and the PE department chair, explaining Xavier's mother's concerns with the regular PE class and her arguments for online PE. The PE department chair emailed back the same day, saying she thought it would be feasible for Xavier to take the online course, as long as he and his parents understood the expectations. Kathy was already aware of the expectations, as she had already sought out the information about the online PE class.

Our PE department chair also suggested that Xavier's mother contact the district's department chair for the online PE program to make sure there would be no problems with the heartrate monitor, and that Xavier would be able to meet the targeted heartrate zone requirements. By that afternoon, Kathy emailed back that she had talked to the department chair for the online PE class, and he felt it would be a good choice for Xavier.

A series of emails followed among the case manager, Xavier's counselor, and the DSS—making sure that all the correct forms were completed, signed, and filed to ensure that Xavier was set for the online PE tenth grade course.

The school sends students a letter at the end of May, indicating the courses for which they are registered for the coming school year as a means of confirming course selections before the master schedule is "built" for the next school year. Kathy received the letter that indicated that Xavier was registered for tenth grade PE, with no indication that it was an online class. She promptly forwarded an email, expressing that she was willing to do what she needed to, but thought she had completed everything that she was required to earlier. Her email ended with: "Should I be worried this might be a sign of struggle to come?" (Such an optimist!) Over the next week and a half, there was a flurry of emails among Xavier's case manager, counselor, the DSS, and me, all confirming that Xavier was, in fact, registered for online PE.

At the end of Xavier's tenth grade year, I received an email from his mother with his fourth quarter PE grade, a 99.58 percent. The email simply said, "Just wanted to share—this was the best place for Xavier to have PE! Thanks for the opportunity!"

While Kathy didn't hesitate to let Xavier's case manager or me know when there was a problem, she also didn't hesitate to let us know when things were going well. That we all appreciated!

A year later (when Xavier was in eleventh grade), I saw Kathy at a school function. She thanked me again for giving him the opportunity, but also confided that he hated it! It was a lot of work (for Xavier *and* his parents), but his parents pushed him (and themselves) and he (they) got through it. Okay, so I hadn't been completely wrong—it was a lot of work. But there is definitely something to be said for supportive parents! At the end of the year, I found a beautiful orchid sitting on my desk—a gift from Kathy, thanking me. An accompanying note stated, "Thanks for listening, thanks for helping our sons [she has two sons in the high school], and thanks for understanding that we will *always* voice our thoughts to those who need it. You're the best!"

Epilogue

The following year (Xavier's senior year), I was at Back to School Night (an activity where parents are invited to follow their child's abbreviated schedule in order to meet their child's teachers and receive a brief overview of the course content) in September. A colleague found me and told me Kathy was looking for me. Inwardly I groaned. Kathy sought me out for two reasons—to complain or to thank me. I hadn't done anything for her to thank me, which only meant she had a complaint. My colleague said, "Don't worry—I told her that you spend the evening visiting teachers' classrooms," which was true. But I also decided to spend time in my office, catching up on work. And that particular night I went to my office, making sure the door was locked behind me. I just wasn't up for a complaint that late in the day!

The next morning, I found a wrapped package in my mailbox, with a note. "Sorry I missed you. Thank you for spending time away from your family tonight to be here for our children." It was from Kathy. I felt like a real heel.

Afterword

It has been several years since my first encounter with Kathy, and I have to say that I have learned a lot in that time, mostly from my interactions with parents and their children. I've learned that just because something hasn't been done before doesn't mean that it's wrong or that it can't be done. I've learned the value of persistence and of not settling on (and only listening to) the first answer I hear. And I've learned that parents can be angry, argumentative, stubborn, overbearing, and aggressive, but that it's not (always) directed at me. Many times, it's a result of the battles they've fought to get their child to where they are today. And disagreements between parents and educators aren't about winning or getting what *you* want—it's about making sure that the child gets what he or she needs. And I realize that I need to be willing to consider a different point of view, whether it is from the teacher, parent, or even the student.

Analysis of Two Perspectives: "Can Physical Education Be Taught Online?"

What Do We Know?

What Don't We Know?

It was quite interesting to see both the differences and the similarities in Kathy's and Margaret's approaches to obtaining the information necessary to determine whether an online PE course would meet Xavier's needs. There was absolutely no disagreement between the two, or the IEP team, as to what areas of Xavier's life were affected by his disability. All agreed that he had mobility issues that affected the pace of his walking and the strength/control of one of his hands. We know that Kathy has had previous "wars" with the school district, and we know that Margaret was essentially new to her position, learning much as she went along.

We know that Kathy did her homework on the requirements of online courses, including the time required, the type of activities, the record-keeping involved, and the need to report progress to the online instructor—and that bowling and archery were *not* among the required tasks. Meanwhile, Margaret learned that the course was perceived by guidance counselors and other staff, including the PE chair, as much more demanding than the traditional class, and that both general and special education students found it to be a very difficult course (but it did not include bowling or archery—things that Xavier could not do). Previous students complained about the course. They failed to keep up with the assignments and reports as required, and often did not pass the course. What the team members did not know was whether Xavier could keep up with the work or how the course would be carried out.

As it turned out, the general education course was partially held off the school site. Students taking the general education PE class would have to walk on the side of a country road for about a half-mile (round trip) to get to the bowling alley. Xavier's hip condition would mean that he would arrive considerably later than the class and have difficulty maneuvering the shoulder of the road. He also had insufficient control and strength in one of his hands to participate in archery. That is, he could not hold the bow with one arm/hand and pull the string with the other—much less place the string in the nock of the arrow. So, in this case, there was total agreement on the difficulties Xavier would face within the general education course, and the team could answer the question "What do we know?" about Xavier, but not about the online course requirements.

Where Do We Want to Go?

Agreement existed on this question too, because tenth grade PE was a requirement for graduation. Xavier must, therefore, successfully complete the course. The disagreement revolved around the two possible answers to the next question.

How Do We Get There?

Here is the question where differences of opinion surfaced. The majority of the IEP team was convinced that they should proceed as usual—with Xavier taking the general education PE course. Kathy was convinced that Xavier would have a better experience with the online program and that he could successfully complete the requirements. So, when she went to the IEP meeting, she brought the information necessary to answer the questions arising from what the team did not know, including what Xavier would need to take and pass the course.

Kathy also addressed the transportation issue by offering to take Xavier to the recreational center, where the physical activities would take place, where the blood pressure and heart rate would be taken, and where the parents would make certain that Xavier completed the requirements of the course. Xavier would keep the records and carry out his part on the computer, as required. The only thing the school would need to do was to adjust Xavier's schedule, so his parents could pick him up from school and transport him to the recreation center. Kathy had it all worked out; all she needed was the IEP team's agreement.

Margaret, after numerous "No's, email correspondences, phone calls, discussions with various school staff, and warnings to Kathy of the difficulties all students had completing the course, and then finally listening to Kathy's full presentation of her rationales concerning the benefits of the online course over the in-class course, said that she would do what she could to obtain the approvals of various individuals who were not in attendance at the meeting (counselors, director of guidance, PE chairperson with oversight of the online courses). In other words, she said "Yes."

Margaret had also conducted her investigation of what was necessary for Xavier to complete the course. What remained an issue, in Margaret's mind, was the difficulty of the course. Clearly, Kathy was in a position to provide the justifications for taking the online course, despite knowing that it would be difficult. Though it certainly would involve more work than the general education class, the course would also be more appropriate, considering Xavier's needs, his physical limitations, and the requirements of the general education PE course.

(In spite of the numerous and relatively minor errors that occurred during Xavier's first year at school—including delays in receiving the promised push-button locks, incorrectly dated reports, and accusations of not providing required accommodations—the school was attempting to do the right thing. From Kathy's perspective, one might just wonder if everything *was* going to become an issue that school year, or, as she phrased it, a "war." Had we not known what really happened—the reasons for the errors and/or how quickly the issues were resolved—a third party could easily have drawn the conclusion that there were systemic problems at this high school. The point to be made, however, is how important it is for both parties to know, to listen to, and actually to *hear* both sides during any interactions, including an IEP meeting.)

How Do We Know That We Are Getting There?

Multiple points were used to measure Xavier's progress, to compensate for the degree of independence provided to Xavier (and other online students) as they worked through the course. Record-keeping was a key measurement of Xavier's progress, as was his attendance at the recreation center. Xavier was required to report his progress to the online teacher regularly, and there were further teacher/ student interactions by phone and email. Xavier also had to pass a final test. His parents, of course, made certain that he attended each day. His final grade was certainly indicative of his meeting the requirements of the course.

What Do We Do When We Get There?

In this case, the requirement was met (passing the course), and Xavier was no longer required to take additional PE classes for the purposes of graduation. Therefore, for Xavier, there are no more demands to meet, at least in regards to his IEP in this particular area. However, it should be noted that, according to his mother, the online course positively impacted Xavier's lifelong physical health by "help[ing] him to think about himself, his own fitness goals, his own personal levels of fitness, and his own lifetime health."

Key Points

- The manner in which a parent or educator approaches an issue (and the individuals involved) greatly impacts how that individual (parent or educator) responds. Emails are easy to send, but can often be misinterpreted due to the manner in which the content is written, its structure (bullets, incomplete sentences, phrases), and, in this example, its intended or unintended tone or affect. If there is any question about any part of the email, ask the sender (via email if you like). If there is a reply and you remain unclear as to the meaning, then *call*. If it is clear to you, write "thank you" or *call* and express your appreciation. Anything more than an exchange of two emails typically demands a phone call, because it is easier to resolve issues with a phone call than to continue with unclearly written emails. If you need to document the conversation, then you can take notes during the conversation. Make sure you understand any resolutions that may be reached during the conversation by repeating the resolution to the parent/teacher. Then, send a summary email bulleting each point made during the telephone conversation. This email is *not* an opportunity to add new issues, however. Just summarize what you agreed over the phone.

- There was value in both parties seeking out what the online course entailed. They simply came to different conclusions. Kathy saw it to be a successful adventure: "We can do that!" The school did not: "This is going to be very hard for Xavier to accomplish." Ultimately, Kathy admitted it *was* as difficult as she was told it would be, but felt it to be successful, because Xavier did complete the course and because he got more out of the course than he would have had he taken the in-class alternative. I am sure that, without his parents' support, Xavier would not have been as successful in the course, and there is nothing wrong with that. Xavier had to do the work himself! His parents simply reinforced his efforts.

- Xavier apparently did not take part in the IEP meetings. This was his tenth grade IEP discussion, and I would have invited him to the IEP to hear his thoughts, his rationale for wanting to try the online option over the typical program. It would have afforded him a chance to practice his self-advocacy skills.

- It would have been very helpful had additional key people (guidance counselor, department chair of student services, person who had oversight of the online courses, as well as the PE chair) attended the IEP meeting—they could have immediately approved Xavier's taking the course. Or, if the online course was not approved, they could have answered any questions about the program or determined steps to take to ensure that Xavier's schedule would reflect the change.

- Interestingly enough, many of the steps of the Structured Collaborative IEP Process were carried out. For example, the team began with a discussion of Xavier's needs and knew the goals (where they wanted to go) that would enable Xavier to graduate (by completing a tenth grade PE course). This was an excellent example of a team using the student's needs, strengths, and weaknesses as the basis for sincere consideration of an alternative PE course, whereby his strengths could enable him to be successful, and his weaknesses did not prohibit him from obtaining the necessary credit for graduation.

- It was only how to get there—how to reach the goals—that was the issue, and that remained the issue until Margaret "listened" to the rationale that Kathy presented. Only then did the team decide to seek approval from other authorities.

- My understanding is that district policies have changed, and when issues similar to this scenario now occur and the IEP team makes such decisions—one way or the other for tenth grade PE—it is simply included in the IEP and implemented the next year. Things can change!

- It is clear that Kathy truly appreciates what the chairperson has done for both her children. How Margaret perceives Xavier's mother is yet to be fully determined. This ambiguity is really the result of Margaret feeling attacked due to Kathy's approach to problems.

- In summary, Kathy was persistent and did her homework, and so did Margaret. A major problem in Kathy's efforts to present something "different" was her having vexed school staff with her approach to previous issues, which made it harder for them to "see" or "listen" to her real points.

- And finally, both adults were more alike than different, because their focus was on Xavier and his needs—they just had different perspectives.

Summary

There is almost a slight undertone of humor to this chapter—as long as you are not the parent or staff from the high school. The errors and issues presented were not so much a problem between the parent and school, but more of a problem between the manner of Kathy's approach and the perceived tone of the emails received by staff. The staff's immediate reaction was to assume a defensive stance. The issues themselves got somewhat lost "under" the emotions.

We don't know if this was the only way Kathy was able to obtain what she needed prior to Xavier's transition to the high school—in which case she simply continued with what worked—or if this was simply a function of her personality. On the other hand, we also learned that Kathy didn't hesitate to thank staff for the perceived good that they did.

In spite of the manner Kathy used to bring issues of concern to the attention of school staff, she was equally grateful for the corrections and good work staff did for her children. Although this is beyond the scope of this book, it is worth mentioning briefly that Kathy's behaviors harm the relationship between herself and the staff. It is unlikely that she will recognize what to do to correct this, even though she knows she can be "bullish." It creates animosity, if not "fear," among the staff, and these reactions are no more beneficial for collaboration than Kathy's approach.

I would recommend that Kathy and those teachers who work with her children (one meeting for each child) be invited to a "cookies and coffee" chat to discuss what gets in the way of a congenial and collaborative atmosphere for their interactions. The goal stated upfront would be to resolve the offensive (real or perceived) behaviors and to re-establish a cordial and collaborative relationship between the school and Kathy. Either that, or develop agreement among the teachers that they would look past the assumed tone of emails and focus on the issues presented.

CHAPTER 12

A Father Whose Son Has a Hearing Impairment Brings Multiple Legal Actions Against the District

In this scenario, the school system said "No!" almost from the start and continued to say it again and again throughout the story. You might start to wonder, as you read the story of Mr. and Mrs. Brite and their son Harris, why they did not just move to another district, where they probably would not have to fight for services. We all know that moving to another district is rarely as simple as it sounds. Maybe it's because Harris's parents kept winning the programming Harris needed. Maybe it's because fighting for what was right allowed Harris's father to show other parents that they, too, could obtain the services their children required. True, there was a great deal of effort behind Mr. Brite's success, but that alone does not make him unique, as you will see while reading this scenario. Whatever the reason, they stayed, they fought, and they won. You'll learn how in this scenario. But it does leave Mr. Brite who tells his story below, with one last question: "Was it worth it?"

Facing Each Challenge Head On

"It's okay, Daddy; don't be sad."

The moment I learned Harris was hearing impaired is like a picture in my mind. It is as clear today, several years later, as it was then. Harris was sitting on the floor in his pajamas, playing with a woman from Early Intervention (EI), and with another sitting behind him. [EI is the local name for the birth to age three program for children with disabilities.] Melinda, his sister, was on the couch looking around, not totally sure what was going on, and looked visibly upset. Harris's Aunt Brenda was sitting on the ottoman, ready to ask the next question. Zuella, Harris's mother, was standing in the doorway with her hand on her mouth and tears on her face. I looked around the room and saw that the only person who wasn't upset was Harris. He was happy playing with the blocks and getting all the attention.

It was a Saturday in October when we found out Harris had a hearing problem. He was about two and a half years old. Two ladies from EI, a program supplied by Pike County, came to our house to evaluate Harris. They came in answer to a request we made about Harris's development. Instead of progressing with his speech, Harris seemed to be saying fewer words and phrases. He also wasn't picking up new words. At first, we just thought Harris was progressing more slowly than Melinda.

The ladies played with Harris as they asked him questions. Harris just sat there and never looked up. One of the ladies sat behind Harris and shook keys. He never turned around. The lady behind Harris said there seemed to be an issue with Harris's hearing.

I stood there and thought, "*This can't be*. He sings songs with his sister and me. We dance around the room to all these songs he asks me to play. We watch TV together. He picks videos for us to watch." I looked at these two women and said, "This can't be. We listen to music. We watch TV. We watch movies. He hears me when I talk to him." One of the ladies said, "Go put on one of the songs he likes." I went into the other room and turned on the stereo and came back in. Harris just sat there and never looked up. She said, "Make it really loud." I went back and turned the music up loud. I knew when I came back in Harris would be up dancing, the way he always does.

A total shock came over me when I returned. It was as if everything just stopped like it does in the movies. Harris was sitting on the floor playing with the blocks. As I stood there and watched Harris sitting, not noticing the music, my heart just broke. "How did I miss this?" I thought. "He can't hear the music. What is he hearing?" All these questions ran through my mind and I just stood there, devastated. These two women came and detected Harris had a hearing problem in less than 15 minutes, and I lived with Harris and never noticed a hearing impairment. It bothers me to this day.

The ladies from EI explained the process. The first thing was to get his hearing checked. They assured us Harris was fine and happy. He wasn't in any pain, so we were meant to relax. After finding out your son has an issue hearing, it isn't easy to relax. We were upset and scared and needed to get answers.

That Monday was a long day. We started at the audiologist, where they confirmed Harris had a hearing loss in both ears. The loss was moderate in his left ear and moderate to severe in his right ear. They explained that Harris would be able to hear with hearing aids. Of course, our first question was, "What was the cause?" They told us we would need to go to an ear specialist.

After examining Harris, the ear specialist said there were no noticeable issues with the ears. Harris didn't have an infection. The ear specialist recommended a computer axial tomography (CAT) scan to tell if there were any internal issues.

We went directly from the specialist to the hospital. The hospital said we needed to make an appointment to get a CAT scan, so we drove to another hospital. The second hospital gave us the same answer, after thinking about it, it made me smile for the first time that day. In my one-track mind, all I wanted to do was get everything done immediately and, of course, I was not thinking about the obvious as I stood there a bit amazed. Who would have thought an appointment is needed to get a CAT scan?

Most hospitals want to put children under sedation when the CAT scan is done. This was not something we were willing to do, so we drove around until Harris was fast asleep and then brought him in. It all worked out well, and this avoided any unnecessary anesthesia.

We had to wait a few days for the CAT scan to be reviewed. The call from the hospital finally came, and they said they had found that Harris had enlarged vestibular aqueducts. My first thought was "What's a vestibular aqueduct?" To top it all off, I couldn't even pronounce "vestibular." We needed to go back to the ear specialist, so he could explain what the vestibular aqueducts do. As the days went by, I felt nothing was happening; so, I started to research on the Internet.

I discovered that children born with enlarged vestibular aqueducts were born with normal hearing. Over time, some people lose their hearing for various reasons. Some possible causes of hearing loss for a person with enlarged vestibular aqueducts include a hit to the head from a fall, a car accident, blowing up a balloon, or even experiencing very loud sounds. Some people go through their whole lives with enlarged vestibular aqueducts without a loss of hearing.

This explained how Zuella and I were able to think Harris could hear, though he had, in fact, lost his hearing. He had lost his hearing over time. During this time, Harris had found ways to compensate, and as he hadn't completely lost his hearing, Zuella and I didn't realize Harris was losing it. This didn't make me feel any better. Not knowing how long Harris had a hearing loss before it was detected bothered me for a long time. I felt like I had let my child down.

The questions were, "Will Harris lose more of his hearing? Will Harris lose all of his hearing?" Almost a year to the day that Harris was fitted with hearing aids, these questions were answered. He was playing in the living room, jumping on the couch as all kids do. He fell and hit his head. He cried for a little bit, but all in all he seemed fine. We kept testing him by covering our mouths when we talked to Harris. His speech teacher worked with him the following day and she said, "He is doing great." So, we didn't think much of the fall. Five days later, Harris's hearing was gone.

I'd been very upset when I found out Harris had a hearing loss. It took me a long time to stop feeling sad. To see Harris lose his hearing completely was even harder. Harris couldn't understand what had happened to him; he had lost his hearing overnight. In the morning, Harris didn't understand why his hearing aids wouldn't work. Here was a three-and-a-half-year-old boy who went from normal hearing to hearing aids to a complete hearing loss. I'd never felt so helpless!

I couldn't explain to Harris, "We can fix this. It is going to take some time, but we can fix this. You will hear again." One day, Harris came to me and, as he stood in front of me, he tilted his head and said, "Daddy, I can't hear you. My ears don't work no more." I wanted to be strong and have Harris know I was going to fix this problem, but that was not possible. Harris saw that I was upset and he put his hand on my shoulder and said, "It's okay, Daddy; don't be sad."

From all the research on the Internet and talking with the other parents, I knew that the only thing to do was to get Harris a cochlear implant. At that time, there were three different types of implants. We asked parents which implant they got for their child. We talked with the implant center. They all said the same thing: "It doesn't matter. All the implants are equally as good. It is up to you." This was not a reassuring answer.

We found out which one most parents got and selected that one. Later, my research reassured me that we probably had picked the best one, as the biggest issue was the batteries. Again, no one, including the doctor, was willing to give a recommendation, not even on which ear to implant. I found the whole situation daunting.

My biggest concern at that point was, "How much time is it going to take to get Harris a cochlear implant?" The process could take more than six months. When we called for an appointment, we were told the surgeon couldn't see us for three weeks. I thought, "Harris can't wait that long!" Zuella called some friends who did us a special favor and arranged for us to meet with the surgeon the next day.

Zuella brought all Harris's files with her. The surgeon explained that we would need a CAT scan. Zuella handed the CAT scan to him. The surgeon took a look at the CAT scan and could see that Harris had "grossly enlarged vestibular aqueducts." The surgeon explained that, with Harris's condition, he would be expected to lose all his hearing at some point, confirming what we had feared. He had lost his hearing.

He took the time to explain somewhat how and why Harris lost his hearing. It basically had to do with the amount of pressure that was put on the cochlea by the vestibular aqueduct. Other than that, he couldn't give us any specifics.

The surgeon then went on to tell us that, before we could proceed with the operation, we would have to get several things together, such as test reports and evaluations and so on. Zuella handed over everything the surgeon asked for.

I am not sure who was more amazed, the surgeon or me. No one could have been more prepared!

I asked her later, "How did you know what to bring to meet with the surgeon?" She said, "We knew there was a chance Harris may lose his hearing and would need an implant. I called the implant center and found out all the things they would need before the surgery, so I could get it all together." Zuella's preparations shaved at least four months off the time it could have taken to get Harris the cochlear implant.

Advocating for Harris in the Public School

Over a six-year period, I have filed for eight impartial hearings, appealed two impartial hearing decisions, filed two state education complaints with the Department of Education, filed a civil complaint under Section 504, and written letters to the state education department all the way up to the commissioner of education. People often ask me, "Was it worth all the effort?" After telling them the results, I then ask, "Do you think it was worth the effort?" [Section 504 refers to a federal law in the U.S. that addresses children with disabilities or children who are perceived to have disabilities. The major difference between Section 504 and other laws that address children with disabilities is that there is no federal/national funding for Section 504 and an accommodation is usually required to address the disability. For example, if a child requires a wheelchair, but not special education, the school must provide access to the school building and to the classrooms required by the child who uses a wheelchair. Another accommodation might be the use of an elevator to enable the child to reach floors other than the first floor. Students who qualify under Section 504 will also have a 504 Accommodations Plan developed by the parents and school. This plan delineates the disability and accommodation(s) to be provided to that child.]

Being new to the whole process of educating Harris, we weren't very clear on what we should be asking for. The *one* thing other parents said was, "Get as much speech as you can." Other than that, we had Harris in the Consortium of Educational Services (CES) program and all seemed fine. [The CES is a program designed to provide special education services to a number of school districts. The districts pay the tuition for those services.]

One parent Zuella met told her about a clinic in California called John Tracy. That summer we took the family to a three-week session at the clinic. This was an amazing experience! At the John Tracy Clinic, Harris attended school, Melinda went to the sibling program, and Zuella and I took classes. We learned about teaching speech, what causes hearing loss, the types of technology that are available, and advocating. It was like taking several college courses in three weeks. We now had a better understanding of our role as parents of a child with hearing loss.

When Harris was three and a half, he started his second year at CES. Zuella and I decided to let Harris take the bus to school, because with the need to get Melinda off to school and us off to work, busing would make our lives easier. Melinda was four years older than Harris, and we needed to be there for her as well. After two months, we became aware of an issue. We found out that Harris was on the bus for over an hour and a half.

He would get on the bus at 7:30 a.m. and arrive at 7:55 a.m. His bus was about the seventeenth bus in line with 25 to 27 buses that waited in front of the school. The buses would sit in the line-up—until 8:25 a.m.—before the teachers would come out and start off-loading the children. Harris wouldn't get off of his bus until after 9:00 a.m. School started at 8:30 a.m. To my shock and dismay, it turned out that 255 children were "trapped" on buses for an hour and a half, and no one seemed to think this was an issue.

We set up a meeting with the principal and found an uncaring bureaucrat. As we explained the situation, the principal kept interrupting and saying, "The teachers are under union contract." We said, "What about the safety of the children? They are on running buses; the fumes can't be good for them." The principal added, "The children are safe, and they have been doing it this way for years and the system works fine." After about an hour, we decided we were getting nowhere and left.

Over the next several months, we were in contact with other parents—some cared; others felt we were just causing trouble. During this time, Zuella and I decided to drive Harris, so he wouldn't be subjected to the situation.

The situation finally was brought to the attention of U.S. Senator Green's office, which sent people to investigate. (When the bus situation wasn't getting handled, a letter was sent to Senator Green's office.) Just think: a simple bus issue was being brought to the attention of a senator! Who would have thought it would go that far?

The bus issue was discovered to be the least of CES's problems. By the end of the year, the program was found to have serious problems, and it needed to be closed down because of all the findings showing how the school failed to meet the children's needs in accordance with local, state, and federal regulations. Just think, the principal wouldn't deal with the bus issue because of a teacher contract, but he was willing to ignore the federal laws.

We needed to find a new placement that would meet Harris's needs. He had aged out of the EI program at age four and would now fall under the public school system. We were going to meet with the school and set up an IEP. Helping Harris develop language skills and ensuring he was getting plenty of speech therapy were of the utmost importance. We went into the Committee on Special Education (CSE) meeting with a list of concerns and required services.

We explained the issue with CES and that we needed to find a different placement. This definitely set the tone for the meeting. We brought up the subject of a private school, and staff quickly asserted that the school would not pay for the placement. Zuella and I explained that we could cover the cost of the school. The next topic of discussion was speech. We explained that Harris would need speech therapy five days a week for 60 minutes each session. The district came back with three sessions a week at 30 minutes each. We went back and forth on this one issue for the next four hours.

We would not let the meeting stop and kept going over why Harris would need the speech sessions. Our main point was that Harris lost his hearing and received a cochlear implant this past year. His hearing age was less than one year, while his chronological age was almost four. Our other point was that CES had some major issues with their program and had caused Harris to fall further behind.

Nobody could really counter our claim about CES not supplying the appropriate services. No one had any reports that showed Harris had made reasonable gains during his second year at CES. The medical setback of needing to get an implant combined with the CES issue had caused Harris's regression. Sadly, at one point school team members had the audacity to point fingers at Harris for losing his hearing.

Frustrated, I said, "It doesn't matter what the reason is that Harris regressed. We are in agreement that Harris did regress, so he should be getting the services due to the regression." Here we are arguing over two additional speech sessions per week for a school year. The total approximate cost to the school was $8,000, and the state reimburses the school for most of that cost.

In the end, the school district finally agreed to our request. Whatever the reason, Harris was going to get the services he needed and would attend the nursery school at Friends Together.

We would cover the cost of the school and the district would supply a speech therapist five days a week for 60 minutes, with therapy sessions at the school after the school day. Thinking back, I now believe we could have pressed the school to cover the costs of the nursery school, but I just wasn't savvy about how it all worked back then. The school year went ahead without a hitch, and Harris made great progress.

At our next annual CSE meeting, we needed to determine where Harris would go for kindergarten. One of the things we'd learned was that if you waited for the school district to come up with out-of-district placements, there was a very good chance you would find they didn't do anything. We had reviewed some schools in the area, and decided on Evergreen Manor. Evergreen Manor was a school for the deaf, and all the services were supplied within the school's program. We got ready for our next CSE meeting with the school district, expecting a very straightforward meeting that should go smoothly.

We talked about Harris's needs and reviewed the programs and services that were available. The district brought up CES, which didn't sit well with Zuella. After the bus incident and later finding out that the program wasn't run correctly, we both objected to sending Harris back to CES following the implementation of its corrections. We talked about Evergreen Manor, and that it seemed to be the right placement for Harris. When the conversation moved to the issue of an extended school year (ESY), to my shock, the chairwoman, Karen Diaz, said that Harris didn't need to go to Evergreen Manor over the summer.

Here we have a deaf child who had two setbacks with his hearing within 18 months. Now, with a cochlear implant, Harris needed to learn to hear in a whole new way and this person didn't feel Harris needed programming over the summer.

I wasn't expecting that. I could see the others in the room put their heads down. It became clear that there was more going on than I knew about. I hadn't brought in anyone from Evergreen Manor, because I didn't see the need. I would not make that mistake again!

Finally Ms. Diaz said, "We will have to agree to disagree," and ended the meeting. I don't know why Ms. Diaz took this approach.

Zuella and I went to see a lawyer, and he said we had a great case for ESY programming—it should be a non-issue. On the other hand, we faced a time constraint. The lawyer let us know that by the time we went to a hearing, the summer would be over. He didn't feel it was a case worth taking.

Several weeks had passed since our CSE meeting and I tried to reach an agreement with Ms. Diaz for the summer to no avail. I finally dropped off a letter stating that I was going to request an impartial hearing through the state Department of Education.

Within an hour, I received a call from Ms. Diaz, who agreed to let Harris go to Evergreen Manor. Elated, Zuella and I called to get Harris set up for the summer. Unfortunately, since the time we started the CSE meeting the program had filled up. We were disappointed and extremely annoyed that Ms. Diaz's delays caused Harris to miss out that summer. We will never know how much Harris lost over the summer. We could only hope that Evergreen Manor would be able to get Harris back on track.

Harris's first year at Evergreen Manor went very well. We went up to the school for several events and meetings and were always greeted with enthusiasm. Harris's speech was improving, and he was picking up new words and phrases all the time. All Harris's setbacks seemed to be behind him.

The summer before Harris's second year at Evergreen Manor was filled with a great deal of stress in our lives. Finances were tight, and we were trying to keep our heads above water. We decided to sell the house, and Zuella and I would go our separate ways. Our major concern was to impact the kids as little as possible. We both agreed on moving into a district that would benefit both children. Someone I knew in the district had grandchildren, who both had cochlear implants, and found the services to be great.

Setting up new homes and preparing for the school year was rough. Melinda did well with her new school and made friends from the onset. Harris didn't have any changes to his school situation since he continued at Evergreen Manor. Overall, the year went well.

When Harris finished first grade at Evergreen Manor, it turned out that he was also aging out of his current program. Past first grade, Evergreen Manor taught total communication, a sign and language method; however, we wanted Harris to be an oral child. To this day I wonder if that was the best decision for Harris.

At the CSE meeting, we discussed moving Harris into a district school. The elementary school Harris would attend would be the Oak Hill School; it had blended and inclusive classrooms—a school that includes children with and without disabilities.

We discussed the services for Harris, and they were overwhelming. Harris would get speech five days a week for 30 minutes, occupational therapy (OT) two days a week for 30 minutes, a teacher of the deaf for two and a half hours a week, and an aide throughout the school day. The district just kept pushing services at us, and, like most parents, when offered services we took as much as we could get. The thought that more wasn't always better had never crossed my mind. Looking back, I would have focused on Harris's specific needs rather than take all that I could get.

Evergreen Manor offered to send a consultant to help Harris and the staff acclimate. This was a free service that Evergreen Manor offered to all the schools when a child transitioned back into the district. With deafness being a low-incidence disability, this was a great opportunity for the teachers and staff at Oak Hill to get some understanding about Harris and his disability. To our surprise, we were told by the Evergreen Manor teacher that Oak Hill didn't want the consultant to visit.

We went to the school and were told that the staff were more than capable of handling Harris's transition and they didn't need anyone coming in to tell them what to do. We assured them this wasn't about someone telling the school how to educate Harris; it was a service that was offered by Evergreen Manor, a school for the deaf. They said, "Union contracts don't allow us to have outside consultants evaluate our teachers." We tried to explain that no one would be evaluated. They said, "One of our teachers filed a grievance against your consultant, and the consultants are not allowed on school property." This was very odd.

Over the next several months, we weren't seeing improvements. Even worse, Harris was constantly complaining about going to school, locking himself in the bathroom. We went to the school to try to resolve these issues, but we got nowhere. Finally, I decided enough is enough and told them that if they weren't going to let the consultant come in, then I would file for an impartial hearing. They said, "That is your right." Not knowing what else to do, I filed my first impartial hearing request.

[An impartial hearing (also called a due process hearing) is a formal proceeding in which disagreements between the parent or guardian and the school district are decided by an impartial hearing officer—or, in some cases, an impartial hearing panel—who is appointed by the particular state's board of education. It is a review of the issues presented by both parents and the educational staff involved with the student. Either side may also use an attorney and bring in external and internal experts to testify for either side. The members of the hearing are not to be involved in, or familiar with, the case and are expected to make a decision(s) that is to be implemented. It is a rather complex process and typically time consuming, but it is an avenue that may be taken to resolve a situation when the local school district and parent/guardian cannot do so.]

Two days before the impartial hearing, I received a call from Richard Rhine, the district assistant director of special education, to inform me they would agree to get a consultant, but not from Evergreen Manor. As the district seemed to have difficulty locating a consultant, I recommended a few. The school district opted to pay for something that was free through Evergreen Manor.

It was clear that the relationship with the Red River School district and us was tenuous, but we wanted to repair the relationship. We set up meetings to review Harris's progress. We talked about it being a team effort and that we were there to help. Harris's teacher, Diane Blake, and speech teacher, Kathy DeSkuto, were clearly not getting over the fact that we had forced a consultant on them. Harris's first year in the district was a disaster, and Harris was paying the price.

The annual CSE meeting for second grade was extremely intense. Over the previous several months, I had done some research on audio verbal (AV) therapy, and we wanted to add this service to Harris's IEP. (This is a specialized type of therapy designed to teach a child to use the hearing provided by a hearing aid or a cochlear implant for understanding speech and learning to talk. The child is taught to develop hearing as an active sense.)

Ms. DeSkuto became very defensive. She used "big words," doing her best to talk over our heads. Every time the meeting started to deviate from talking about AV therapy, I brought it back to the subject and I was able to get it added to the IEP. It's important to note here that while this new school provided students with special services, their program was not designed for students with hearing impairments. In the beginning, this school threw an abundance of services at us, and we felt confident that they were doing their jobs. In reality, however, they used unqualified staff to provide these services. For example, Ms. DeSkuto had no experience working with deaf children. Unfortunately, it took time for us to figure that out.

Judy Ramirez was one of two AV therapists in our district at the time and, from my understanding, one of the best in the country. Ms. Ramirez came twice a month and worked with Ms. DeSkuto during Harris's speech sessions. What frustrated me most was how Ms. DeSkuto had fought to keep the AV therapist off Harris's IEP but when she finally started to work with the therapist, she couldn't stop talking about how great she was. Why should I have cared as long as it helped Harris?

By October, it was apparent to me that this was going to be another wasted year. With all the services on Harris's IEP, why wasn't he making any real improvements? What was the problem? Was it Harris? Was it the teacher?

I noticed that Harris wasn't bringing home any spelling words. His reading teacher, Grace Mullen, gave him three books at the beginning of each week that he was to practice with at home. She would use these books in the reading session with Harris during the day. I was never completely clear about what we were meant to do at home. Harris would say, "We need to read my books." He would go and get them and hold them to his head and recite them to me, never opening them. Harris could tell you what was in the books by memory, but when I opened them and asked Harris to read the words on a random page, he was lost. He couldn't read them.

These books were repetitive, and by the middle of the week he could recite them without even opening them up. I was beside myself with frustration and called Zuella. She felt everything was going fine and I should stop looking to cause trouble. I was totally surprised by Zuella's attitude. I did my best to work with Harris over the next couple of months, with no real improvements. With Zuella and I not on the same page, I was lost with what to do next.

One night in December, I received a call from Zuella. She was upset about the lack of improvements Harris was making. The next thing I knew she was yelling at me, "Harris isn't reading, and you had better do something about it!" I am not sure what caused the sudden change, but I was happy that we were in agreement.

Between the holidays and vacations, it took forever to set up the CSE meeting. We met in the beginning of March. Before we even had a chance to discuss the issues, we were told the district didn't feel they could educate Harris. They wanted to move him to an out-of-district placement. "Why the sudden change?" I wondered. I asked, "What are you going to do about the remainder of the school year?" They said, "We are going to focus on next year." They didn't even have a plan for the remainder of the school year other than to make no changes.

Zuella and I left the meeting upset and confused. More importantly, we finally realized the people we trusted didn't know what to do and were looking for a way out. It was clear that neither of us expected the district suddenly to admit they couldn't help Harris. We then went our separate ways with a plan to speak the next day on how we would proceed with the school district.

I called around, looking for some advice and it was clear Harris's biggest issue was that he wasn't reading. As I reviewed websites looking for answers, I found tons of information and statistics on literacy. I talked to some reading teachers and even brought Harris to a reading specialist. The reading specialist we met said Harris was much delayed and she didn't feel she would be able to help him.

Zuella found a program called Lindamood-Bell®[1]. I did some research and talked with Ken DiStello, the director of the clinic, about Harris's problems. As time was of the essence, we immediately got Harris evaluated. His reading scores were bleak, but at least we knew what we were up against.

I requested another CSE meeting. At the meeting Richard Rhine asked me to explain why I wanted the meeting. I said that they needed to come up with a plan to educate Harris for the remainder of the year and for summer while they were looking for an out-of-district placement. Harris wasn't reading, and doing nothing to address this was not acceptable.

From there, the meeting turned into a blame game. Kathy DeSkuto blamed Evergreen Manor for making it sound like Harris was further along than he was. She blamed Harris for not trying. The reading teacher said she was working very hard with Harris, but that he gets tired quickly. There were more pointing fingers than anything else.

I pointed out that everybody was focusing on the past and not on what needed to take place moving forward. I gave everybody the test scores from the Lindamood-Bell® assessment. Everybody agreed that they looked accurate. I then asked if people knew about the Lindamood-Bell® program and no one seemed to be familiar with it. I suggested that Harris attend the program. Mr. Rhine said the school would have to check into the program. The meeting ended with no plan on how to move forward.

It was clear to me that I needed to understand the CSE process better if I was going to help Harris. I called advocates and anybody who had gone through the process. The more I talked with people, the more confusing the whole situation got. Realizing the school was not going to do the right thing, I decided to go with my gut and file for an impartial hearing.

Here is how I would describe what an impartial hearing is: you file an impartial hearing request. An impartial hearing officer is assigned to the case. The school district presents their case, and you present your case. Just like court, you and the school district can both present evidence and call witnesses. There is no jury, just the impartial hearing officer. This person will take everything into account and make a decision. When considering an impartial hearing, like anything else, you will need to decide if you feel the system is fair and impartial.

---

1 www.lindamoodbell.com, accessed July 2, 2013.

I let the school know that if they weren't going to change Harris's education plan and provide solutions, I would file for an impartial hearing. Mr. Rhine said, "Stop threatening me!" "I'm not threatening you," I said. He said, "If you're going to file for an impartial hearing, then just do it." I recognized that the relationship with the district would never be productive.

I filed the impartial hearing complaint that day. I knew from here on out I would be fighting with the district to get services for Harris. With this in mind, I decided to plan out how I would deal with the school personnel. I have worked for large corporations, and it got me thinking that I needed to avoid talking like a parent and just focus on the facts and not get emotional. I needed to review the services for Harris and only pick ones that I truly believed would be appropriate. I couldn't get mad or let my emotions get in the way of helping Harris.

I met with the school for a resolution meeting (which did not help) and then went to mediation. When a request for an impartial hearing/due process is initiated, by law, the school needs to meet with a parent in a "resolution meeting" in an effort to resolve issues before going ahead with an impartial hearing. For all intents and purposes, it is a formality.

Mediation is not required by law and neither party has to go to mediation. Everyone will tell you that it is in your best interests, but having gone through the system, I would question that. Mediation is where both parties agree to meet in front of a third party to work out their differences. I was very open to both a resolution meeting and mediation in the beginning, but became jaded in the end as neither was successful, with no changes as the result.

It was clear that, as the school was not going to budge, we would be going to the impartial hearing and I needed to prepare for something I knew nothing about. Evidence needed to be put together, lists of witnesses needed to be supplied, and questions needed to be written for the witnesses. Not being a lawyer, it was a very scary experience. When the day of the hearing finally arrived, I was so scared, nervous, and upset that I got sick several times before I walked out of the house. [Special education advocates are not permitted to attend the impartial hearing in this particular state.]

The first day of the proceedings was full of formalities. We passed evidence back and forth, reviewed the witness list, and discussed future hearing dates. The hearing dragged on with not much happening. If all hearings are like this, then there is no wonder it takes so long.

By the end of the day, we were able to read our opening statements. The school went first. My opening statement seemed to strike a chord with the school's attorney. She kept objecting about my requests for Lindamood-Bell® as a related service. I wasn't sure why she had an issue with my bringing it up at the opening statement. Dr. Monk, the impartial hearing officer, clarified that my request was acceptable under certain circumstances. I knew there was something I was missing, but I couldn't figure out what. After reading our opening statements, the hearing was adjourned, and we were to return the next day to start questioning witnesses.

It was clear the school was concerned about my opening statement. It kept me awake all night as I read and reread my notes. With very little sleep, it was time to go back for what I expected to be a very long day. We all arrived and the hearing began.

The hearing officer asked if there was anything we needed to go over before the first witness was called. The school's attorney said she did have something that needed to be discussed. All I thought was, "Here we go, another delay tactic." Then, she said, "My client would like to see if we could come to a settlement with the Brites." Wow!

The shock of her statement sent shivers through me. Two months of going back and forth with no compromise, and all of a sudden they wanted to settle. I knew it had to do with my opening statement, but for the life of me I didn't know what exactly made them change their minds. With that, the impartial hearing ended in a settlement. Most settlement agreements have a section where both parties agree not to speak about the settlement agreement, so I can add nothing more.

Harris's summer was fundamental in terms of his reading program. Within the first week of beginning the Lindamood-Bell® program, Harris knew the alphabet. He learned more than 50 sight words. By the second week, Harris and I were reading books together. By the fourth week, Harris sat in a book store and read me *Green Eggs and Ham*.[2] Harris's summer at Lindamood-Bell® increased his reading skills in decoding by two grade levels and he was on the road to becoming a reader!

Mid-summer, I sent a letter to Mr. Rhine, informing him of Harris's progress and letting him know we needed to set up a CSE meeting immediately. I prepared for this meeting by bringing test scores and the director of the Lindamood-Bell® program, Ken DiStello.

We showed everyone the test scores and Mr. DiStello explained how the program helped Harris. Mr. Rhine listened and in the end said, "Harris's new placement will be able to supply the services that Harris needs and there is no need to continue with Lindamood-Bell®." We went back and forth for a while and it was clear the school was not going to budge. With that, I handed them the impartial hearing notice and waited for the CSE meeting to end. There was no point in getting emotional or fighting. I thought, "Don't waste time; just move to the next step as quickly as possible." [As it turns out, the district expected the parents to locate acceptable placements. Mr. Brite noted that "…I have yet to find any of the schools to do anything proactive. It wasn't just us; with any parent I talked to it was the parent who found the placement. Our issue was the placements couldn't supply everything."]

---

2 Dr. Seuss (1960) *Green Eggs and Ham*. New York, NY: Random House.

Over the next month, I put together the materials for another impartial hearing. As the school settled the last time, I hoped they would again. Instead, the impartial hearing was a full battle that took three months. The school district and I both supplied our evidence and called all our witnesses. Each party was then asked to supply our closing brief to the impartial hearing officer within 30 days. The hearing officer then had 30 days to make her decision. To me, this meant Harris would go at least 60 more days without services. First the hearing and now this; we were looking at six months of time going by while a child sat idly by, waiting for services. I thought my case was very solid, and I believed the impartial hearing officer would decide in Harris's favor.

Harris had increased his decoding skills over two grade levels when in the Lindamood-Bell® program. Mr. DiStello's testimony seemed very clear cut. The district called Harris's old reading teacher as their expert witness. She, in my mind, did not present herself well. After working with Harris for a year, she couldn't get Harris to learn 50 sight words and Harris learned more than 250 sight words at Lindamood-Bell®. Harris wasn't able to read any books in two years at Oak Hill School, but after one summer on the Lindamood-Bell® program, Harris was able to read a 64-page Dr. Seuss book.

With all of this in mind, I was shocked when the impartial hearing officer did not find in favor of "The Parent." Having gone through a total of six months of the hearing process, only to get a decision not in favor of supplying my son with needed services, was devastating. If there was ever a time I felt like giving up, this would have been it.

(When Harris had finished the first eight weeks at Lindamood-Bell®, he was upset that his time there was over. Harris said, "These people are nice to me, and they help me; I want to come back." I promised Harris I would get him back to Lindamood-Bell®. I said to an eight-year-old boy, "Hey buddy, don't worry; I'll get you back here. I promise.") After losing the impartial hearing, I was drained and overcome by depression. My income ($17 an hour) barely covered my fixed costs and there was no way I could afford a lawyer at $375 an hour. I believed my case was solid. Everything that I put together—from the test scores to the reports, and even the school district's inability to educate Harris—was all neatly presented to the impartial hearing officer. Yet the decision came down in favor of the school district. I was completely demoralized. I had lost my ability to keep my promise to Harris. I had failed, and it devastated me.

I was sitting at my computer late at night and a picture of Harris came up. He was smiling at me; you know that innocent smile a child has? That picture shocked me back to life. I spent the entire night working on my appeal. I pulled all the paperwork together and went into work the next day without sleeping.

Now, I needed to sit back and wait. After the impartial hearing officer's decision, I expected to lose the appeal; so, I decided to review what I would need to do if the appeal were lost and started putting together the paperwork to go to federal court. Every night, I would go to the mail box and see if the envelope I was looking for had arrived.

One freezing night in March, I finally found the letter in the mailbox. As I read through the decision, I saw the words, "The impartial hearing officer's decision is annulled… It is so ordered… Harris will receive compensatory damages…" and so on. I jumped up and yelled, "Harris won! Harris won!" I was ecstatic.

I think about what would have happened to Harris if I hadn't appealed the impartial hearing officer's decision. I was very close to quitting, and that could have cost Harris dearly. Quitting has *never* crossed my mind again. Moving forward, at all other meetings, I recognized that I could get a "No" or a decision that did not favor Harris. If it did, I would hand back my motion for whatever came next. I never gave them a moment's rest.

Even while the impartial hearing was going on, there were still CSE meetings that needed to be attended. Nothing stops while you fight it out in an impartial hearing. I decided, as the school district wasn't going to work with me, I was going to do whatever it took to get Harris the services he needed. Complaints can be filed if you feel the school district is not doing their job correctly. It wasn't about me being petty; it was about doing anything and everything to help Harris. Every civil complaint or state education complaint that I filed, the school district had to answer. It was important to keep in mind these complaints needed to have validity. They had to be true and worthy complaints. I reviewed all the laws I could and looked for valid reasons to file complaints. I found myself up at the school, at CSE meetings, to deal with the state review officer's (SRO) decision on the appeal. Mr. Rhine was obviously upset that the SRO found in Harris's favor. As we reviewed the SRO decision, I pushed for the service provider to be Lindamood-Bell®. Mr. Rhine refused, but didn't have an alternative, so we were at a standstill.

He was getting frustrated that I wouldn't let it go and he "lost his cool." In his frustrated state, when asked why he would not approve services from Lindamood-Bell®, he said, "Because I don't have to." Never was I so glad that a meeting was being taped. With that, I planned to file a state complaint the moment the meeting ended.

Still, in the same CSE meeting, we moved to discuss Harris's next year's placement. The committee was in agreement that Harris would continue with an out-of-district placement. Mr. Rhine continued to disagree with the provision of Lindamood-Bell® services for Harris. It was clear that the only course of action was another impartial hearing request. My head was spinning, just trying to keep up with all the filings.

After a complaint is filed, several months go by while you await a decision. While I was in this "holding pattern," the only thing I could think about was that my child was missing out on services. Frustration set in and now I was waiting to start another impartial hearing and awaiting a state complaint decision. [This is another avenue to lodge a complaint; it is where you are not requesting a due process/impartial hearing, but instead you are asking the state to review your complaint, to investigate, and to reach a conclusion.]

After a few months, we were again sitting in front of an impartial hearing officer. I was expecting the first day of the hearing to be another long, boring day of passing papers back and forth. The hearing officer took the hearing in a different direction and wanted us to talk about settling the case. This seemed to me to be a futile effort, as we had already been through a resolution and a mediation session.

To my surprise, the school district's attorney once again said those words, "My client would be willing to settle with the Brites." Again, I am baffled as to why, all of a sudden, the district was willing to settle. Then, they hit me with the reason. They wanted me to drop the state complaint as part of the settlement. In my mind, if Harris got the services he needed, it was worth dropping all the complaints, so I agreed.

While the hearing officer was there, the district drew up the settlement agreement. In front of the hearing officer, I called the state education department to withdraw the complaint. I was informed that the complaint had already been decided and it could no longer be withdrawn.

Two days later, the decision arrived. I am sure the district was upset when they found out that the complaint was sustained. The investigator found the district to be in violation of both federal and state laws, along with state education regulations. Now, the district had a "mark" against them.

Harris's story is long from over, but it is more of the same. There are more CSE meetings and likely more impartial hearings and more state complaints to come. I am a thorn in the district's side that won't go away. I am sure many will see Harris's story as a never-ending, bitter battle, where Harris's father and the school district cannot work together. This is not the relationship I wanted to have with my son's school. Our inability to work together only hurt one person—Harris—and for that I am very sorry.

Addendum

Many people have asked me about working with advocates and educational lawyers. I did indeed talk with advocates on many occasions. In the beginning, they gave me some great advice and direction. Maren Spencer was an advocate at Tyler Advocacy, and she was of great help to me. I brought in my files, and she helped me coordinate the paperwork. As time went on, though, it got to the point where my experiences have now eclipsed her knowledge. The advocates were, at some points, asking me to report back to them on my outcomes, so they could pass on my information to others.

Lawyers were another issue. My very first experience with the lawyer who took our $375 and said, "I can't help Harris," jaded me. I went back to the school district and basically threatened them with an impartial hearing, and they conceded almost immediately. That lawyer could have done the same thing and maybe Harris would have gone to Evergreen Manor that first summer. I did what he wouldn't even try to do.

I spoke to other attorneys along the way. You would be amazed at all the advice they gave me, even knowing that I was going to continue on my own, without hiring them. I had one lawyer who spoke with me for more than an hour on the phone, giving me advice and telling me what I should ask for. He even asked to review my notes to ensure I got his points correct. He understood I didn't have the funds to pay him. By my eighth impartial hearing, I had found the funds to hire him, but he'd retired.

I hired two lawyers for my last impartial hearing. The first one took $2,000 and, after four months, had accomplished nothing. I had to fire him. The second got the job done, but during the hearing he got busy and put Harris's case aside and took longer to come to a settlement than I was usually able to do.

In total, I won a state education complaint and an SRO decision, and accepted three settlement agreements. Harris left Oak Hill School at the end of second grade, unable to read. He didn't know the letters of the alphabet or the sounds of the letters. The district said that Harris maybe knew 50 sight words when he left. However, following his getting the services we fought for, he started the seventh grade reading at the seventh grade reading level. So, was it worth it? I'll let you decide.

Analysis of "Facing Each Challenge Head On"

Richard Brite faced many obstacles, including: coming to realize that his child was losing his hearing and that he and his then wife had been unaware of it; divorcing the mother of his children; and contending with issues at the school building level on up to the district and state levels. Often, he needed to pursue the process of contesting similar problems, because the building-level personnel would simply refuse to address them just "because I said so," as one administrator nearly said.

Mr. Brite also had much going for him, even though that "much" was internally driven. But for his fortitude and desire to obtain the services Harris needed, I think we can all agree that Harris would unlikely be reading today.

Please understand that several parents in this book have been struggling with their school systems much like Mr. Brite, and those issues were brought out in each scenario. The similarities, interestingly enough, include feeling that something was wrong and seeking assistance only to find that, in this case, Harris had a hearing loss. Harris's parents initially had no idea that he was losing his hearing or that he had a disability.

The shock, however, was similar to that experienced by our other families, and the questions poured out: "What do I do next, and how fast can I get it done?" The only difference is that this story is told by a single father, one who, very much like our other parents in this book, would fight feverishly for the services his son needed while maintaining his support for Harris's sister as well. Mr. Brite managed to keep his focus on his children.

Harris's Problem Is What?
We Did Not Have a Clue!

Harris's story started when his parents perceived that he had a communication problem. Mr. and Mrs. Brite contacted the EIP (a national program overseen by each state and available at the local levels, which assists parents and children from birth to age three who are identified with disabilities) for an evaluation. By taking this step, they learned their son had a hearing loss. They needed the input of medical experts to learn more.

A CAT scan confirmed that Harris had enlarged vestibular aqueducts. Without going into great detail, these are narrow, bone-like ducts that connect the inner ear deeply inside the skull. We learned, too, that loud sounds, falls, and other rather common occurrences could cause deafness in children with this condition. On the other hand, some children can have enlarged vestibular aqueducts and not suffer a loss of hearing. Mr. and Mrs. Brite were told early on that hearing aids would be helpful, and even later on that it was very likely that Harris would lose his hearing entirely.

Typically, I would not extend an explanation of a child's condition, but this particular condition is not commonly known by the general population and is medical in nature. The cause—like most disabilities—is not totally understood. In addition to the degree of hearing loss, language development is another variable. This is a common corollary, or consequence, experienced by those with hearing loss which can be regained through medical intervention.

Unfortunately, the inevitable happened. Harris had a minor fall and completely lost his hearing within five days. This loss of hearing also had a dramatic impact on his language development.

With the help of friends, Mrs. Brite found a surgeon who could see them sooner than expected, but only for very brief time. Having sought out, in advance, what documents would be required, she was able to present all the information the surgeon needed, expediting the surgery for the cochlear implant by several months. In essence, by bringing all the documents, reports, and records, Mrs. Brite was able to explain to the surgeon what Harris "looked like" and "who he was"—an important discussion covered very early in this book.

Planning and preparation are absolute strengths of both Mr. and Mrs. Brite, and, because of these competencies, they were successful in creating positive change for their child more quickly. Later, Mr. Brite continued to use this strength to be as successful when dealing with the school district on his own.

Mr. and Mrs. Brite—like most parents who first learn that their child has a disability—were novices in terms of their knowledge of the disability, what services were available, and how to obtain them. They were also unfamiliar with any laws or policies related to the particular district's "universe" of special education. Like most parents, at first the Brites accepted whatever was offered them by the school system. And, like many parents in this book, it wasn't long before they suspected that their child was not benefiting from the services and the IEP provided by the school system. But the Brites also sought out the information and connections they would need to provide their son with the interventions and services he required.

Shortly after initially learning about Harris's hearing loss, Harris's mother, Zuella, was told about the John Tracy Clinic in California. That summer the family attended a three-week session at the clinic, where they—as a family—learned how to deal with a family member's hearing loss. This family workshop/training was beneficial as Harris transitioned to the use of hearing aids and then the cochlear implant.

What Do We Know?
Transportation and Teachers' Contracts

The first incident that caused the Brites to look more closely at the school system was the degree of time that children (aged three to five) were sitting on the school bus—approximately for an hour and a half. (This is the total time from being picked up at home to being let off the school bus.) As it turned out, the Brites learned that the buses had actually arrived at the school, but Harris and his peers were not exiting the bus until after school had been in session for 30 minutes. This was due to the teachers' contracted time to begin working.

Where Do We Want to Go?

Clearly, this is an extreme amount of time to remain on the bus. As we learned, the children were sitting outside the school. Staff waited for the teachers' contracted start time to go into effect before beginning to release the children from the buses so they could enter the school. The Brites wanted to shorten the total bus time by releasing the children when the buses arrived, so the children could enter school in a timely manner, defined as having entered the school building and been readied for the start of school—on time.

At first, this might not appear to be an IEP issue, but it is on several levels. The most egregious, or unacceptable, offense is that the IEP's length of time was administratively reduced by Harris's not exiting the bus until after school had begun. There was an apparent reduction of the IEP time that was not based on Harris's needs. The other issue of relevance to the IEP is the reasonableness (an arguable point during a hearing or court) of the amount of time a child of this age is required to sit on a bus. The latter is not part of a national law (time spent on transportation), but may well conflict with the school's local policy and/or the state's.

How Will We Get There?

The most reasonable step toward achieving the goal of reducing the time on the bus would be to speak with the building principal, which the Brites did. They made the assumption that the teachers could meet the buses earlier and reduce the time the children were to sit outside the school waiting to enter. This would also enable the children—including Harris—to be in the building and readied for the start of the full school day.

The problem was that the principal based his reasoning of the situation on the teachers' contract—which, by the way, cannot override the IEP. Here is where the Brites needed to request a copy of two policies. If they had requested all policies related to transportation, then they could have seen if there were a policy related to the allowable length of time on the bus—total travel time—and the time the students may be held on the buses prior to exiting. If they had requested to see the teachers' entire contract, then they could see where it referenced the starting and ending time. Both of these documents are public information and may not be withheld from review by the parents. Should the principal refuse, the next step would be to contact the district superintendent to explain the situation and again request those policy documents.

Although there are likely other upper management staff who could answer the questions, contacting the superintendent will result in the quickest response. (The materials will likely be sent by another of the superintendent's administrative staff. However, the Brites would have made the superintendent aware of the concern, which might have resulted in a quicker resolution than if they had contacted the directors/supervisors of special education, transportation, and personnel separately first.)

In lieu of this, the family simply decided to drive Harris to school. Clearly this was an option, but the school system was responsible for resolving this issue. Ultimately, the program was closed after several levels of state investigation for a multitude of reasons that extended well beyond those experienced by the Brites.

What Do We Know?

Exiting the Early Intervention Program

By the time the Brites experienced their first IEP meeting, they knew that Harris's previous school had been closed due to an extensive number of compliance issues. They also knew that Harris had not made significant progress, due to the poor programming and his complete loss of hearing. So, Mr. and Mrs. Brite proposed that Harris be placed in a different program outside of the CES jurisdiction.

Where Do We Want to Go?

How Will We Get There?

Because of the closing of the preschool CES program, it was important that another program be selected. The parents no longer wished to have Harris served under the jurisdiction of the CES program. His language skills were no better than they had been when he began a year ago, and he was not reading. Mr. and Mrs. Brite also wanted an increase in speech and language services to expand on the agreed speech/language needs. In a way, this was proposed as compensatory services, but not presented in that manner.

Before the Case Study Team (CST), or IEP team, could refute the private placement, the Brites offered to pay for the tuition. Because the CES program had been closed due to a number of citations, the team was less likely to say "No" to parents who wanted to pay for their own private placement. However, when it came to the extra speech and language programming, the CST team said "No." Mr. Brite, however, would only reiterate the issue of regression and the need for additional speech-language pathologist (SLP) time, so the CST finally agreed to provide the speech services as requested.

A Few Notes

It was difficult for the CST (IEP) team to argue against the distinct possibility of regression, even though it was not presented in any measurable format, so they agreed to the parents' paying for private placement. Regression was a key factor when requesting a program outside the CES's program oversight, because it was clear that the CES was severely lacking—or the program would not have been closed.

This is an extreme step that provided the Brites with the foundation for asking for a private placement (a program not under the auspices of CES). They could have undertaken a number of steps to have the school pay for private tuition, just as the increase in speech and language services (the additional hours over what was proposed) could have been brought to bear as compensatory education, making up for the time, services, and insufficient growth exhibited by Harris.

Granted, the Brites were unaware of the services and laws and regulations in place to accommodate situations experienced by their family due to the failure of the district to satisfy the IEP (including the additional problem with transportation and the shortened length of the school day resulting from it). Again, this would have been a time to ask about policies and laws related to major regression for the time span of a year and the closing of a school that had not met the needs of the students. Had the Brites done so, they likely would have found the section on private placement or out-of-district placement and, under that, a section regarding transportation and the responsibility of the school system to provide such. If at all in doubt, just ask for laws and policies related to ineffective schools or forced termination of schools not meeting the law, or something similar.

The Brites' request of private placement (out-of-district school) paid for by the school system could have been made on the basis of compensatory education, particularly in response to the closing of the school and the lack of growth (regression) achieved by Harris. They could have requested out-of-district placement from one or all of the following concurrently:

1. The CST.

2. The director of special education.

3. The superintendent of the school district.

Assuming that the Brites would have been denied private placement and the additional speech and language services, then they could have taken one or both of the following steps:

1. Request that an investigation be carried out by the state Department of Education (this is not a due process, but a request for the state Department of Education to conduct an independent investigation).

2. Request a due process hearing (this is a request made to the state to have an independent hearing officer—or, in some states, a panel—hear the case). The complainant (the Brites) may or may not be represented by an attorney. That is the parents' choice.

Granted, there is a time factor involved in seeking each of these requests. The first three might well result in denial, requiring one or both of the last two options, which can vary considerably in time over that of the first three. Please keep in mind that it is important to document that you have a written/documented request and have attempted to work the issue out with the school. However, in the U.S., you may put all five into action at the same time if you wish. With some exceptions, due to timelines by which the state must reply, you may also withdraw all.

Mr. Brite, in retrospect, realized that he had the option of having the school pay for the private school tuition. He would have known this if he had had more knowledge of the laws and regulations. Again, Mr. Brite could have asked for copies of related laws and policies—had the school continued to say "No!"—to have learned of the options he had available if the district disagreed with the parents.

The Legal Approaches Taken by Mr. Brite

The remainder of this review and analysis will focus on the legal steps Mr. and Mrs. Brite—and then Mr. Brite alone—took to ensure that Harris received his services. Again, Harris's needs are not the issue in the remainder of this analysis, because the school staff agreed about what those needs were; rather it is the manner in which Mr. Brite had to go about obtaining the services to meet those needs, *making this a unique and valuable chapter of the book.*

What Do We Know?

At the end of the year, the Brites sought ESY services to ensure that there would be no regression over the summer; that is, no loss in Harris's reading and communication skills (though this is assumed, because Mr. Brite did not provide any specific measures to speak of). The Brites were basing growth and lack of growth on Harris receiving a cochlear implant and its effects on language.

How Will We Get There?

In readiness for the next year of school (kindergarten), the Brites had located a school for the deaf, where Harris could receive all the services he needed. However, the chairwoman of the CST, Ms. Diaz, said at the onset of the meeting that Harris did not need summer programming (ESY). The Brites recognized that Harris was still learning to communicate with the cochlear implant, and their rationale was that this was not the time to end language services, because, as it was a new skill, there could easily be regression should services be terminated. (One step that Mr. Brite failed to do—something he later recognized as part of his own learning process—was to invite someone from Harris's previous school to speak about his growth, needs, and present skill levels. Without a person who knew Harris and his learning well, it was more difficult for the remainder of the team to understand the significance of the data.)

The final statement, marking the end of the meeting, was when the chairwoman said, "We will have to agree to disagree." Once again, here was a time where the

Brites should have asked for a copy of the policies/laws pertaining to when the school and parents fail to agree.

How Will We Get There? (Continued)

The Brites elected to seek the assistance of an attorney, who agreed that it was a solid case and one that could be won easily. The difficulty was the time it would have taken to work through the process. Summer would have been over and the opportunity to take advantage of the extended summer school options/program would have been lost. However, there was an alternative that unfortunately, the attorney did not even raise. They could have brought a suit against the school for compensatory education, making up for the lost time of summer school. The compensatory time could have been made up over the regular school year—after school, for example.

This is not to emphasize the need for pursuing legal options, but so that the reader understands that there is an amount of time/program and services to be provided based on the child's needs. ESY is a program of services made available to address possible regression. That is, the services are provided to prevent regression of skills learned over the school year or to retain a recently "learned skill," where gains might have been lost, such as the development of Harris's language skills with his relatively recent cochlear implant.

It is a service that, for the Brites, could have been sought through litigation in order to continue Harris's learning, based on the concern that without continued learning, what had been gained during the school year could have been lost or that his skills might have regressed. As well, it could have been addressed by appealing to the district or lodging a complaint to the regional oversight program, if there was one, or directly to the state Department of Education. The point is that there are often multiple avenues that can be pursued when conflicts arise.

Mr. Brite elected to continue with the district and to ask Ms. Diaz to reconsider her decision, but she did not change her decision until he told her that he was going to request an impartial hearing (or due process). Unfortunately, by then, all the slots for the summer school program had been filled.

At this point, Mr. Brite could have sought compensatory education services by taking the issue to the state Department of Education in the form of a complaint or to request an impartial hearing. Yet, the Brites elected not to pursue any further steps. A reasonable concern for Harris was that missing additional instructional time might become cumulative.

Fortunately, Harris's first year attending Evergreen Manor went well. His speech was improving, and he was using new words. As Mr. Brite noted, "…Harris's setbacks seemed to be behind him." This would be somewhat surprising given his suspected issue of regression.

(Mr. Brite notes that a divorce took place the summer before Harris's second year at Evergreen Manor. Fortunately, both parents agreed to keep the interests of the children at the forefront. Although this caused the family to move, Harris was able to continue at Evergreen Manor, and, although his sister would change schools, the overall year went well considering the circumstances.)

What Do We Know?
Where Do We Want to Go?
How Will We Get There?

At the end of the second year at Evergreen Manor (his first grade year), Harris aged out of their program. Another issue that the family had to face was the methodology of communication, whereby a sign and language (Total Communication) system was offered. In lieu of the combined language system, the Brites wanted Harris to have a pure oral form of communication.

The result was that Harris would be transferred from the private school to the district program at the Oak Hill School, which provided a "blended class" (or inclusion) and a large host of services that were offered and provided to him. These services included speech therapy five days a week, OT twice a week, services from a teacher of the deaf, and an aide assigned to Harris throughout the day.

The concern here is that there was no indication of identified needs—no reason specified for why Harris needed all these services, or what the services were intended to accomplish. Again, Mr. Brite, in looking back, realized that he "… would have focused on specific needs and have them addressed rather than take all [the services] I could get." The question "What do we know?" was ignored.

This is a key issue in the Structured Collaborative IEP Process. What we know and don't know determines the goals to be accomplished, and the answers to both questions are then the basis for the answers to "How will we get there?" Here, the school offered the services without the team considering the answers to the first two questions, "What do we know/don't we know?" and "Where do we want to go?"

Beyond that, the third question ("How will we get there?") was assumed to be the receipt of all available services, instead of services that addressed actual needs. The services provided did *not* match what we (the reader) know to be Harris's problems. And, to worsen the planning of Harris's IEP, the Oak Hill School refused to allow a representative from the previous school, Evergreen Manor, to take part in meeting Harris's real needs.

What Do We Know?
Where Do We Want to Go?
How Will We Get There?

As it turned out, Harris's program was not working. Mr. Brite saw no improvements and Harris was now complaining about going to school. Both were new experiences for Harris, and Mr. Brite returned to Oak Hill School and told the school that they would either allow a consultant to assist the school or he would file for an impartial hearing (due process). The school responded, "That is your right." So, Mr. Brite was still working on answering the third question, "How are we going to improve Harris's language and reading skills?" In other words, what services should be in place that would match his needs ("What do we know?") and accomplish the goals ("Where do we want to go?") to improve his reading and communication skills?

Although it does not *always* work the way it did, Richard Rhine, the assistant director for special education, called to agree to allow a consultant to work with staff. The condition was that it must be someone who was not involved with Evergreen Manor. The district wanted someone impartial, who was not there to "evaluate" staff and who did not have experience working with Harris. Oddly enough, it was left to Mr. Brite to locate a consultant, whose services would be paid for by the district.

Two issues arose from the district's decision. First, the school passed on working with someone who knew Harris's program intimately—what worked, what didn't, and why. This meant they lost out on the insights such a person would have concerning the selection of IEP participants. Second, the school chose to pay for a service that Evergreen Manor would have provided for free.

This is a consequence of the "paranoia" that can present itself when *any* consultant is brought into a school or school system. Just be aware of this and how it might stem from a fear that what is observed is shared outside of the school (a condition that could easily be written in the contract with the consultant), that real problems will be discovered, and the program or staff will be assessed. Imagine how you would feel if the school were to suggest a consultant visit your home to observe your family's interactions. It makes sense that there might be concerns and hesitancy.

The people with the greatest concerns and worries were ultimately raving about the assistance provided by the consultant, who was selected by Mr. Brite. It is clear from the outcomes that the consultant was an excellent choice—one who focused on benefiting Harris by actually helping the staff work on his needs. In other words, the focus remained on Harris's goals and needs—not on the individual teacher or program—which is the major function and purpose of the Structured Collaborative IEP Process.

We finally achieve a program that has been "revised" to meet Harris's needs and have answered the third question, "How will we get there?" Completing the plan is only part of the process, though, because it brings us to the next question, "How do we know that we are getting there?" In other words, "How are we measuring the progress made toward meeting Harris's needs?" This is something Mr. Brite brought to the attention of the school: Harris was not making progress.

How Do We Know That We Are Getting There?

Mr. Brite, determined to know how the program was working, conducted a bit of research on his own and discovered that the speech therapist, Kathy DeSkuto, actually had no prior experience of working with children who were deaf. Although she had worked with Harris for two years, Harris had been unable to learn the letters of the alphabet.

Other staff members were assigned to Harris for the convenience of the school. This included assigning Harris a teacher of the deaf, who was already contracted to work with two other students. It was not that the teacher of the deaf actually had a role/purpose in helping Harris. More specifically, Mr. Brite noted that, because Harris was placed in a blended class (inclusion), the teacher of the deaf provided services more like those of a classroom aide.

As Mr. Brite pointed out, all of it sounded good (the number of services), yet the program was not accomplishing what it was intended to in *accordance with Harris's needs*. (Please note that the services must meet the needs, which is part of the purpose of following the steps of the Structured Collaborative IEP Process.) Furthermore, Mr. Brite saw that the services provided by the teacher of the deaf conflicted with what the family had learned at the John Tracy Clinic, which raised a great concern. There were simply too many issues that Mr. Brite was unwilling to accept, including the services of a "reading teacher," that resulted in no progress.

In fact, it turned out that the books Harris brought home to practice reading had simply been memorized—when his father asked him to read the words on the page, Harris could not read them. When Mr. Brite called his ex-wife to share his concerns, she felt everything was fine and to "let it go"—that is, until one night in December, when she called to complain about Harris's lack of achievement and demanded that Mr. Brite do something.

What Do We Know?
How Will We Get There?
Where Are We Going?

Unmistakably, based on the title of this section if nothing else, the CST meeting addressed Mr. Brite's concerns about Harris's lack of progress out of order. At the onset, the chairwoman told the parents that the team felt that they could not educate Harris, and recommended that he be transferred to an out-of-district placement, where his needs could be met. Furthermore, they stated that, until they could locate a program for Harris, he would remain in the present program—which was not working, according to the chairwoman.

It was inappropriate for the final decision of placement to be decided outside of the CST meeting before the CST meeting even began, and before the team discussed the progress that Harris had or had not made. (A fully formed CST team must include the parents to be a part of the discussion and decisions.) This was neither the process that should have been followed, nor was it the manner in which the IEP should have been written or revised. The red flags of blatant impropriety are unfurling all over the place. The parents left the meeting, unsure of what to do.

What Do We Know? (Good Question!)

Mr. Brite, of course, began researching reading problems, which he considered to be Harris's greatest issue. It was his ex-wife, Zuella, who learned of the Lindamood-Bell® program. Harris was tested, and, not surprisingly, his scores were low, but at least there was now some measure of his reading levels. With this information, Mr. Brite contacted Mr. Rhine, the assistant director of special education, stating that, until another program/placement was located, a different program needed to be implemented for the remainder of the school year and summer (ESY).

At the CST meeting, instead of sharing data showing Harris's growth or lack thereof, Mr. Brite explained to us that staff began blaming each other *and* Harris for his failure to make progress. Mr. Brite stated his concern that if we want to know where we are, we need information—measurable and observable data—and not to "point fingers." It is no wonder there was no progress being made and that staff were not focused on "Where are we and where do we need to go?"

In spite of Mr. Brite's distributing the Lindamood-Bell® testing information and the district's apparent agreement with the results, the district stated they were unfamiliar with the program and would need to seek more information. This decision does fit well under the questions "What do we know?" and "What don't we know?" Unfortunately, this would further delay Harris's receiving an appropriate program and, instead, guaranteed the continuance of an unsuccessful program. In the end, the team ended the meeting without a "next steps" plan.

With that in mind, Mr. Brite proceeded with an impartial hearing (due process). It is extremely important to know that this does not mean that the team was to stop instructing Harris or seeking to understand the benefits of the Lindamood-Bell® program; neither does this mean that staff and the parents ceased holding additional CST meetings to resolve programming/parental issues and concerns. All may run concurrently—impartial hearing or due process requests do not cause all other activities to stop.

Mr. Brite realized that he now needed more information on how the CST teams functioned and began by asking friends, advocates, and others who had experienced the CST process, only to become, as he noted, "more confused." In my opinion, you can easily become lost by approaching answers as Mr. Brite did, because he was receiving only bits and pieces of information. You should be seeking answers from those who offer you federal, state, or local policy materials, or web links, phone numbers, and agency or department names to contact to obtain a copy of all regulations related to special education.

With that information you can locate (though not necessarily easily) relevant regulations. You can always call the school district to ask where particular pieces of information in the regulations are located, or even the state Department of Education. There are as well, in the U.S., Parent Information Centers (PICs) in every state, whose role is to assist parents of children with disabilities. Staff at the PICs are knowledgeable about the federal and state laws and regulations and can assist you in obtaining copies of those laws. One can also obtain applicable education laws at the U.S. Department of Education at www.ed.gov. Ultimately, however, Mr. Brite decided to pursue an impartial hearing.

A better initial approach would have been to ask the CST chairwoman for a copy of all laws, policies, and regulations related to the CST process. Because the information is found throughout and interrelated to all parts of the law, Mr. Brite should have received a complete set of state and local regulations and policies on special education. A great deal of work would have been ahead of him, but this information is available in digital form from the state and federal websites, and by using "searches" he would have been able to find relevant passages more quickly.

The point is, had he asked, the chair would have had to provide all the information needed and related to the IEP and the CST processes. That is why I tell parents and advocates to ask for a copy of the law, regulation, or policy when in doubt, or when you hear something that sounds odd to you. Your request must be complied with.

A later exchange between Mr. Brite and Mr. Rhine made it clear that the district had no intention of dealing any further with the issue, and was willing to face an impartial hearing (due process) procedure. The idea of working in collaboration with Mr. Brite was no longer an option in which the district was interested.

Correctly, Mr. Brite thought it necessary to remove emotion and affect from his thinking and to address Harris's needs and the impact/results of the program made available in Harris's IEP. It is not necessarily easy to dismiss all the anger and anxiety but these do get in the way of making your point(s) and good decisions. By dismissing them, the listener (or reader of your written material) is attentive to the issues and does not have to wade through the affect—which usually only serves to anger that person and influence his or her thinking and reply. It also makes it easier for the hearing officer, or panel, to review the regulations and to reach their findings when they can readily understand the issues you are raising. You might think that this is the time to expose your full emotions, but they get in the way of you outlining the failure(s) of the school or district to educate your child.

This is the perfect time to use the questions of the Structured Collaborative IEP Process: State the "answers" to each question on which agreement was reached by the team. Continue until you reach a question where there is disagreement. State the reasons for disagreement (which are also the reasons you requested the impartial hearing) clearly.

The hearing officer/panel will appreciate knowing where the points of agreement were, where the parties ceased to be in agreement, and what caused you to request the hearing. Use this same process when filing a complaint with the state Department of Education. Make it as easy for the readers of the complaints to see where agreement exists and when it does not. You can be certain that they will use the points of CST/IEP agreement in making their decisions.

Other options available to a school or parent are mediation or a facilitated IEP meeting. The school or parent may request these, usually prior to a request being made for a due process/impartial hearing. I will not go into a description of either at this point, except to ask you this question: What part of your child's IEP are you willing to give up through a mediation process?

If a due process or impartial hearing is requested of a state in the U.S., the state must offer a resolution meeting to the district and parents. These are meetings designed to give the school and parents an opportunity to reach an agreement. Parents may opt not to pursue the resolution meeting, and it is difficult to advise whether or not to take advantage of the offer. It depends on too many conditions and experiences.

Mr. Brite found neither mediation nor the resolution meeting to be successful, but the timelines on carrying out the due process/impartial hearing continued, and Mr. Brite prepared for the hearing. Typical of Mr. Brite, he made a concerted effort to pull all his materials together—you will recall that he is an organized person and knew he should have as much information as possible about what was known about Harris, the points of agreement with the school, what goals were established to meet Harris's needs, what services were provided to meet those needs, and, finally, documentation showing Harris's progress or lack of progress. Mr. Brite was ready—admittedly nervous—but ready.

In short, the first day of the hearing was spent with explanations of the process and exchanges of materials—mostly listening to the routine processes of hearing. The second day of the hearing, the school district decided to offer Harris the Lindamood-Bell® program, which is what Mr. Brite was seeking because it had been shown to be effective with Harris. The summer program, using the Lindamood-Bell® program with Harris, resulted in significant growth, including improvements in his decoding and reading skills. It also provided current data to answer the question: "What do we know (now)?"

Mr. Brite, in planning the programming for the upcoming school year, had sent a letter to the building principal, requesting a CST meeting. At the CST meeting, Mr. Brite also brought the progress data from the summer program and Mr. DiStello, the director of the Lindamood-Bell® program, to present Harris's growth though that program. Once the information was shared, the principal advised Mr. Brite that Harris would be moved to another placement.

Mr. Brite argued the decision with as little emotion as possible—but made no progress. Being prepared, he then handed the principal an impartial hearing notice. Again, Mr. Brite prepared for the hearing, which this time went on for days. At first, Mr. Brite lost the hearing, but he decided to submit an appeal, which, after quite some time, he won. The next step, of course, was to hold yet another CST meeting to discuss the findings and to develop Harris's IEP.

Naturally, Mr. Brite wished to continue with the Lindamood-Bell® system—and why not? He had the data to show it was successful. Oddly, Mr. Rhine refused—without providing alternatives for consideration. Mr. Brite remained with the same proposal, and he was able to because he had supporting data. Mr. Rhine replied to Mr. Brite's multiple requests for using Lindamood-Bell® saying, "Because I don't have to." This is, of course, an inappropriate reply.

At a minimum, Mr. Rhine should have explained why the Lindamood-Bell® was not appropriate for continuing with Harris, in which case the team would have had to use the data to justify its inappropriateness. Options for consideration should have been presented and shown how they would benefit Harris's reading through typical IEP discussions. "Because I don't have to" is far from supporting a discussion of options (the requirement of the laws and regulations of the federal and state laws) and a rationale for program selection.

Again, the answer to "What do we know?" exists. The goal of reading was established as a need, and the Lindamood-Bell® program was selected to achieve the goal. Lastly, data were available to show measures of growth. Although Harris was not yet reading at his grade level (understandably so, given his hearing and rather recent cochlear implant), Mr. Rhine ignored the information relating to the first four questions of the IEP process, which were directly related to the service/program that would be provided to Harris. And the team—including Mr. Rhine—agreed that the out-of-district placement was appropriate, ignoring the discussion of Harris's program.

Mr. Brite decided to take two steps. The first was to submit another impartial hearing request. The second was to send a complaint to the state Department of Education. (Remember, these actions may be applied concurrently, along with the continuance of CST meetings. Recall, too, that the Department of Education must conduct an investigation and complete a report of its findings.) At this point, it was clear that Mr. Rhine was making an independent decision, without a team discussion, regarding the method/approach to be used to achieve the goal, and this is not how a CST/IEP team should function. Certainly, this is an out-of-compliance behavior, which would be one of the negative findings of the state Department of Education.

To be brief, the impartial hearing meeting was held and, once again, the district's attorney elected to provide the Lindamood-Bell® program. There was a caveat, and that was that Mr. Brite would rescind his administrative complaint to the state Department of Education, to which he agreed. However, when the call was made (where the hearing members could hear), Mr. Brite was told that the state had timelines it had to abide by and had completed the review. The district and Mr. Brite were soon to discover that the state had found in favor of Mr. Brite (on Harris's behalf), as did the impartial hearing officer.

Key Points

- One individual in particular is a major destructive component in this story, and that is Mr. Rhine, the assistant director of special education. He routinely made IEP decisions without regard to data that supported Harris's success with the Lindamood-Bell® program. He made decisions independent of the CST team, contrary to the very reason and federal rationale for a CST meeting. And he made placement decisions prior to discussing and answering the question "Where are we?"

- We never learned why the assistant director adamantly rejected the Lindamood-Bell® reading program or what made him persist with a change of school. The question was not asked, neither did he offer a rationale.

- Mr. and Mrs. Brite, like most parents of children with disabilities, conducted a great deal of personal research to learn about Harris's disability. They sought to learn what other parents were doing and what services were available to them. The problem is, they were picking up bits and pieces—not enough information to have the "whole" picture (i.e., federal, state, and local laws, regulations, and policies).

- In the beginning, the Brites attempted to work within the school system's procedures—for example, accepting a poorly designed transportation system and the subsequent reduction in time allotted for the IEP program, without questioning the rules for transportation.

- Once Mr. and Mrs. Brite realized that the principal could provide no logical explanation for his decisions (other than a teacher's contract for starting time), they proceeded to transport Harris themselves. But no effort was made to seek those policies.

- Following a thorough investigation, the CES-run preschool program was closed due to a number of findings that revealed that the school program was out of compliance with federal and state laws and regulations. It sounds as if many laws, regulations, and policies were not being followed.

- The Brites recognized that they needed to take the lead on where Harris would receive services for the following year, although their decision amounted to their paying for an out-of district placement. This was their own error, because they had not yet thought to ask for copies of regulations or policies regarding when a district and parents disagree. (School systems have policies for transportation, cheating, graduation, and sports activities, and the list goes on.)

- When in doubt, *ask* for copies of any laws, regulations, and policies *any* time an issue arises that strikes you as odd or unusual, or that you simply do not understand. Perhaps, by doing so, the transportation issue could have been resolved, as it is likely that there is a district policy for the length of time a child is to be on a bus or some other form of transportation.

- A perfect example of this is to ask for regulations that address a request for out-of-district placement for the provision of IEP services. In retrospect, Mr. Brite did realize that he should have asked the district to pay for the private placement. He had more than enough documentation to show that the previous program was not capable of meeting Harris's needs, did not enable Harris to make progress, and had failed to meet a great number of regulations—so much so that the state's citations and findings led to the closing of the program.

- Once the Brites determined that the relationship with the school district was less than tenuous, they continued to make reasonable requests of the school, providing more than ample information for answering the questions of the Structured Collaborative IEP Process: where Harris was functioning ("What do we know?"), that reading and communication were key goals ("Where do we want to go?"), and locating a program (eventually) that showed progress toward the goals of speech and reading ("How will we get there?").

- The barrier to having those requests approved was Mr. Rhine's singular voice denying the use of the Lindamood-Bell® program. Yet he never proposed a rationale for his decision.

- In each example presented, the Brites were successful in winning their administrative complaint with the state Department of Education and with the number of findings in their favor through impartial hearings (due processes). Mr. Brite repeated that approach, following his presenting the team with a reasonable request. In fact, he presumed, by previous experiences, that he would be told "No." Because of Mr. Rhine's prior practices, Mr. Brite would provide him with a written request for an impartial hearing during the meeting.

- Finally, unless a major intervention (facilitation or seeking an expert in collaboration) is put into place to address the parent/school relationship, or a new administrator seeks to change the relationship between the district and parents, the only recourse available to Mr. Brite will likely remain legal actions. That is unfortunate, but may be the only way to achieve IEPs that meet Harris's needs.

- As pointed out, it was Harris who experienced the greatest loss, due to the time absent from the receipt of the needed services while the legal, but necessary, actions took place.

Summary

One might think that the district would prefer to re-establish a favorable relationship with Mr. Brite and in a collaborative fashion—perhaps taking advantage of the IEP facilitation processes and learning to use the Structured Collaborative IEP Process as a proactive step for reducing disagreements. That, however, was not the approach that Mr. Brite expected from the district, and the district has not yet shown interest in doing so. It would not be easy, especially in the beginning. But even using the Structured Collaborative IEP Process alone, Mr. Brite could have enabled the IEP team, through the basic "structure" of taking small steps, to reach agreement. Simply agreeing to the child's needs ("What do we know?") would have been a huge first step toward collaboration.

However, Mr. Brite has become quite familiar with the system of complaints and due processes and no longer expects to resolve issues short of these two steps. And, at this point, the school district only know how to say "No." Until both learn successfully to experience a CST/IEP meeting, neither has a reason to believe that there is a better way to deal with their issues. Not until both sides have put a new process into practice and can see what actually working together could be like, will they even imagine a different and better way.

I chose to include this story to show the reader what is involved when making impartial hearing/due process requests and administrative complaints to the state. The resolutions may have been acceptable, but three things are common results when multiple due process and administrative complaints are presented:

1. The relationship between the parents and school is weakened.

2. The time taken from both the school's and parents' normal activities to prepare and present evidence for these hearings can be extensive.

3. The time to process the legal approaches often results in the child's needed program to be on hold until the decision is made.

This is not to say that these legal actions should be avoided. In this example, Mr. Rhine was most likely to say "No" regardless of the Brites' request. If faced with that kind of "No," then the only way to receive the "Yes!" your child needs may be through legal action, which should be used. (I cannot determine why Mr. Rhine's saying "No" and causing impartial hearings was acceptable to the district.)

In summary, you can use federal, state, and local regulations to help understand what steps and procedures are required in the special education process. My suggestion is to ask for them. You might be surprised to learn that, sometimes, policies referred to during a meeting don't exist.

Final Thought—Please Read

These stories do *not* represent the majority of parent and school interactions. I have worked with educators from across the country and have met some incredible educators (teachers, administrators, related service personnel) whom I would have total faith in, should my child require special education services. This book does *not* represent the norm of Individualized Education Program (IEP) meetings or parent and school interactions. The process presented in this book can readily be used by both parents and educators and will benefit all children with disabilities, and even those without disabilities. It provides an excellent framework from which to address any child's needs, regardless of ability. In fact, this system is one that can benefit and be applied to any meeting where a child's needs are under discussion, by either parents or educators.

Afterword

Striking Observations of Interest

I want to share some additional observations that were found in at least two scenarios. They don't fully represent themes found in all Individualized Education Programs (IEPs), but surfaced sufficiently to warrant mentioning here. I observed:

- Many parents blamed themselves, their choices, and their decisions simply because they did not yet know that their child had a disability.

- Many parents blamed themselves, their choices, and their decisions simply because they did not yet have the information they needed to understand or know why or what they were seeing in their child. This is understandable, but unfortunate.

- A team's decisions were overridden/redirected because of the "status" of an IEP team member, or because of who a team member knew, or what university or college degree an IEP member held. And that could cut both ways—school system or parent(s).

- Policy pressure from "above" (administration) forced a decision without consideration of the individual child's needs. This was especially true with respect to placement decisions (least restrictive envornment [LRE]).

- LRE was misunderstood and misapplied, because of a failure to understand its intent and meaning.

- Medical professionals missing, even in contemporary times, the signs of autism and other disabilities, and failing to diagnose children appropriately.

- There were parents who provided homeschooling successfully (at least a few decades ago they could), and reintegrated their child back into public schools in a planned and organized way, including the re-entry and transition from home to school.

- There were parents and advocates who were successfully and unknowingly using many parts of the Structured Collaborative IEP Process that you learned about by reading this book.

- All parents had significant strengths and persistance, and there was much needed to bring change and get the "Yes" from the school that their child needed.

- Parents who eventually recognized the need for an advocate and who realized that—as with physicians, educators, and parents—there are strong and weak ones.

- Parents and/or educators can be zealots to the detriment of the child.

- Parents and/or educators can be zealots for the betterment of the child.

- There were parents who moved to another school or wished they had, even after the "Yes!" was obtained—sometimes it is simply necessary to move elsewhere because the district are too ingrained in their own needs.

- There were times when it was necessary to request help from an advocate or attorney—even then, getting the "Yes!" can be difficult or even impossible without a full hearing.

- Sometimes the school should say "No" and fails to do so, because they don't know how to use the process presented throughout this book.

- Although other parents did not state this specifically, many were very absorbed with their child's symptoms and behaviors, and this led to extreme frustration when they felt that they were not "listened to" by professionals who they, as parents, felt should "know."

Perhaps, most importantly, I saw that not one of the parents lost his or her passion for their child, no matter what the circumstances.

It is my hope that the stories of the "Bryns" in our world, to whom this book is dedicated, and the parents who graciously provided the scenarios found in this book will help you to work collaboratively with your school's IEP team. It is also my hope that the resulting IEP is developed based on your child's needs so that the program meets your child's needs.

I wish you all the very best.

Index